O-Parts HUNTER

SEISHI KISHIMOTO

CHARACTERS of O-Parts HUNTER

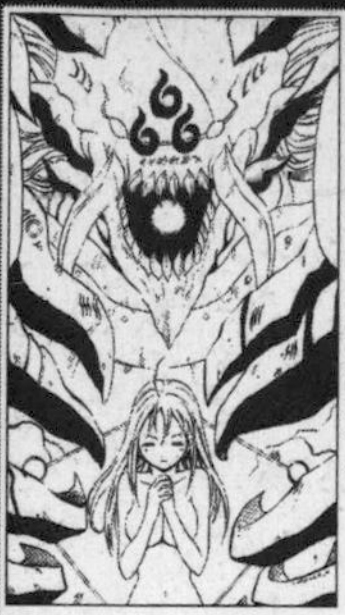

Satan is looking for an opportunity to take over Jio's body, but Ruby is holding Satan in check.

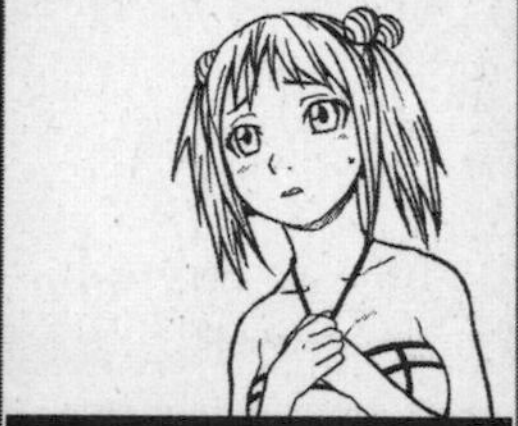

Ruby Crescent: A treasure hunter in search of the Legendary O-Part and her missing father. Currently, her body is with the Stea Government, and her soul is resting inside Jio's body.

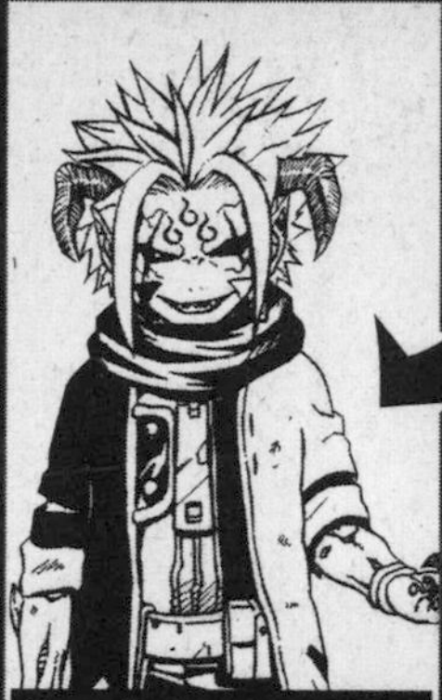

Satan: An alternate personality that exists inside Jio's body. The ultimate weapon of the Kabbalah who holds earth-shattering powers.

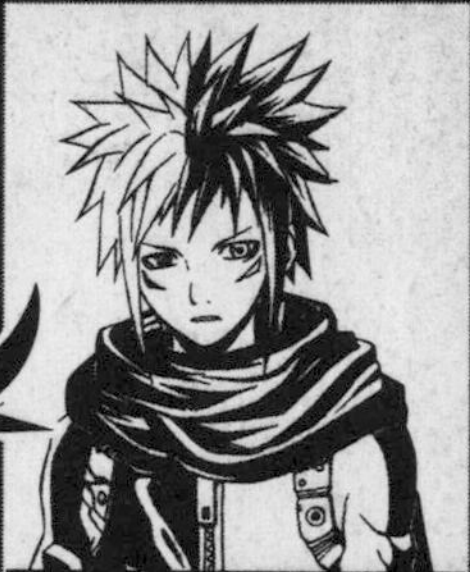

Jio Freed: A wild O.P.T. boy whose dream is world domination. He has been emotionally hurt from his experiences in the past, but has become strong after meeting Ruby. Ever since the Rock Bird incident, he has had Ruby's soul inside him.

Jio's Friends

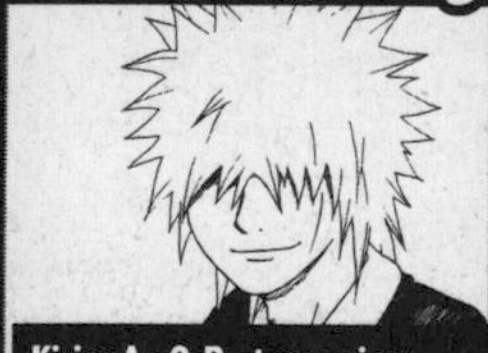

Kirin: An O-Part appraiser and a master of dodging attacks. He trained Jio and Ball into strong O.P.T.s.

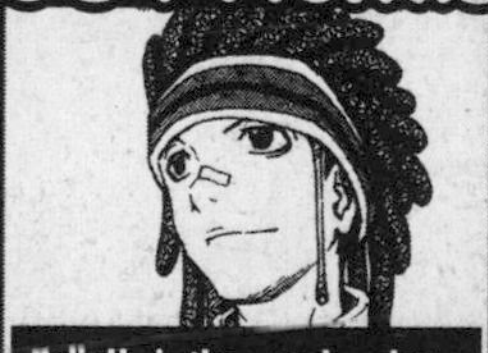

Ball: He is the mood-maker of the group and a kind person who cares about his friends.

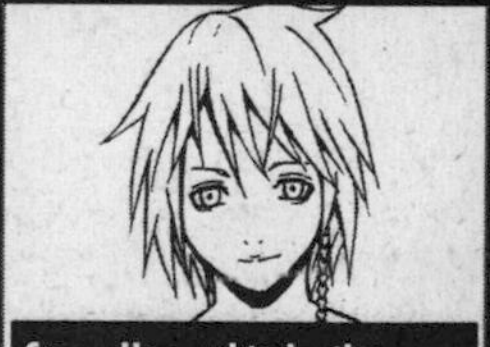

Cross: He used to be the Commander in Chief of the Stea Government's battleship. His sister was killed by Satan.

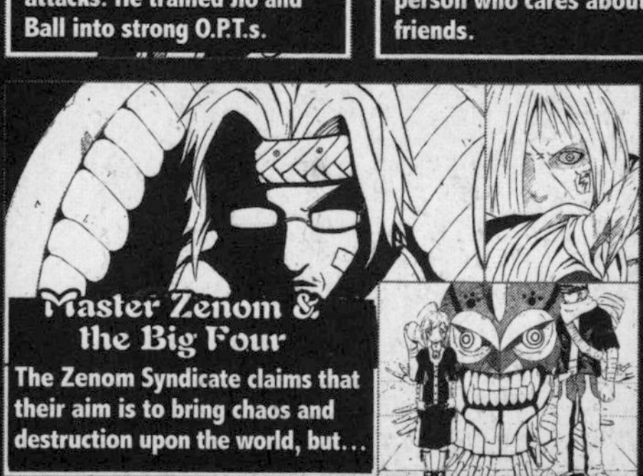

Master Zenom & the Big Four

The Zenom Syndicate claims that their aim is to bring chaos and destruction upon the world, but...

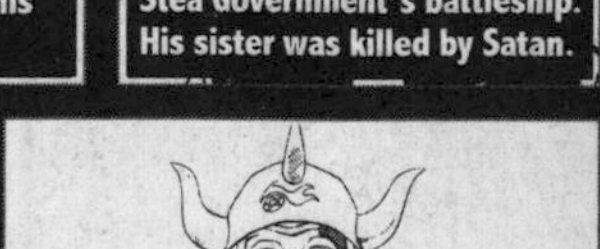

Stea Government Leader Amaterasu Miko

The very person who turned the Stea Government into a huge military state. Rumor has it that she has been alive for at least a century...

KABBALAH

the keyword of 666

A legacy left by the Ancient Race who are said to have come from the Blue Planet. The Kabbalah is the Ultimate Memorization Weapon, which absorbs every kind of "information" that makes up this world, and evolves along with the passing of time! It consists of two counterparts, the Formal Kabbalah and the Reverse Kabbalah.

10i
Nahema
(Materialism)
9i
Lilith
(Instability)
7i
Baal
(Lust)
8i
Adramelech
(Avarice)
6i
Belphegor
(Odious-
ness)
4i
Astaroth
(Apathy)
5i
Asmodeus
(Cruelty)
2i
Beelzebub
(Stupidity)
3i
Lucifuge
(Rejection)
1i
Satan
(Atheism)
666

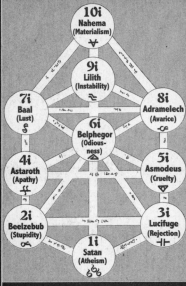

Reverse Kabbalah

The symbol of destruction with the names of the powerful archdemons listed on the sephirot from one to ten.

1
Metatron
(Crown)
3
Zaphkiel
(Understand-
ing)
2
Raziel
(Wisdom)
5
Samael
(Might)
4
Zadkiel
(Benevo-
lence)
6
Michael
(Beauty)
8
Raphael
(Splendor)
7
Haniel
(Victory)
9
Gabriel
(Foundation)
10
Sandalphon
(Kingdom)

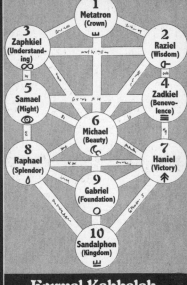

Formal Kabbalah

The symbol of creation with the names of the great archangels listed on the sephirot from one to ten.

STORY

Ascald: a world where people fight amongst themselves to get their hands on mystical objects left behind by an ancient civilization...the O-Parts.

In that world, a monster that strikes fear into the hearts of the strongest of men is rumored to exist. Those who have seen the monster all tell of the same thing–that the number of the beast, 666, is engraved on its forehead.

***

Jio and his friends enter Stea Government HQ in order to free Ruby. Amaterasu Miko, Stea's leader, sends her chief of staff Longinus, the true Angel Michael and May's long-missing brother Tsubame to stop them. These are all overcome, but this leads to the discovery that Miko has replaced her human body with a robot one. Jio destroys the robot body, but the question is... where is Miko now?

O-Parts HUNTER

16

Table of Contents

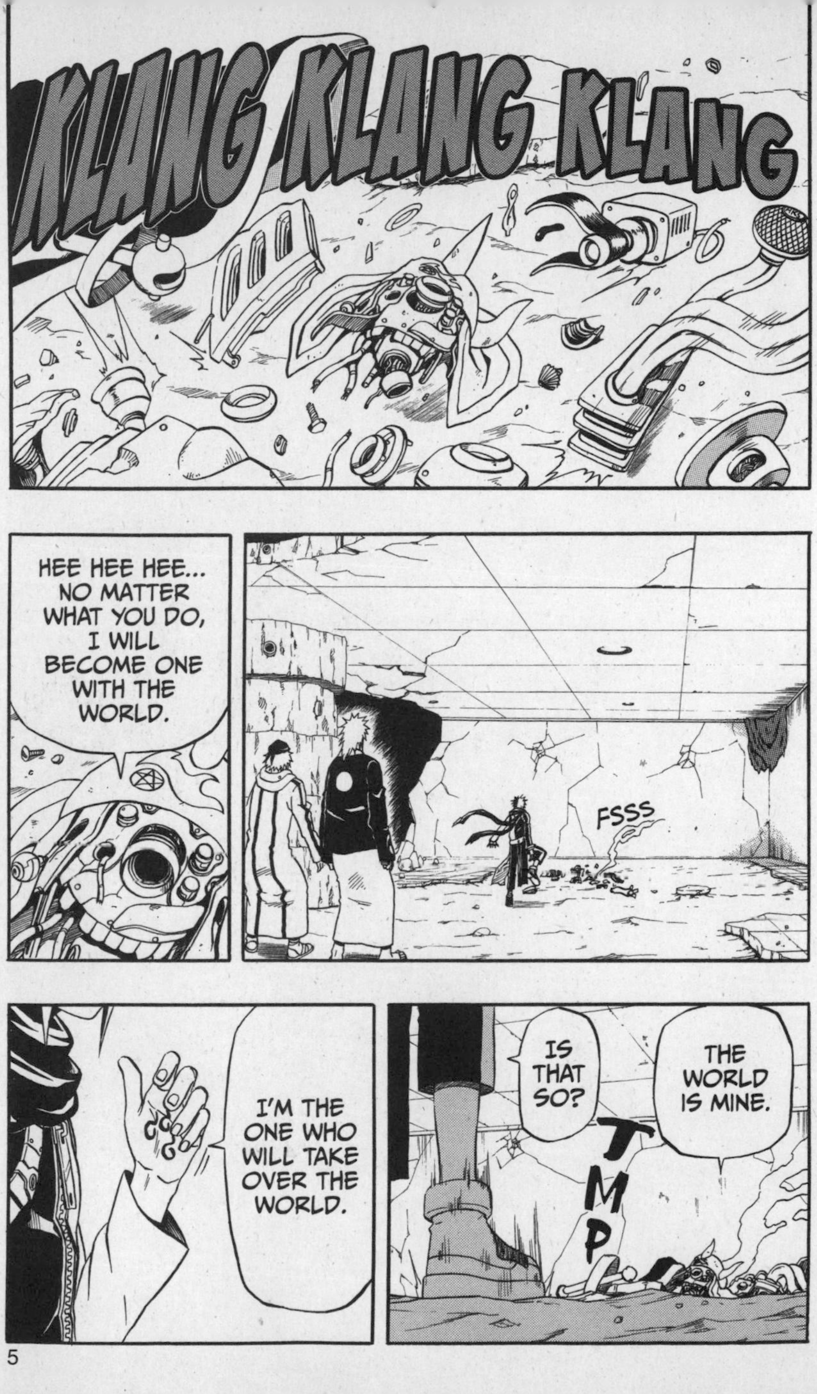
KLANG KLANG KLANG
FSSS
HEE HEE HEE... NO MATTER WHAT YOU DO, I WILL BECOME ONE WITH THE WORLD.
THE WORLD IS MINE.
IS THAT SO?
TMP
I'M THE ONE WHO WILL TAKE OVER THE WORLD.

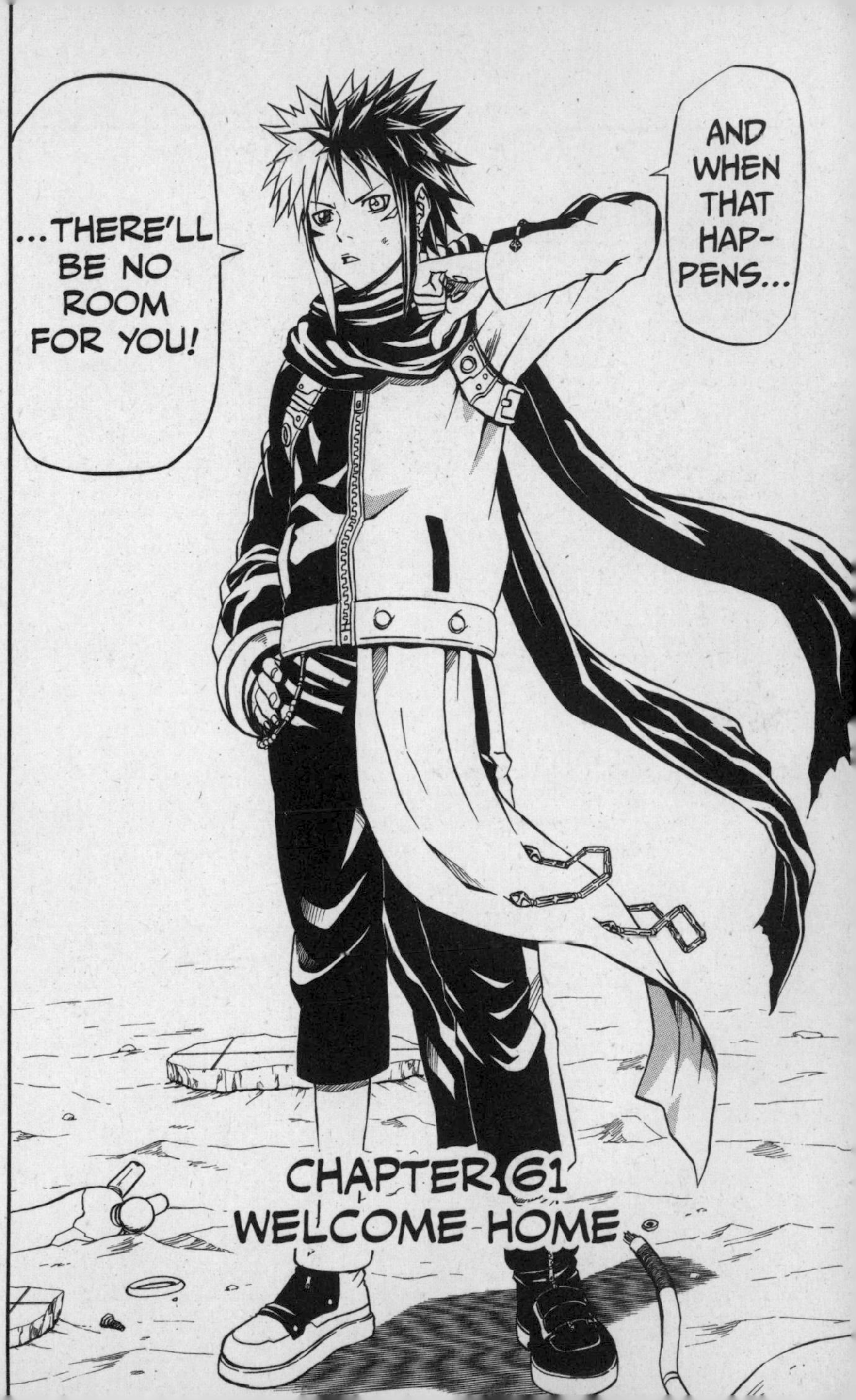
AND WHEN THAT HAP-PENS...
...THERE'LL BE NO ROOM FOR YOU!
CHAPTER 61
WELCOME HOME

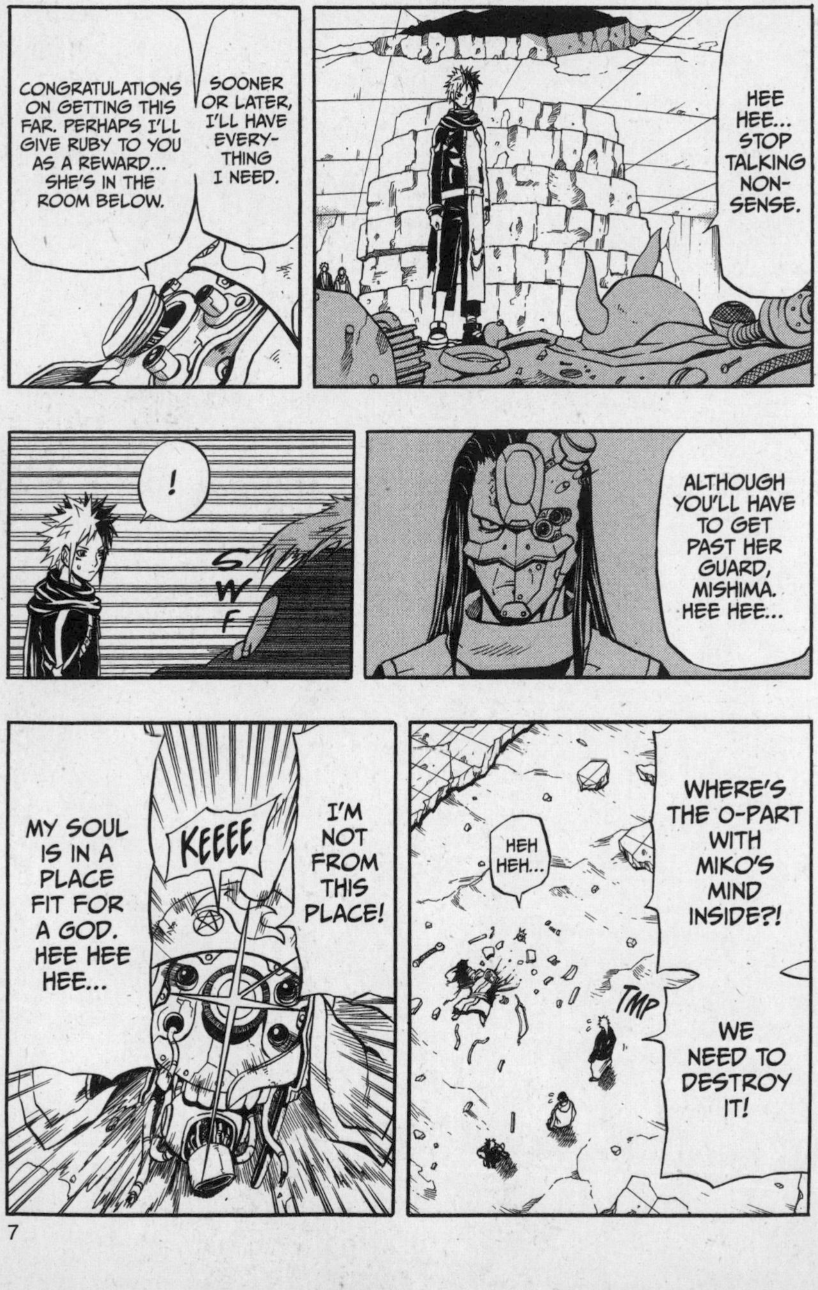
HEE HEE... STOP TALKING NONSENSE.
SOONER OR LATER, I'LL HAVE EVERY-THING I NEED.
CONGRATULATIONS ON GETTING THIS FAR. PERHAPS I'LL GIVE RUBY TO YOU AS A REWARD... SHE'S IN THE ROOM BELOW.
ALTHOUGH YOU'LL HAVE TO GET PAST HER GUARD, MISHIMA. HEE HEE...
!
SWF
WHERE'S THE O-PART WITH MIKO'S MIND INSIDE?!
HEH HEH...
WE NEED TO DESTROY IT!
TMP
I'M NOT FROM THIS PLACE!
KEEEE
MY SOUL IS IN A PLACE FIT FOR A GOD. HEE HEE HEE...

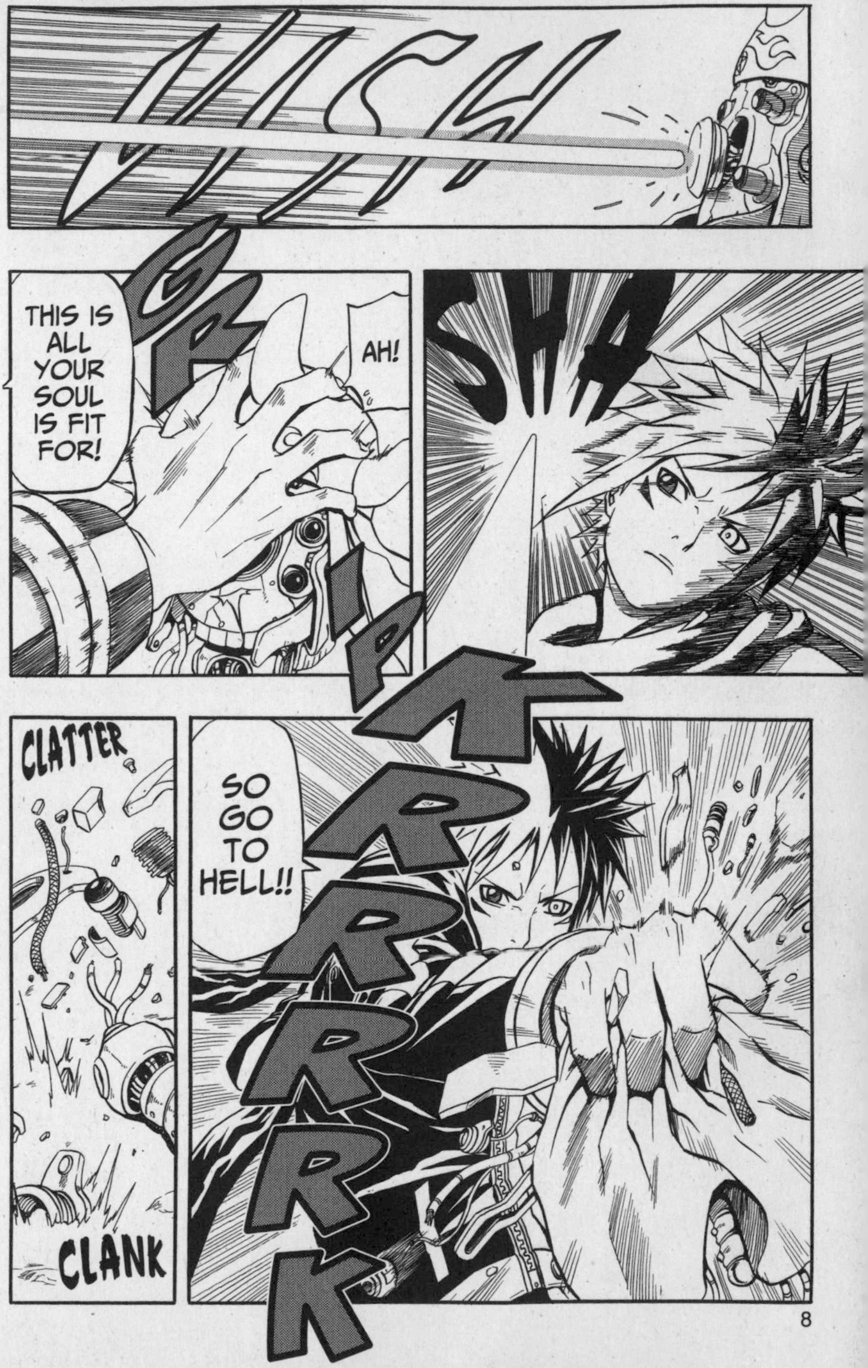
WHSH
SHA
GRIP
AH!
THIS IS ALL YOUR SOUL IS FIT FOR!
KRRRRK
SO GO TO HELL!!
CLATTER
CLANK

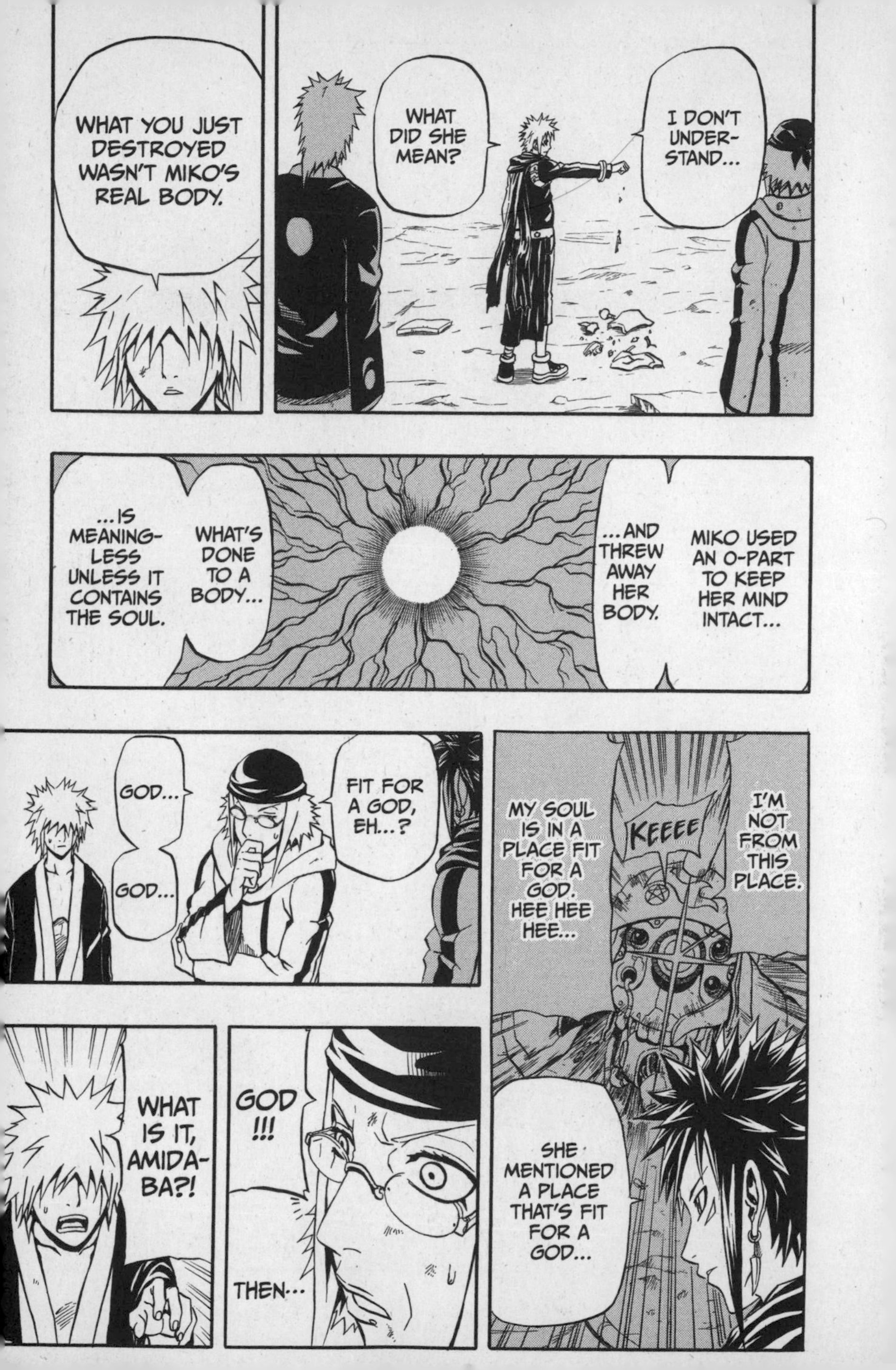
I DON'T UNDER-STAND...
WHAT DID SHE MEAN?
WHAT YOU JUST DESTROYED WASN'T MIKO'S REAL BODY.
MIKO USED AN O-PART TO KEEP HER MIND INTACT...
...AND THREW AWAY HER BODY.
WHAT'S DONE TO A BODY...
...IS MEANING-LESS UNLESS IT CONTAINS THE SOUL.
I'M NOT FROM THIS PLACE.
KEEEE
MY SOUL IS IN A PLACE FIT FOR A GOD. HEE HEE HEE...
SHE MENTIONED A PLACE THAT'S FIT FOR A GOD...
FIT FOR A GOD, EH...?
GOD...
GOD...
GOD!!!
THEN...
WHAT IS IT, AMIDA-BA?!

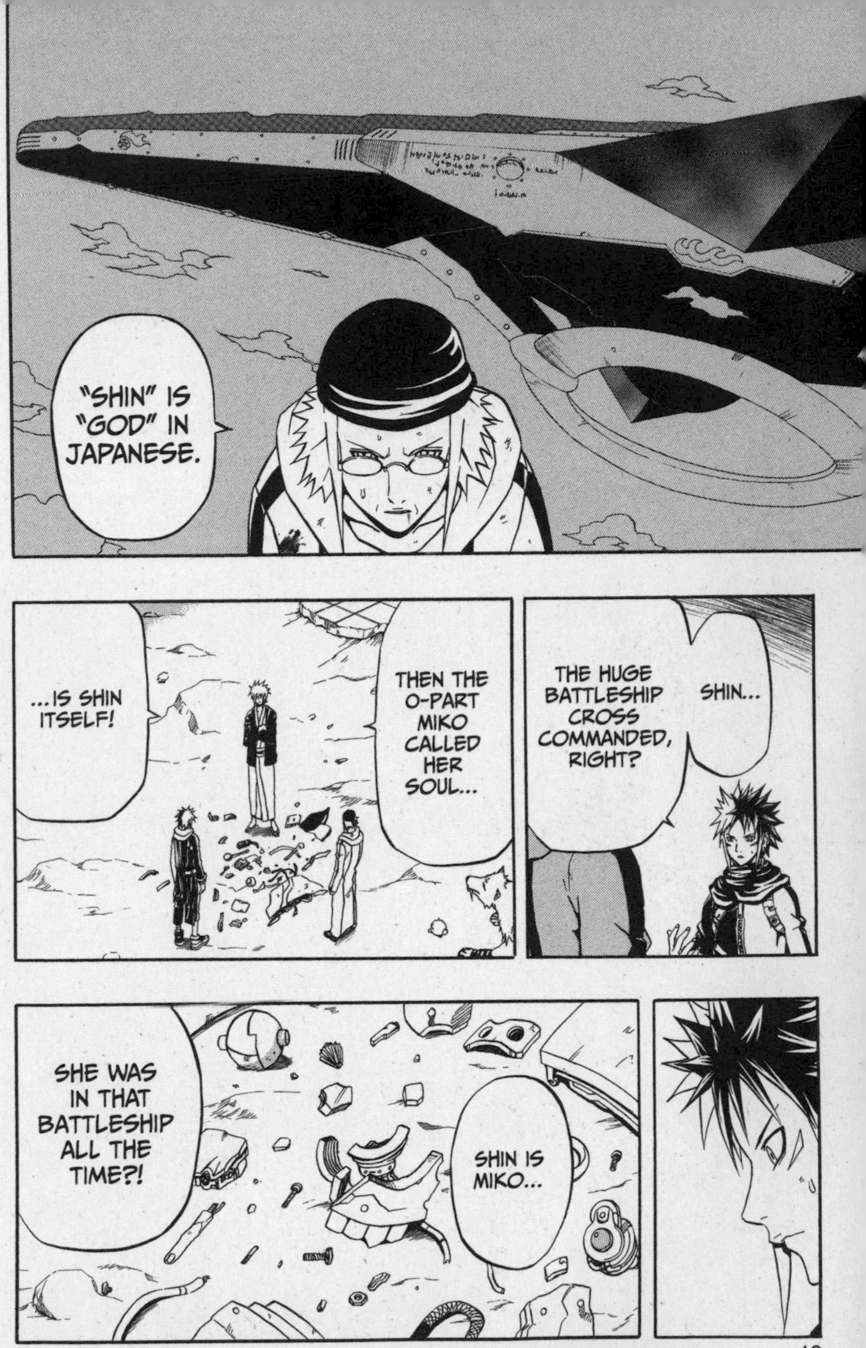
"SHIN" IS "GOD" IN JAPANESE.
SHIN...
THE HUGE BATTLESHIP CROSS COMMANDED, RIGHT?
THEN THE O-PART MIKO CALLED HER SOUL...
...IS SHIN ITSELF!
SHIN IS MIKO...
SHE WAS IN THAT BATTLESHIP ALL THE TIME?!

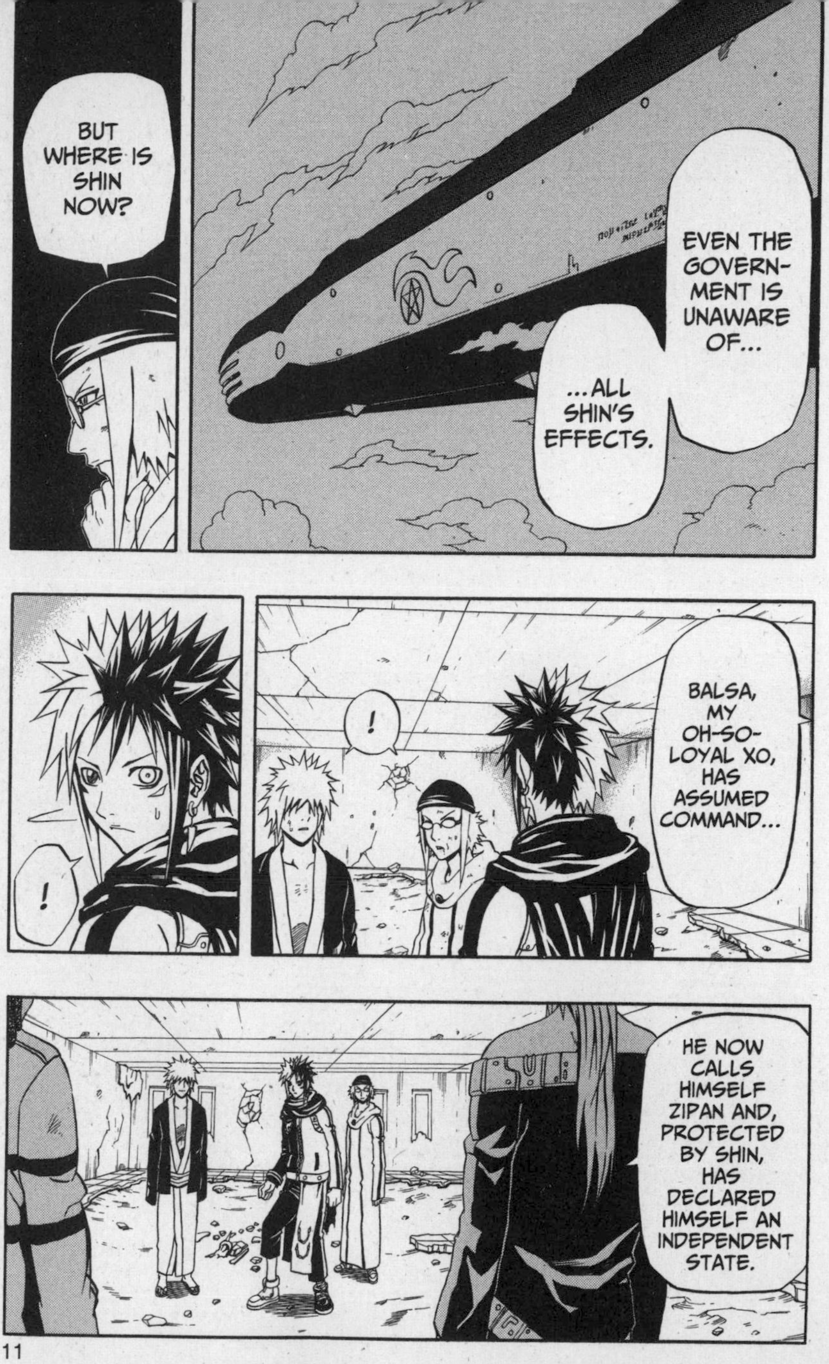
EVEN THE GOVERN-MENT IS UNAWARE OF...
...ALL SHIN'S EFFECTS.
BUT WHERE IS SHIN NOW?
BALSA, MY OH-SO-LOYAL XO, HAS ASSUMED COMMAND...
!
!
HE NOW CALLS HIMSELF ZIPAN AND, PROTECTED BY SHIN, HAS DECLARED HIMSELF AN INDEPENDENT STATE.

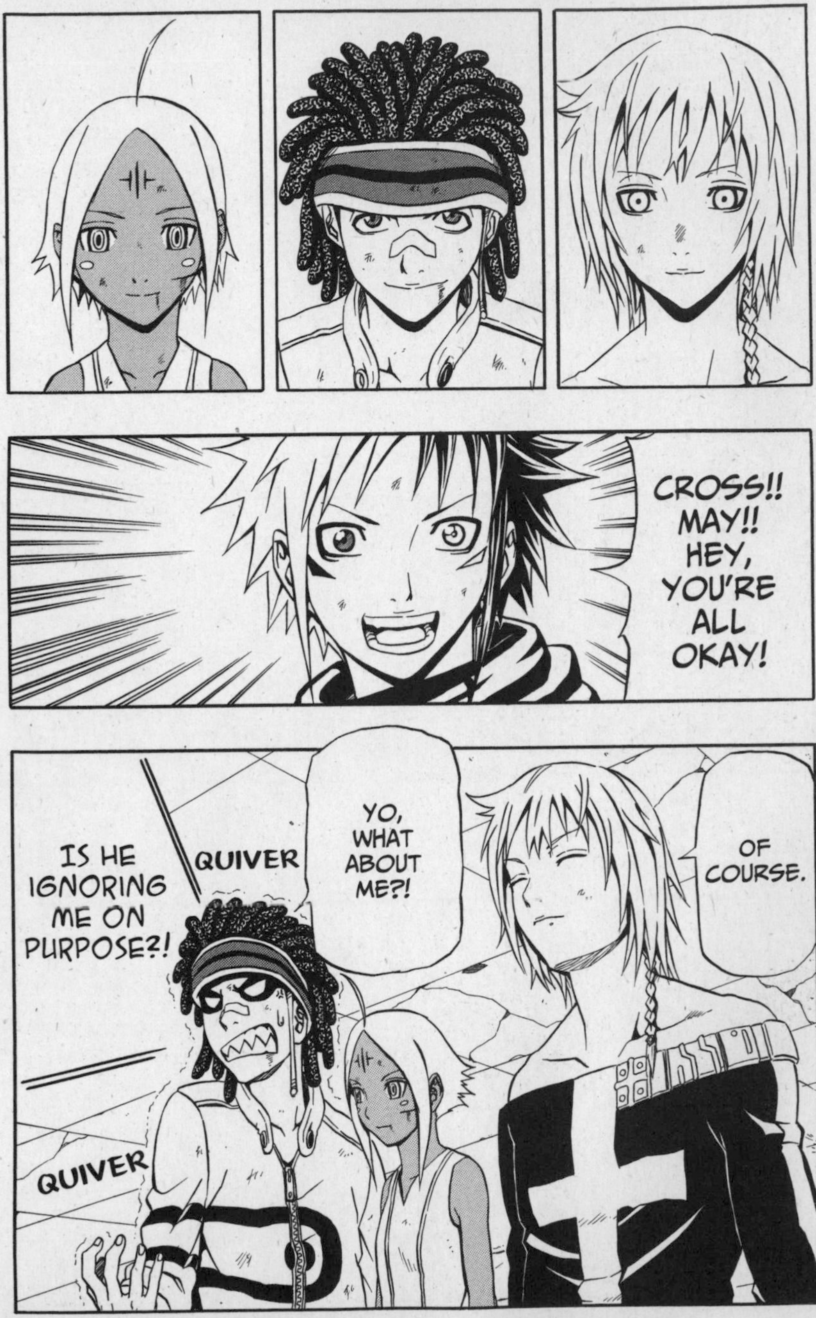
CROSS!! MAY!! HEY, YOU'RE ALL OKAY!
OF COURSE.
YO, WHAT ABOUT ME?!
QUIVER
IS HE IGNORING ME ON PURPOSE?!
QUIVER

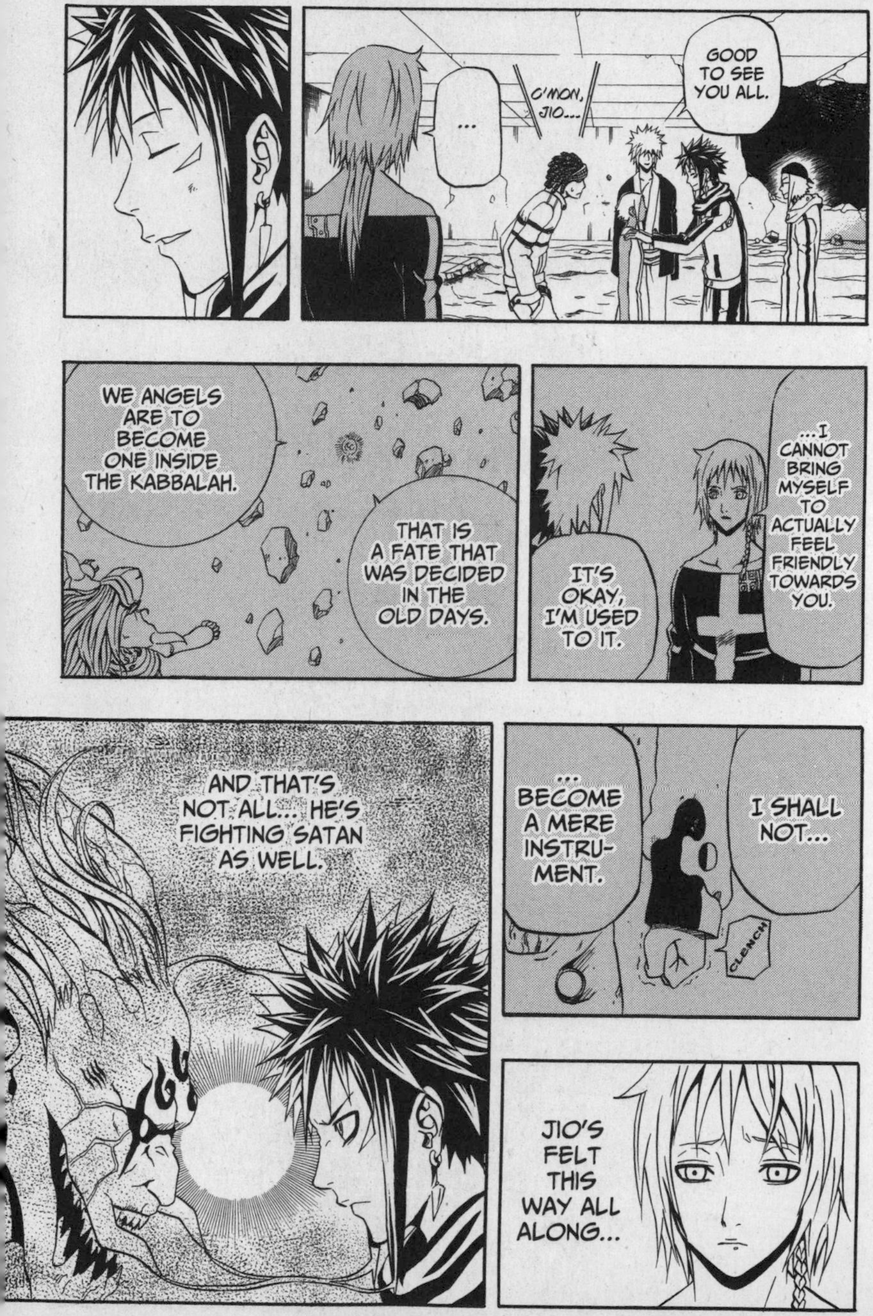
GOOD TO SEE YOU ALL.
C'MON, JIO...
...
...I CANNOT BRING MYSELF TO ACTUALLY FEEL FRIENDLY TOWARDS YOU.
IT'S OKAY, I'M USED TO IT.
WE ANGELS ARE TO BECOME ONE INSIDE THE KABBALAH.
THAT IS A FATE THAT WAS DECIDED IN THE OLD DAYS.
I SHALL NOT...
...BECOME A MERE INSTRUMENT.
CLENCH
JIO'S FELT THIS WAY ALL ALONG...
AND THAT'S NOT ALL... HE'S FIGHTING SATAN AS WELL.

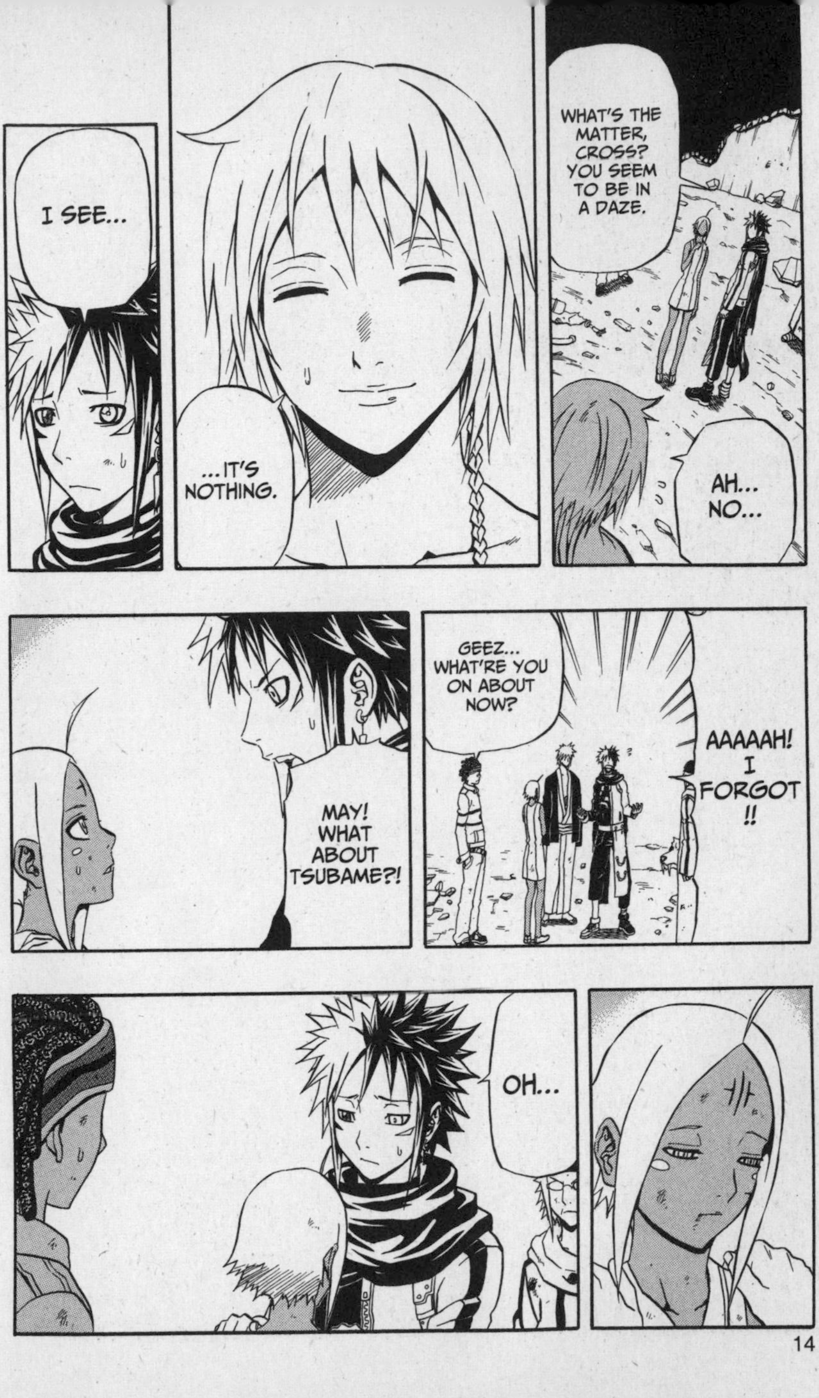
WHAT'S THE MATTER, CROSS? YOU SEEM TO BE IN A DAZE.
AH... NO...
...IT'S NOTHING.
I SEE...
AAAAAH! I FORGOT !!
GEEZ... WHAT'RE YOU ON ABOUT NOW?
MAY! WHAT ABOUT TSUBAME?!
OH...

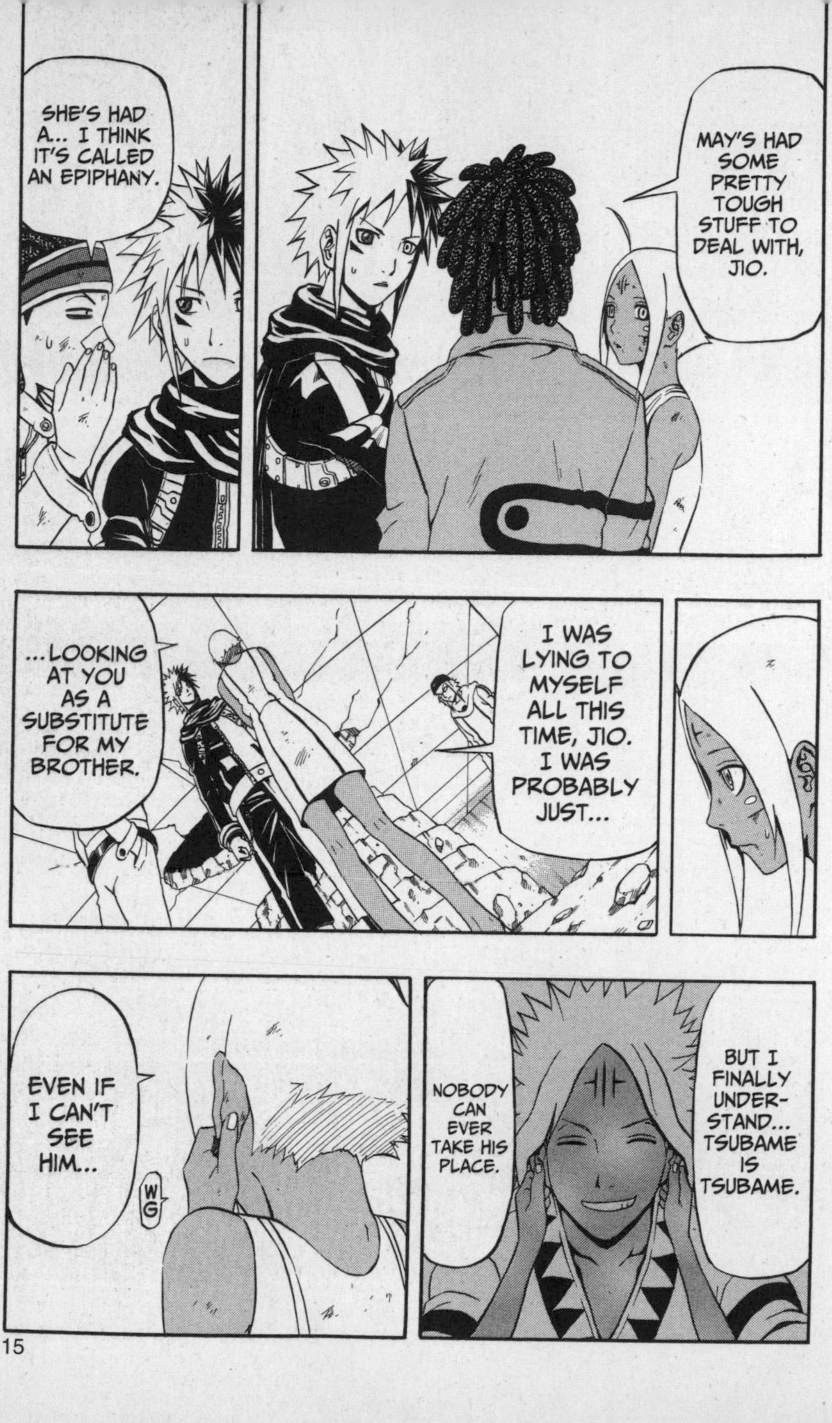
MAY'S HAD SOME PRETTY TOUGH STUFF TO DEAL WITH, JIO.
SHE'S HAD A... I THINK IT'S CALLED AN EPIPHANY.
I WAS LYING TO MYSELF ALL THIS TIME, JIO. I WAS PROBABLY JUST...
...LOOKING AT YOU AS A SUBSTITUTE FOR MY BROTHER.
BUT I FINALLY UNDER-STAND... TSUBAME IS TSUBAME.
NOBODY CAN EVER TAKE HIS PLACE.
EVEN IF I CAN'T SEE HIM...
WG

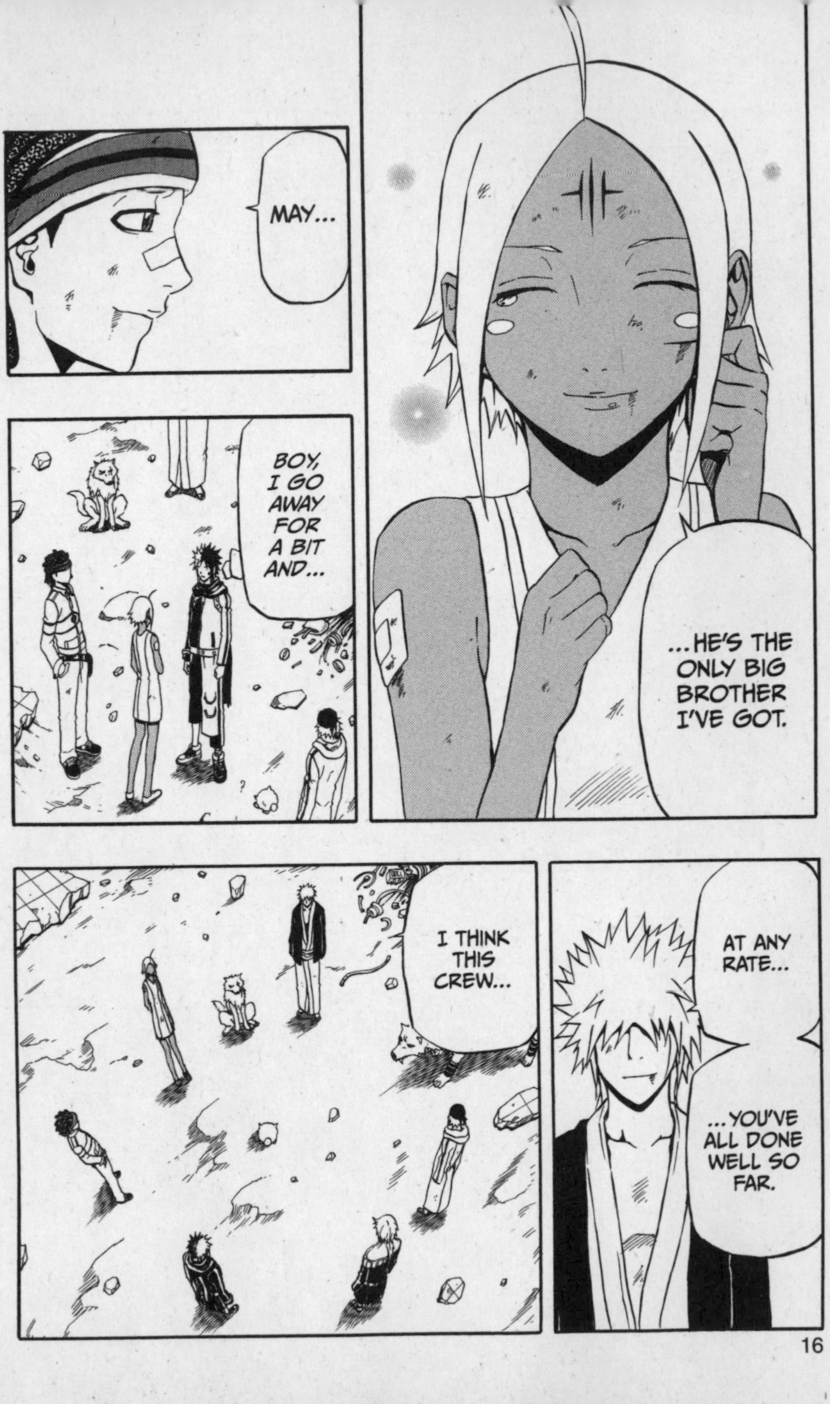
...HE'S THE ONLY BIG BROTHER I'VE GOT.
MAY...
BOY, I GO AWAY FOR A BIT AND...
AT ANY RATE...
...YOU'VE ALL DONE WELL SO FAR.
I THINK THIS CREW...

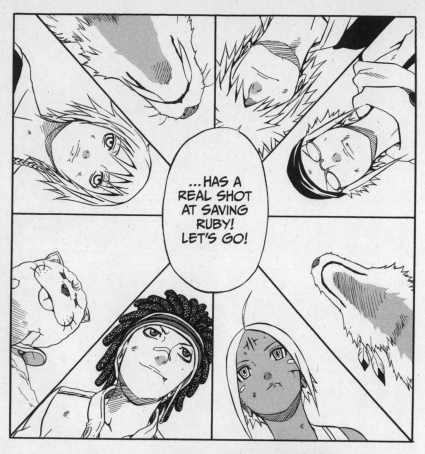

...HAS A REAL SHOT AT SAVING RUBY! LET'S GO!

YEAH!!

STEA HEAD-
QUARTERS'
BASEMENT,
HUH?

...OUR
GOAL.

THIS
IS...

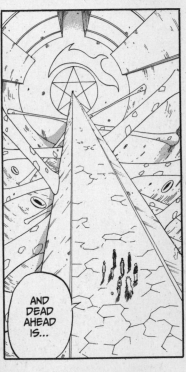

AND
DEAD
AHEAD
IS...

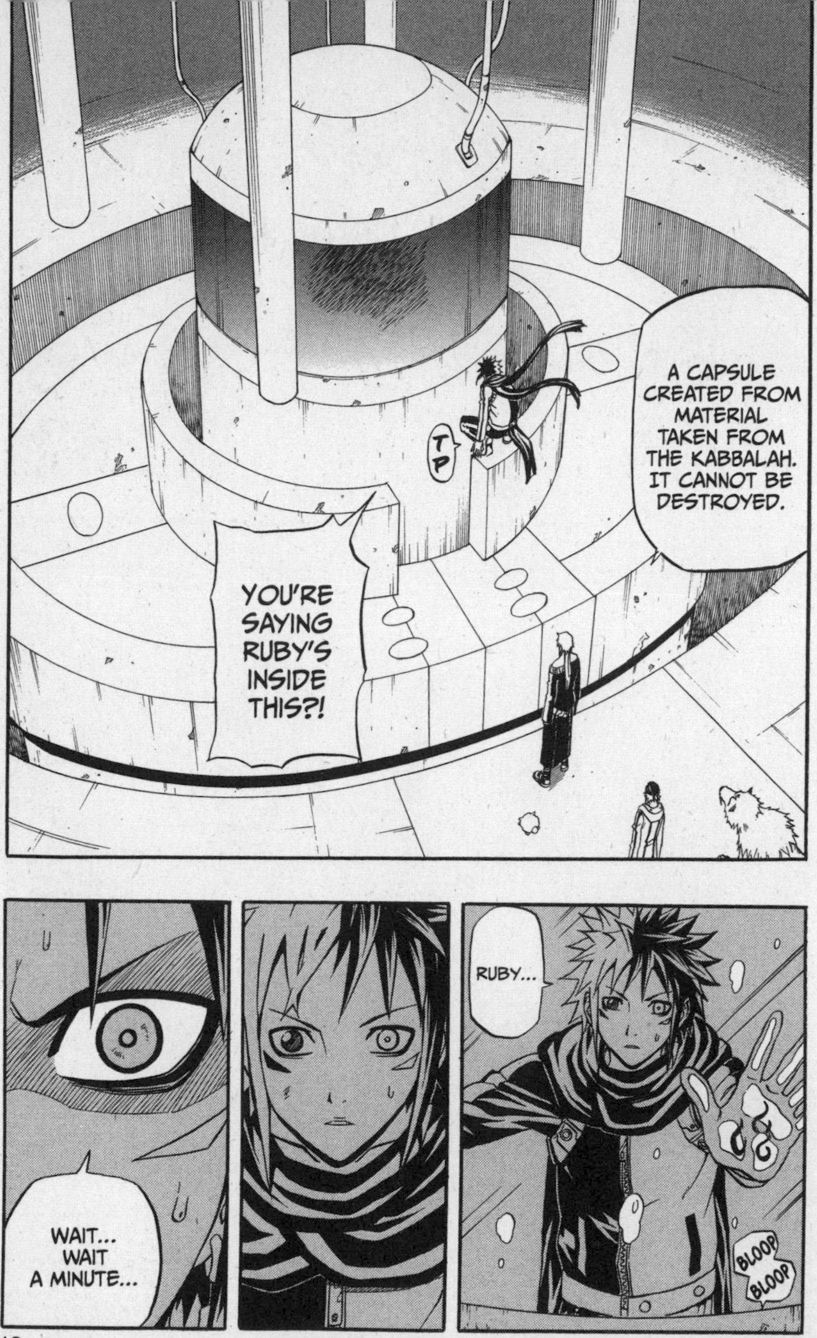
A CAPSULE CREATED FROM MATERIAL TAKEN FROM THE KABBALAH. IT CANNOT BE DESTROYED.
TP
YOU'RE SAYING RUBY'S INSIDE THIS?!
RUBY...
BLOOP BLOOP
WAIT... WAIT A MINUTE...

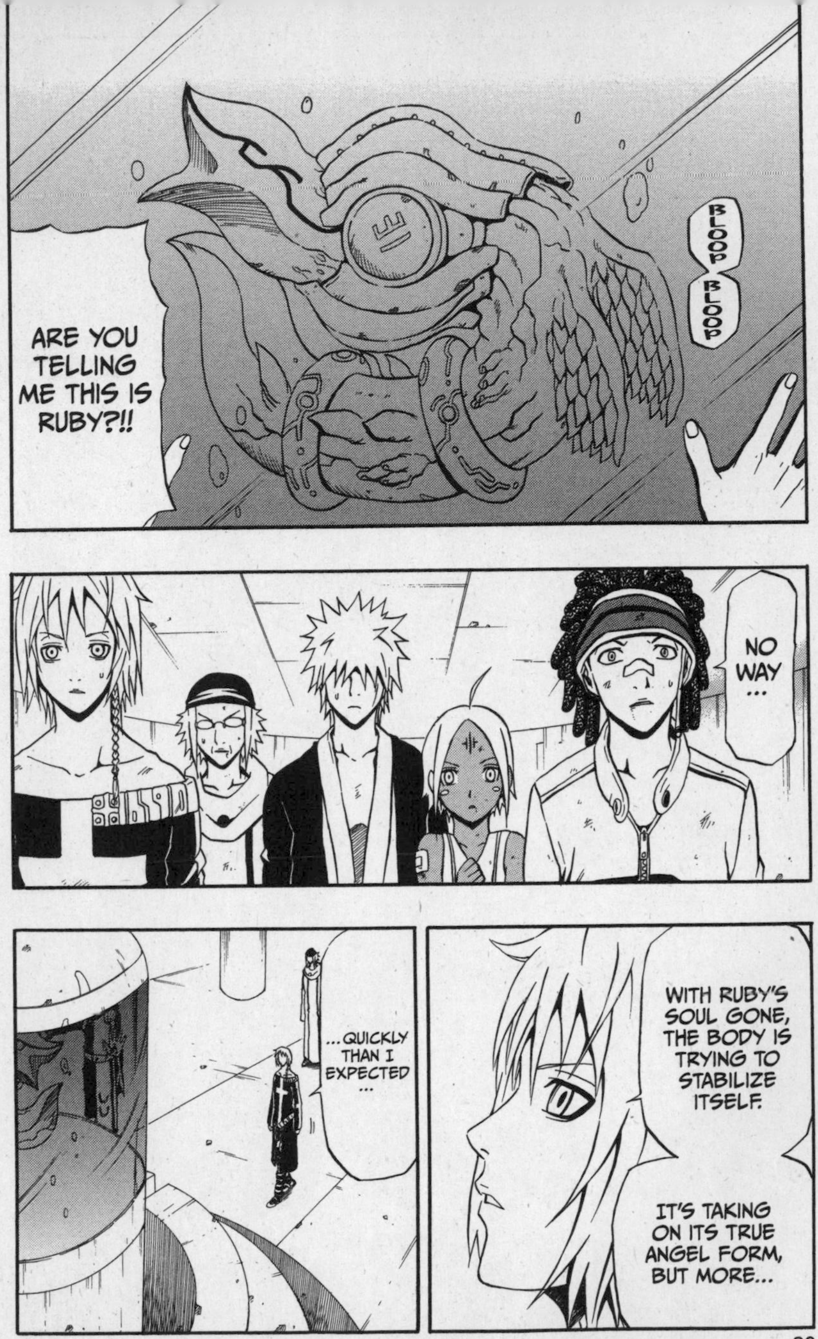
BLOOP BLOOP
ARE YOU TELLING ME THIS IS RUBY?!!
NO WAY ...
WITH RUBY'S SOUL GONE, THE BODY IS TRYING TO STABILIZE ITSELF.
IT'S TAKING ON ITS TRUE ANGEL FORM, BUT MORE...
...QUICKLY THAN I EXPECTED ...

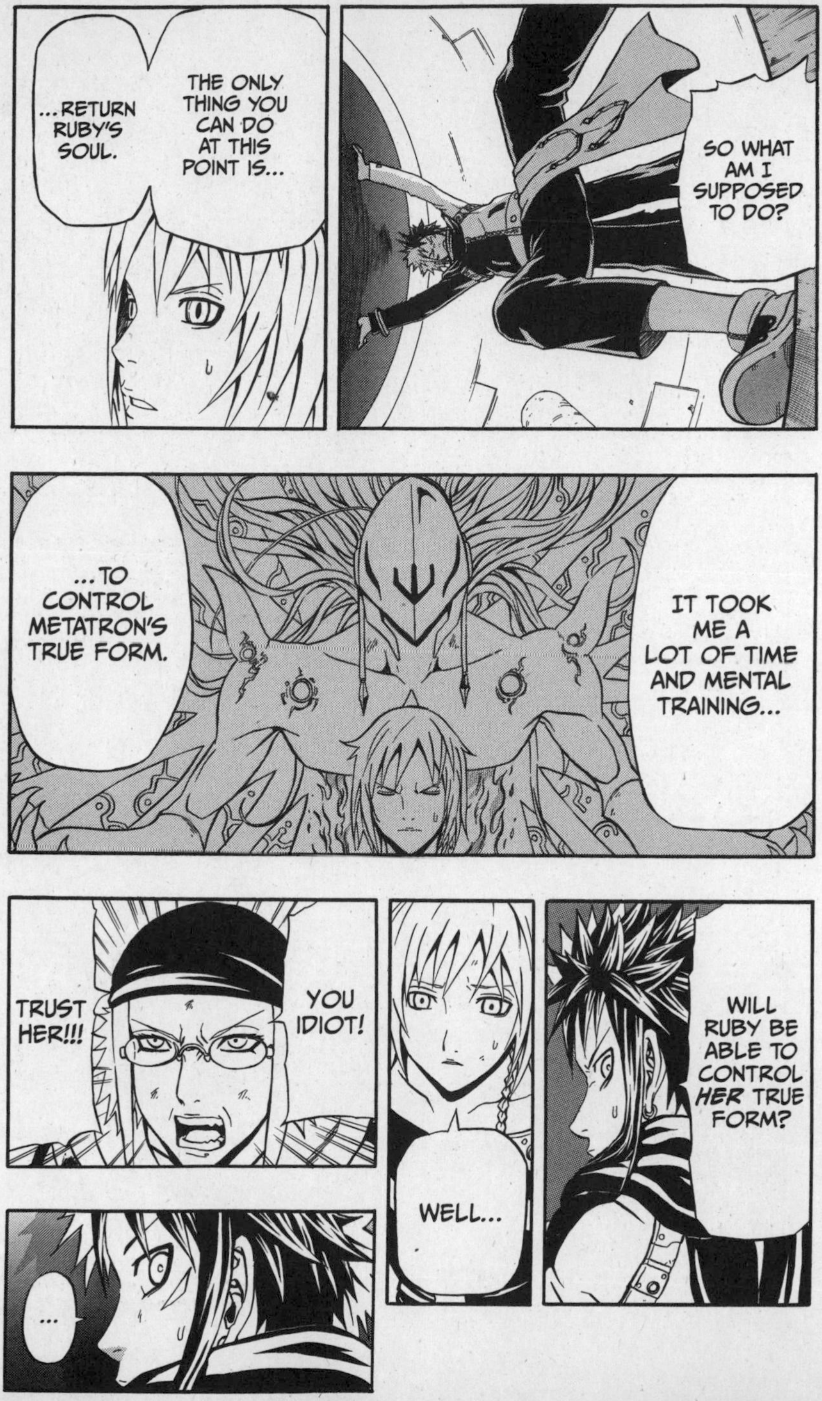
SO WHAT AM I SUPPOSED TO DO?
THE ONLY THING YOU CAN DO AT THIS POINT IS...
...RETURN RUBY'S SOUL.
IT TOOK ME A LOT OF TIME AND MENTAL TRAINING...
...TO CONTROL METATRON'S TRUE FORM.
WILL RUBY BE ABLE TO CONTROL *HER* TRUE FORM?
WELL...
YOU IDIOT!
TRUST HER!!!
...

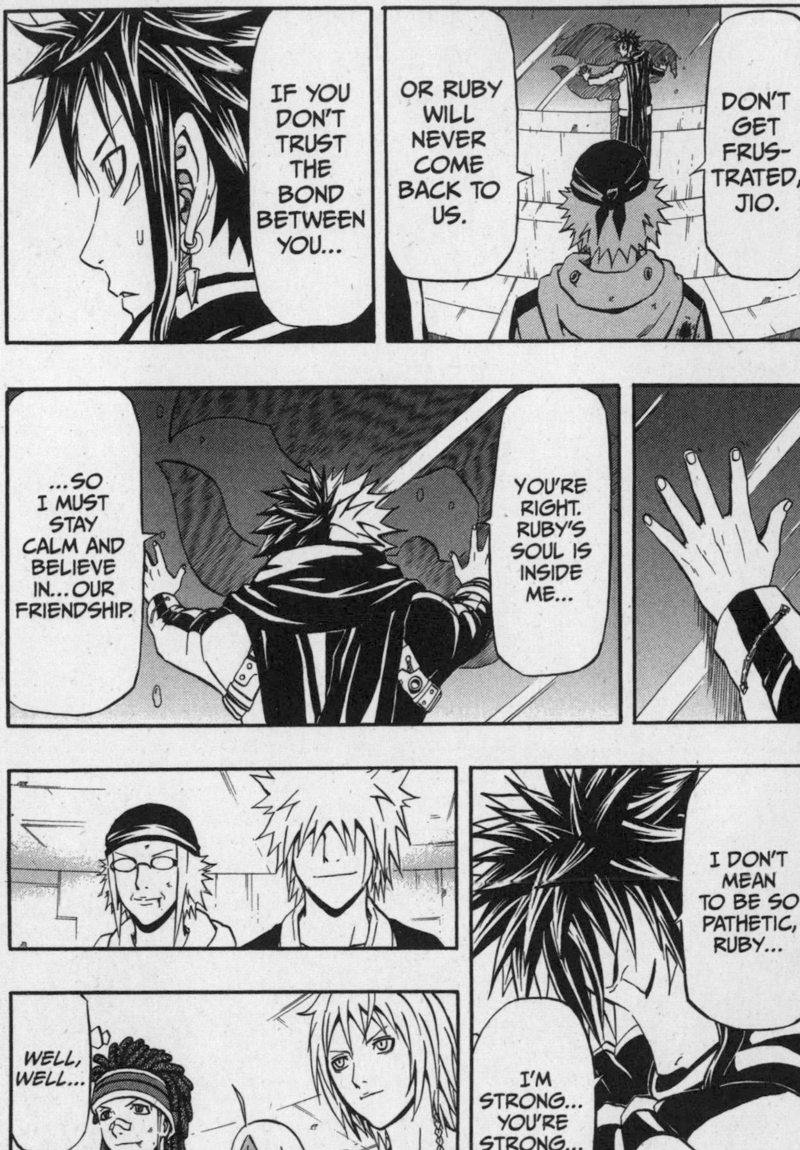
DON'T GET FRUS-TRATED, JIO.
OR RUBY WILL NEVER COME BACK TO US.
IF YOU DON'T TRUST THE BOND BETWEEN YOU...
YOU'RE RIGHT. RUBY'S SOUL IS INSIDE ME...
...SO I MUST STAY CALM AND BELIEVE IN...OUR FRIENDSHIP.
I DON'T MEAN TO BE SO PATHETIC, RUBY...
I'M STRONG... YOU'RE STRONG...
WELL, WELL...

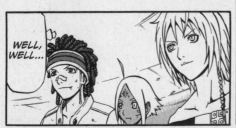

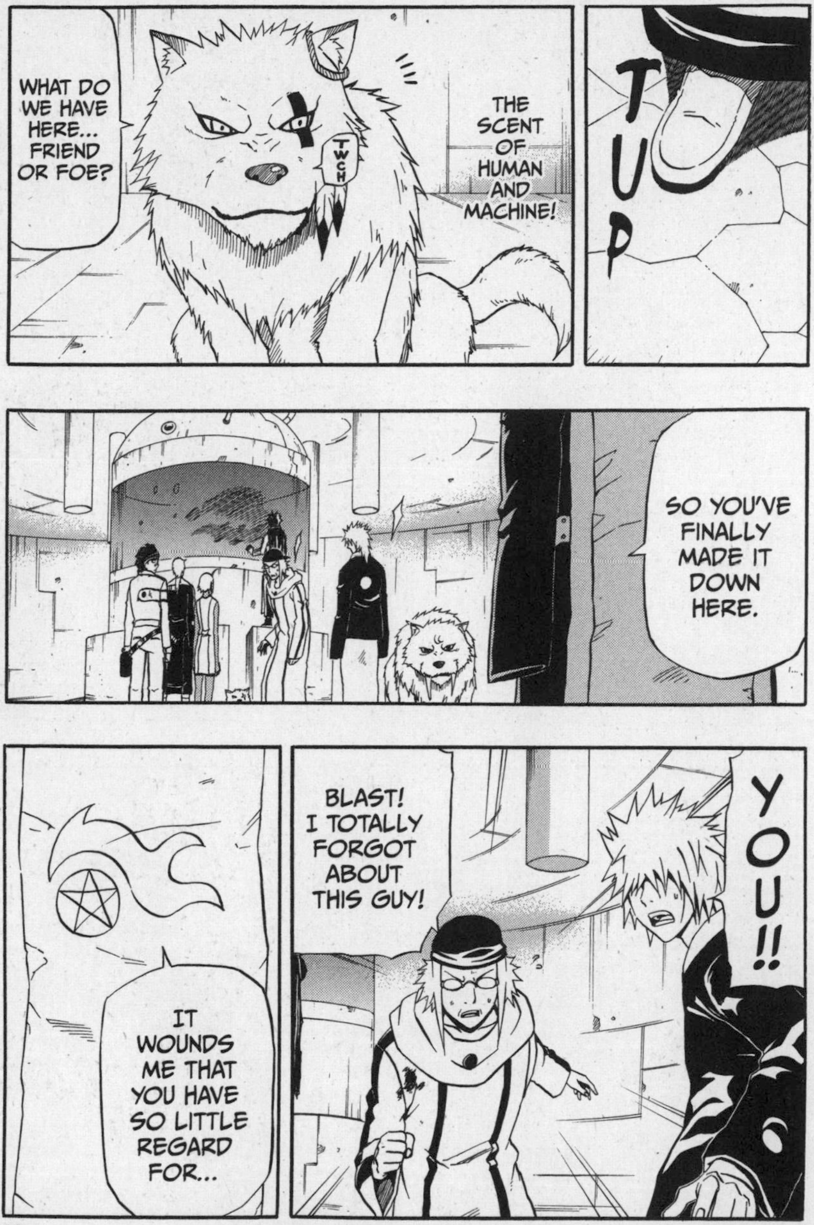
TUP
THE SCENT OF HUMAN AND MACHINE!
TWCH
WHAT DO WE HAVE HERE... FRIEND OR FOE?
SO YOU'VE FINALLY MADE IT DOWN HERE.
YOU!!
BLAST! I TOTALLY FORGOT ABOUT THIS GUY!
IT WOUNDS ME THAT YOU HAVE SO LITTLE REGARD FOR...

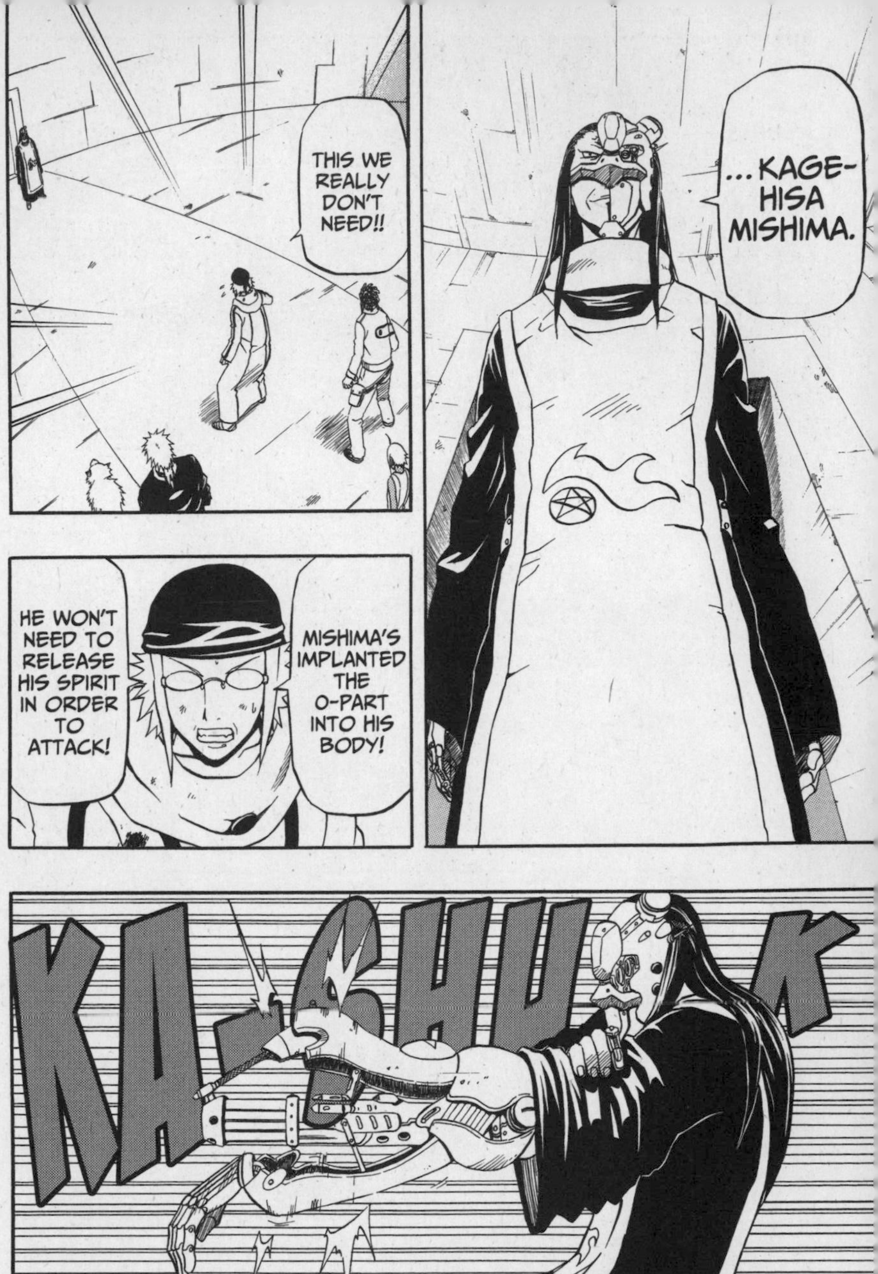

...KAGE-HISA MISHIMA.
THIS WE REALLY DON'T NEED!!
MISHIMA'S IMPLANTED THE O-PART INTO HIS BODY!
HE WON'T NEED TO RELEASE HIS SPIRIT IN ORDER TO ATTACK!
KA-CHU K

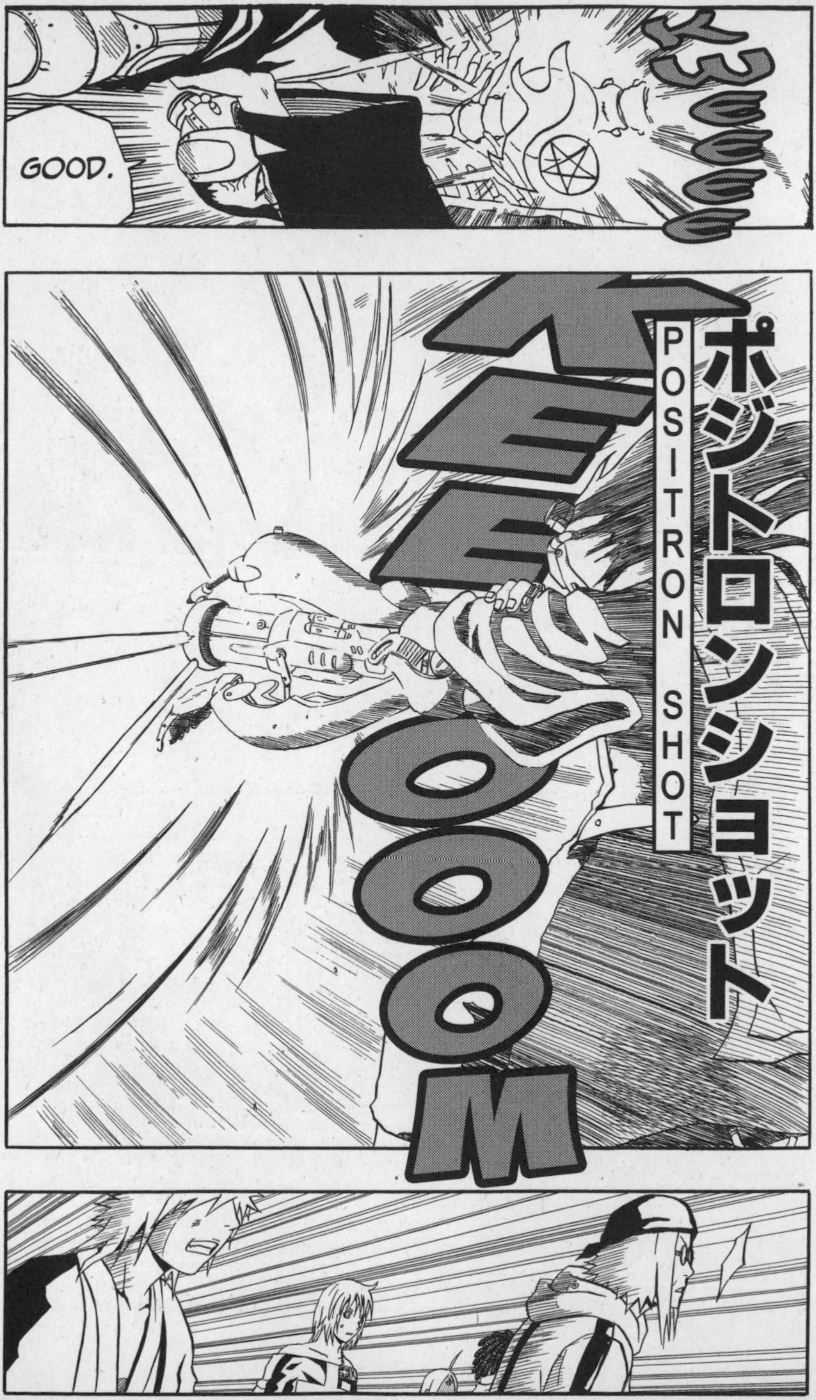
GOOD.
ポジトロンショット
POSITRON SHOT

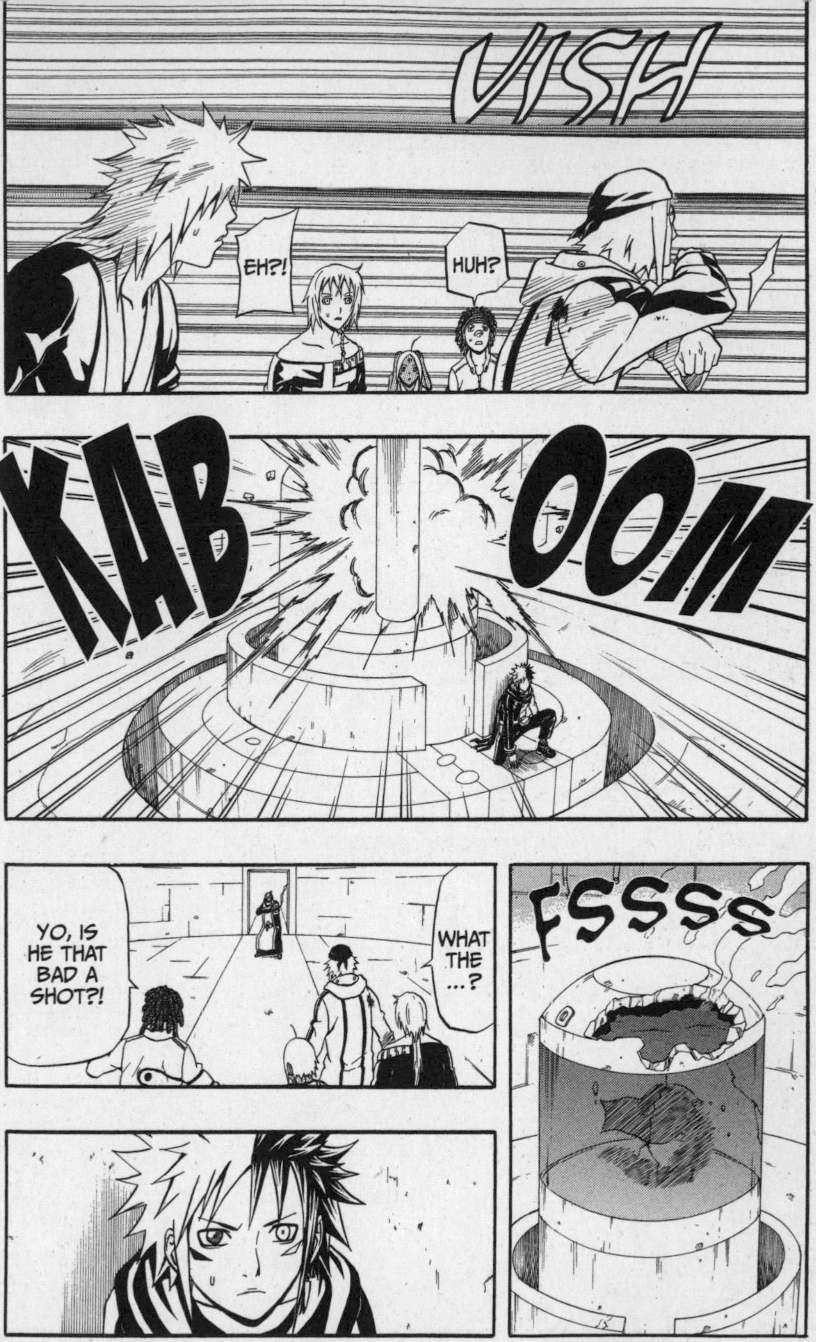
VISH
HUH?
EH?!
KABOOM
FSSSS
WHAT THE ...?
YO, IS HE THAT BAD A SHOT?!

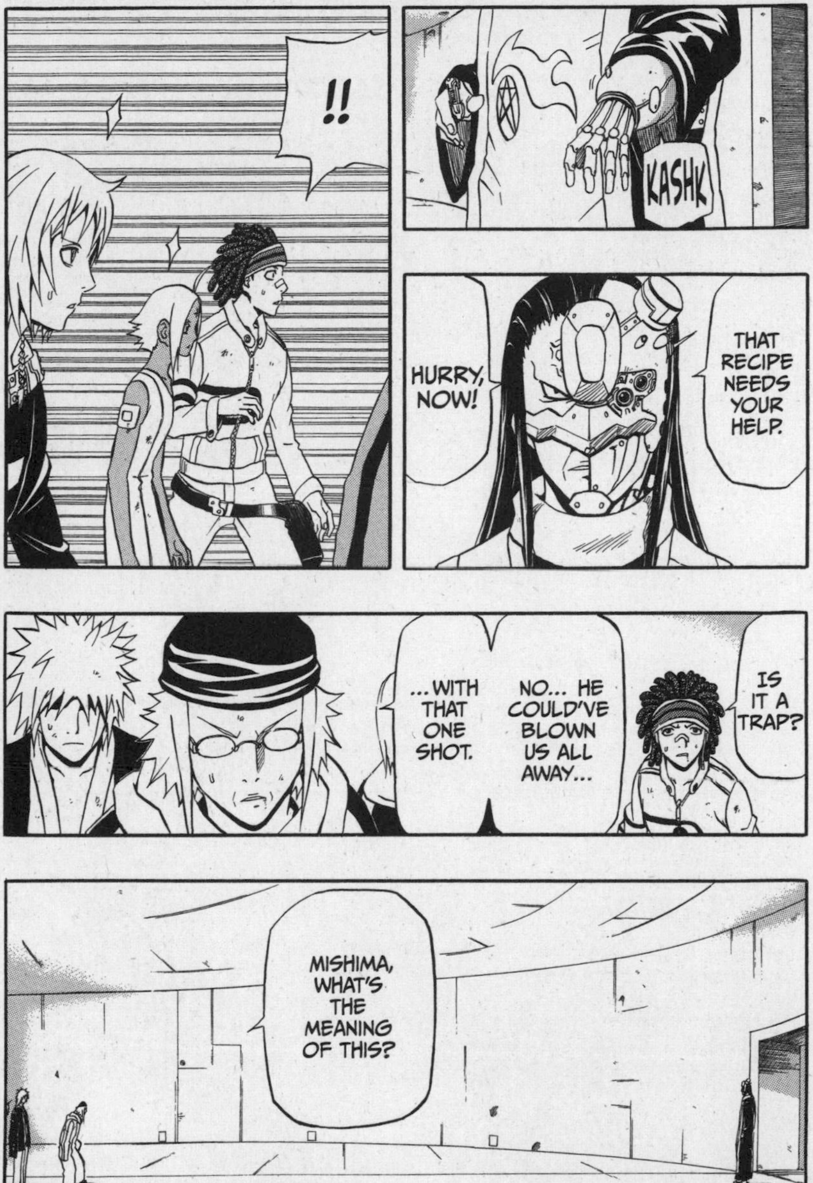
KASHK
THAT RECIPE NEEDS YOUR HELP.
HURRY, NOW!
!!
IS IT A TRAP?
NO... HE COULD'VE BLOWN US ALL AWAY...
...WITH THAT ONE SHOT.
MISHIMA, WHAT'S THE MEANING OF THIS?

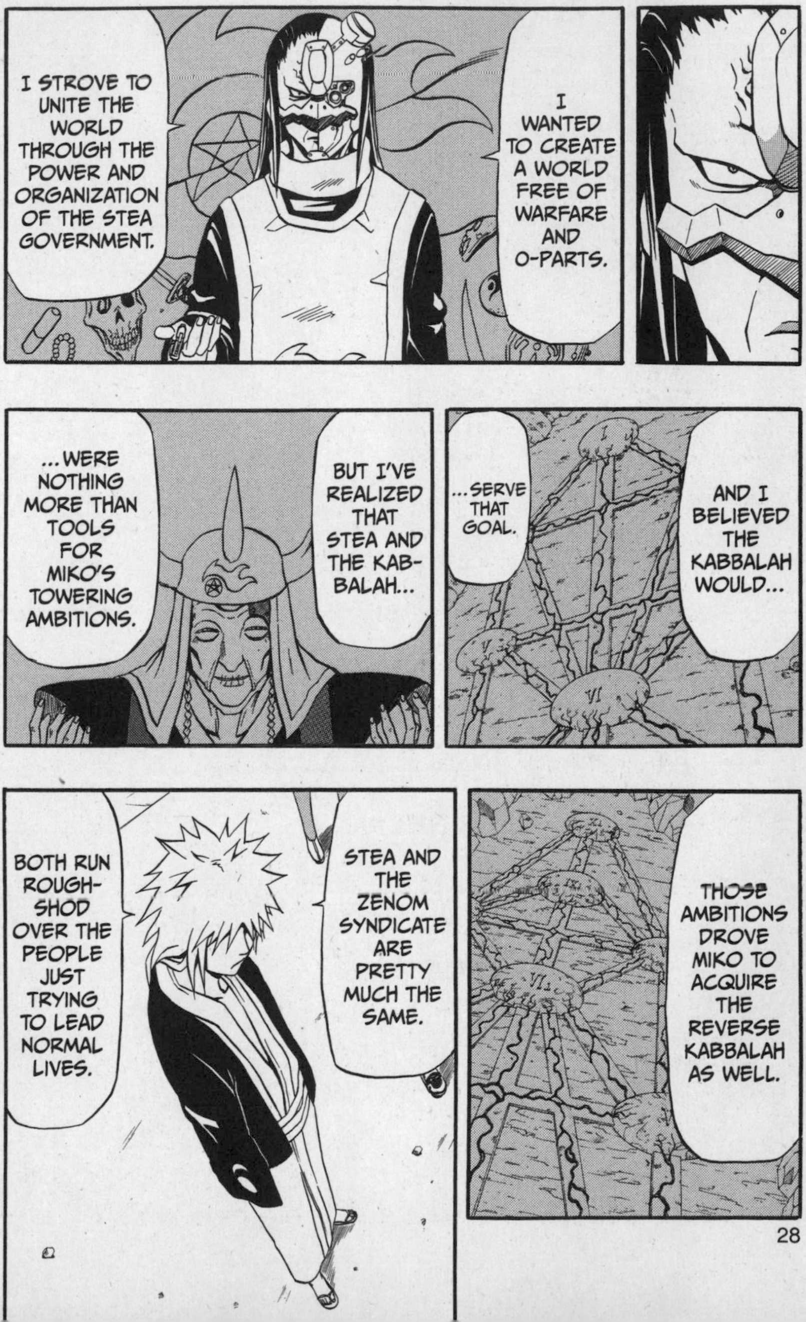
I WANTED TO CREATE A WORLD FREE OF WARFARE AND O-PARTS.
I STROVE TO UNITE THE WORLD THROUGH THE POWER AND ORGANIZATION OF THE STEA GOVERNMENT.
AND I BELIEVED THE KABBALAH WOULD...
...SERVE THAT GOAL.
BUT I'VE REALIZED THAT STEA AND THE KAB-BALAH...
...WERE NOTHING MORE THAN TOOLS FOR MIKO'S TOWERING AMBITIONS.
THOSE AMBITIONS DROVE MIKO TO ACQUIRE THE REVERSE KABBALAH AS WELL.
STEA AND THE ZENOM SYNDICATE ARE PRETTY MUCH THE SAME.
BOTH RUN ROUGH-SHOD OVER THE PEOPLE JUST TRYING TO LEAD NORMAL LIVES.

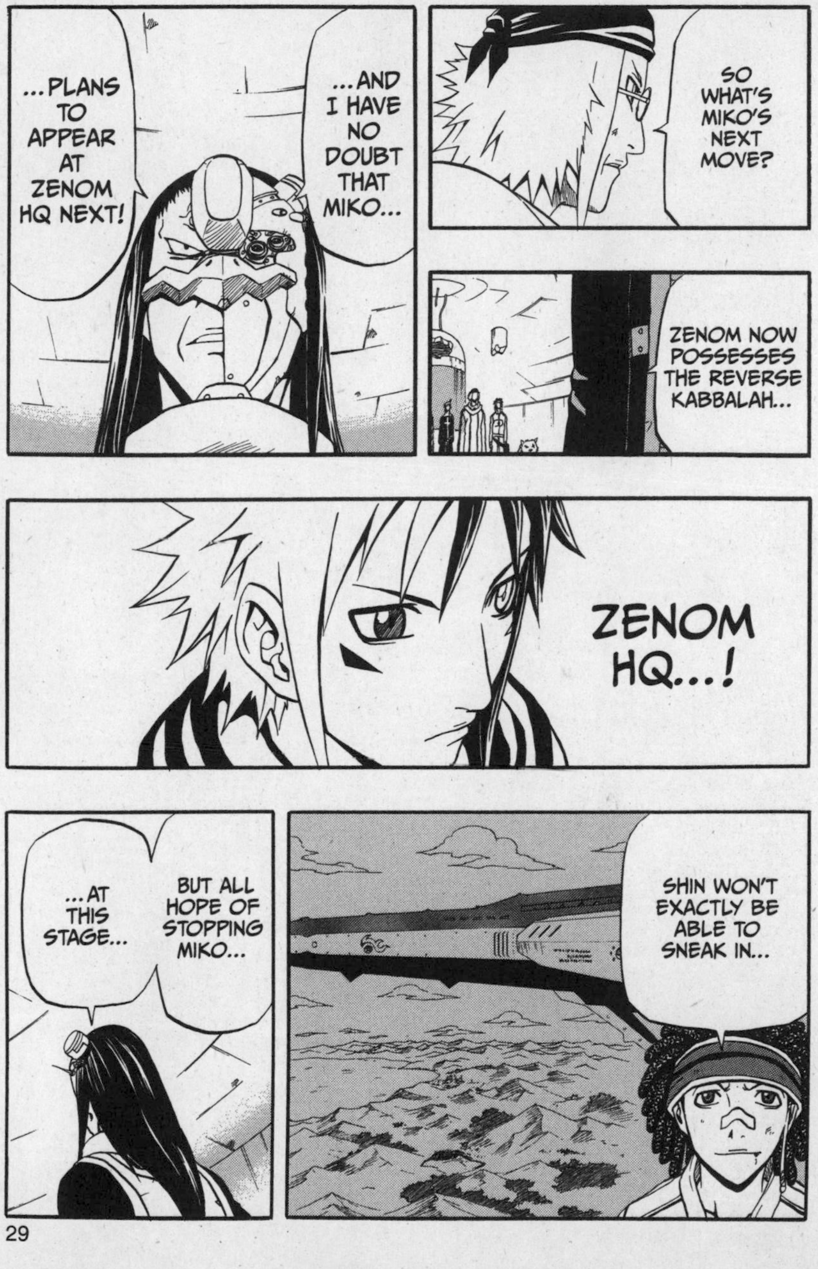
SO WHAT'S MIKO'S NEXT MOVE?
ZENOM NOW POSSESSES THE REVERSE KABBALAH...
...AND I HAVE NO DOUBT THAT MIKO...
...PLANS TO APPEAR AT ZENOM HQ NEXT!
ZENOM HQ...!
SHIN WON'T EXACTLY BE ABLE TO SNEAK IN...
BUT ALL HOPE OF STOPPING MIKO...
...AT THIS STAGE...

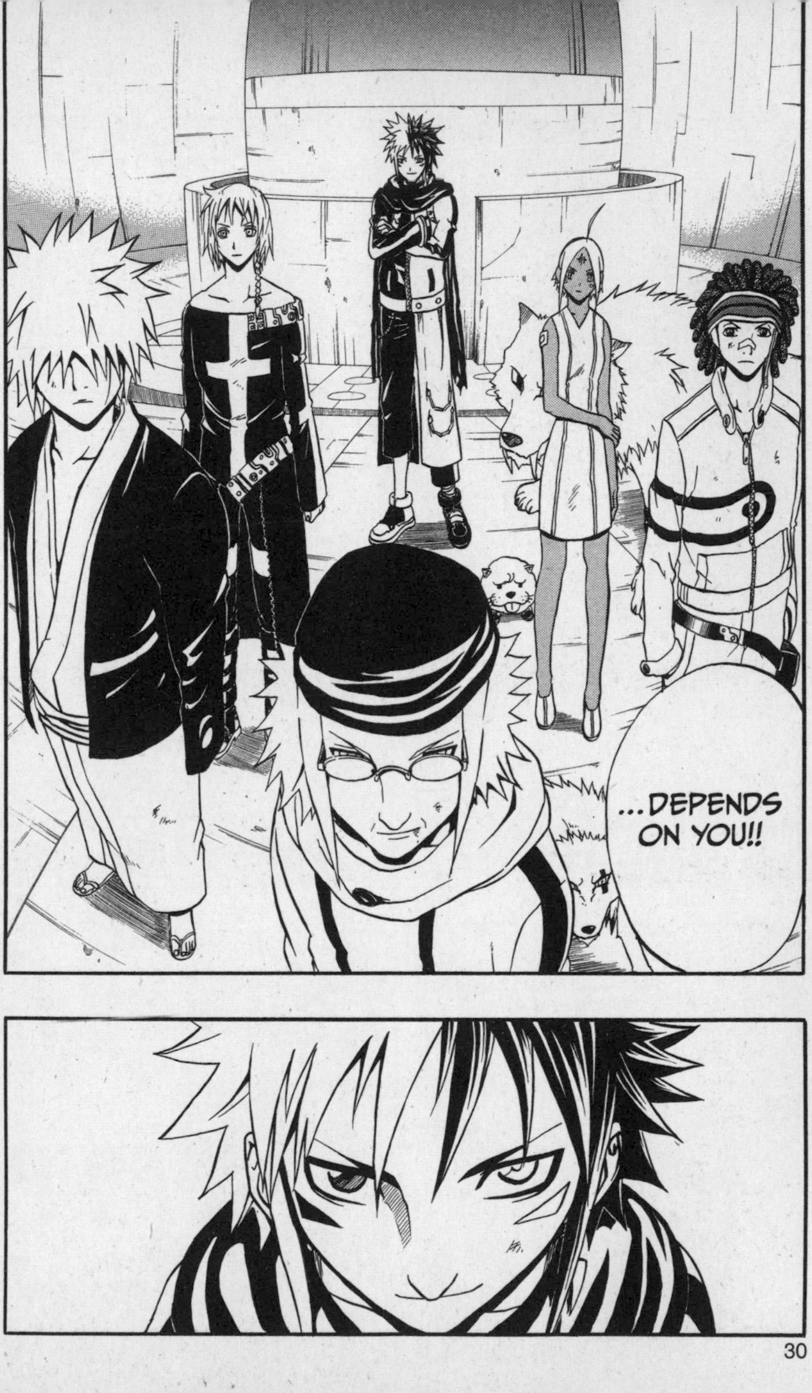
...DEPENDS ON YOU!!

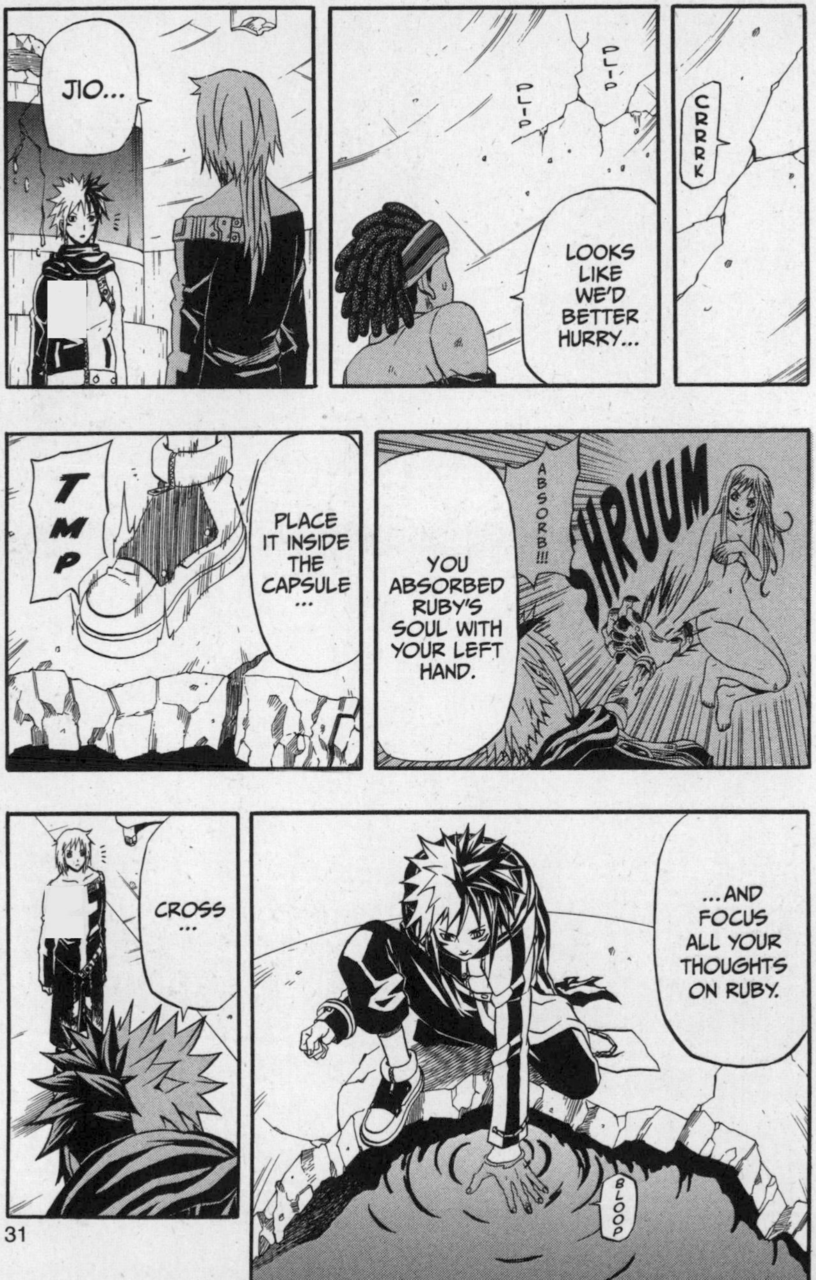
CRRRK
PLIP PLIP
LOOKS LIKE WE'D BETTER HURRY...
JIO...
ABSORB!!!
SHRUUM
YOU ABSORBED RUBY'S SOUL WITH YOUR LEFT HAND.
TMP
PLACE IT INSIDE THE CAPSULE...
...AND FOCUS ALL YOUR THOUGHTS ON RUBY.
BLOOP
CROSS...

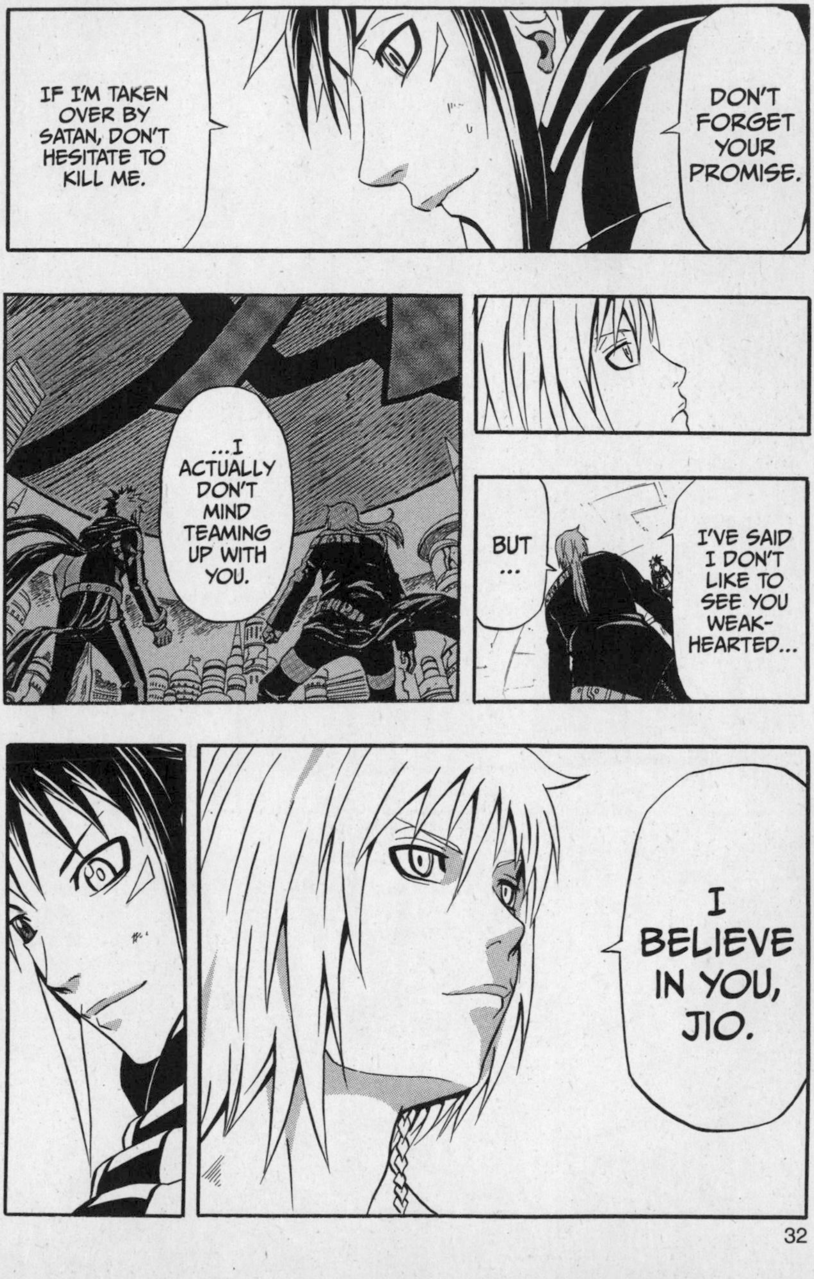
DON'T FORGET YOUR PROMISE.
IF I'M TAKEN OVER BY SATAN, DON'T HESITATE TO KILL ME.
I'VE SAID I DON'T LIKE TO SEE YOU WEAK-HEARTED...
BUT ...
...I ACTUALLY DON'T MIND TEAMING UP WITH YOU.
I BELIEVE IN YOU, JIO.

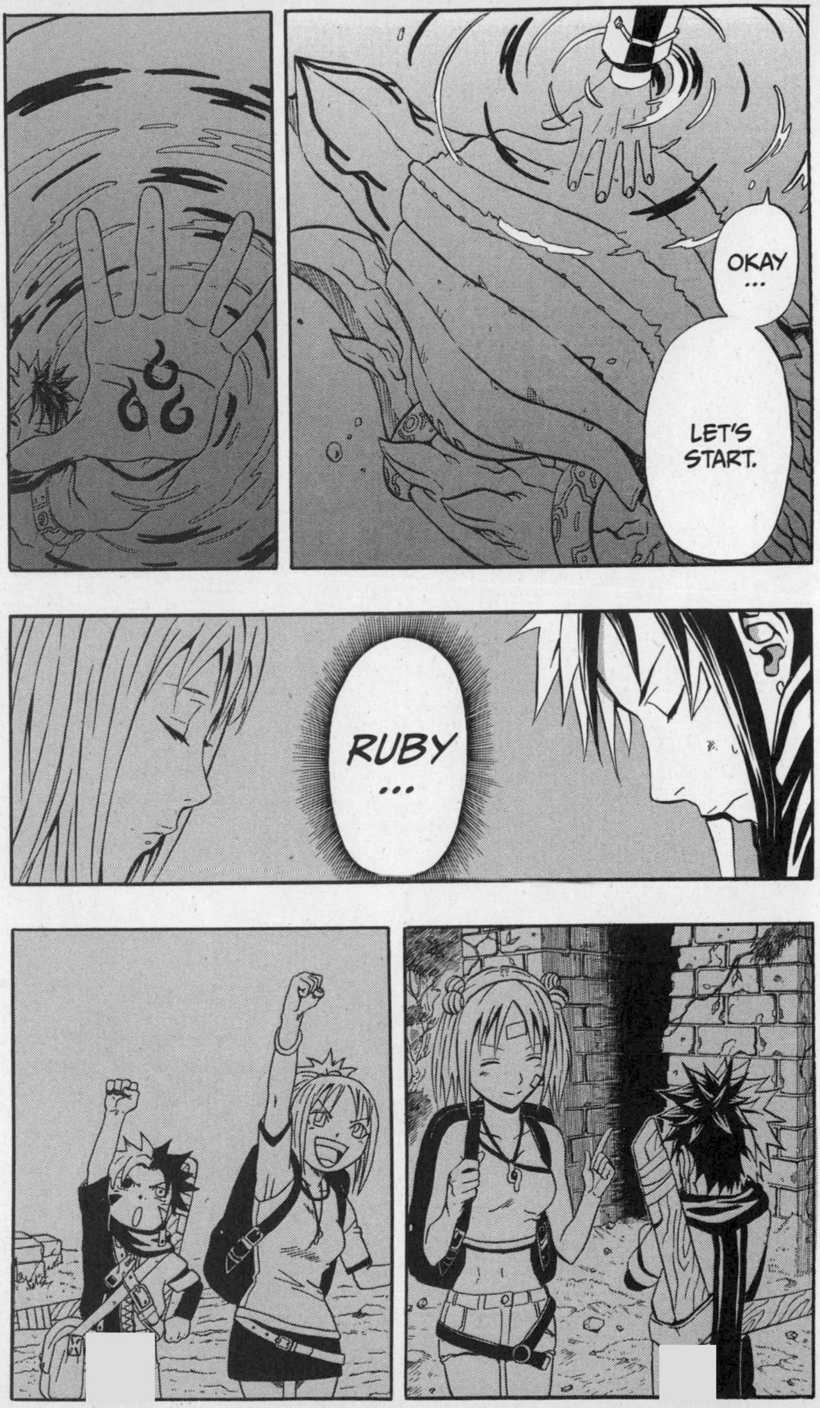
OKAY ...
LET'S START.
RUBY ...

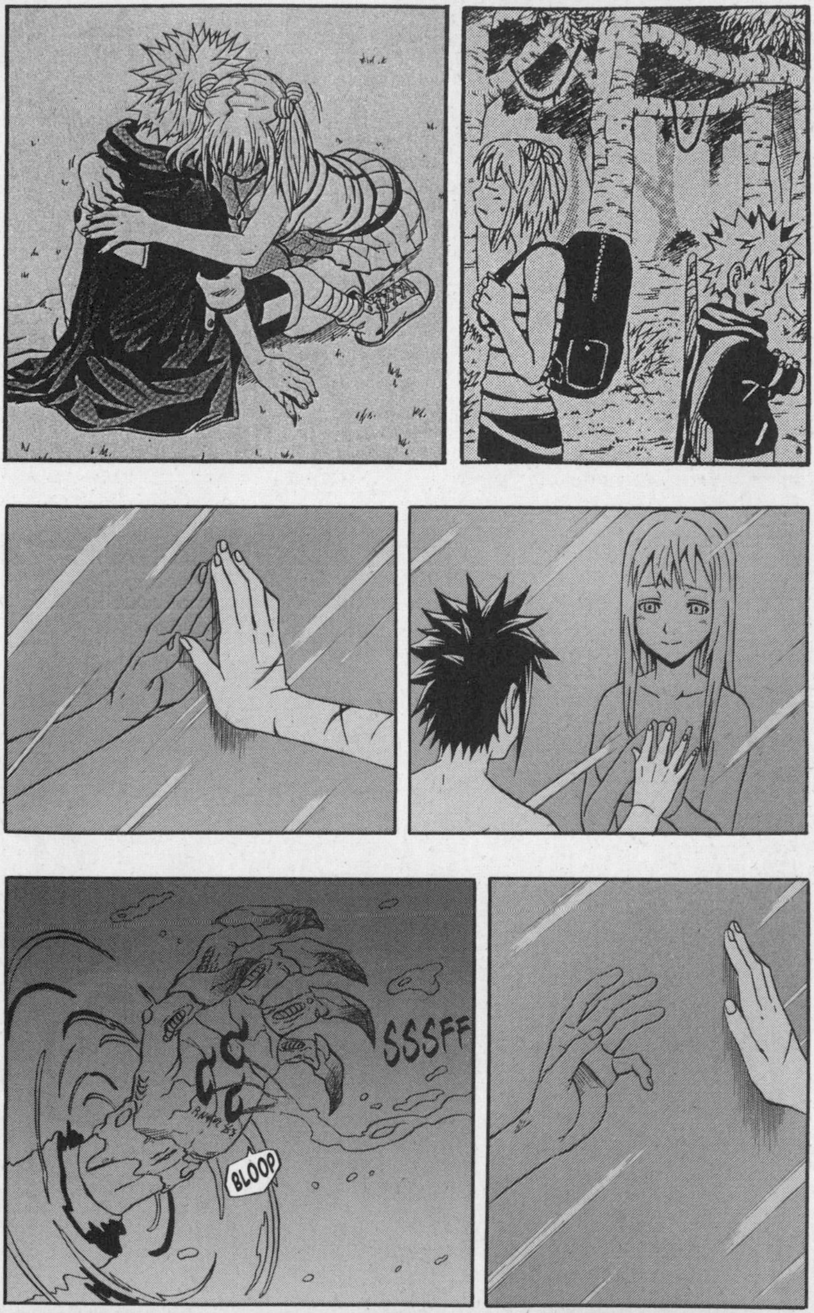
SSSFF
BLOOP

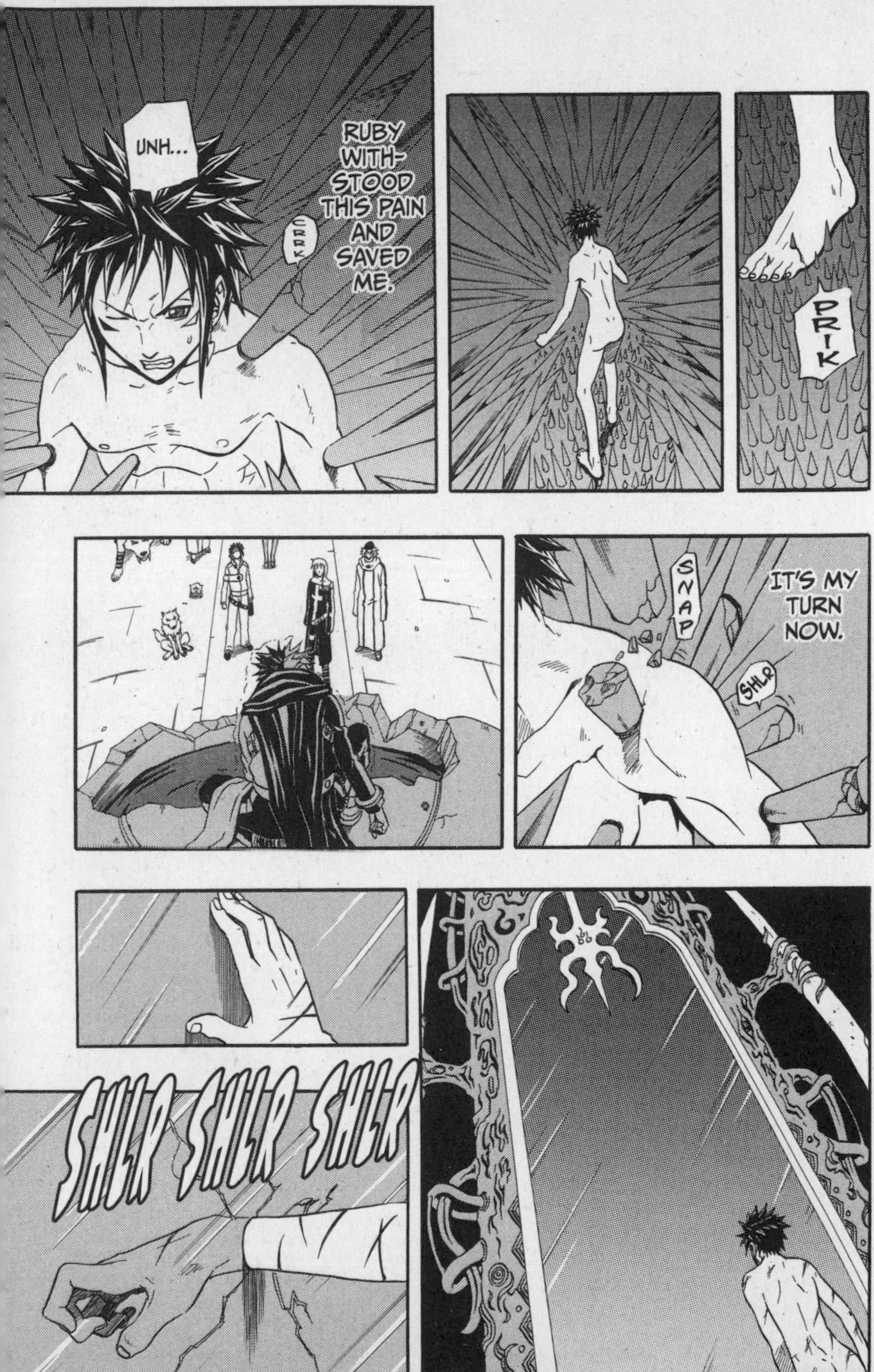
PRIK
RUBY WITH-STOOD THIS PAIN AND SAVED ME.
UNH...
CRRK
IT'S MY TURN NOW.
SNAP
SHLR
SHLR SHLR SHLR

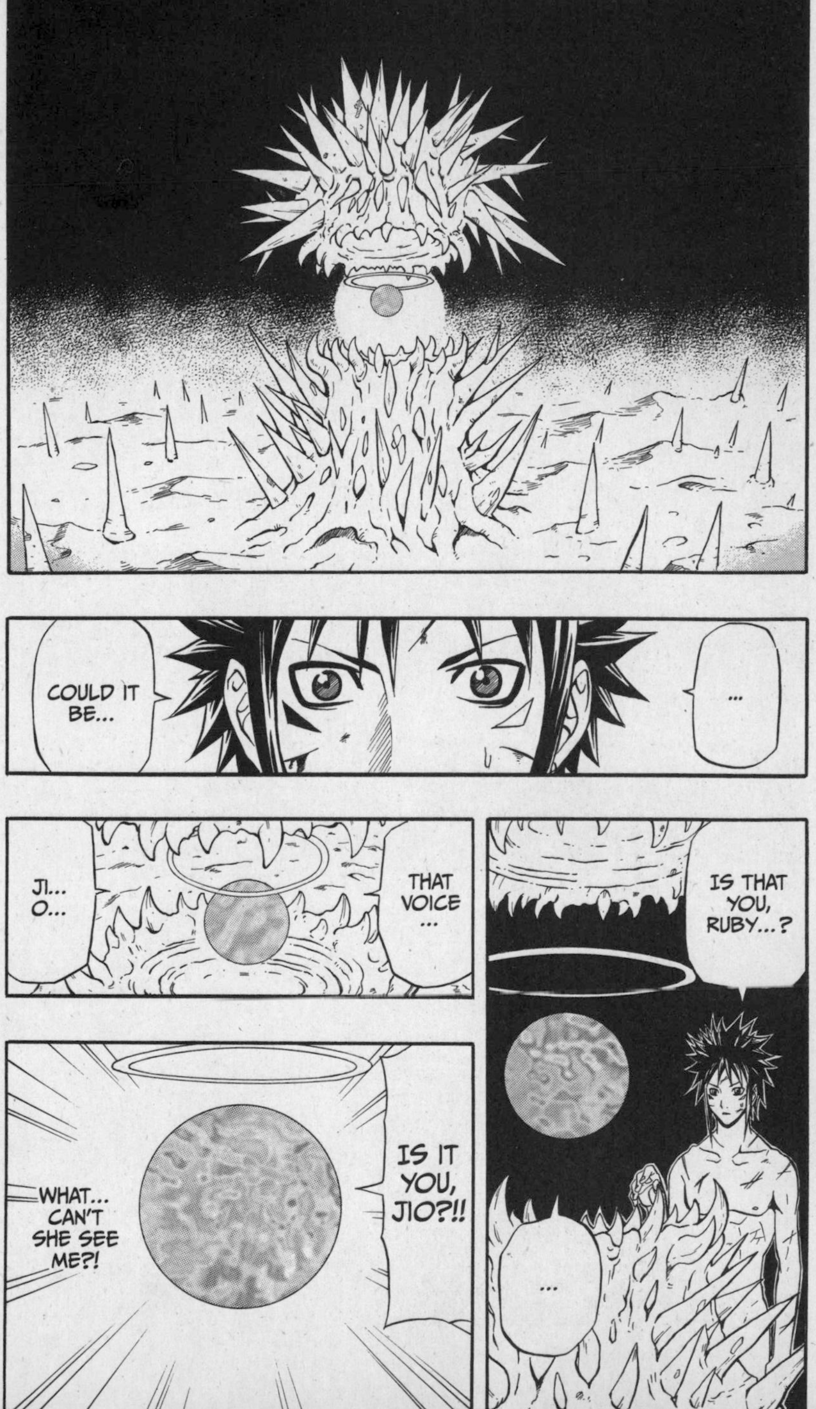
...
COULD IT BE...
IS THAT YOU, RUBY...?
...
THAT VOICE ...
JI... O...
IS IT YOU, JIO?!!
WHAT... CAN'T SHE SEE ME?!

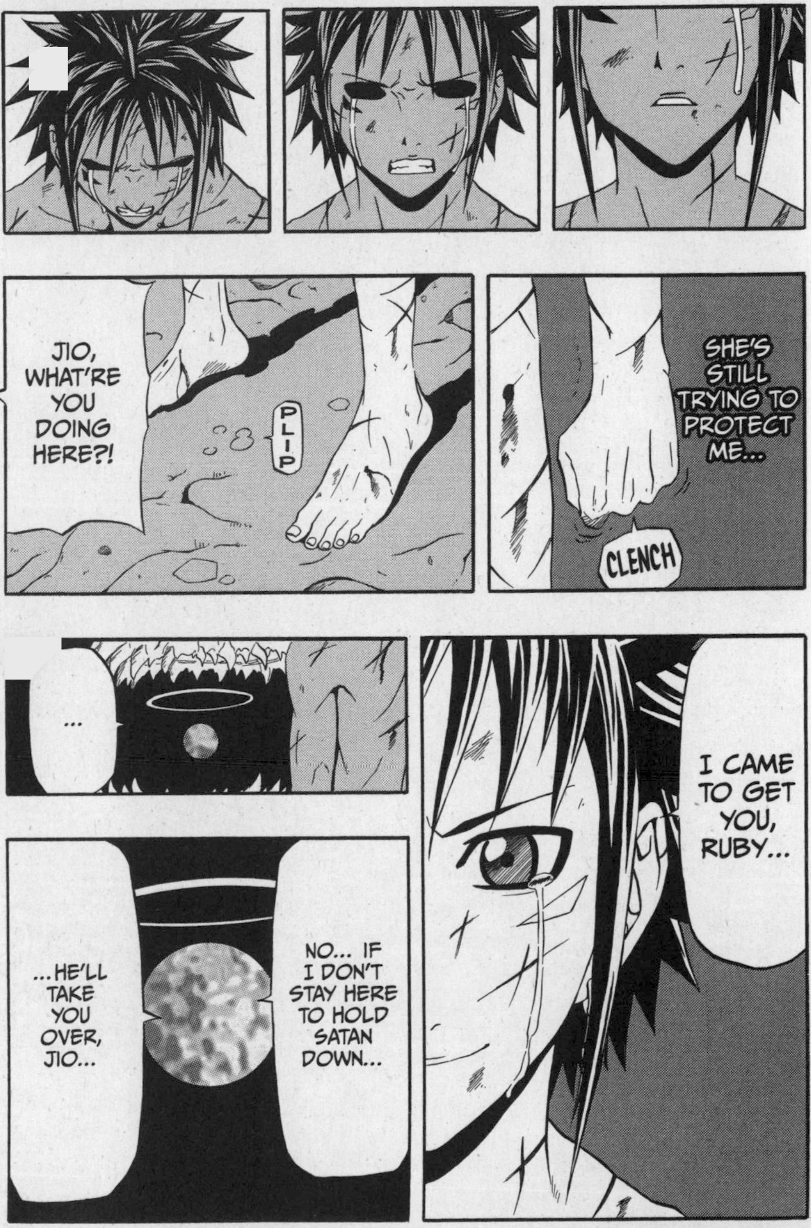
SHE'S STILL TRYING TO PROTECT ME...
CLENCH
JIO, WHAT'RE YOU DOING HERE?!
PLIP
I CAME TO GET YOU, RUBY...
...
NO... IF I DON'T STAY HERE TO HOLD SATAN DOWN...
...HE'LL TAKE YOU OVER, JIO...

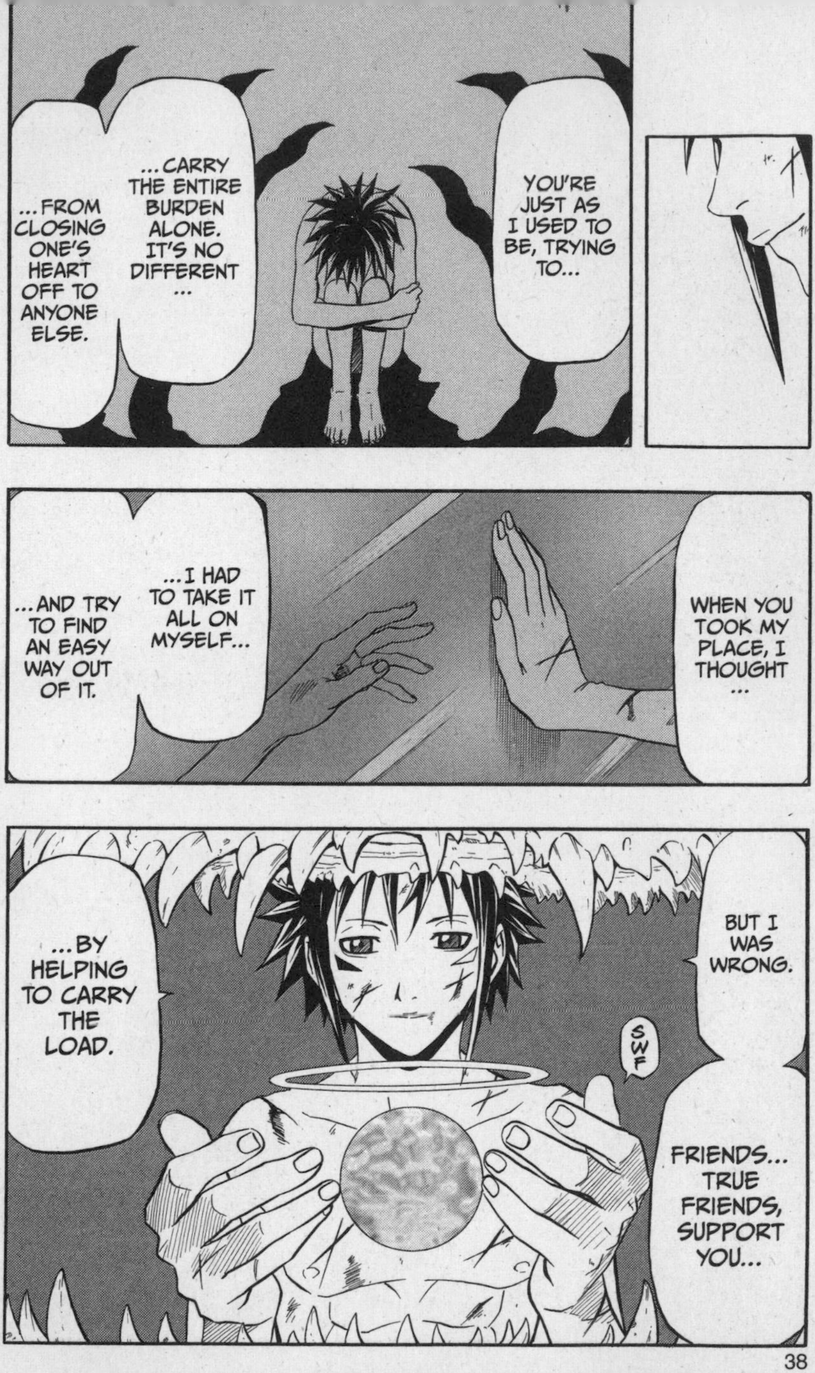
YOU'RE JUST AS I USED TO BE, TRYING TO...
...CARRY THE ENTIRE BURDEN ALONE. IT'S NO DIFFERENT ...
...FROM CLOSING ONE'S HEART OFF TO ANYONE ELSE.
WHEN YOU TOOK MY PLACE, I THOUGHT ...
...I HAD TO TAKE IT ALL ON MYSELF...
...AND TRY TO FIND AN EASY WAY OUT OF IT.
BUT I WAS WRONG.
SWF
FRIENDS... TRUE FRIENDS, SUPPORT YOU...
...BY HELPING TO CARRY THE LOAD.

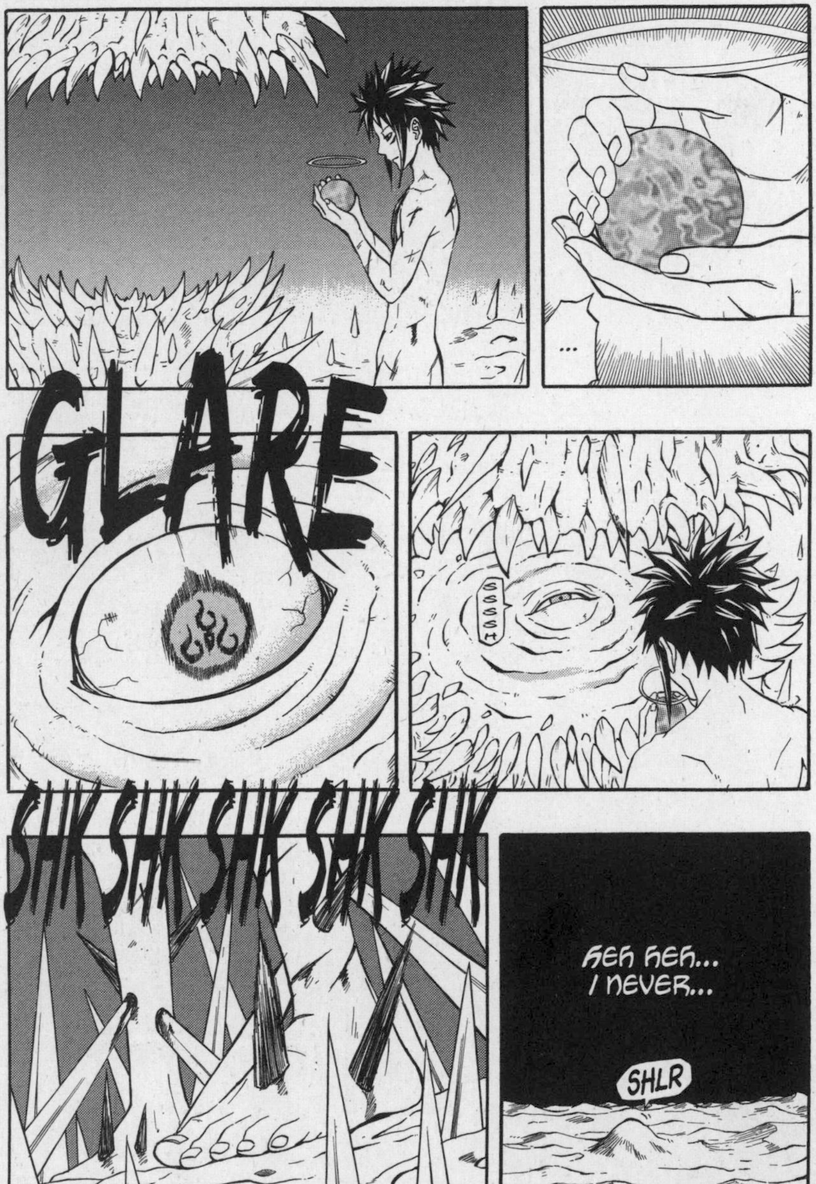
...
SSSSH
GLARE
HEH HEH...
I NEVER...
SHLR
SHK SHK SHK SHK SHK

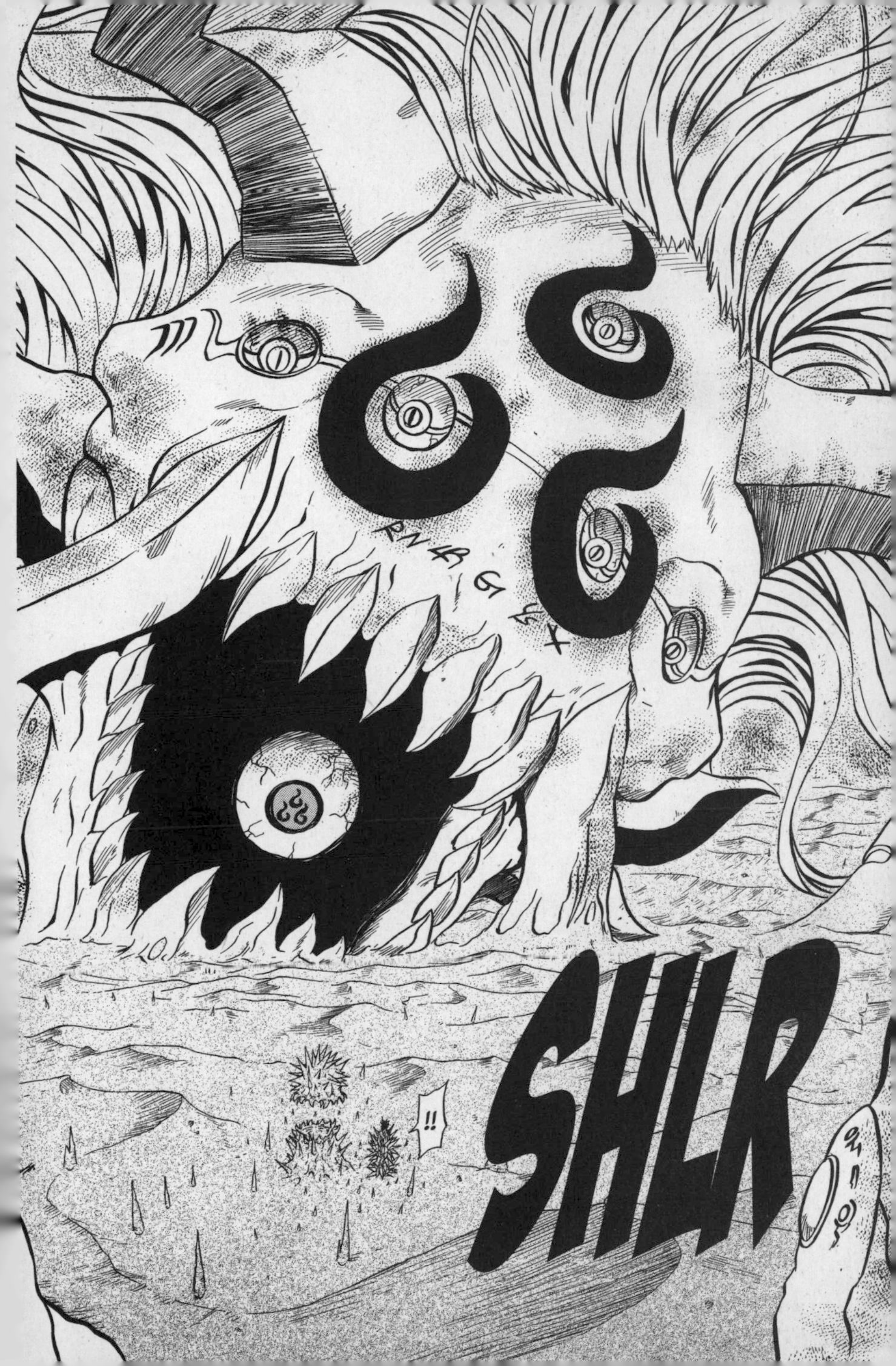
SHLR
!!

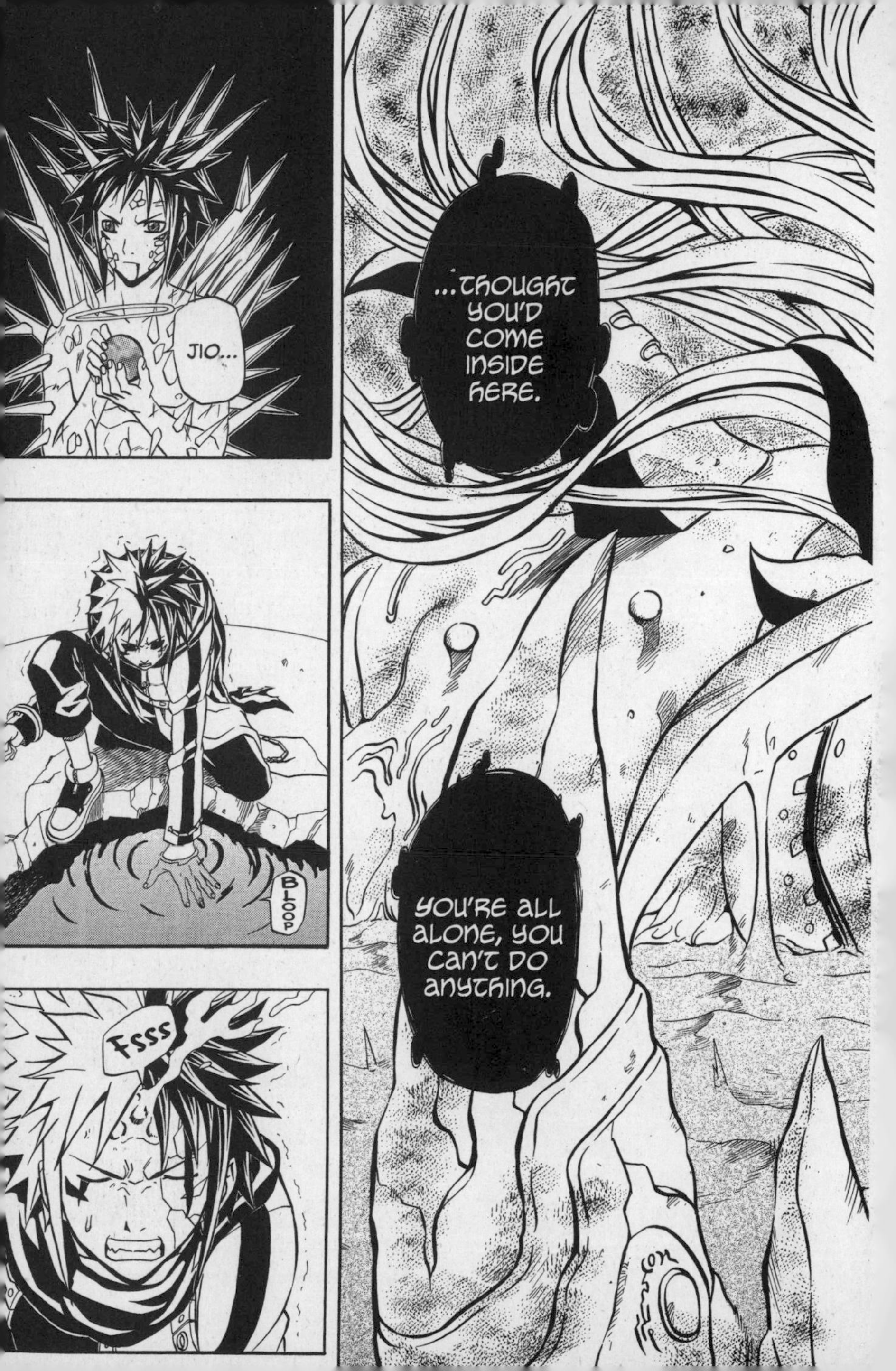
...THOUGHT YOU'D COME INSIDE HERE.
YOU'RE ALL ALONE, YOU CAN'T DO ANYTHING.
JIO...
BLOOP
FSSS

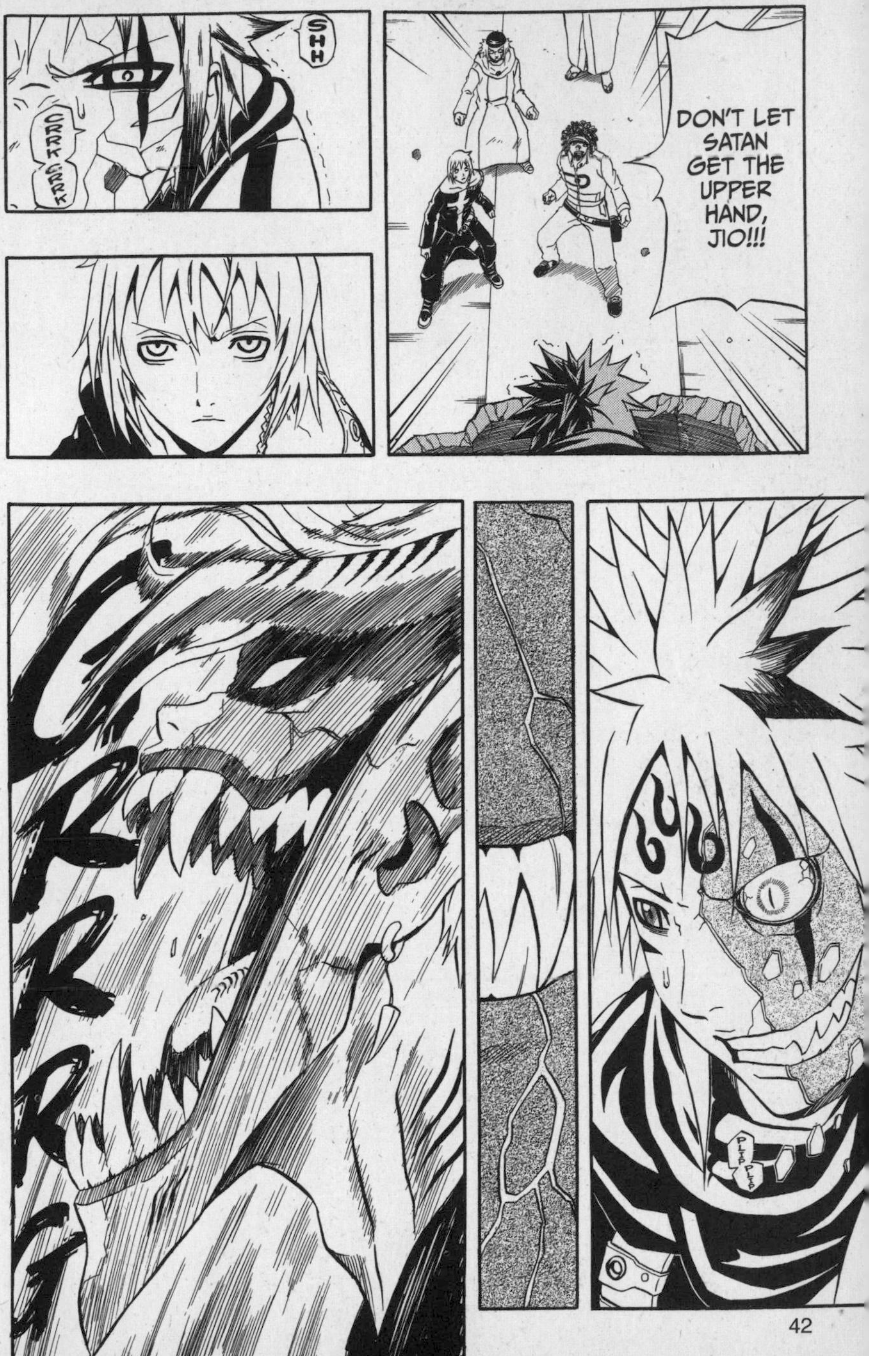
DON'T LET SATAN GET THE UPPER HAND, JIO!!!
SHH
CRRK CRRK
PLIP PLIP

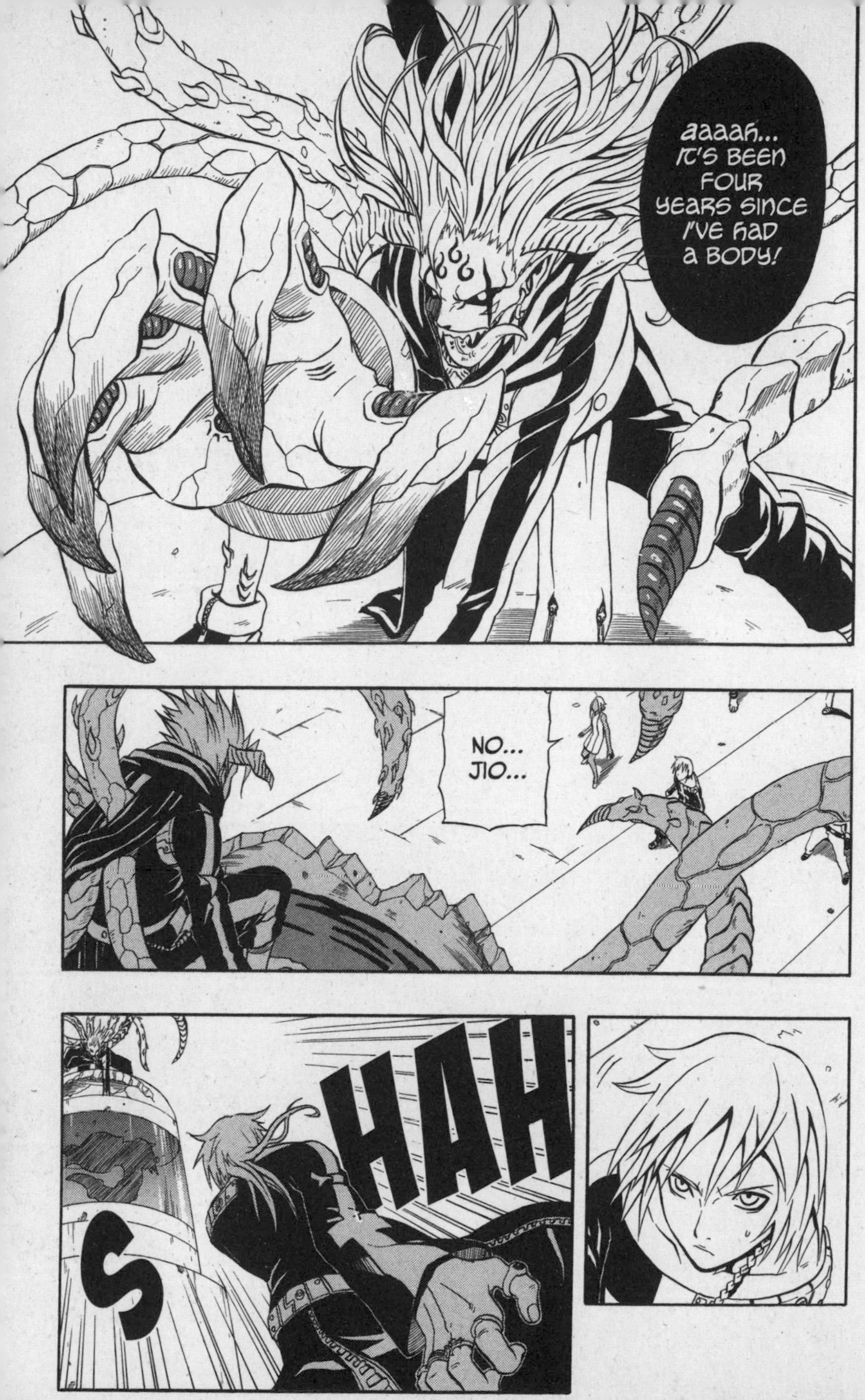
aaaah... IT'S BEEN FOUR YEARS SINCE I'VE HAD A BODY!
NO... JIO...
HAH
S

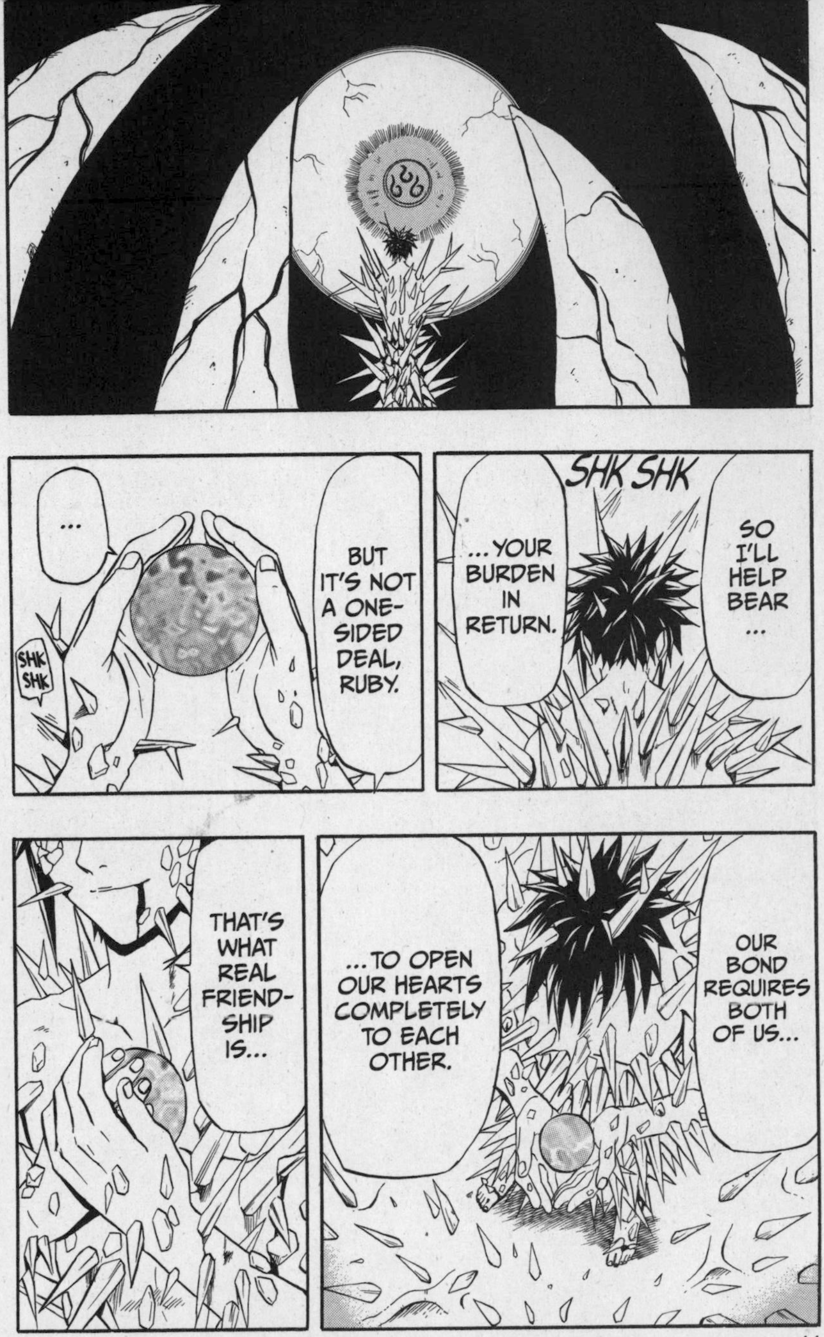
SHK SHK
SO I'LL HELP BEAR...
...YOUR BURDEN IN RETURN.
BUT IT'S NOT A ONE-SIDED DEAL, RUBY.
...
SHK SHK
OUR BOND REQUIRES BOTH OF US...
...TO OPEN OUR HEARTS COMPLETELY TO EACH OTHER.
THAT'S WHAT REAL FRIENDSHIP IS...

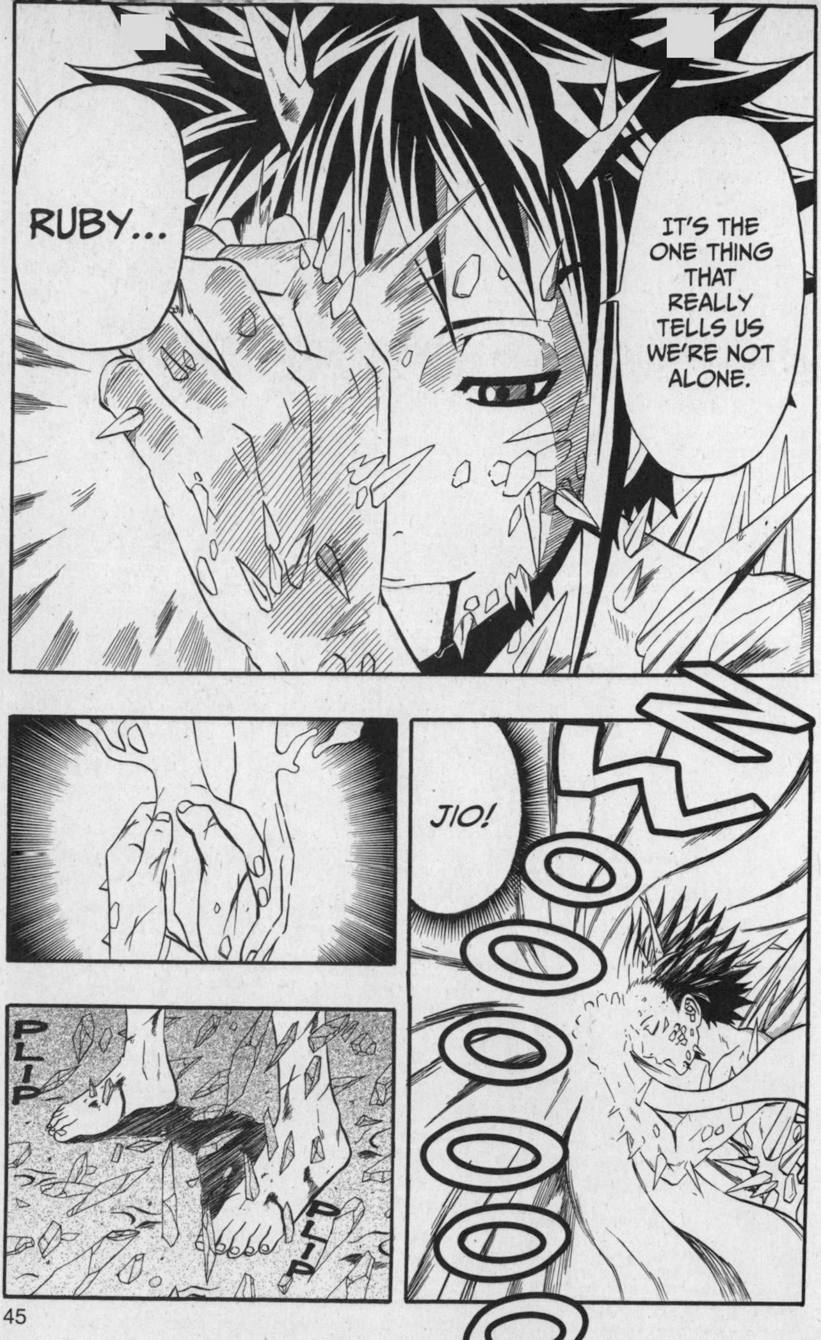

IT'S THE ONE THING THAT REALLY TELLS US WE'RE NOT ALONE.
RUBY...
NN
JIO!
PLIP
PLIP

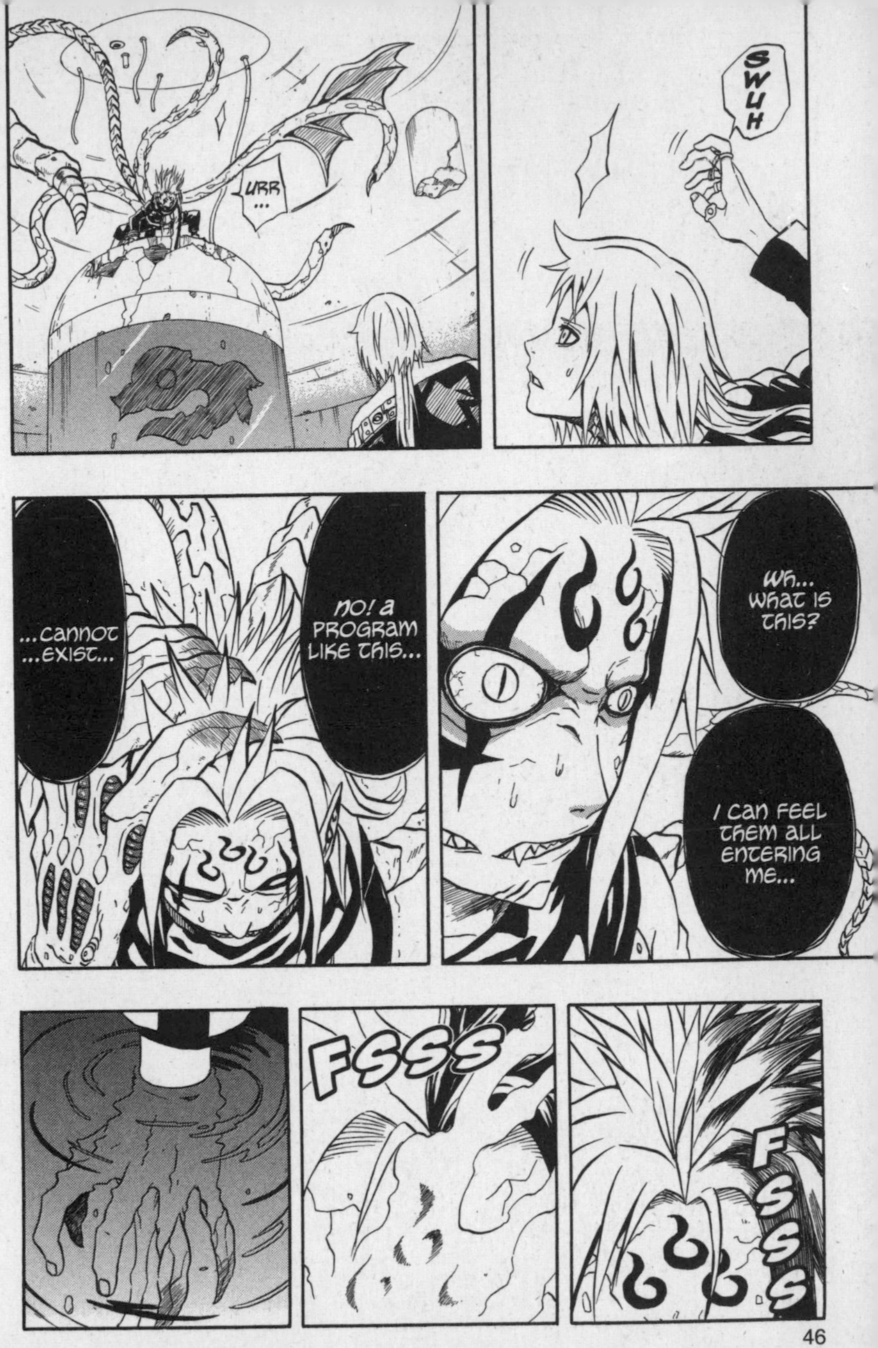
SWUH
URR...
WH... WHAT IS THIS?
I CAN FEEL THEM ALL ENTERING ME...
NO! A PROGRAM LIKE THIS...
...CANNOT ...EXIST...
FSSS
FSSS

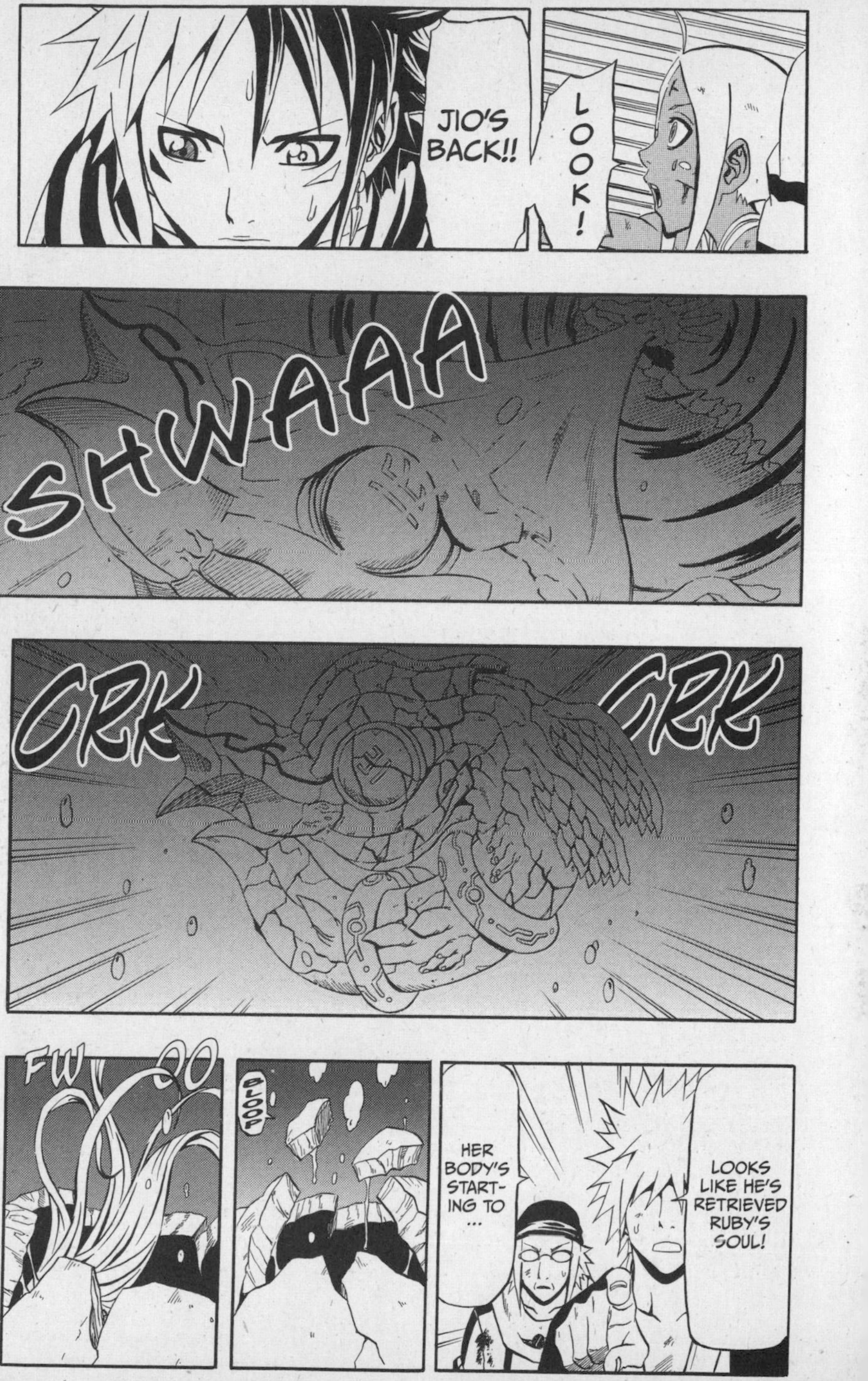
LOOK!
JIO'S BACK!!
SHWAAA
CRK
CRK
LOOKS LIKE HE'S RETRIEVED RUBY'S SOUL!
HER BODY'S STARTING TO ...
BLOOP
FWOO

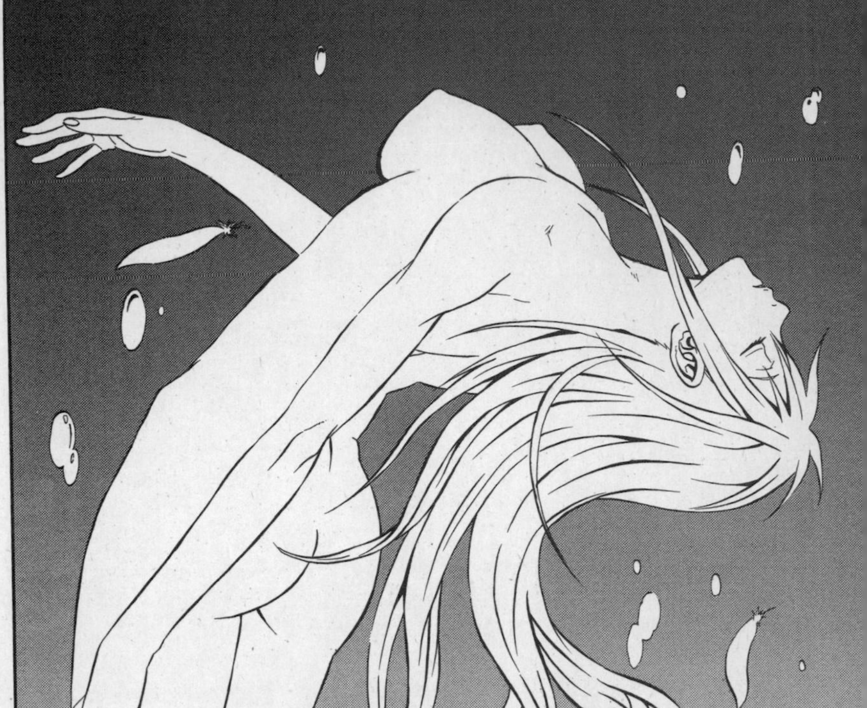

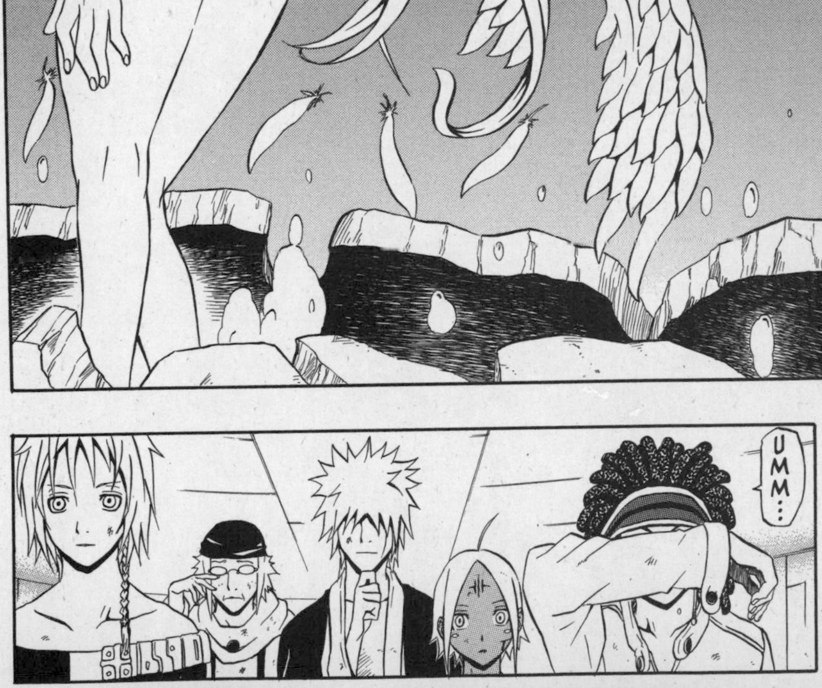
UMM...

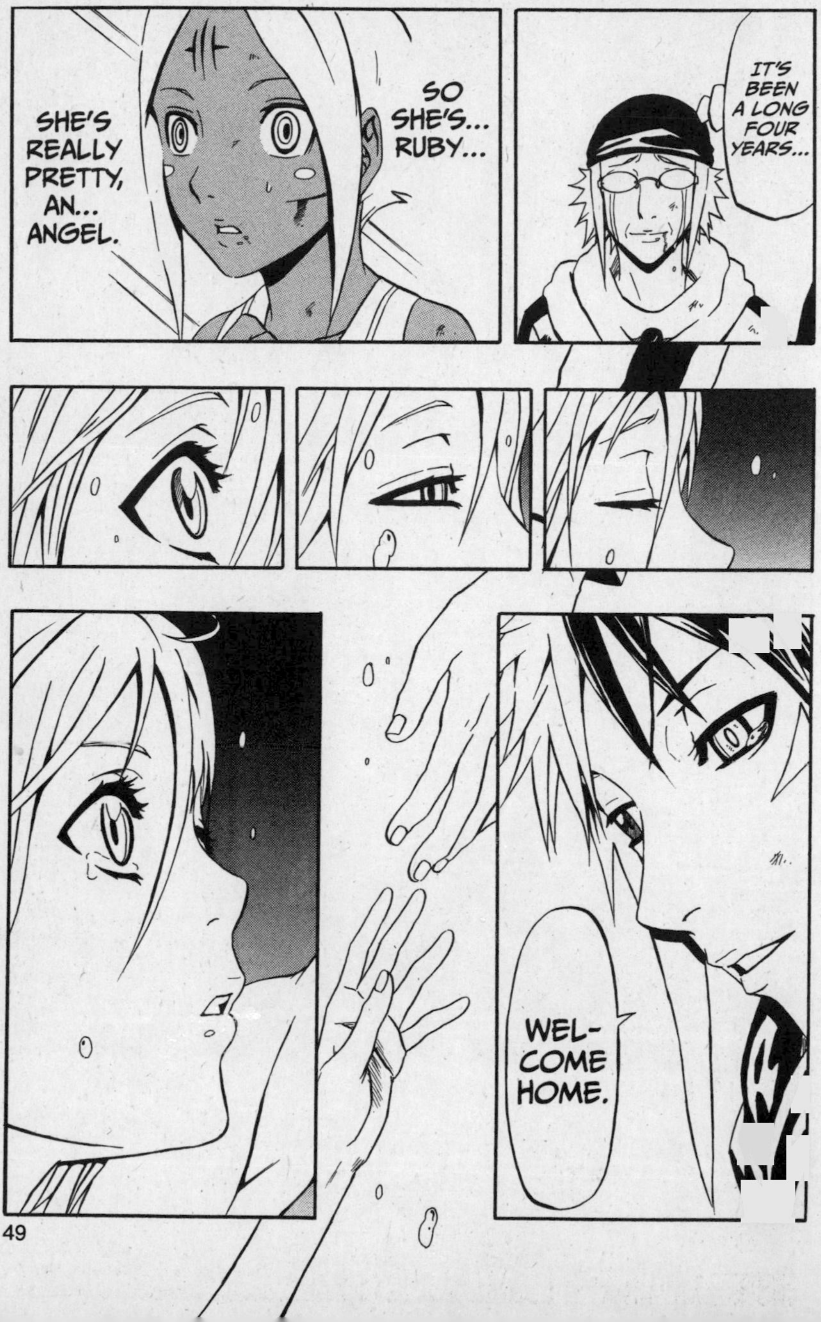
IT'S BEEN A LONG FOUR YEARS...
SO SHE'S... RUBY...
SHE'S REALLY PRETTY, AN... ANGEL.
WEL-COME HOME.

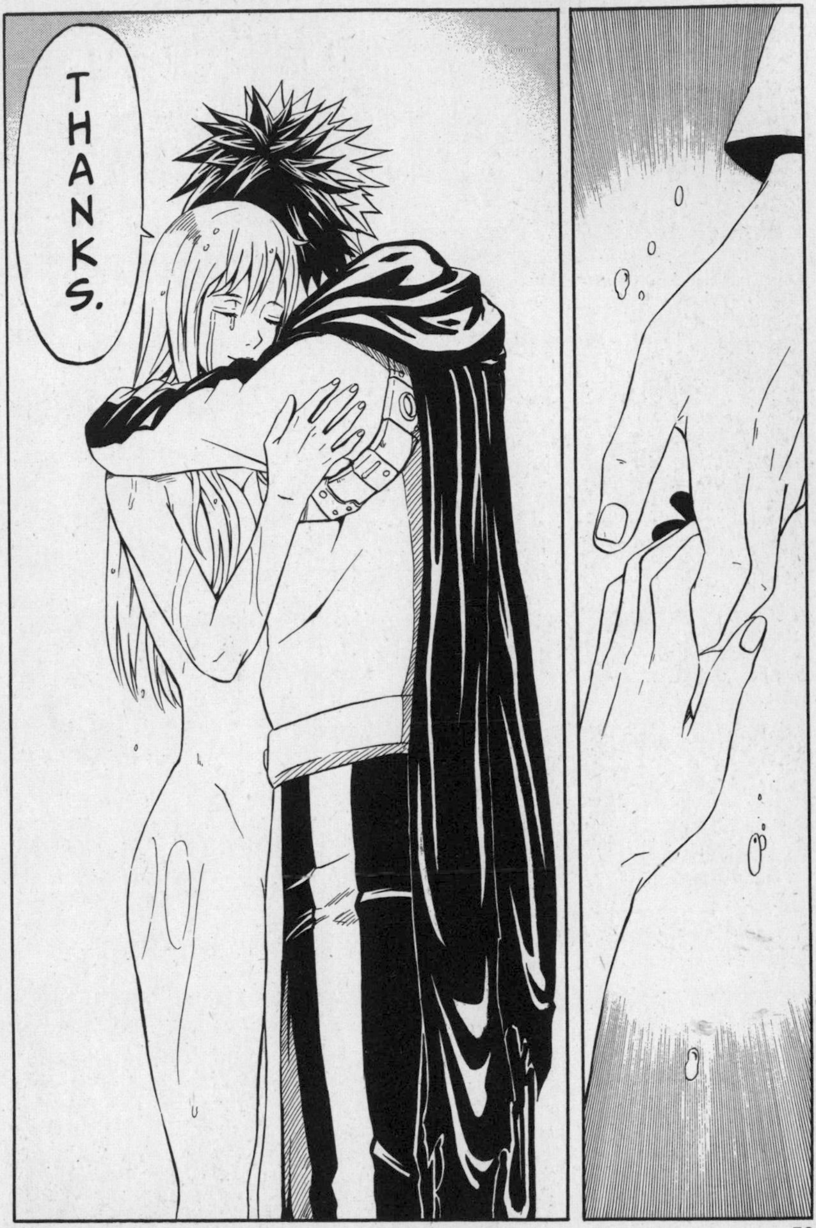
THANKS.

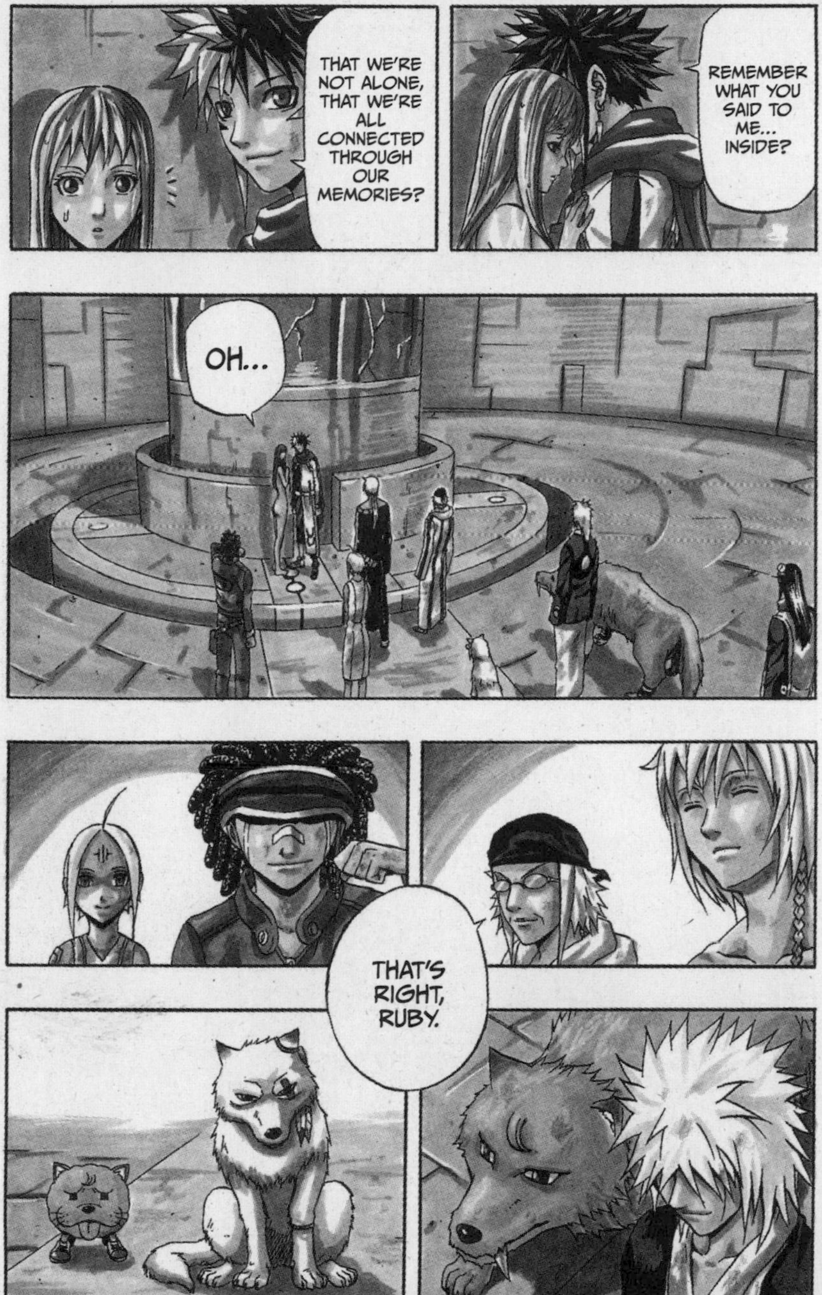
REMEMBER WHAT YOU SAID TO ME... INSIDE?
THAT WE'RE NOT ALONE, THAT WE'RE ALL CONNECTED THROUGH OUR MEMORIES?
OH...
THAT'S RIGHT, RUBY.

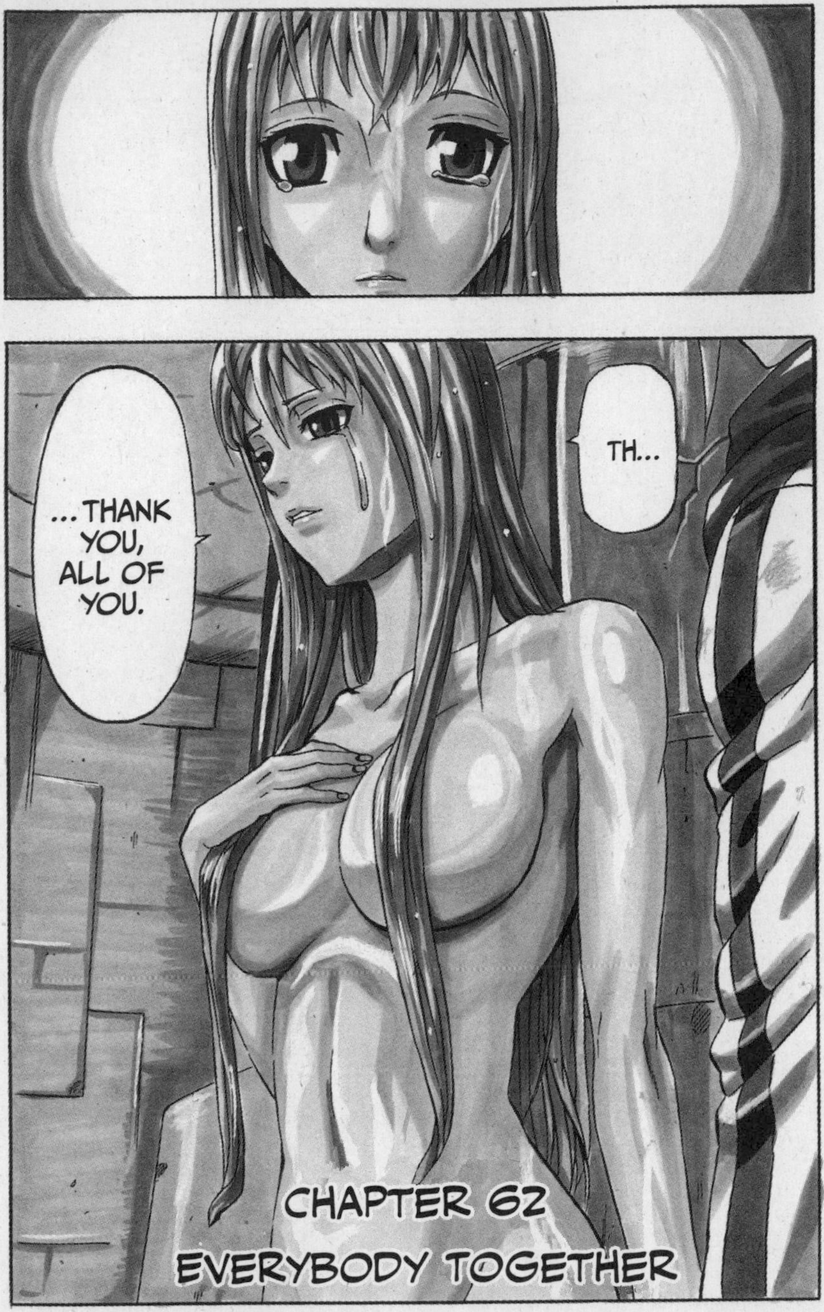
TH...
...THANK YOU, ALL OF YOU.
CHAPTER 62
EVERYBODY TOGETHER

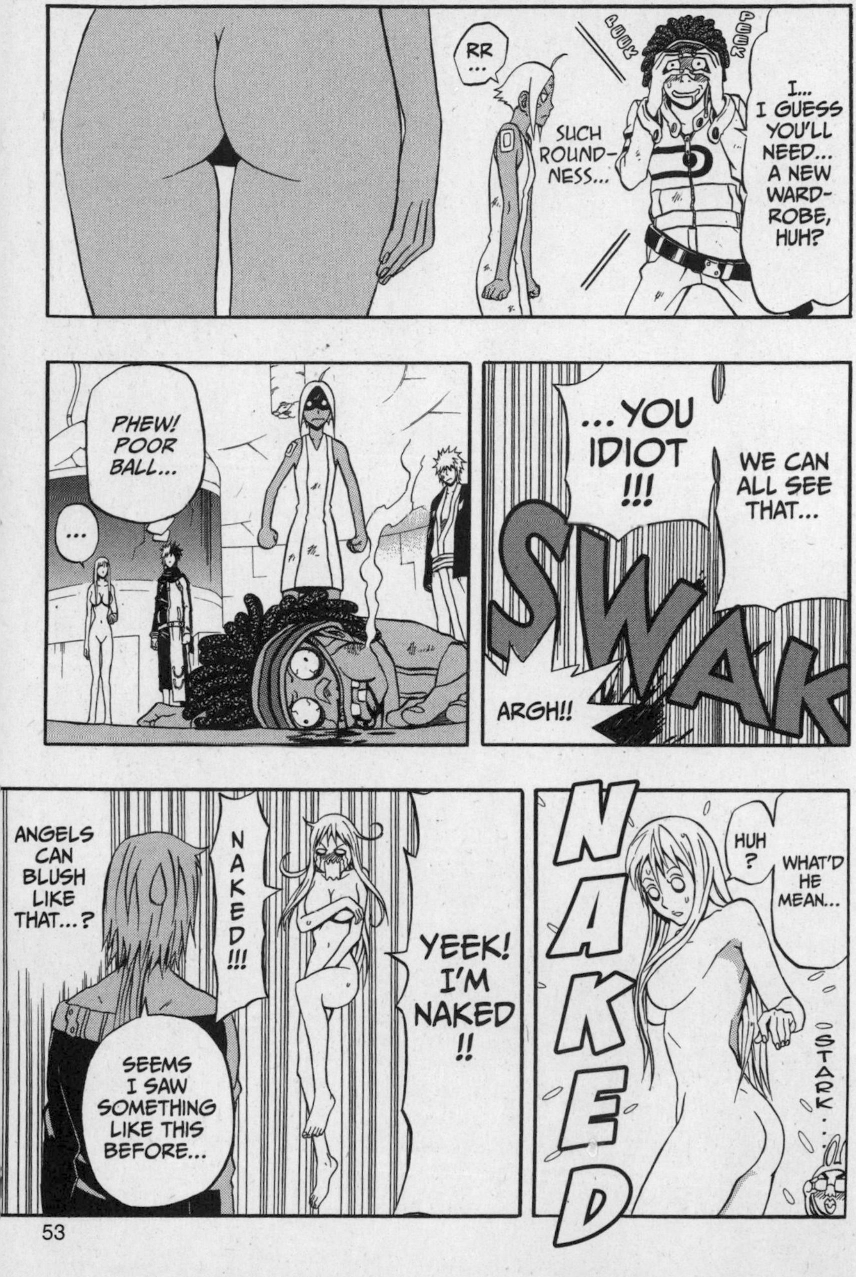
PEEK
I... I GUESS YOU'LL NEED... A NEW WARDROBE, HUH?
SUCH ROUNDNESS...
RR...
WE CAN ALL SEE THAT...
...YOU IDIOT !!!
SWAK
ARGH!!
PHEW! POOR BALL...
...
HUH?
WHAT'D HE MEAN...
NAKED
STARK...
YEEK! I'M NAKED !!
NAKED!!!
ANGELS CAN BLUSH LIKE THAT...?
SEEMS I SAW SOMETHING LIKE THIS BEFORE...

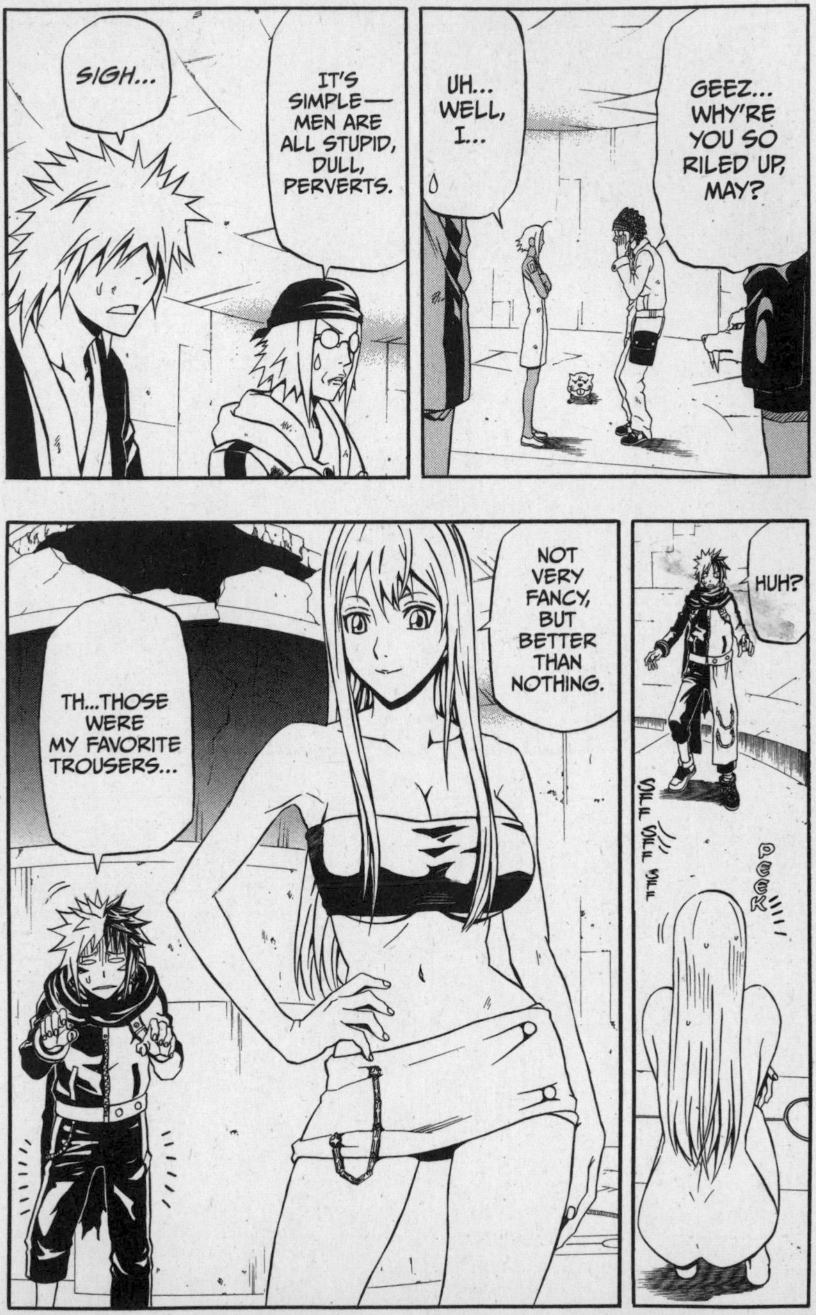
GEEZ... WHY'RE YOU SO RILED UP, MAY?
UH... WELL, I...
IT'S SIMPLE— MEN ARE ALL STUPID, DULL, PERVERTS.
SIGH...
HUH?
PEEK
NOT VERY FANCY, BUT BETTER THAN NOTHING.
TH...THOSE WERE MY FAVORITE TROUSERS...

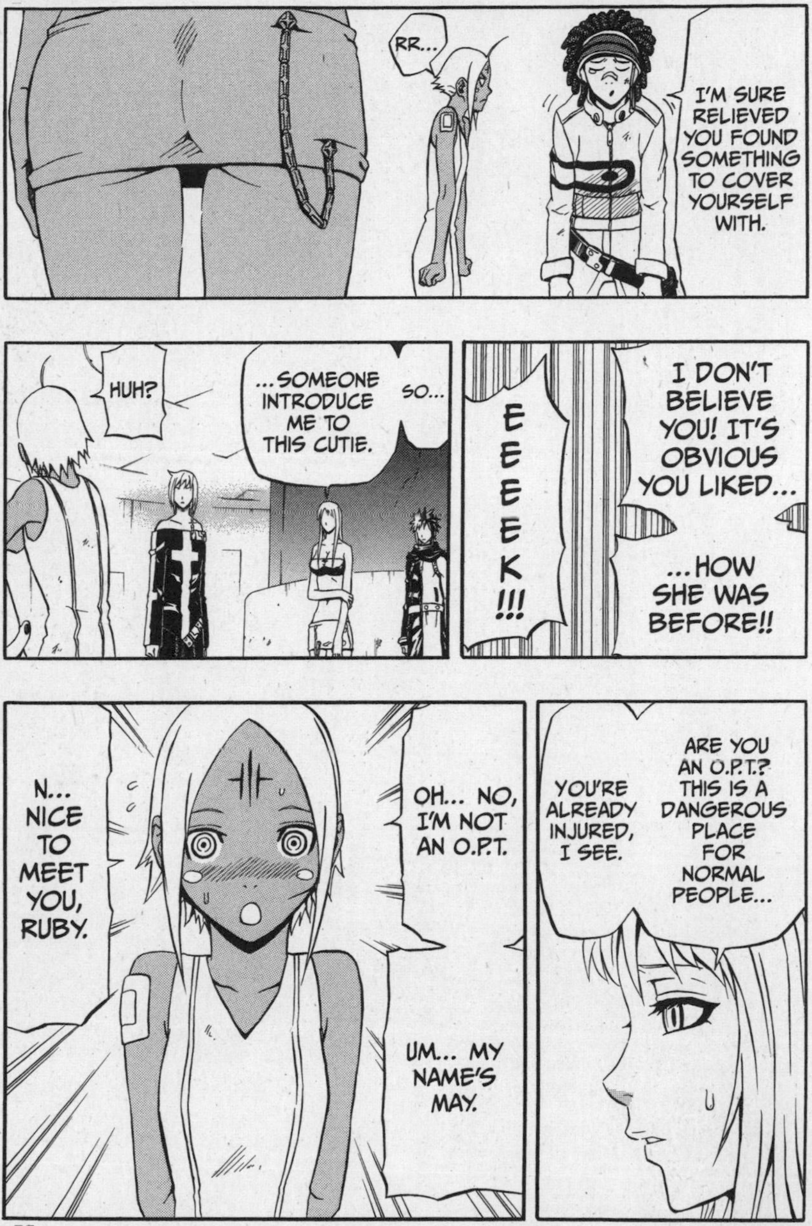
I'M SURE RELIEVED YOU FOUND SOMETHING TO COVER YOURSELF WITH.
RR...
I DON'T BELIEVE YOU! IT'S OBVIOUS YOU LIKED...
...HOW SHE WAS BEFORE!!
EEEEK!!!
SO...
...SOMEONE INTRODUCE ME TO THIS CUTIE.
HUH?
ARE YOU AN O.P.T.? THIS IS A DANGEROUS PLACE FOR NORMAL PEOPLE...
YOU'RE ALREADY INJURED, I SEE.
OH... NO, I'M NOT AN O.P.T.
UM... MY NAME'S MAY.
N... NICE TO MEET YOU, RUBY.

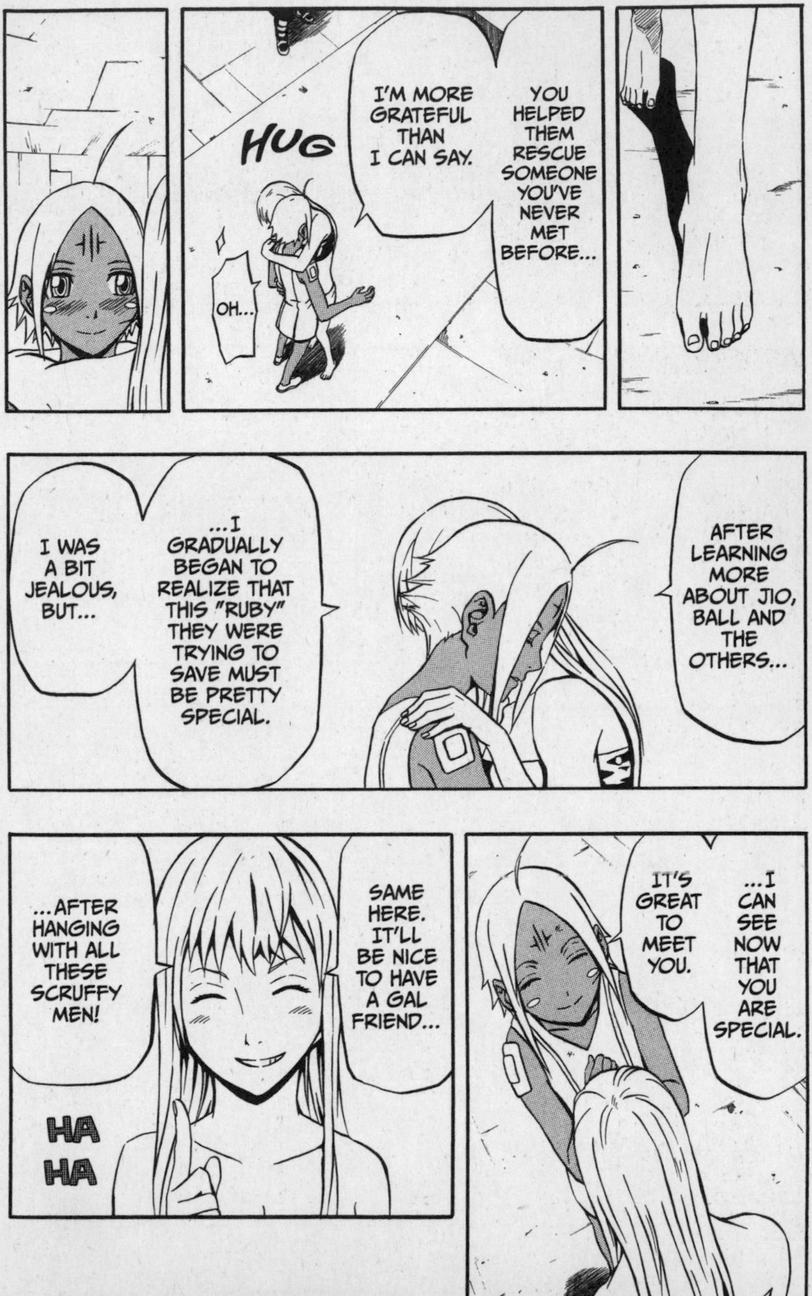
YOU HELPED THEM RESCUE SOMEONE YOU'VE NEVER MET BEFORE...
I'M MORE GRATEFUL THAN I CAN SAY.
HUG
OH...
AFTER LEARNING MORE ABOUT JIO, BALL AND THE OTHERS...
...I GRADUALLY BEGAN TO REALIZE THAT THIS "RUBY" THEY WERE TRYING TO SAVE MUST BE PRETTY SPECIAL.
I WAS A BIT JEALOUS, BUT...
...I CAN SEE NOW THAT YOU ARE SPECIAL.
IT'S GREAT TO MEET YOU.
SAME HERE. IT'LL BE NICE TO HAVE A GAL FRIEND...
...AFTER HANGING WITH ALL THESE SCRUFFY MEN!
HA HA

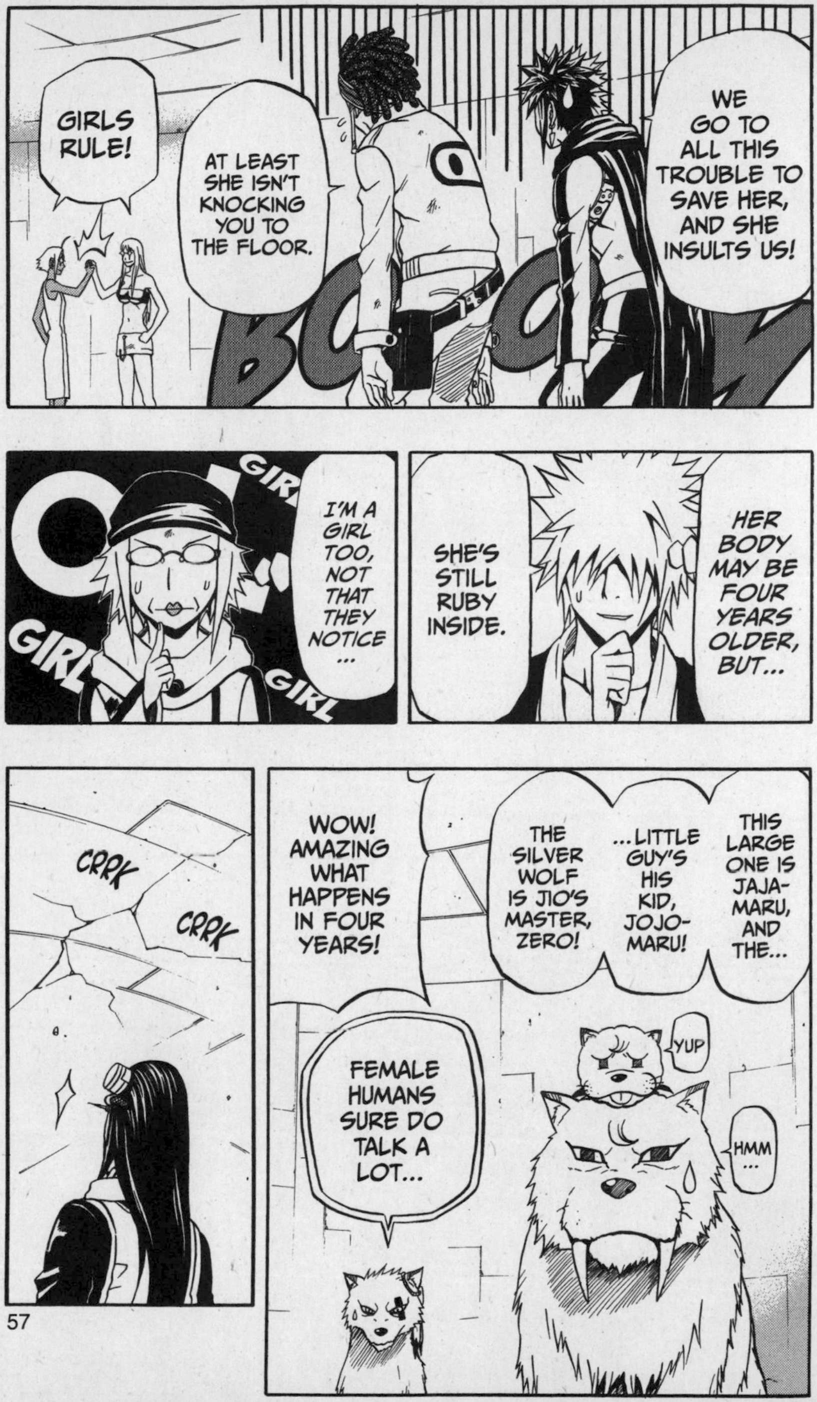
WE GO TO ALL THIS TROUBLE TO SAVE HER, AND SHE INSULTS US!
AT LEAST SHE ISN'T KNOCKING YOU TO THE FLOOR.
GIRLS RULE!
BOOM
HER BODY MAY BE FOUR YEARS OLDER, BUT...
SHE'S STILL RUBY INSIDE.
I'M A GIRL TOO, NOT THAT THEY NOTICE...
GIRL
GIRL
GIRL
THIS LARGE ONE IS JAJA-MARU, AND THE...
...LITTLE GUY'S HIS KID, JOJO-MARU!
THE SILVER WOLF IS JIO'S MASTER, ZERO!
WOW! AMAZING WHAT HAPPENS IN FOUR YEARS!
YUP
HMM...
FEMALE HUMANS SURE DO TALK A LOT...
CRRK
CRRK

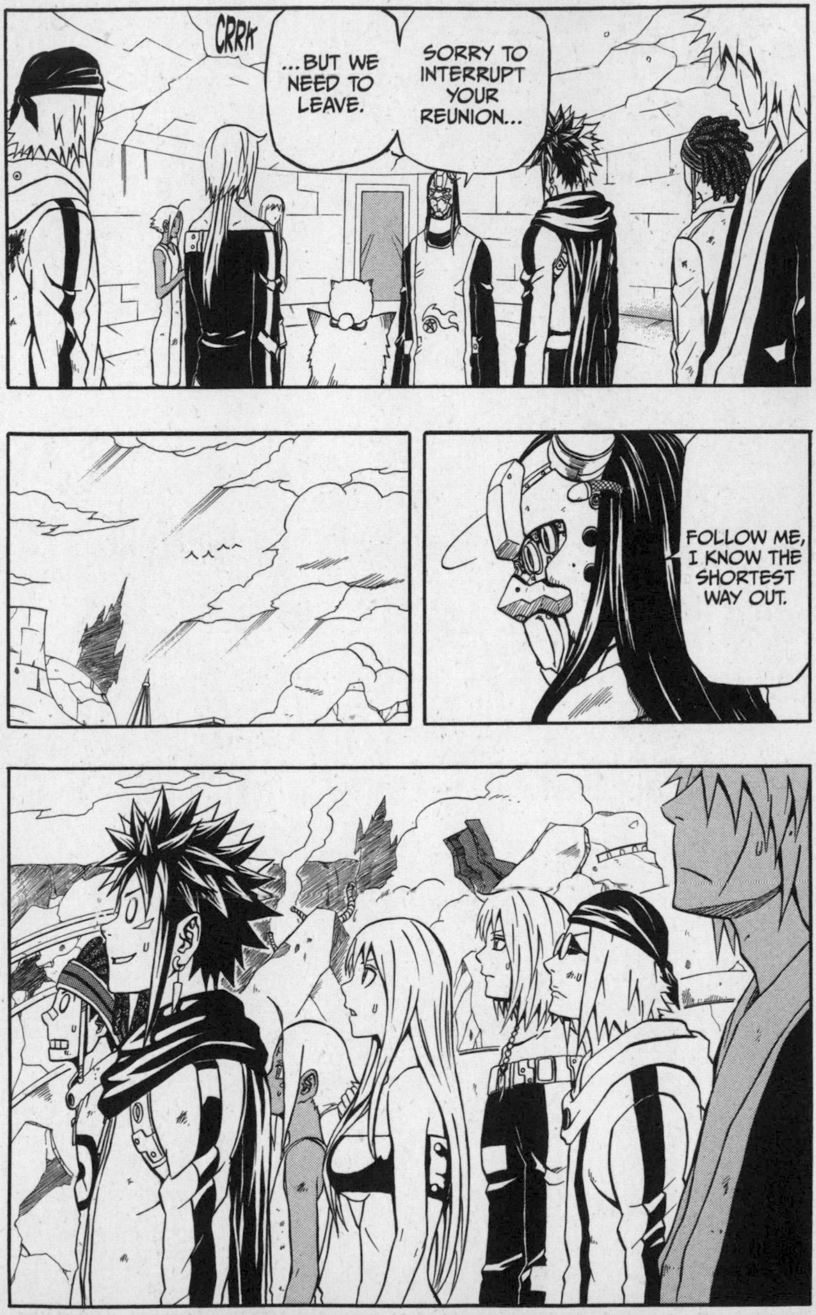
SORRY TO INTERRUPT YOUR REUNION...
...BUT WE NEED TO LEAVE.
CRRK
FOLLOW ME, I KNOW THE SHORTEST WAY OUT.

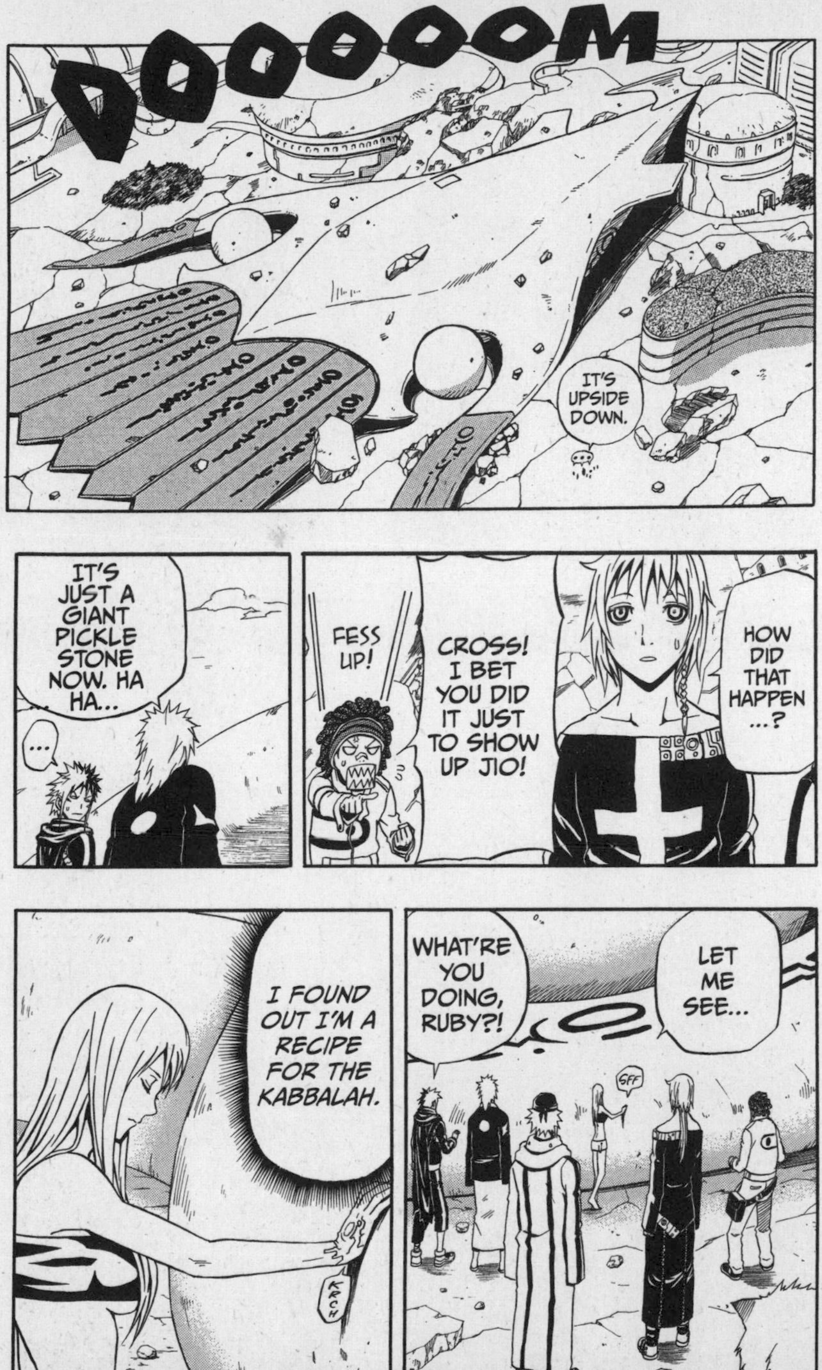
DOOOOOM
IT'S UPSIDE DOWN.
HOW DID THAT HAPPEN ...?
CROSS! I BET YOU DID IT JUST TO SHOW UP JIO!
FESS UP!
IT'S JUST A GIANT PICKLE STONE NOW. HA HA...
...
LET ME SEE...
WHAT'RE YOU DOING, RUBY?!
SFF
I FOUND OUT I'M A RECIPE FOR THE KABBALAH.
KRCH

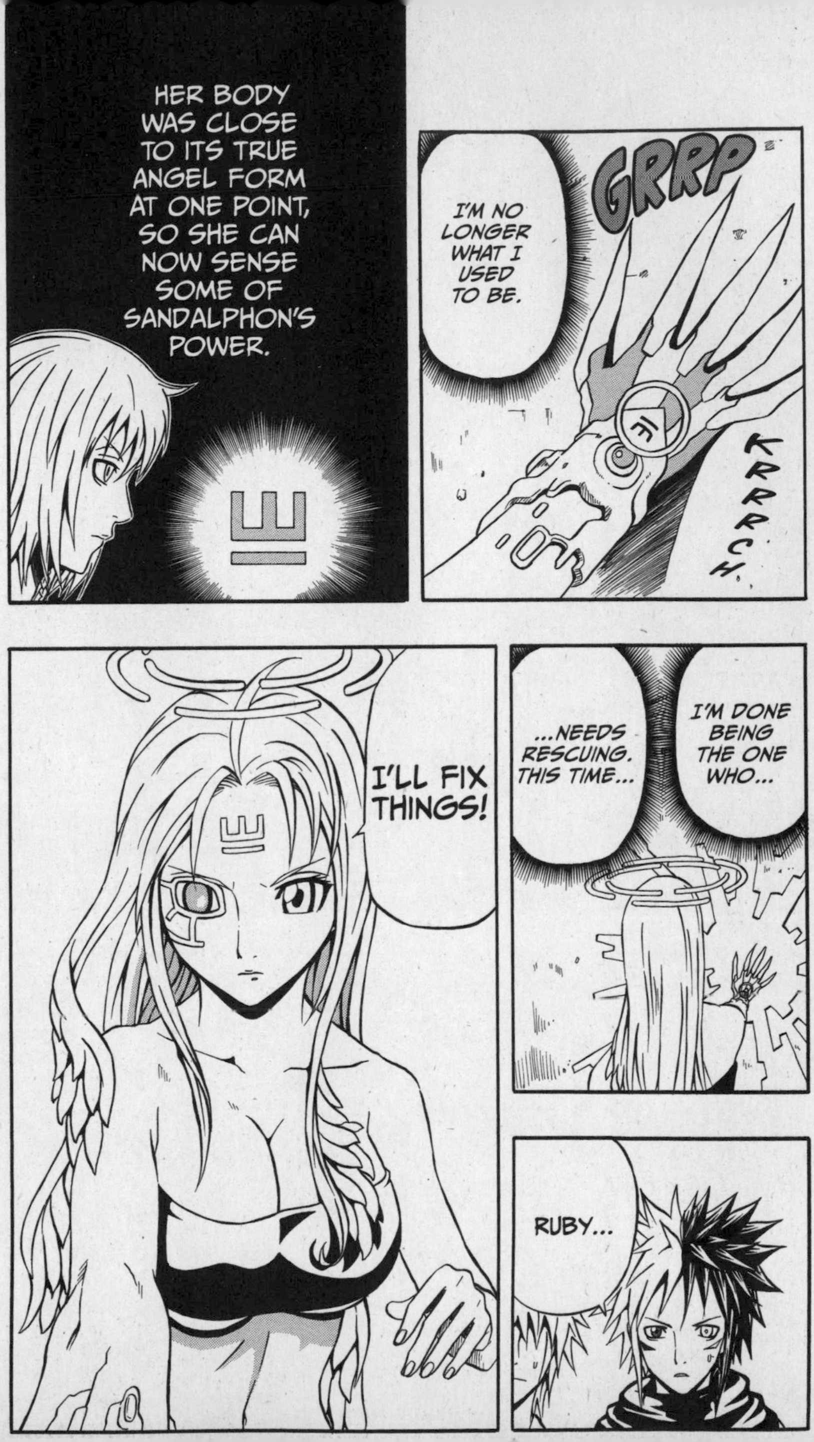
GRRP
I'M NO LONGER WHAT I USED TO BE.
KRRRCH
HER BODY WAS CLOSE TO ITS TRUE ANGEL FORM AT ONE POINT, SO SHE CAN NOW SENSE SOME OF SANDALPHON'S POWER.
I'M DONE BEING THE ONE WHO...
...NEEDS RESCUING. THIS TIME...
RUBY...
I'LL FIX THINGS!

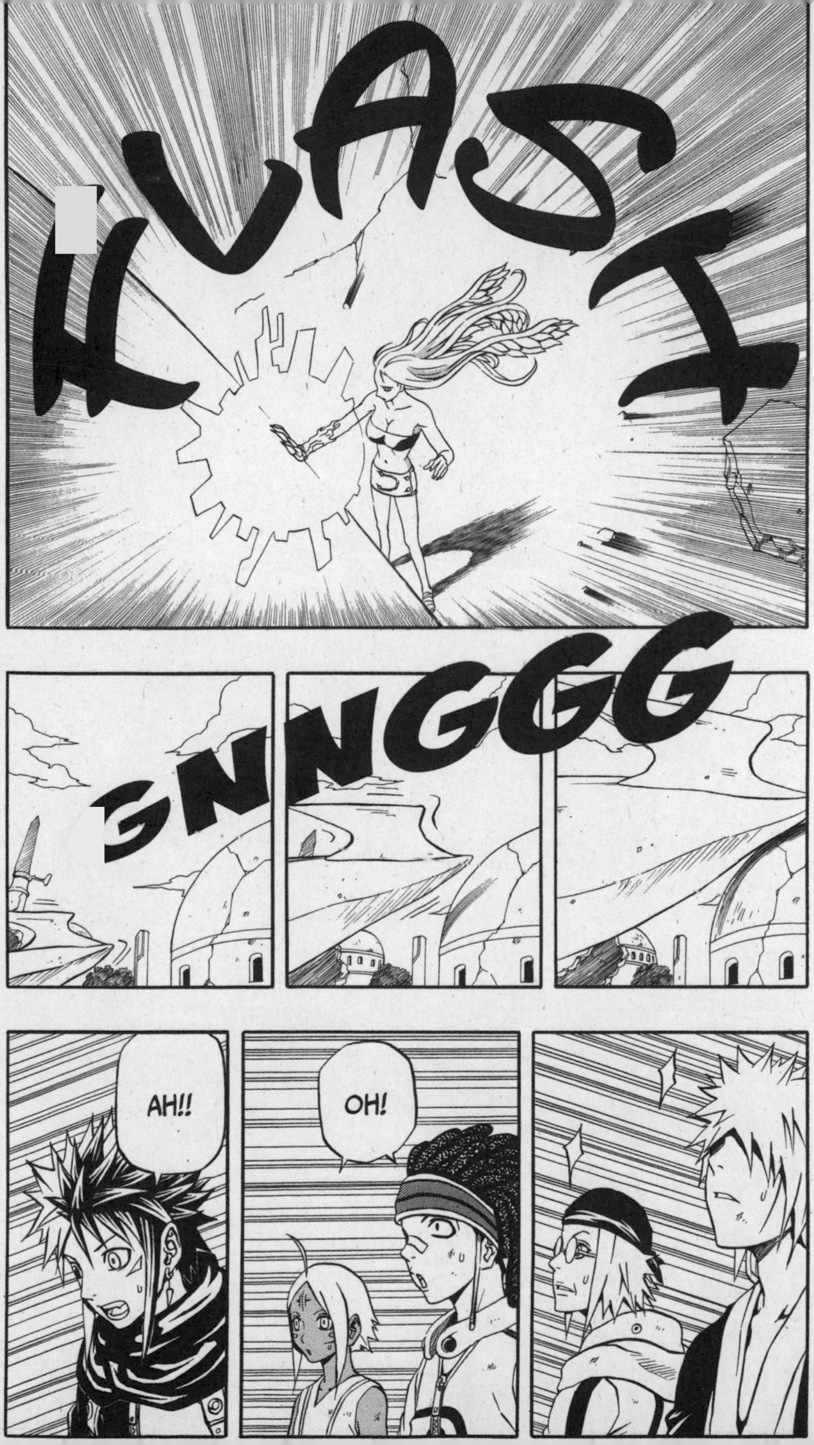

FLASH
GNNGGG
OH!
AH!!

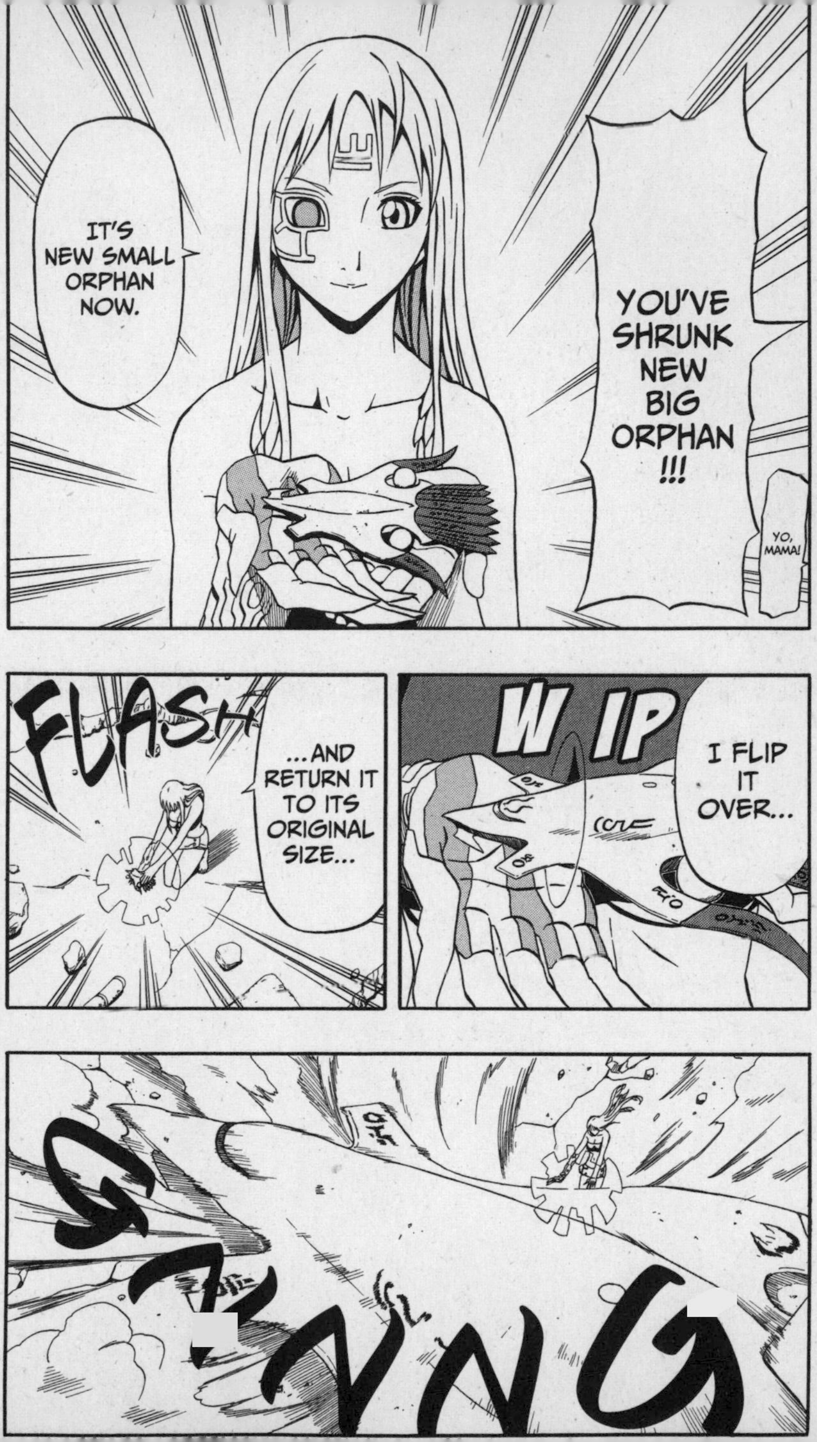
YOU'VE SHRUNK NEW BIG ORPHAN !!!
YO, MAMA!
IT'S NEW SMALL ORPHAN NOW.
W IP
I FLIP IT OVER...
FLASH
...AND RETURN IT TO ITS ORIGINAL SIZE...

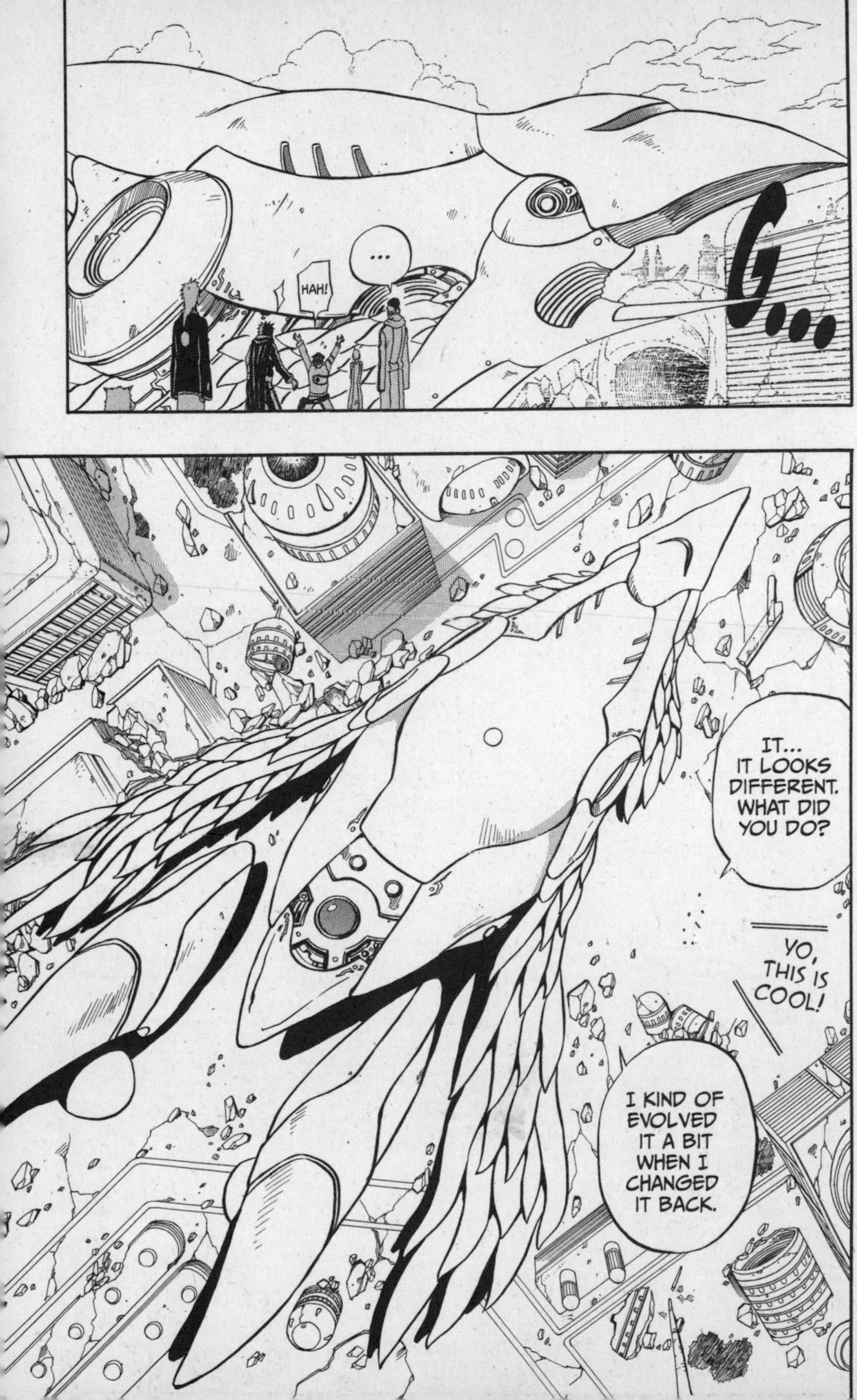
G...
...
HAH!
IT... IT LOOKS DIFFERENT. WHAT DID YOU DO?
YO, THIS IS COOL!
I KIND OF EVOLVED IT A BIT WHEN I CHANGED IT BACK.

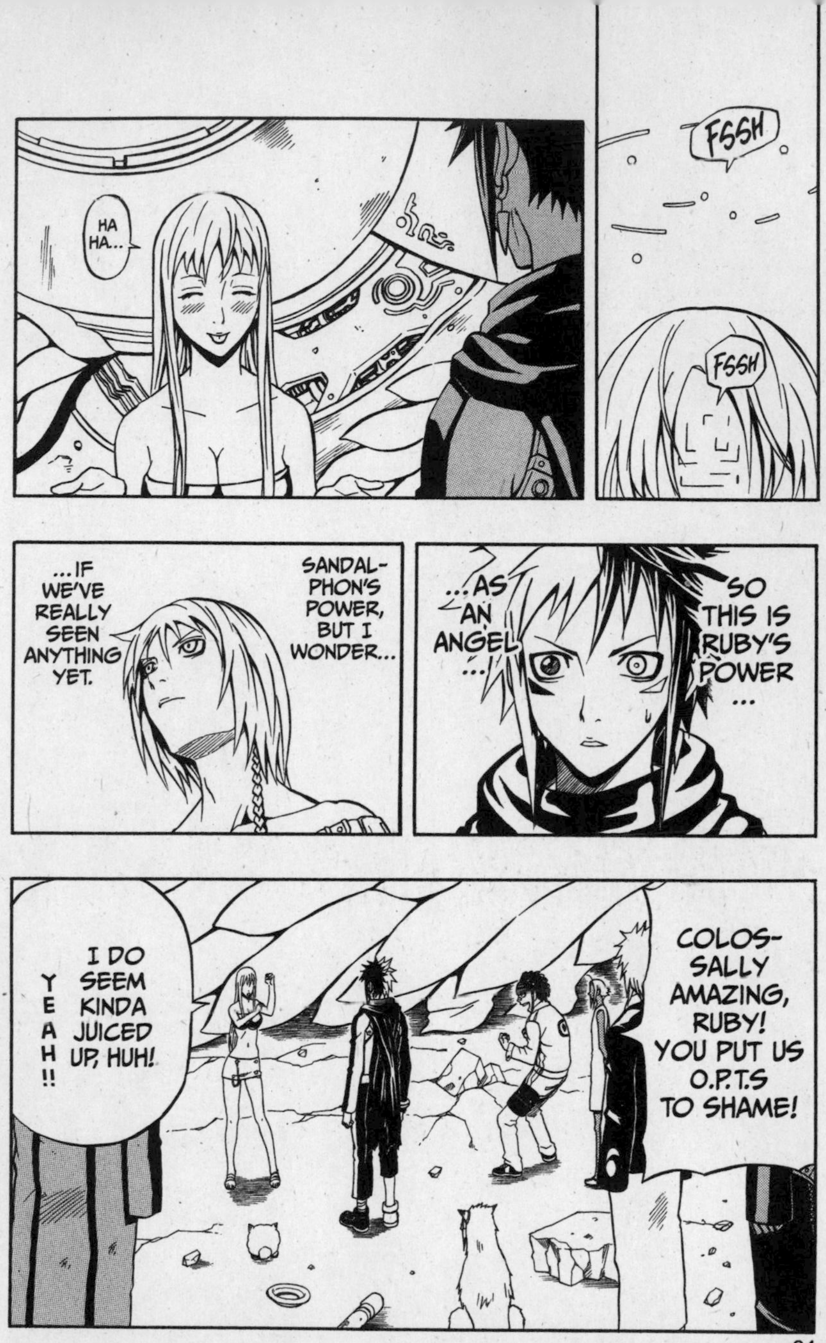
FSSH
FSSH
HA HA...
SO THIS IS RUBY'S POWER...
...AS AN ANGEL...
SANDAL-PHON'S POWER, BUT I WONDER...
...IF WE'VE REALLY SEEN ANYTHING YET.
COLOS-SALLY AMAZING, RUBY! YOU PUT US O.P.T.S TO SHAME!
YEAH!!
I DO SEEM KINDA JUICED UP, HUH!

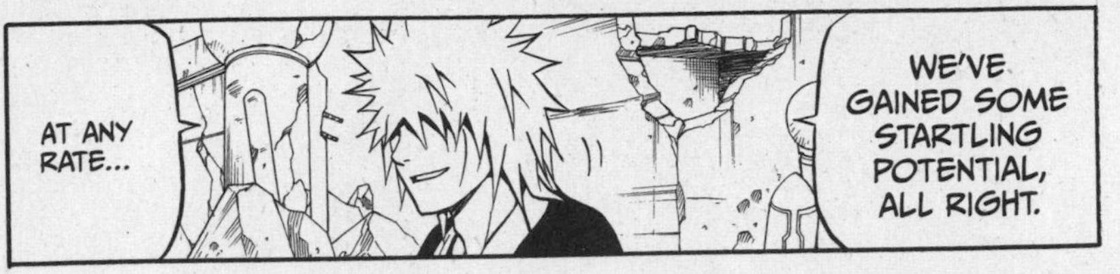
WE'VE GAINED SOME STARTLING POTENTIAL, ALL RIGHT.
AT ANY RATE...

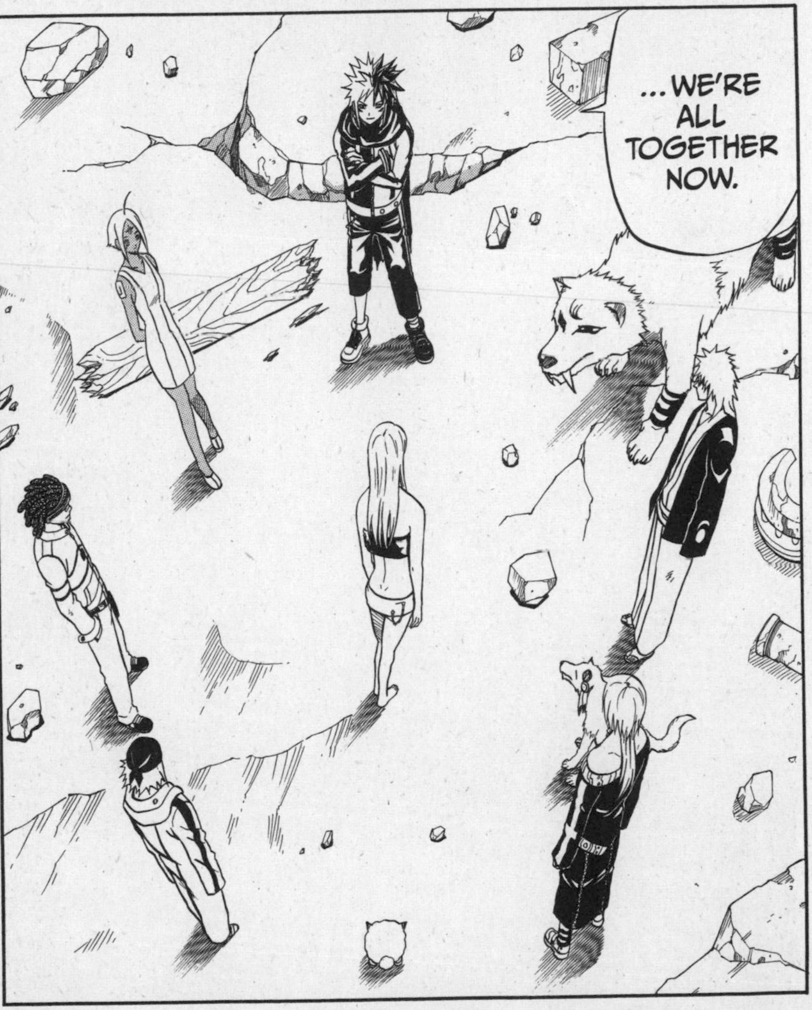
...WE'RE ALL TOGETHER NOW.

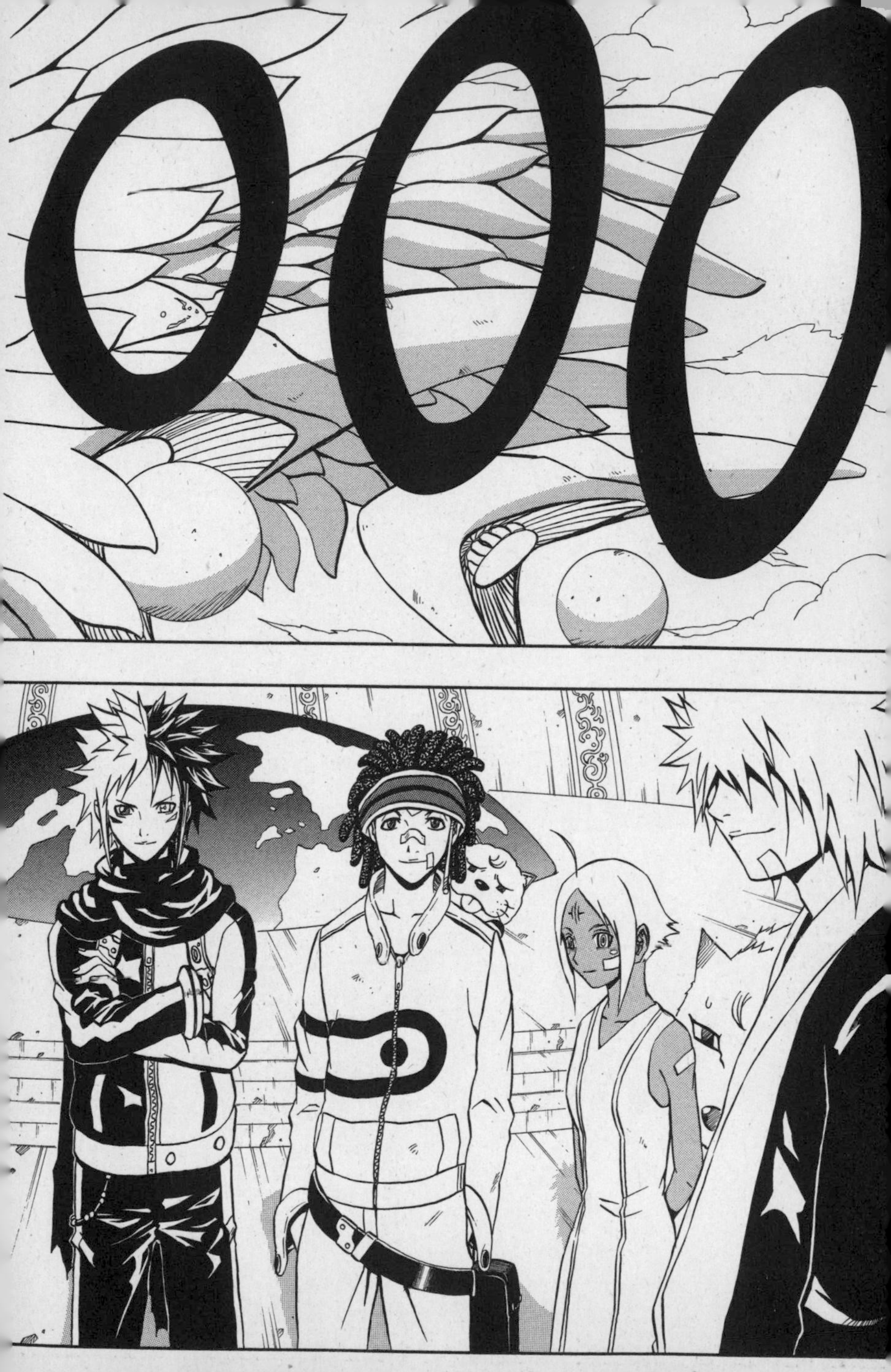
OOO

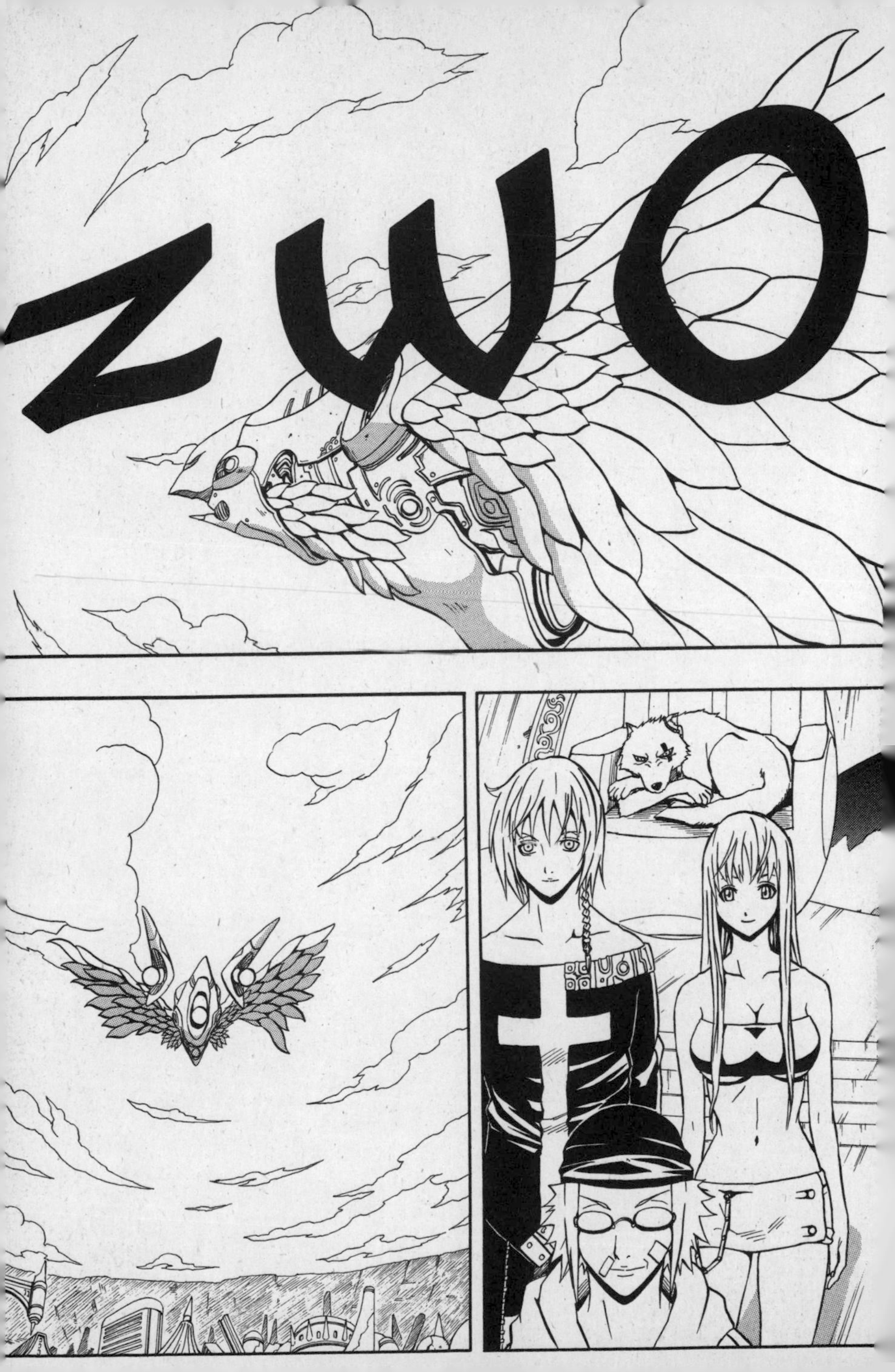
ZWO

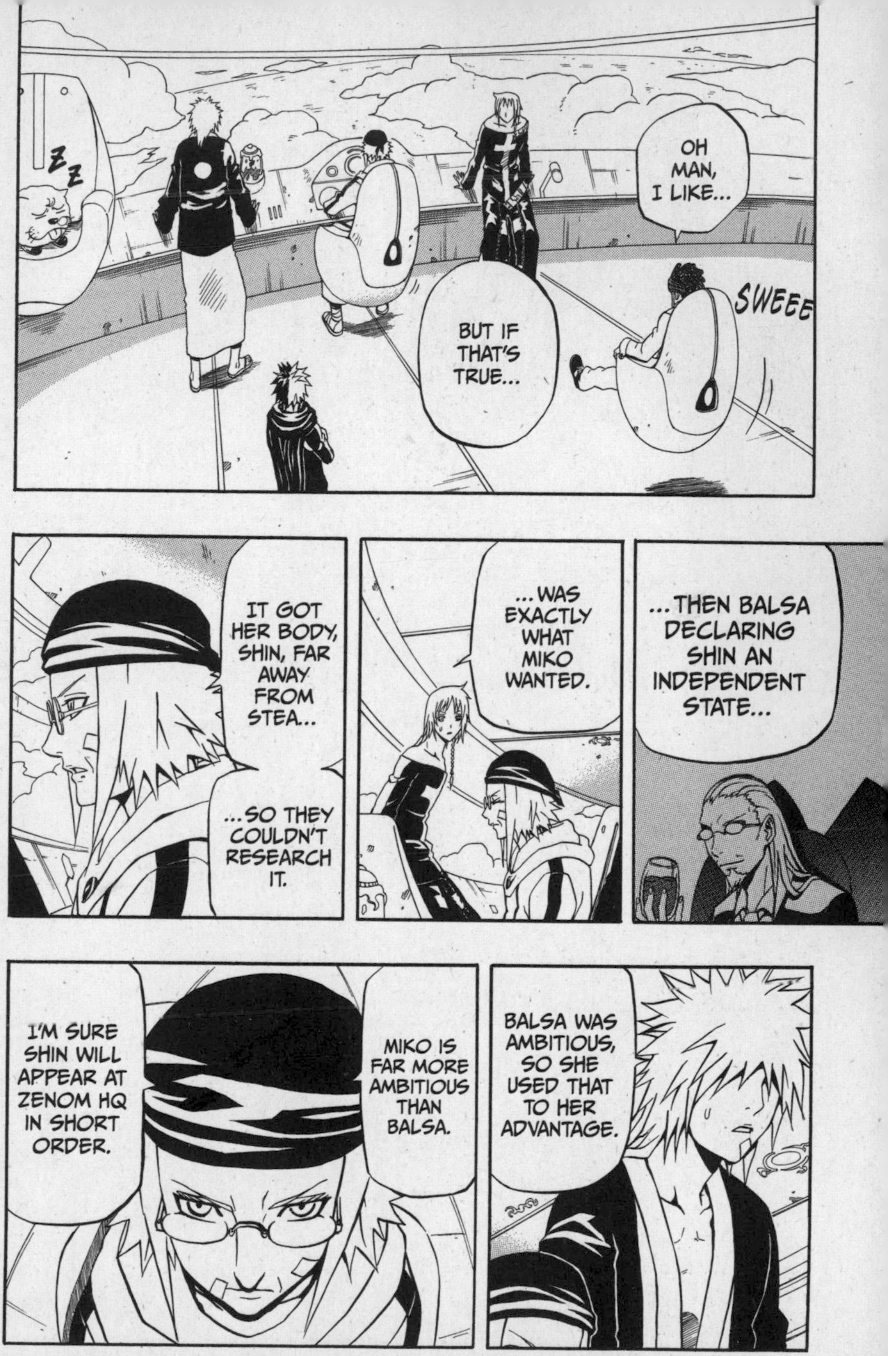
OH MAN, I LIKE...
SWEEE
BUT IF THAT'S TRUE...
...THEN BALSA DECLARING SHIN AN INDEPENDENT STATE...
...WAS EXACTLY WHAT MIKO WANTED.
IT GOT HER BODY, SHIN, FAR AWAY FROM STEA...
...SO THEY COULDN'T RESEARCH IT.
BALSA WAS AMBITIOUS, SO SHE USED THAT TO HER ADVANTAGE.
MIKO IS FAR MORE AMBITIOUS THAN BALSA.
I'M SURE SHIN WILL APPEAR AT ZENOM HQ IN SHORT ORDER.

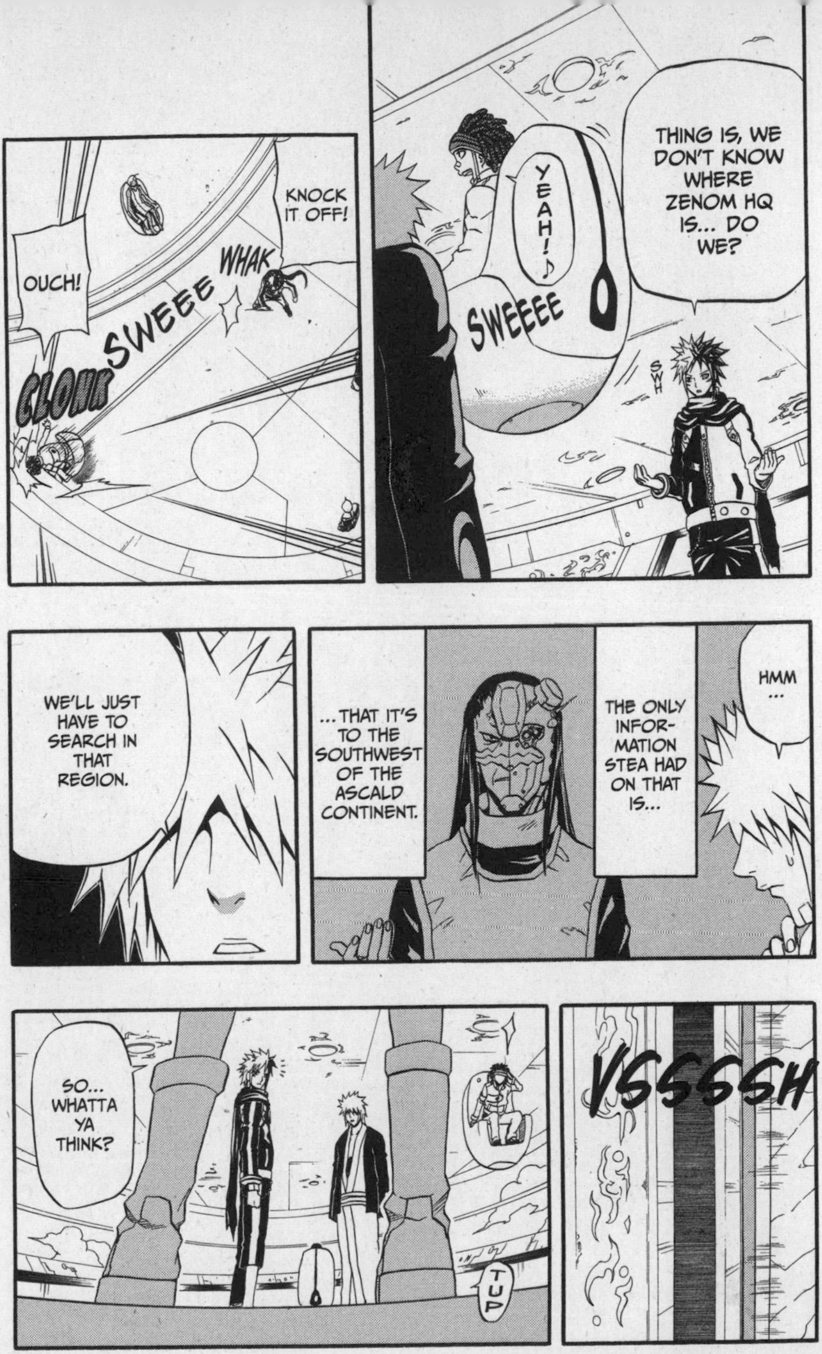
THING IS, WE DON'T KNOW WHERE ZENOM HQ IS... DO WE?
YEAH! ♪
SWEEEE
SWH
KNOCK IT OFF!
WHAK
OUCH!
SWEEE
CLONK
HMM ...
THE ONLY INFORMATION STEA HAD ON THAT IS...
...THAT IT'S TO THE SOUTHWEST OF THE ASCALD CONTINENT.
WE'LL JUST HAVE TO SEARCH IN THAT REGION.
VSSSSH
SO... WHATTA YA THINK?
TUP

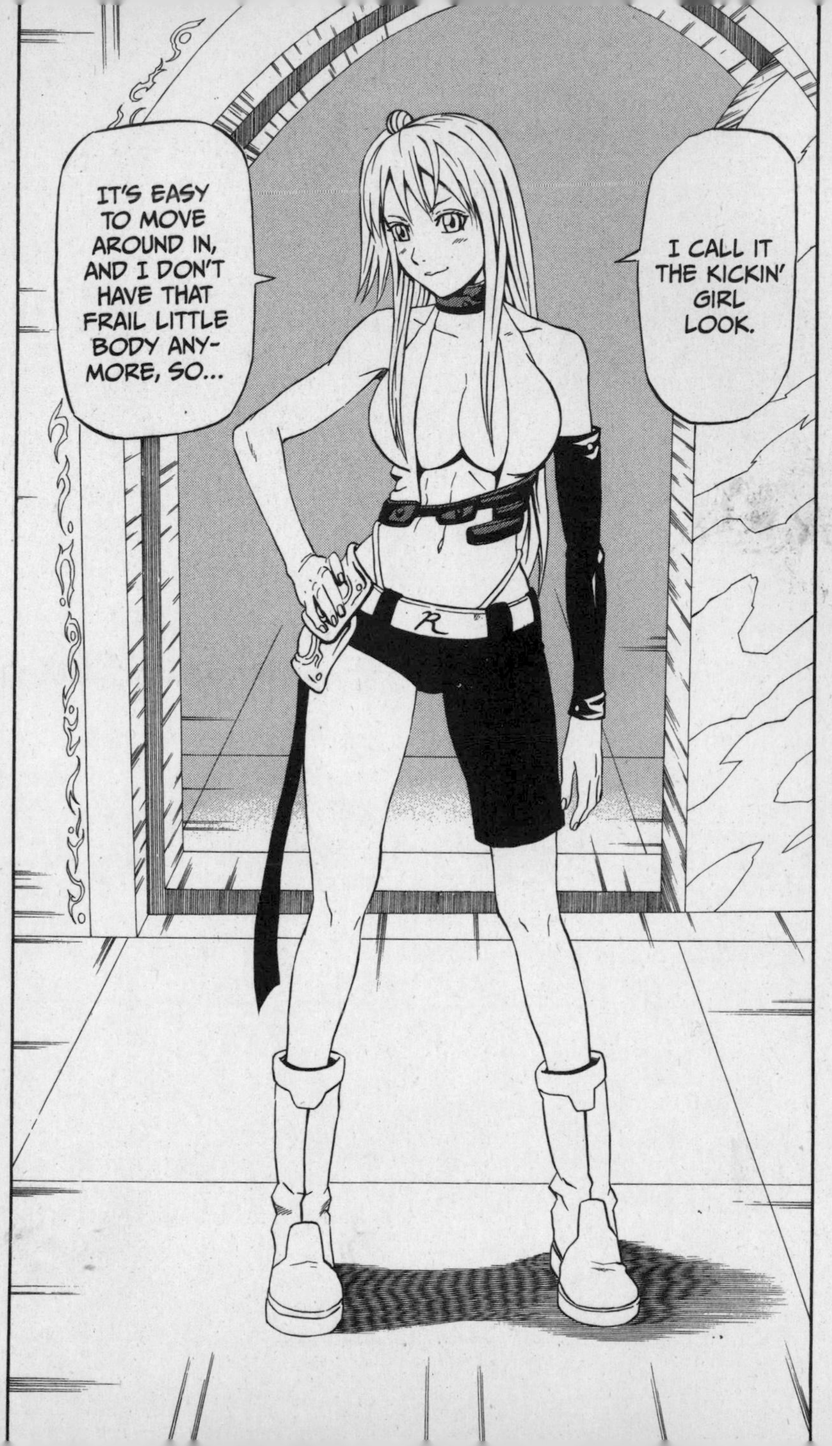
I CALL IT THE KICKIN' GIRL LOOK.
IT'S EASY TO MOVE AROUND IN, AND I DON'T HAVE THAT FRAIL LITTLE BODY ANY-MORE, SO...

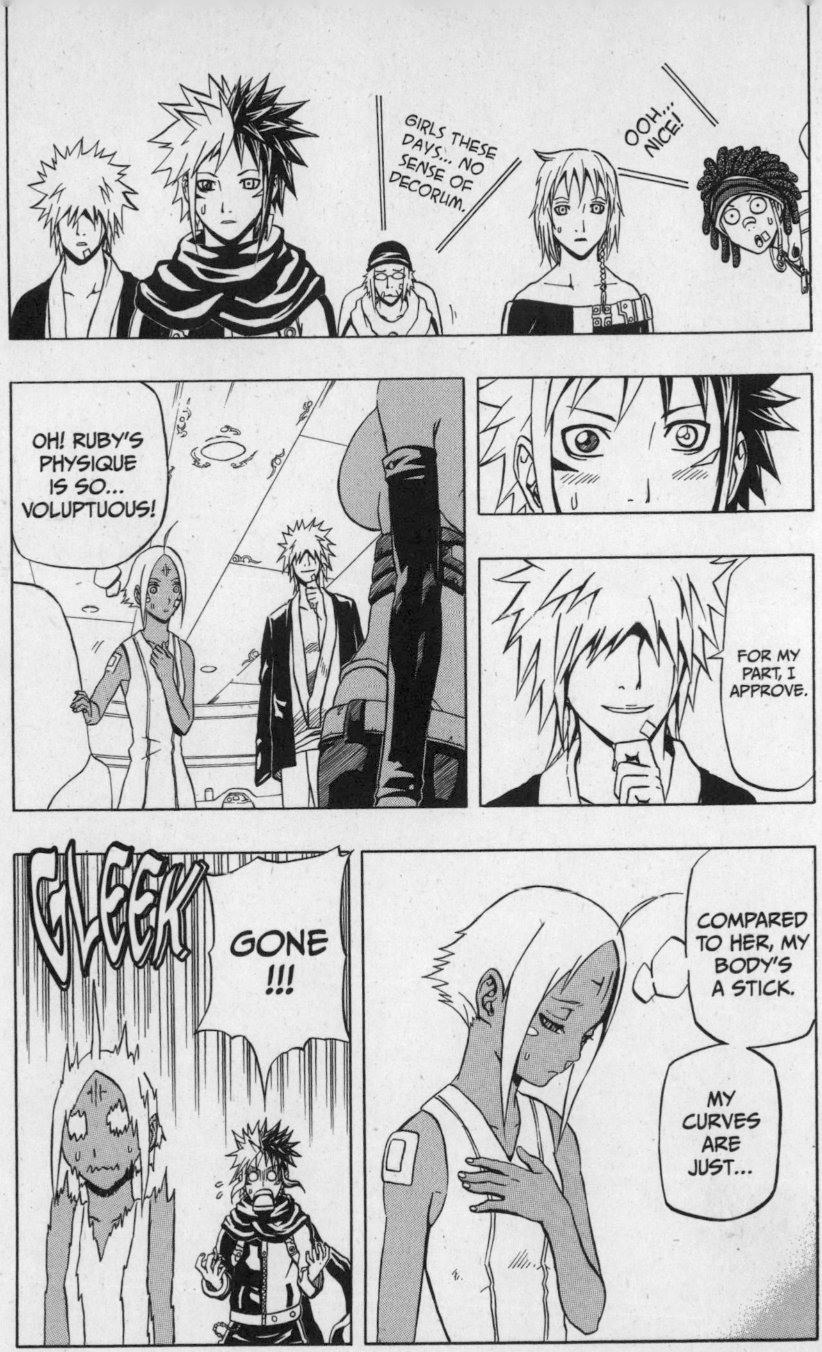
OOH... NICE!
GIRLS THESE DAYS... NO SENSE OF DECORUM.
FOR MY PART, I APPROVE.
OH! RUBY'S PHYSIQUE IS SO... VOLUPTUOUS!
COMPARED TO HER, MY BODY'S A STICK.
MY CURVES ARE JUST...
GONE !!!
GLEEK

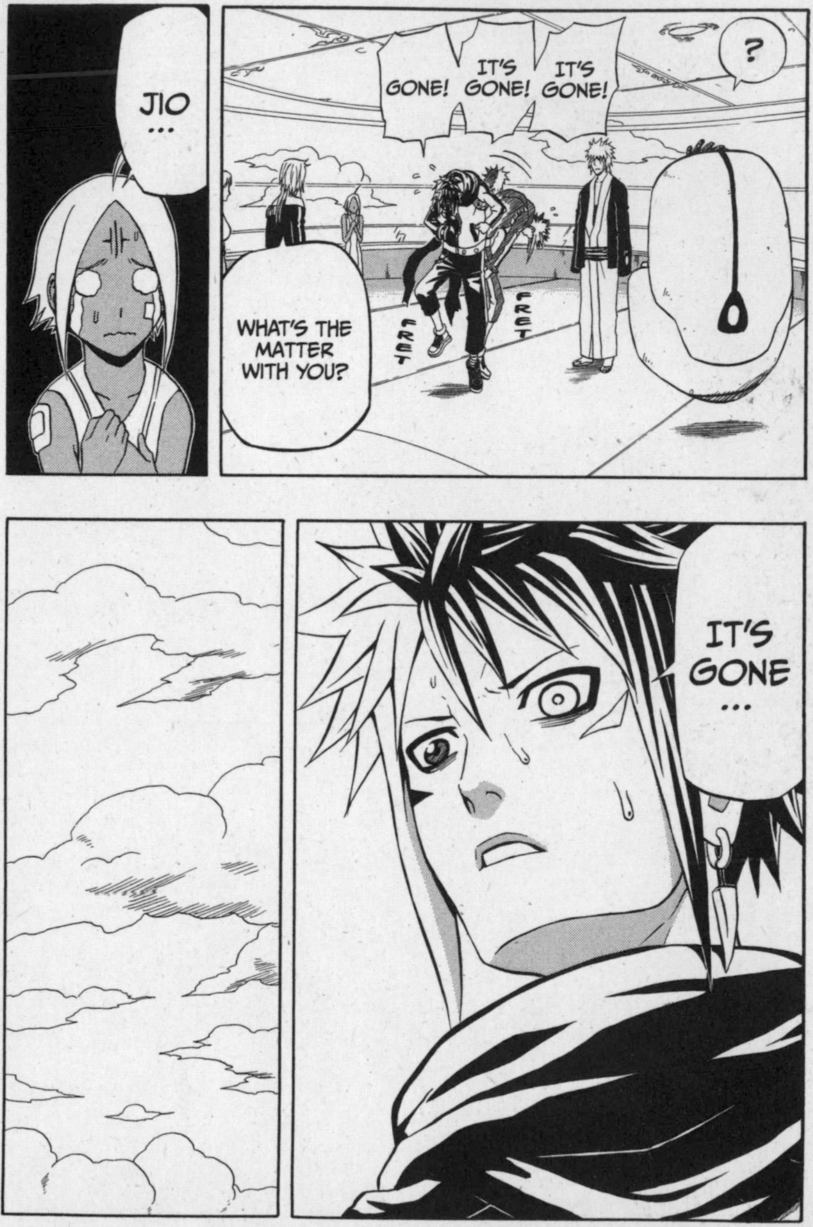
?
IT'S GONE! IT'S GONE! IT'S GONE!
FRET
FRET
WHAT'S THE MATTER WITH YOU?
JIO ...
IT'S GONE ...

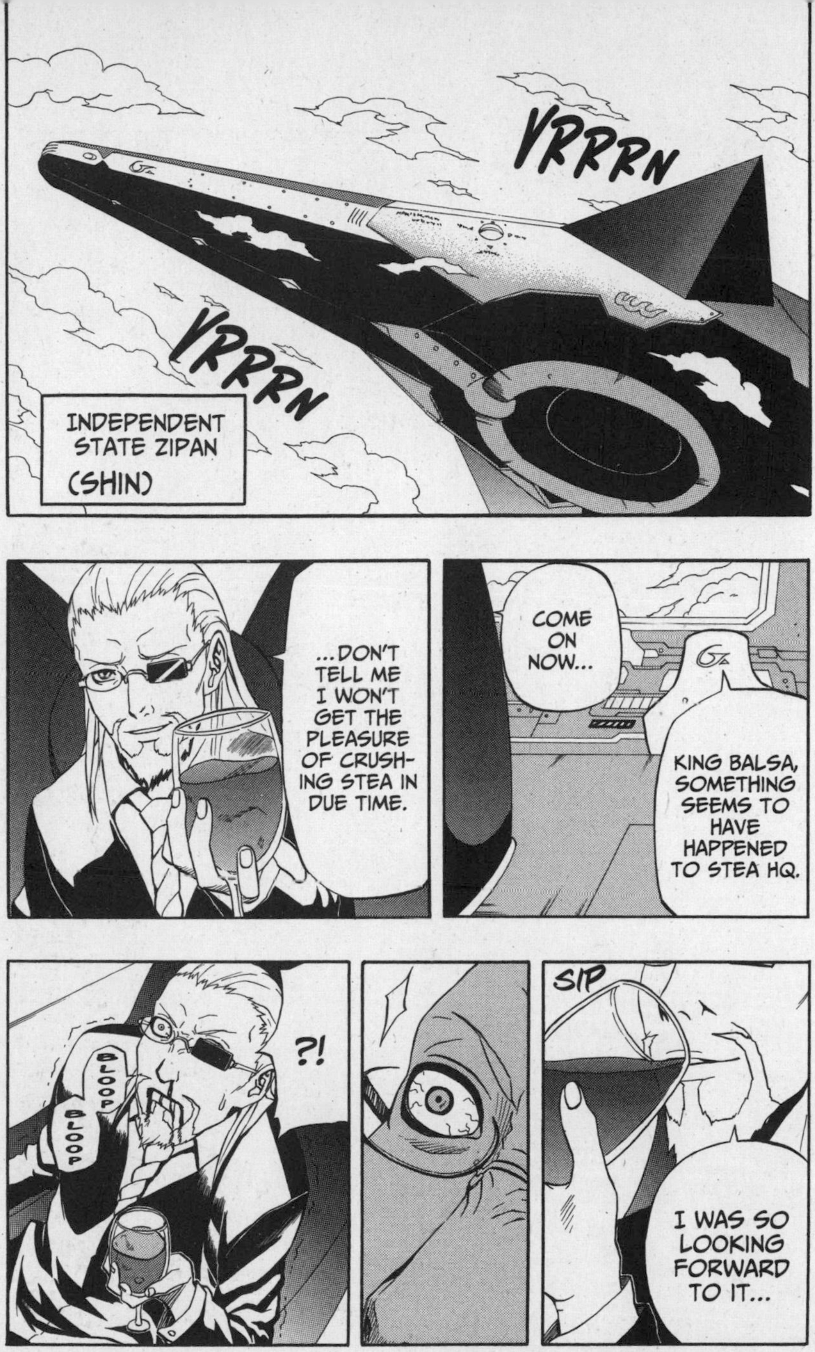
VRRRN
VRRRN
INDEPENDENT STATE ZIPAN (SHIN)
KING BALSA, SOMETHING SEEMS TO HAVE HAPPENED TO STEA HQ.
COME ON NOW...
...DON'T TELL ME I WON'T GET THE PLEASURE OF CRUSHING STEA IN DUE TIME.
SIP
I WAS SO LOOKING FORWARD TO IT...
?!
BLOOP
BLOOP

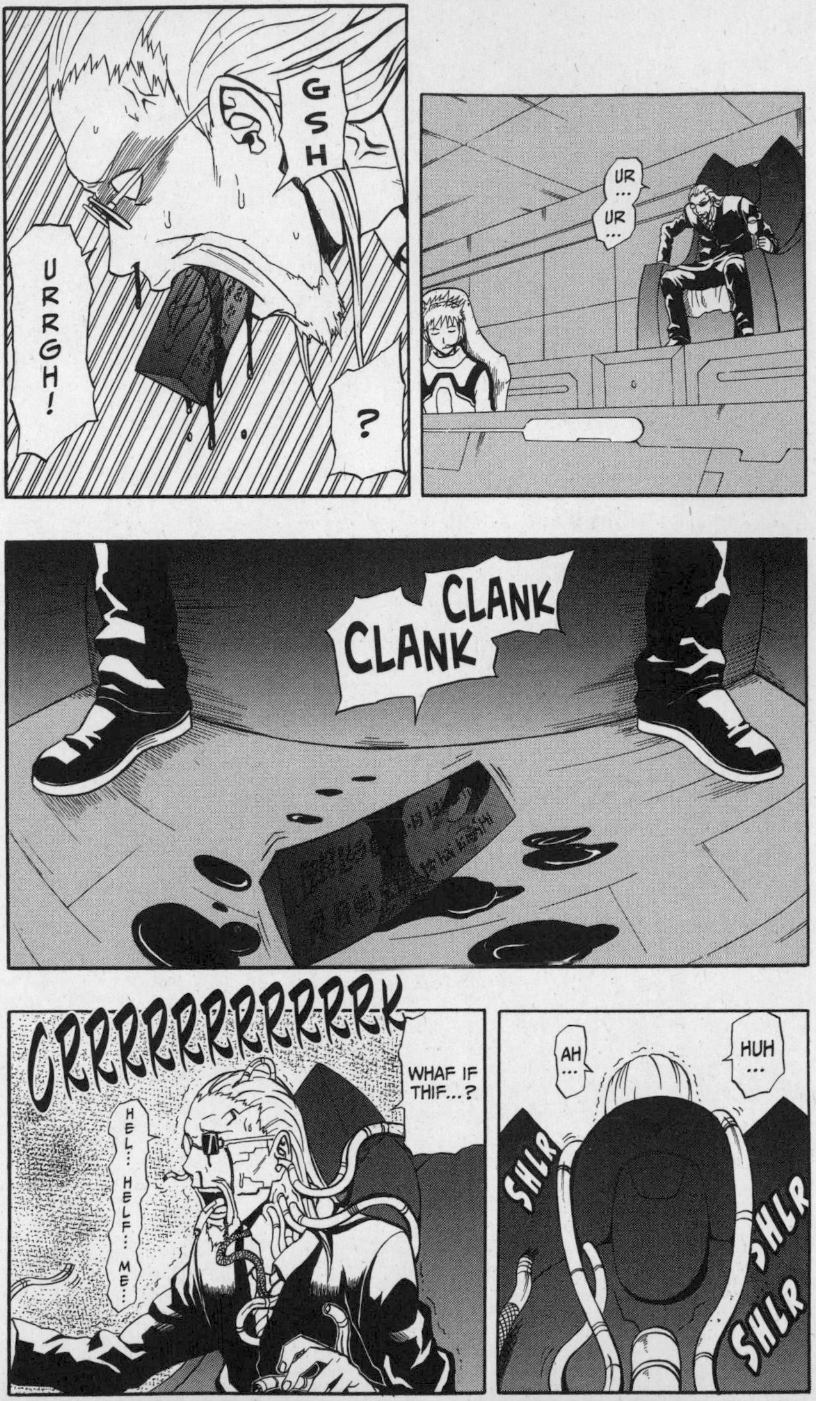
UR... UR...
GSH
?
URRGH!
CLANK CLANK
HUH...
AH...
SHLR
SHLR
SHLR
SHLR
WHAF IF THIF...?
CRRRRRRRRRRRK
HEL... HELF... ME...

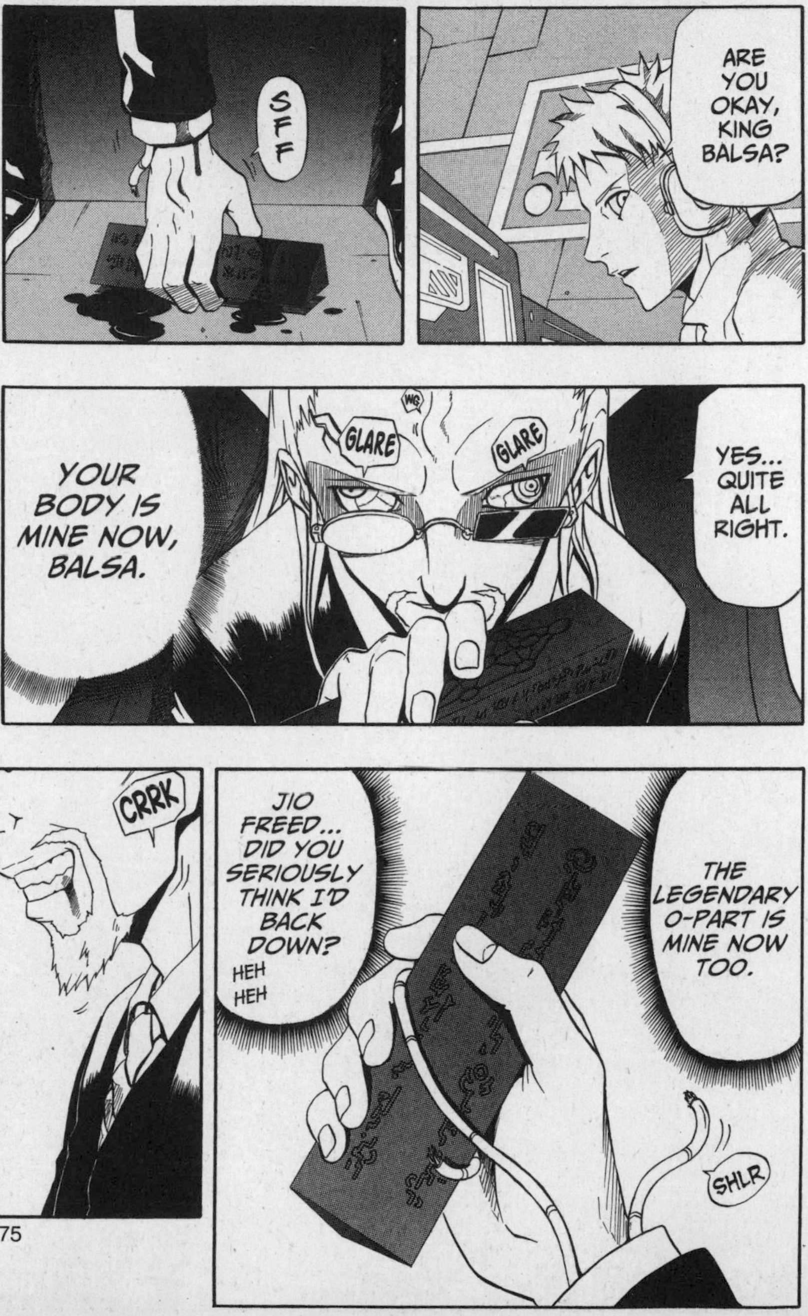
ARE YOU OKAY, KING BALSA?
SFF
YES... QUITE ALL RIGHT.
GLARE
GLARE
WG
YOUR BODY IS MINE NOW, BALSA.
THE LEGENDARY O-PART IS MINE NOW TOO.
JIO FREED... DID YOU SERIOUSLY THINK I'D BACK DOWN?
HEH HEH
SHLR
CRRK

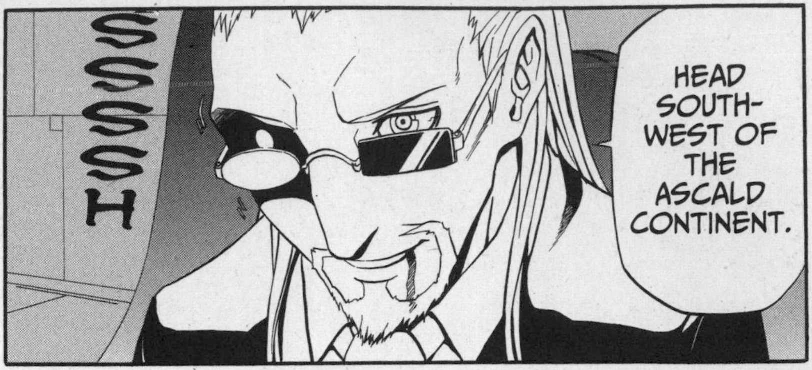
SSSSSH
HEAD SOUTH-WEST OF THE ASCALD CONTINENT.
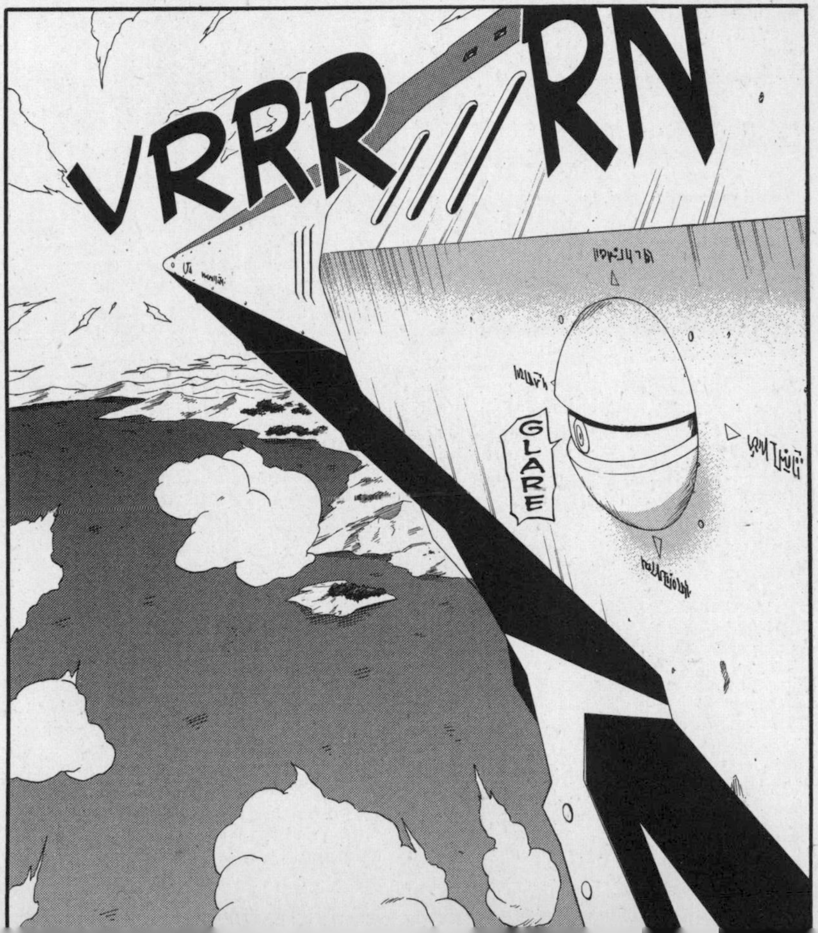
VRRR///RN
GLARE

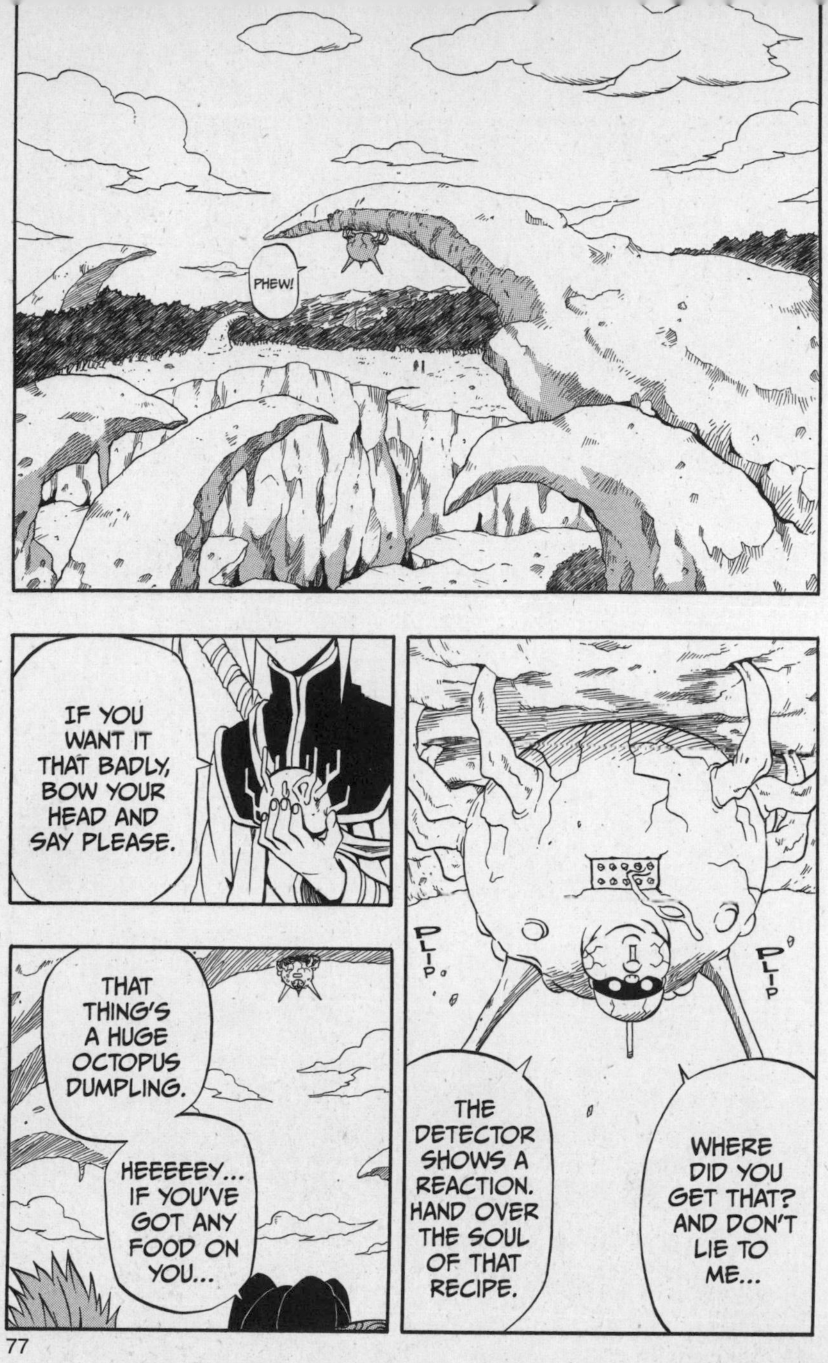
PHEW!
PLIP
PLIP
WHERE DID YOU GET THAT? AND DON'T LIE TO ME...
THE DETECTOR SHOWS A REACTION. HAND OVER THE SOUL OF THAT RECIPE.
IF YOU WANT IT THAT BADLY, BOW YOUR HEAD AND SAY PLEASE.
THAT THING'S A HUGE OCTOPUS DUMPLING.
HEEEEEY... IF YOU'VE GOT ANY FOOD ON YOU...

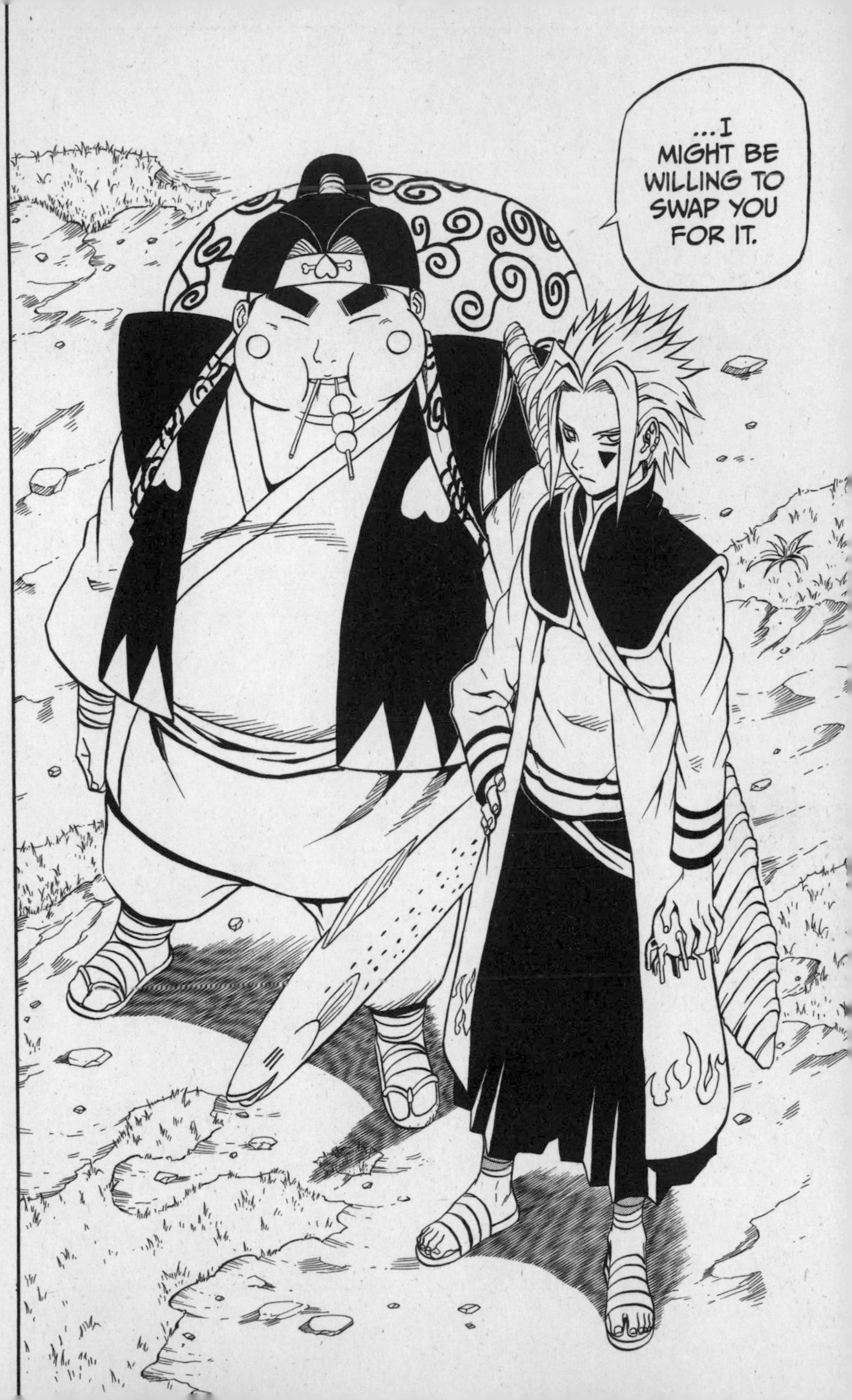
...I MIGHT BE WILLING TO SWAP YOU FOR IT.

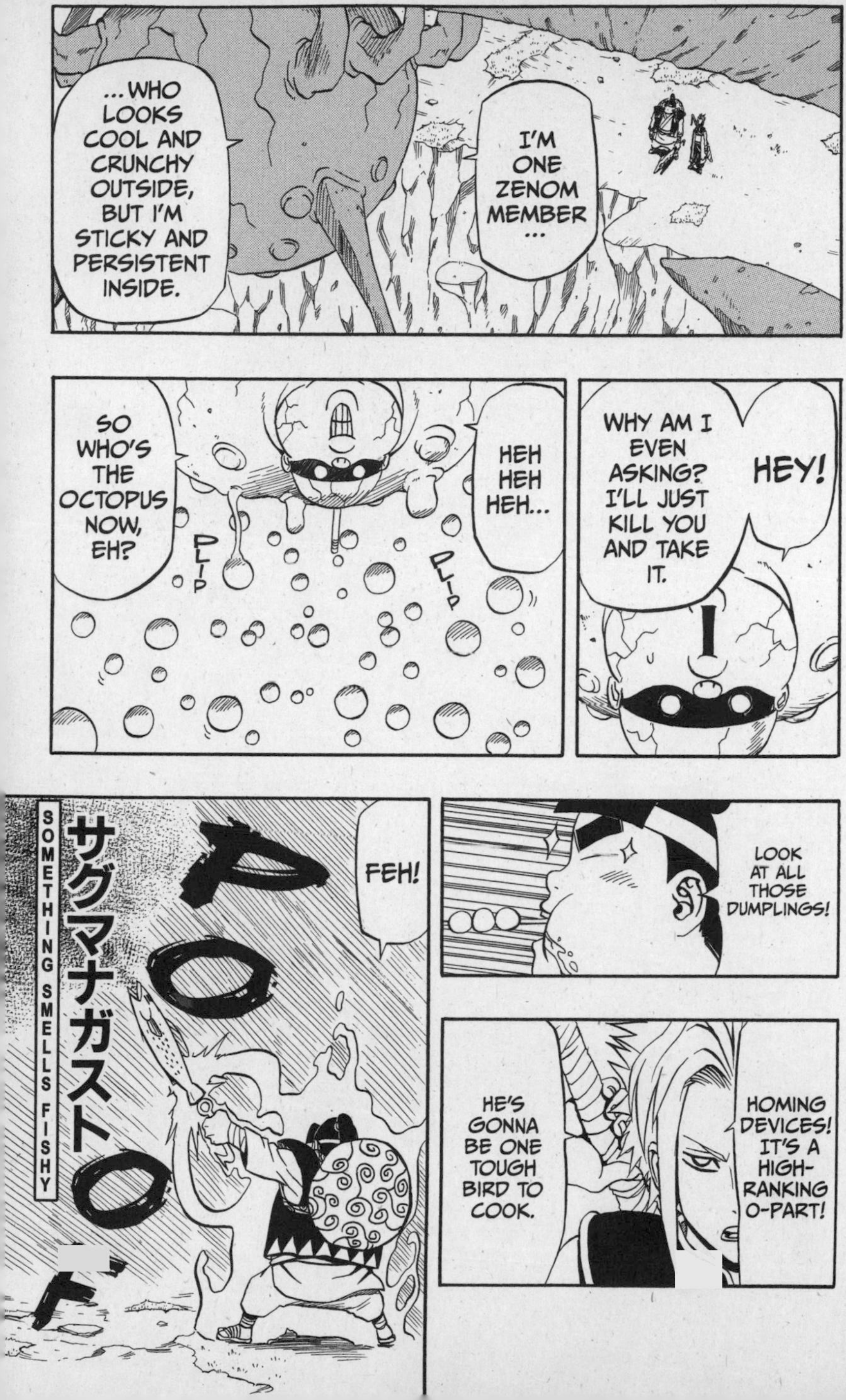
I'M ONE ZENOM MEMBER ...
...WHO LOOKS COOL AND CRUNCHY OUTSIDE, BUT I'M STICKY AND PERSISTENT INSIDE.
HEY!
WHY AM I EVEN ASKING? I'LL JUST KILL YOU AND TAKE IT.
HEH HEH HEH...
PLIP
SO WHO'S THE OCTOPUS NOW, EH?
PLIP
LOOK AT ALL THOSE DUMPLINGS!
HOMING DEVICES! IT'S A HIGH-RANKING O-PART!
HE'S GONNA BE ONE TOUGH BIRD TO COOK.
FEH!
サグマナガスト
SOMETHING SMELLS FISHY

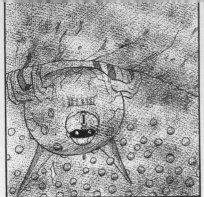

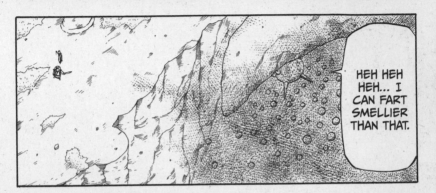

HEH HEH HEH... I CAN FART SMELLIER THAN THAT.

BURNING CROW
タキガラス

...YOU!!

WELL, I FEEL SORRY FOR...

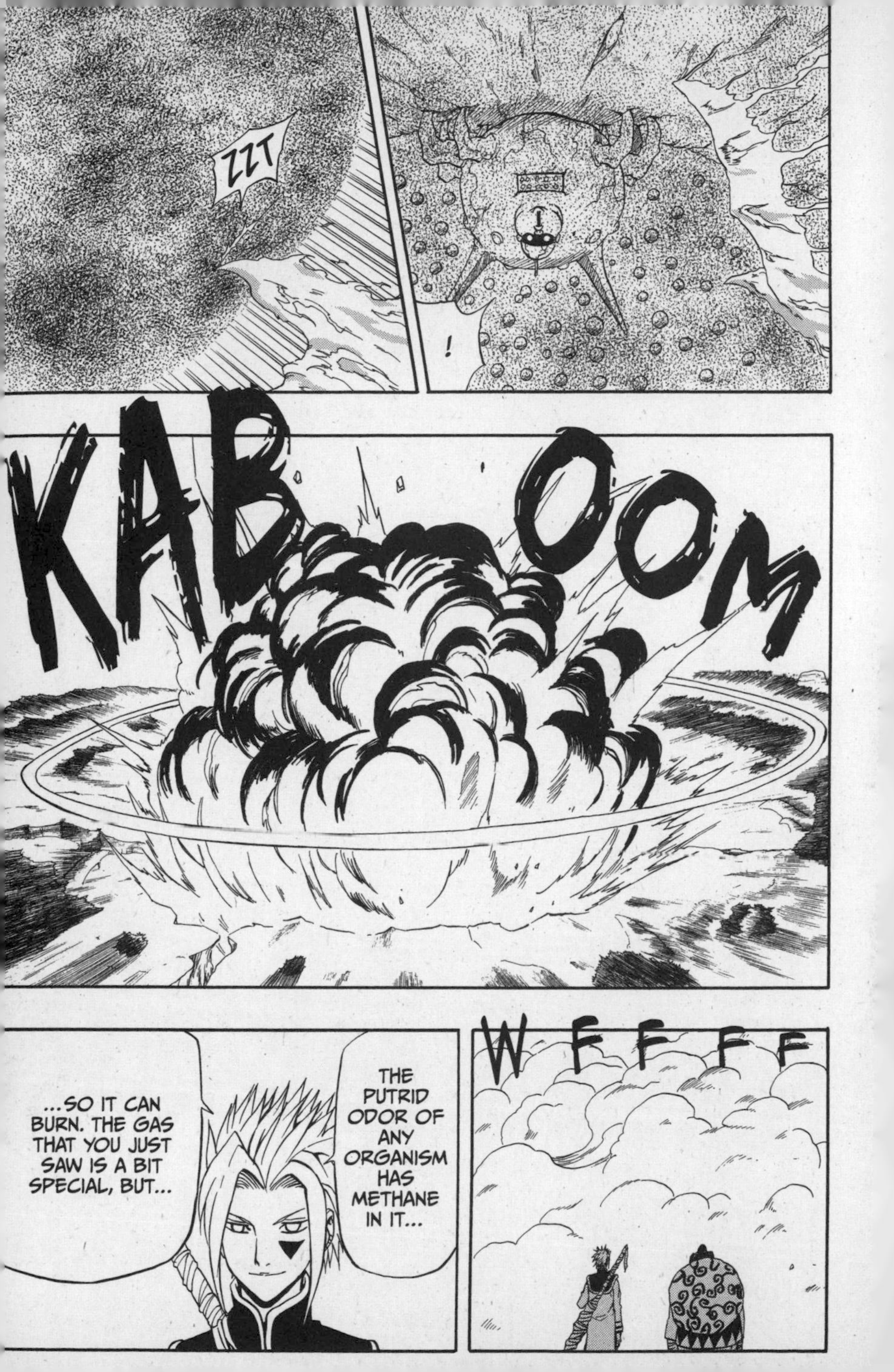
!
ZZT
KABOOM
WFFFF
THE PUTRID ODOR OF ANY ORGANISM HAS METHANE IN IT...
...SO IT CAN BURN. THE GAS THAT YOU JUST SAW IS A BIT SPECIAL, BUT...

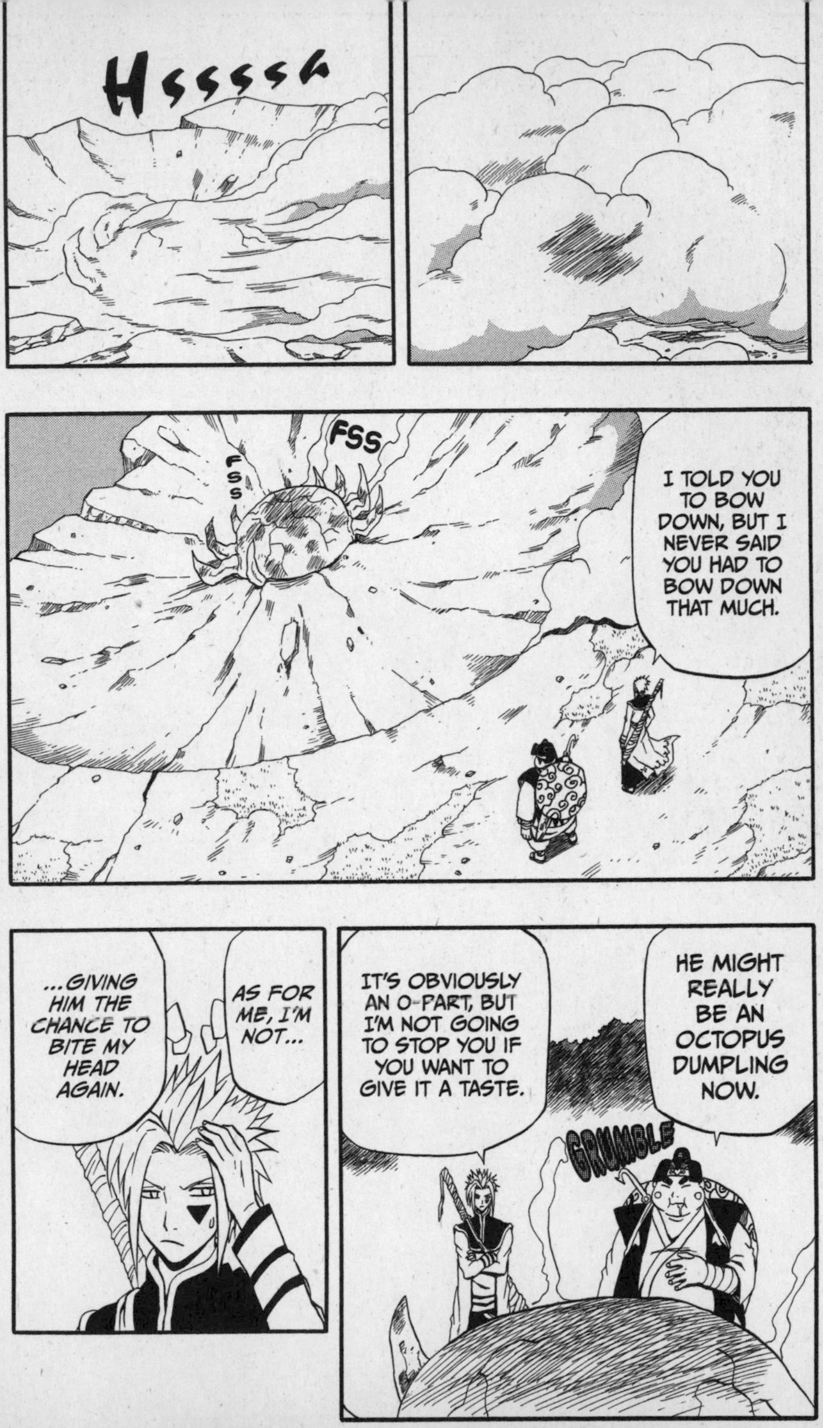
HSSSSH
FSS
FSS
I TOLD YOU TO BOW DOWN, BUT I NEVER SAID YOU HAD TO BOW DOWN THAT MUCH.
HE MIGHT REALLY BE AN OCTOPUS DUMPLING NOW.
IT'S OBVIOUSLY AN O-PART, BUT I'M NOT GOING TO STOP YOU IF YOU WANT TO GIVE IT A TASTE.
GRUMBLE
AS FOR ME, I'M NOT...
...GIVING HIM THE CHANCE TO BITE MY HEAD AGAIN.

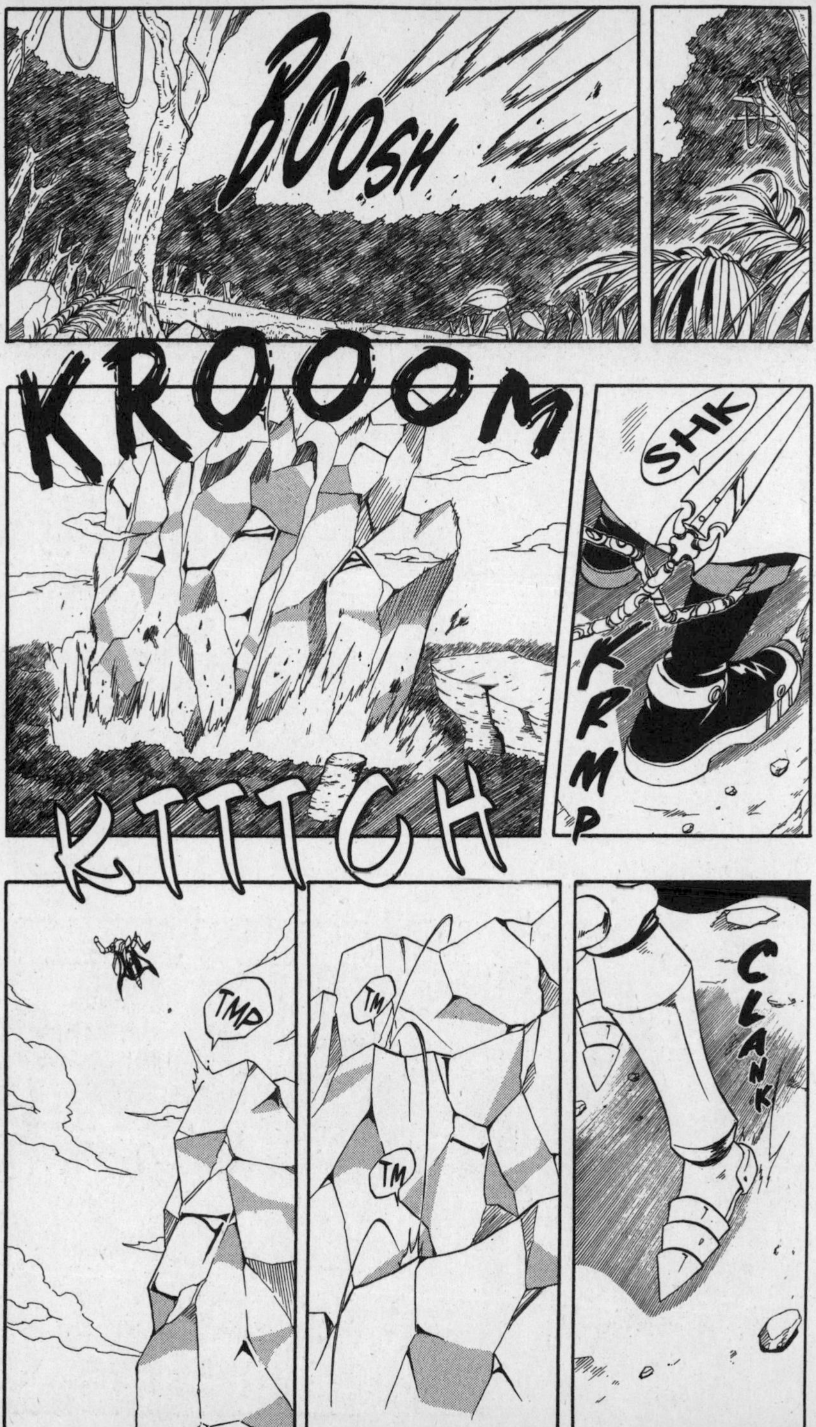
BOOSH
SHK
KRMP
KROOOM
KTTTCH
CLANK
TM
TM
TMP

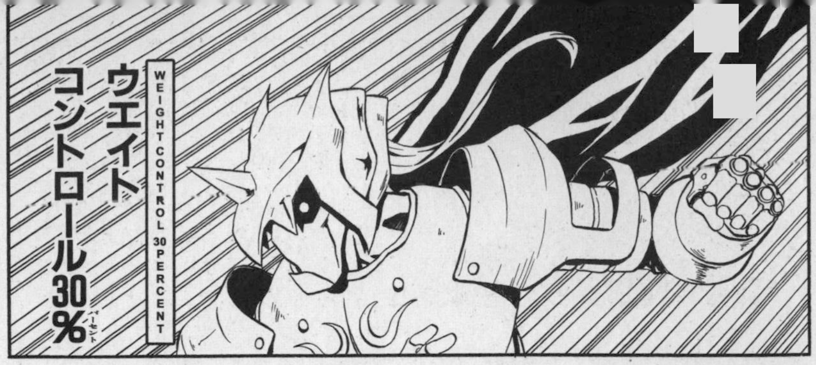
WEIGHT CONTROL 30 PERCENT
ウエイトコントロール30%(パーセント)

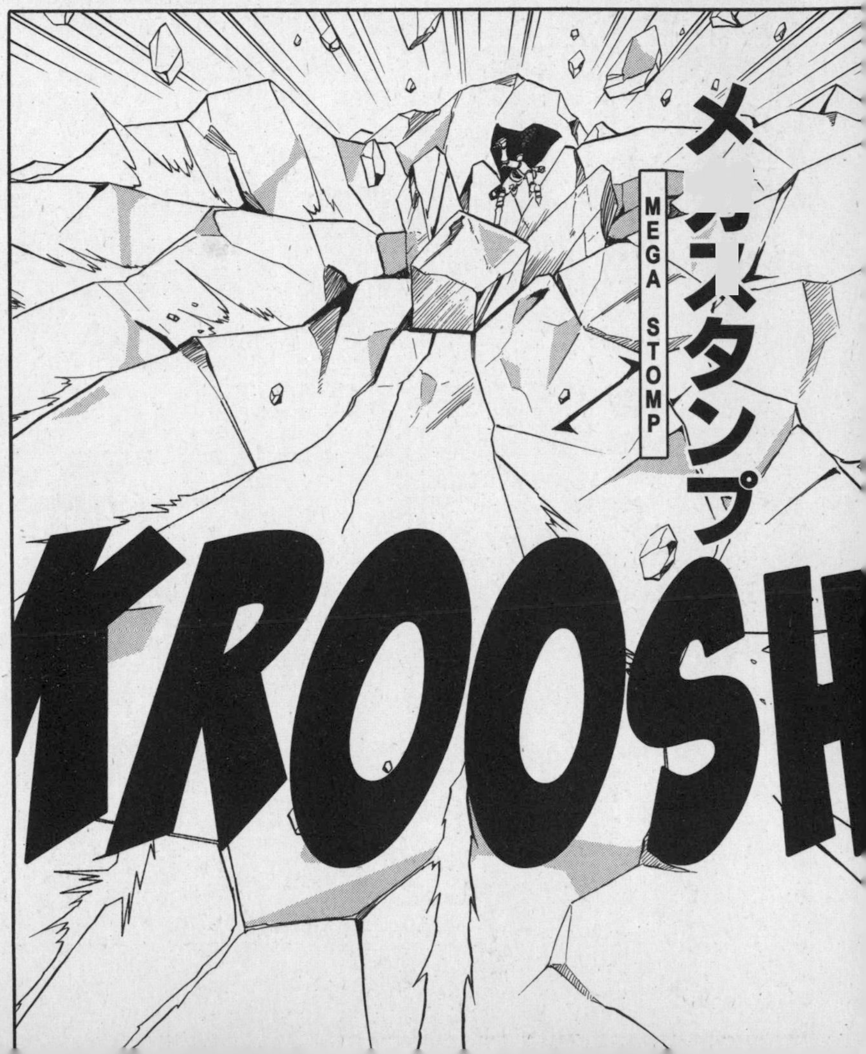
MEGA STOMP
KROOSH

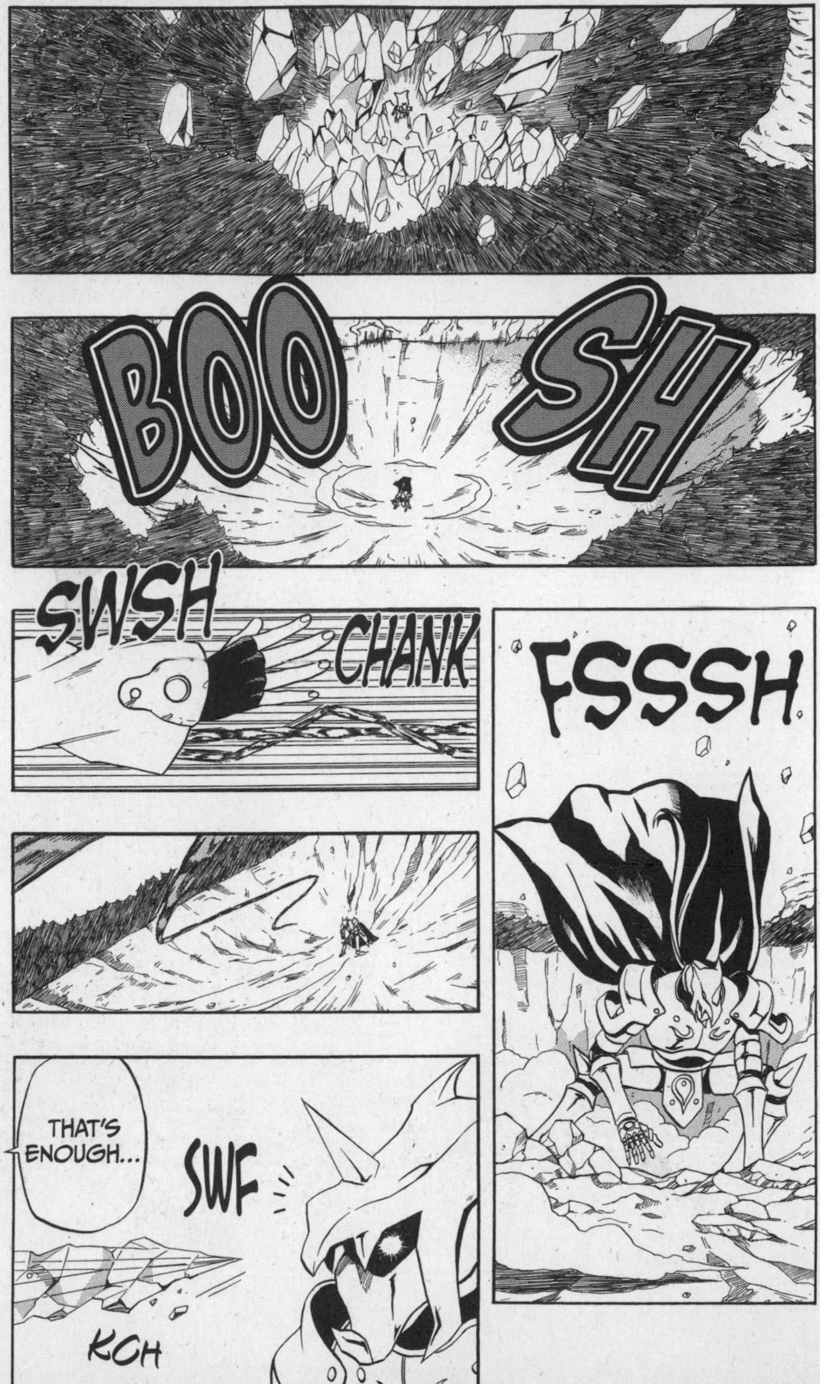
BOOSH
FSSSH
SWSH
CHANK
THAT'S ENOUGH...
SWF
KOH

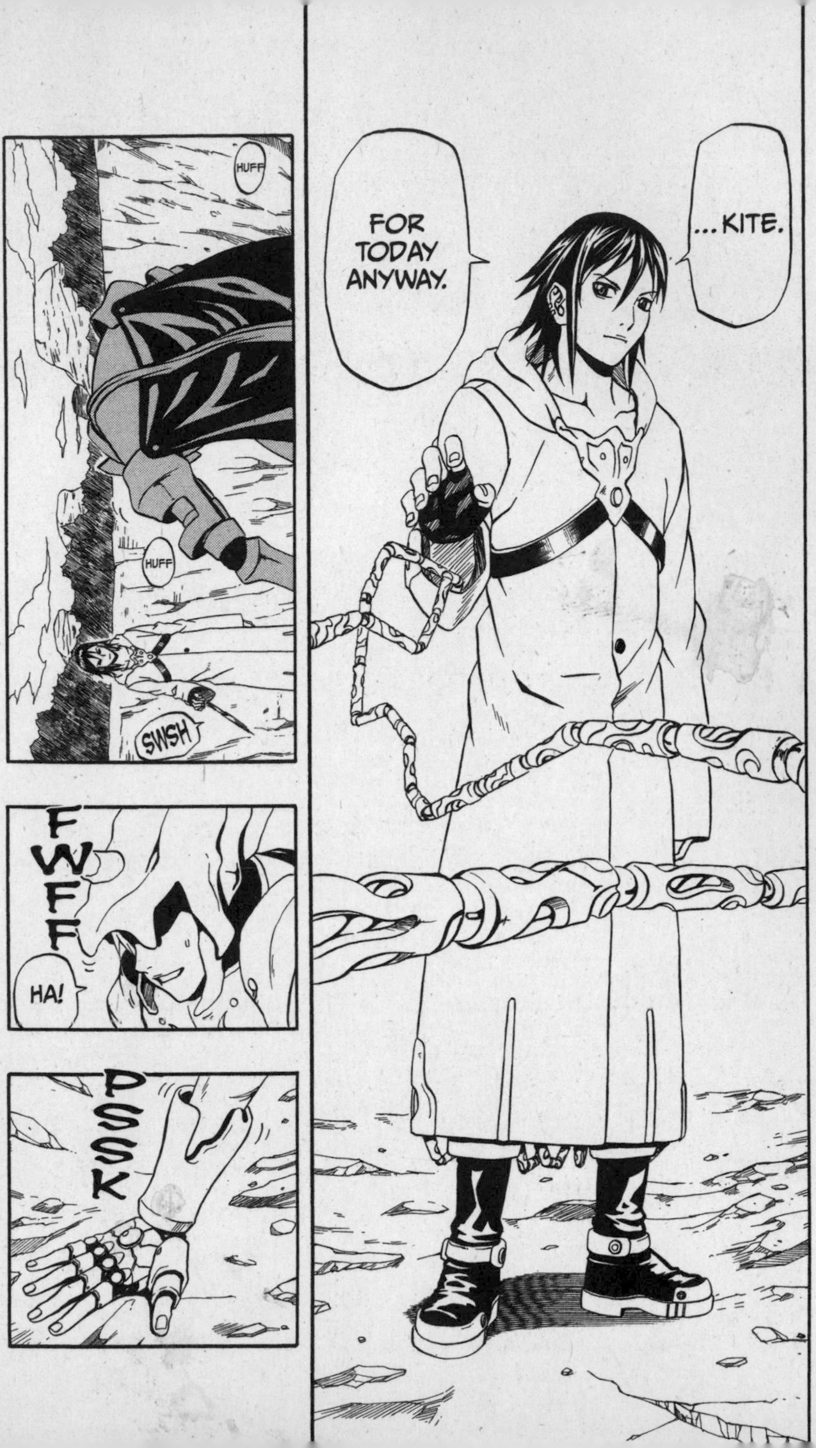
...KITE.
FOR TODAY ANYWAY.
HUFF
HUFF
SWSH
FWFF
HA!
PSSK

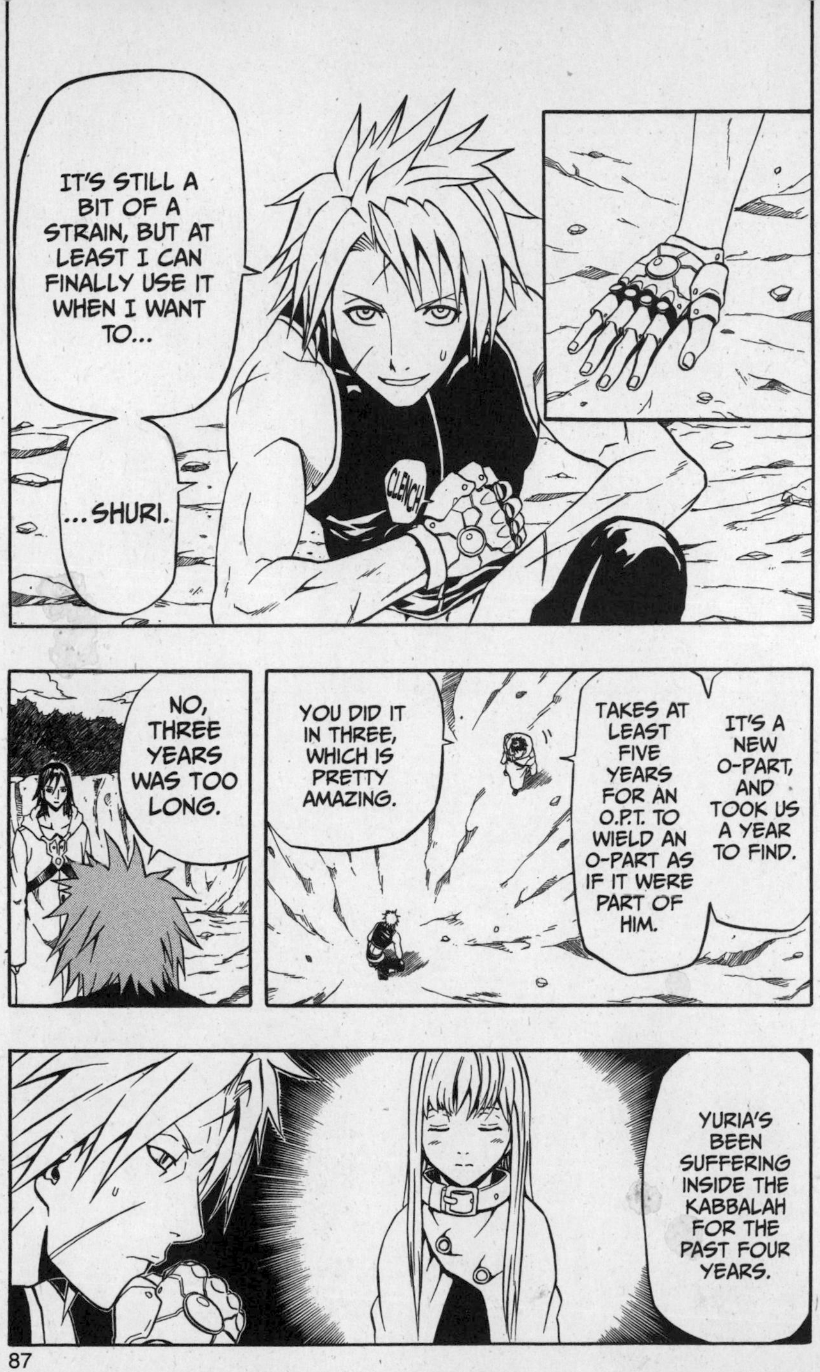
IT'S STILL A BIT OF A STRAIN, BUT AT LEAST I CAN FINALLY USE IT WHEN I WANT TO...
...SHURI.
CLENCH
IT'S A NEW O-PART, AND TOOK US A YEAR TO FIND.
TAKES AT LEAST FIVE YEARS FOR AN O.P.T. TO WIELD AN O-PART AS IF IT WERE PART OF HIM.
YOU DID IT IN THREE, WHICH IS PRETTY AMAZING.
NO, THREE YEARS WAS TOO LONG.
YURIA'S BEEN SUFFERING INSIDE THE KABBALAH FOR THE PAST FOUR YEARS.

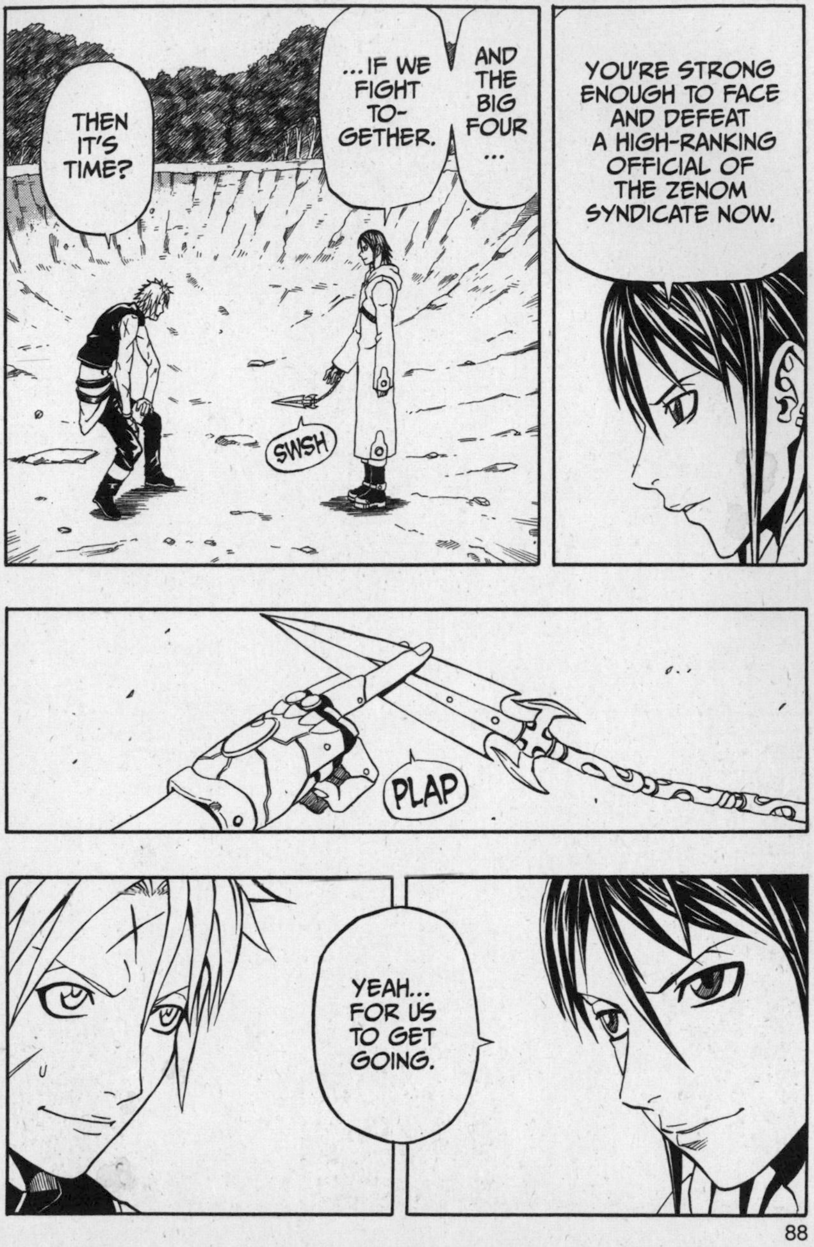
YOU'RE STRONG ENOUGH TO FACE AND DEFEAT A HIGH-RANKING OFFICIAL OF THE ZENOM SYNDICATE NOW.
AND THE BIG FOUR ...
...IF WE FIGHT TO-GETHER.
THEN IT'S TIME?
SWSH
PLAP
YEAH... FOR US TO GET GOING.

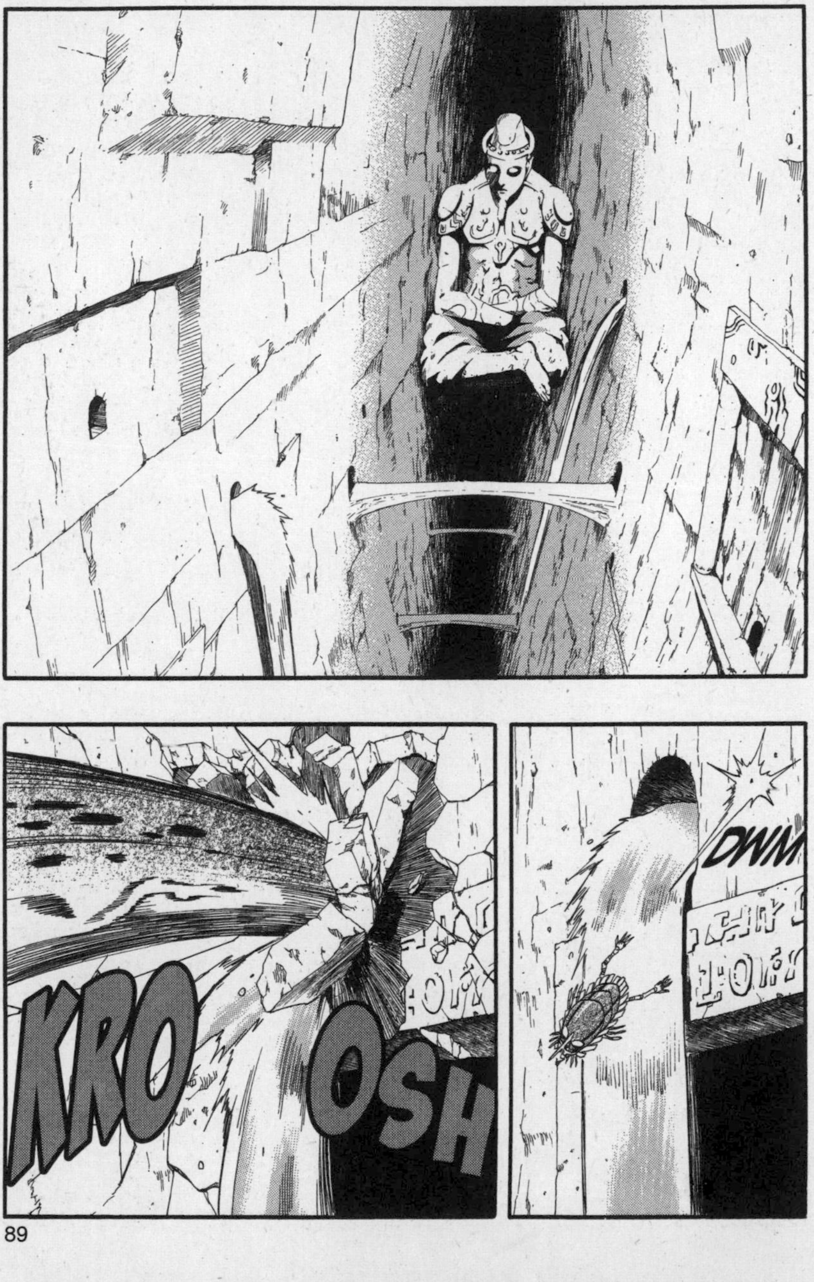
DWM
KRO
OSH

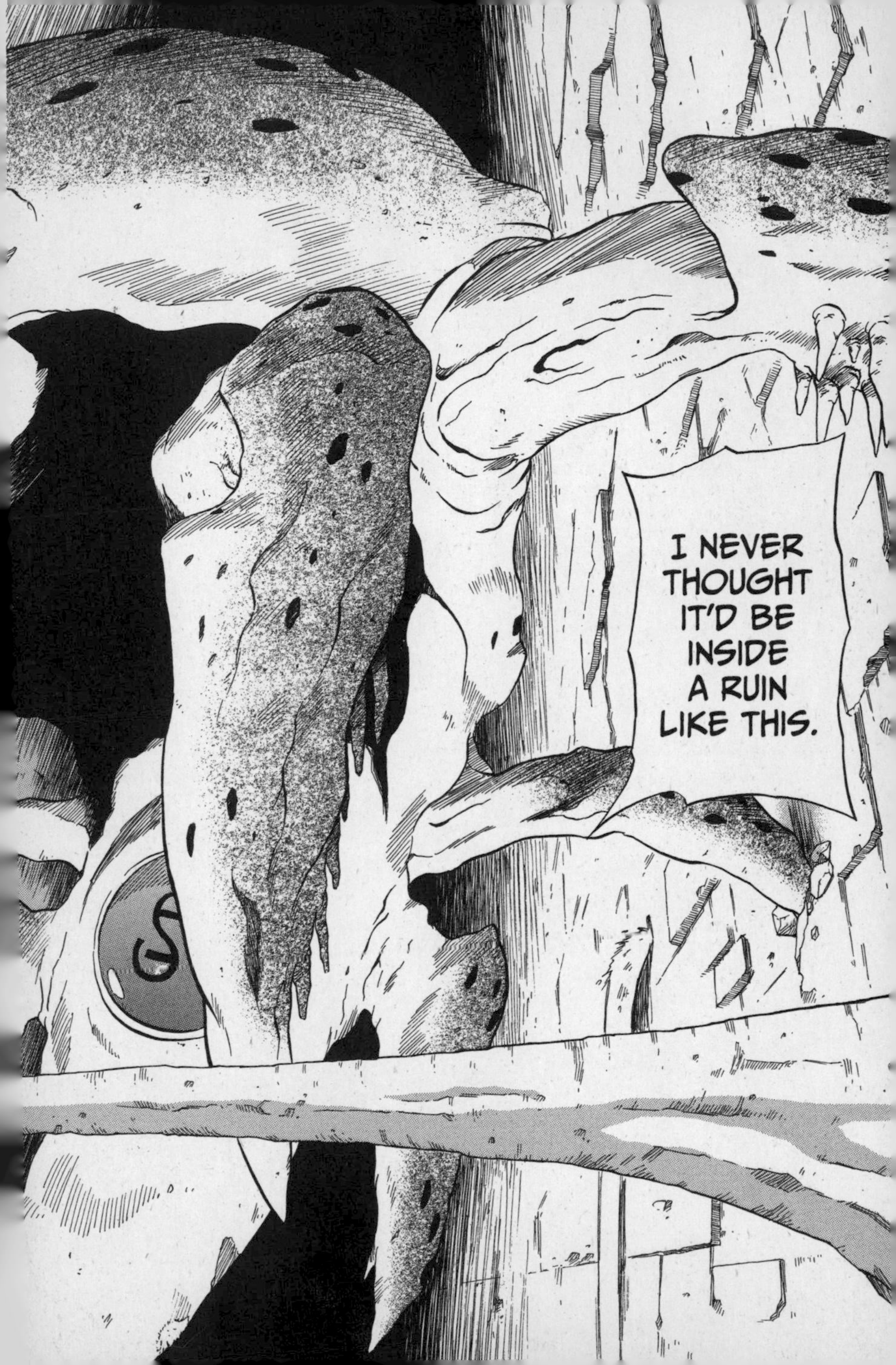
I NEVER THOUGHT IT'D BE INSIDE A RUIN LIKE THIS.

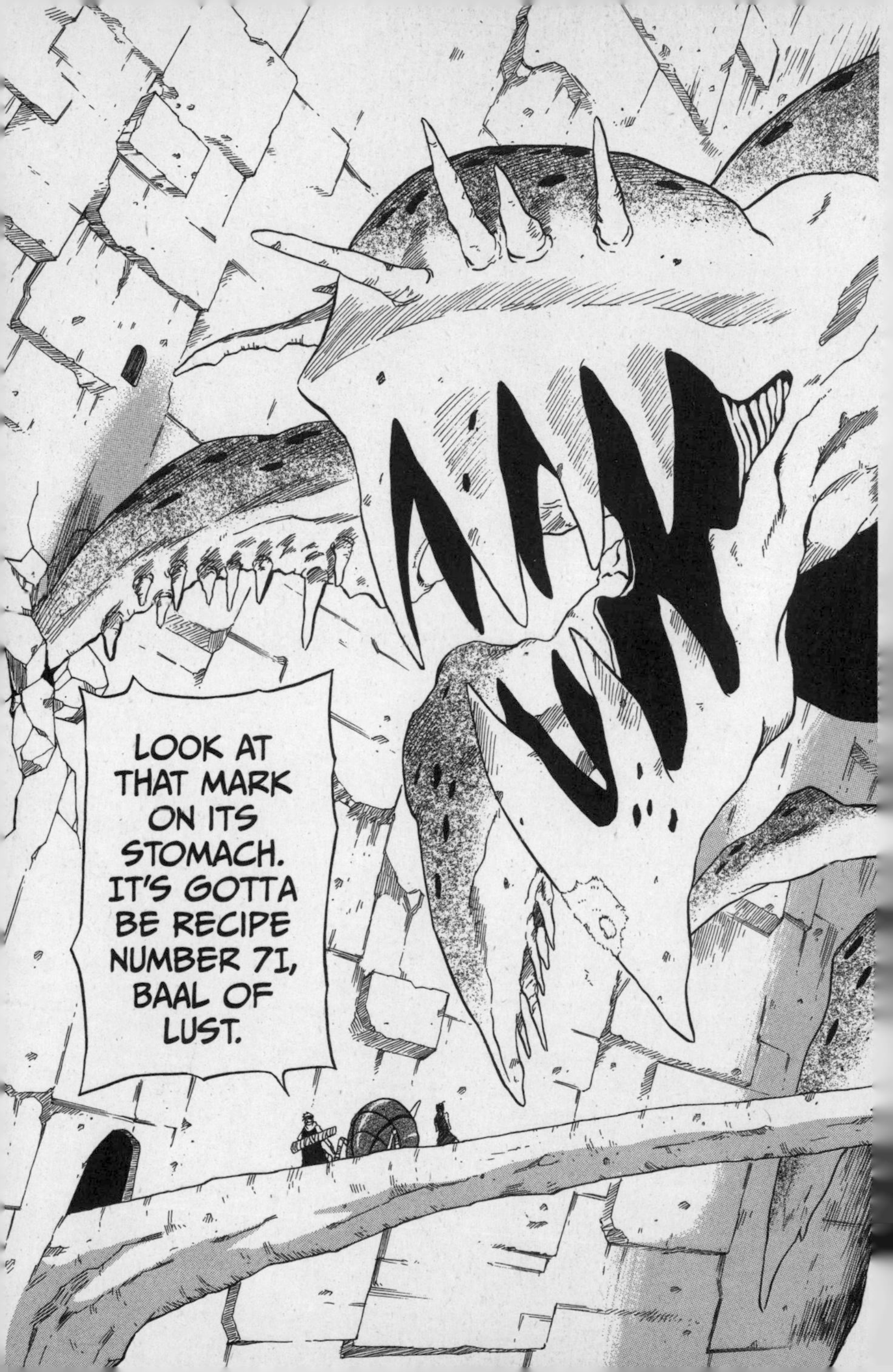
LOOK AT THAT MARK ON ITS STOMACH. IT'S GOTTA BE RECIPE NUMBER 71, BAAL OF LUST.

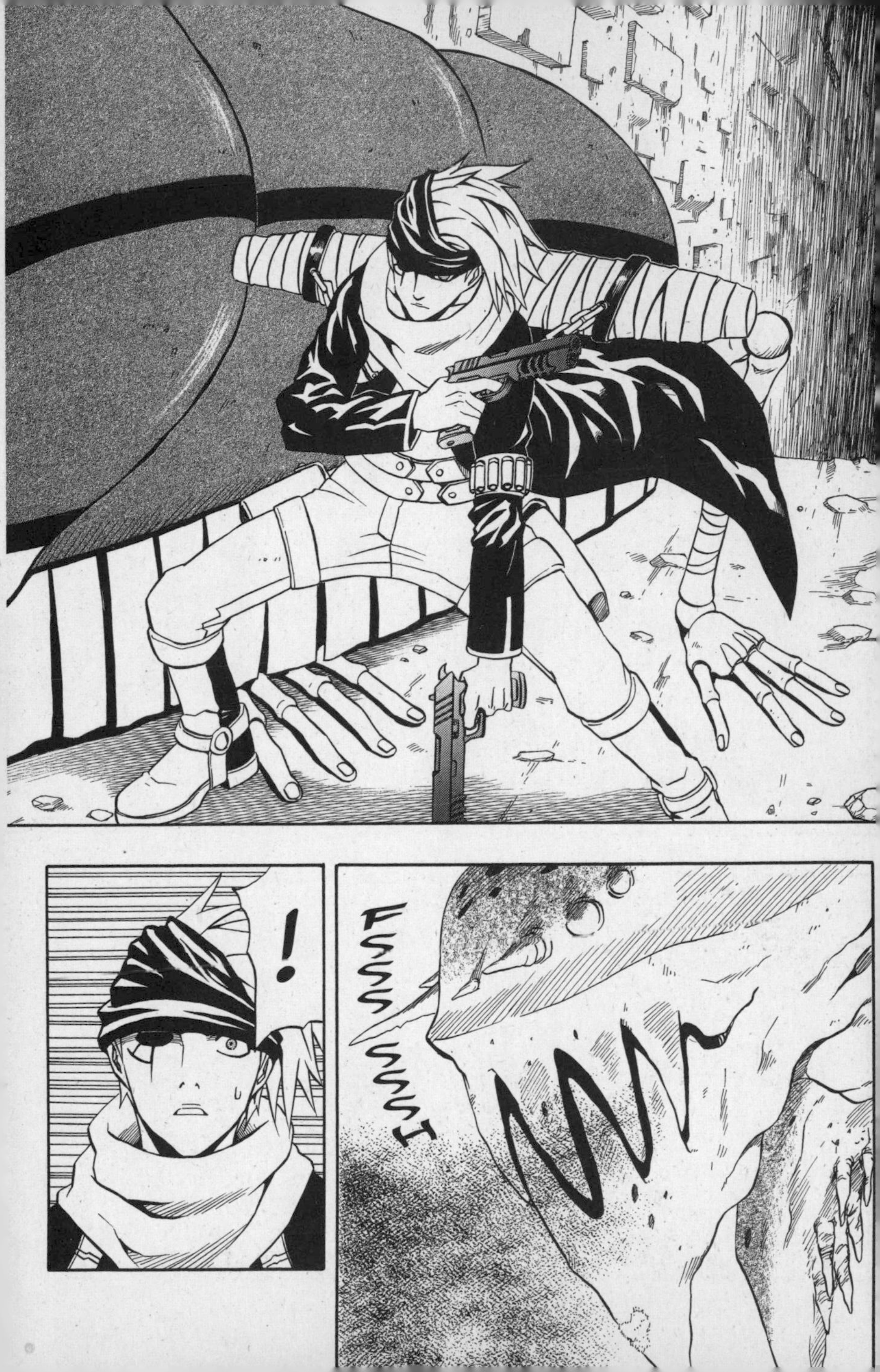
FSSSSSSI
!

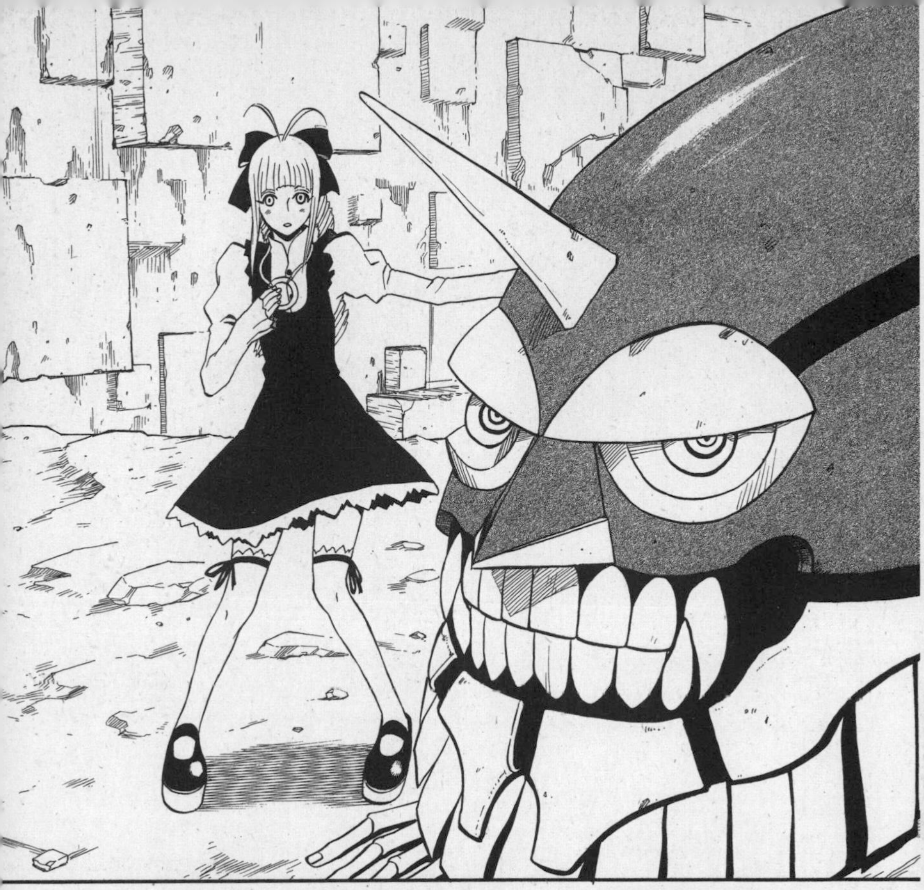

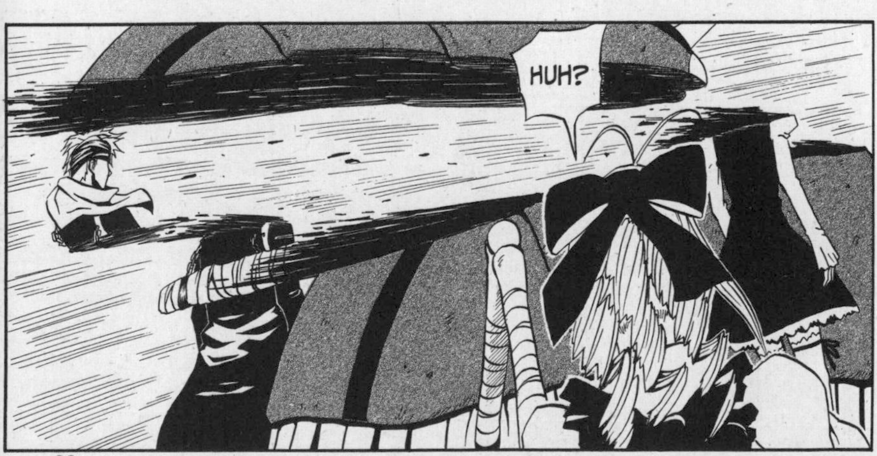
HUH?

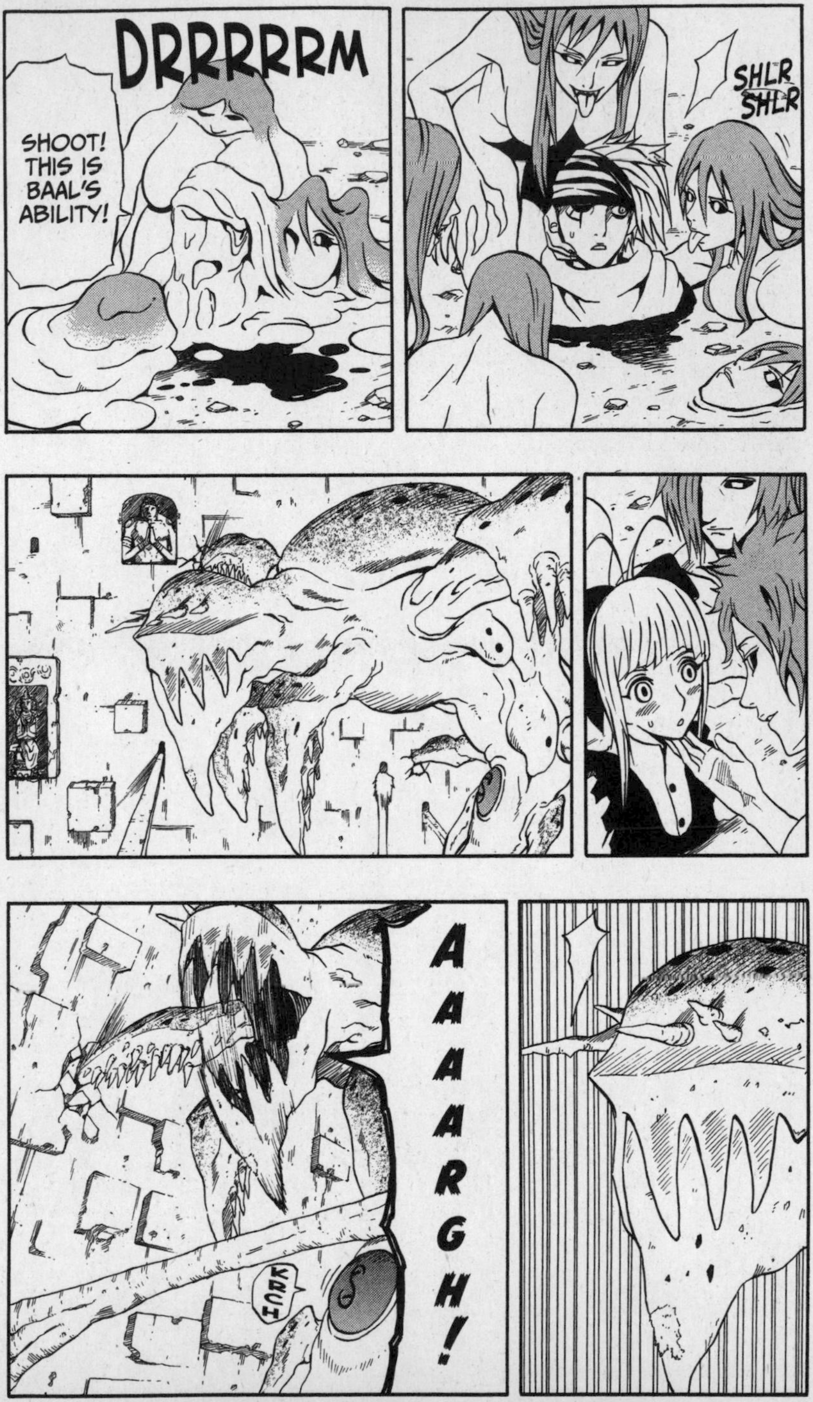
SHLR SHLR
DRRRRRM
SHOOT! THIS IS BAAL'S ABILITY!
AAAARGH!
KRCH

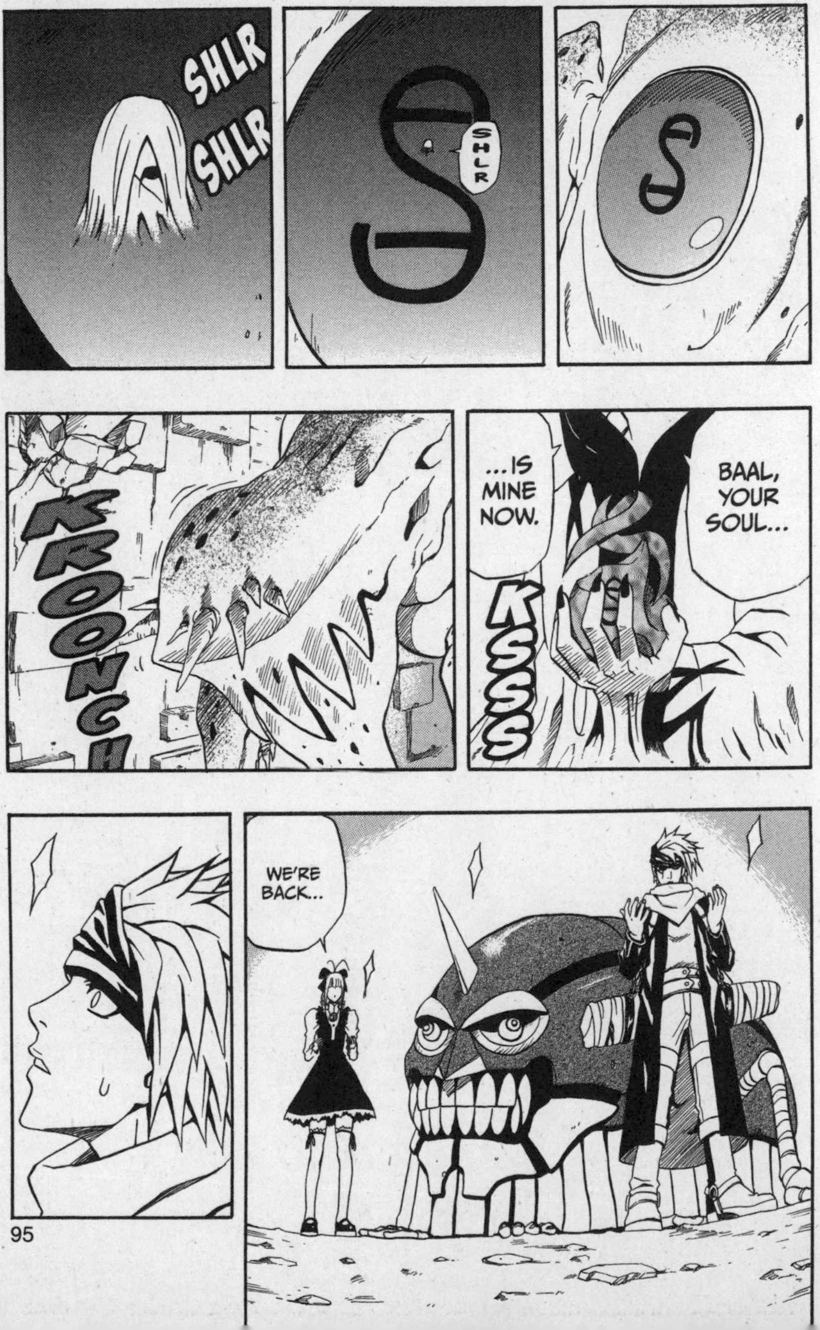
SHLR
SHLR SHLR
BAAL, YOUR SOUL...
...IS MINE NOW.
KSSS
KROONCH
WE'RE BACK...

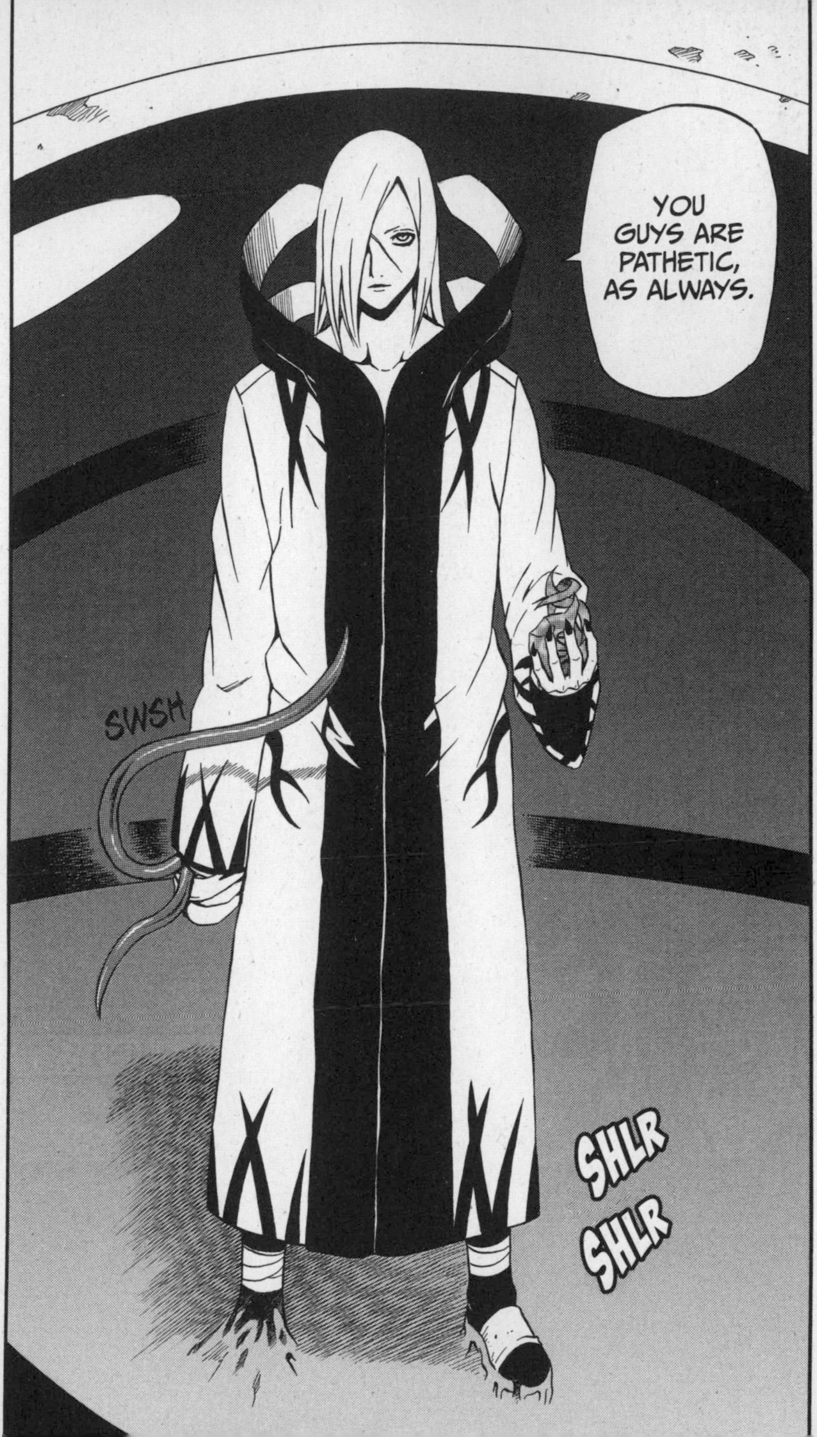
YOU GUYS ARE PATHETIC, AS ALWAYS.
SWSH
SHLR SHLR

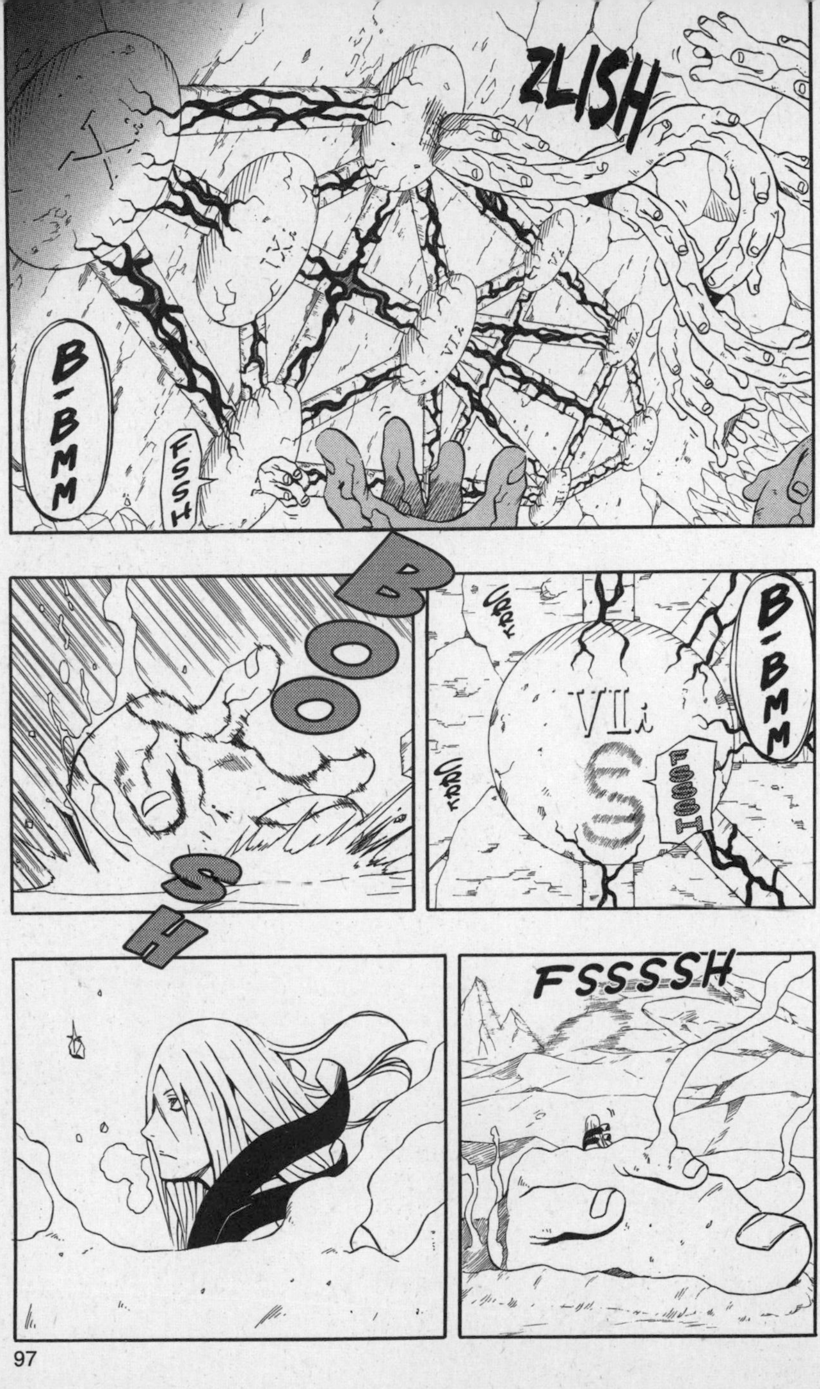
ZLISH
B-BMM
FSSH
B-BMM
FSSST
CRRK
CRRK
BOOSH
FSSSSH

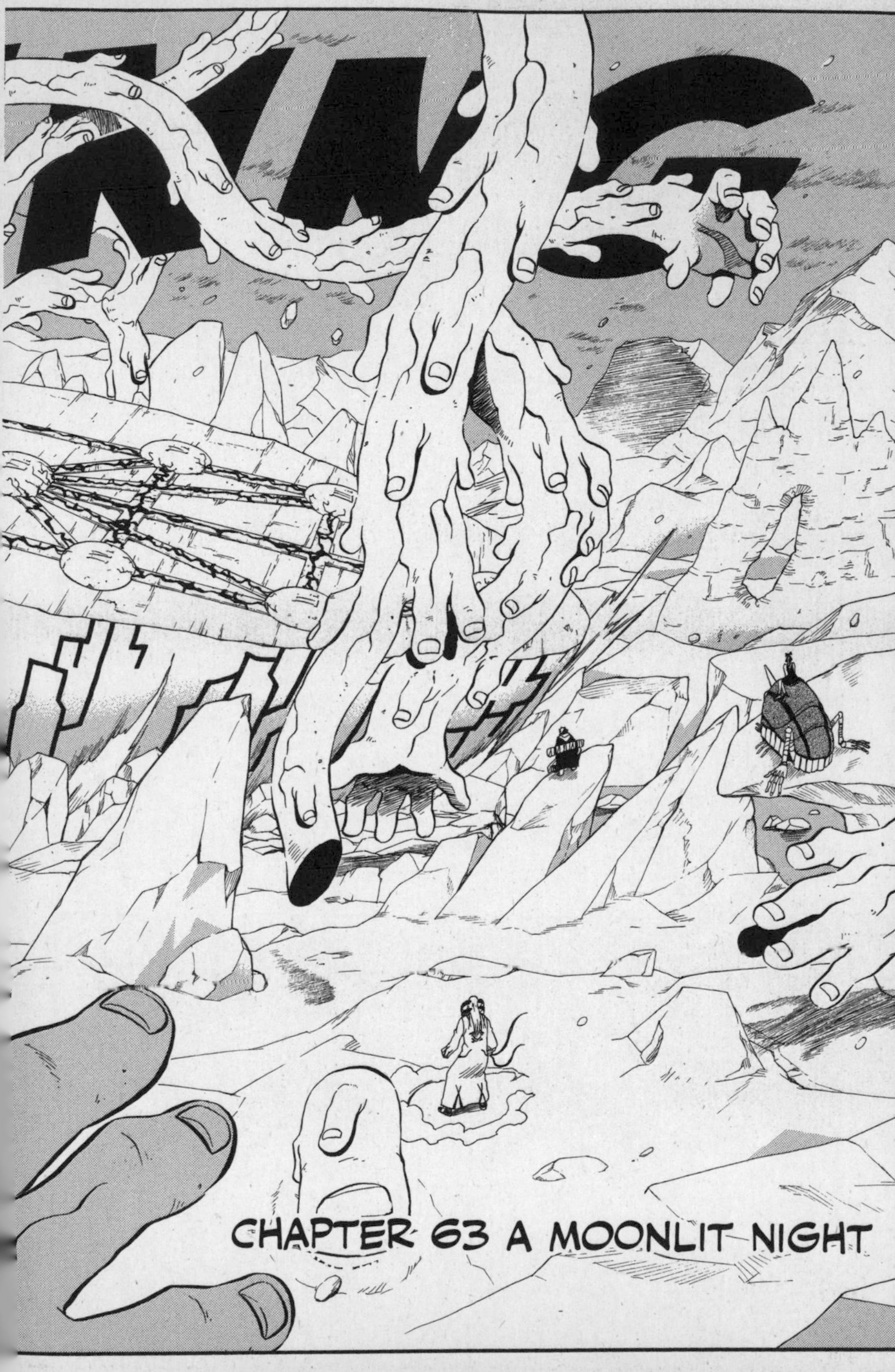
CHAPTER 63 A MOONLIT NIGHT

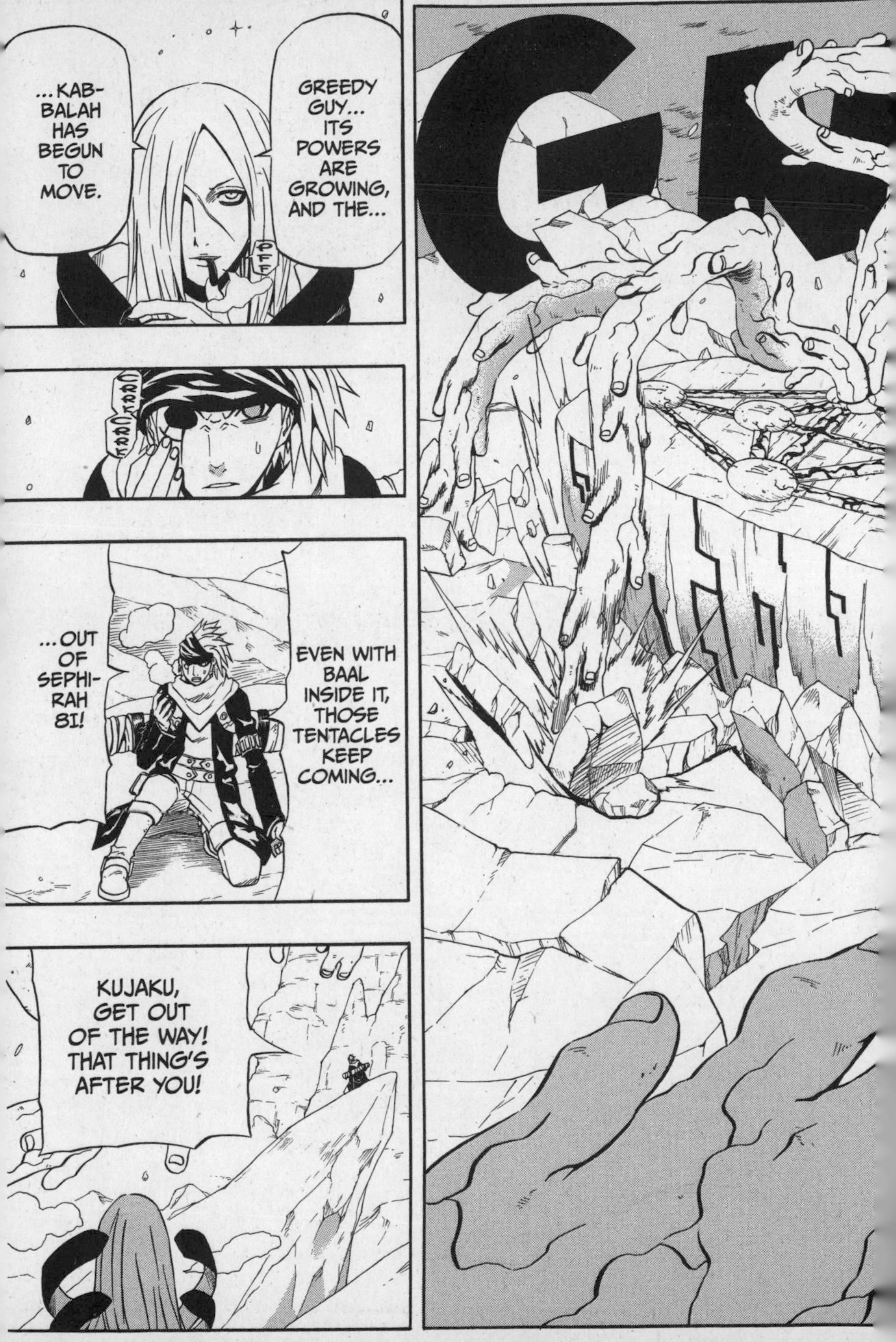
GR
GREEDY GUY... ITS POWERS ARE GROWING, AND THE...
...KAB-BALAH HAS BEGUN TO MOVE.
PFF
CRRK CRRK
EVEN WITH BAAL INSIDE IT, THOSE TENTACLES KEEP COMING...
...OUT OF SEPHI-RAH 81!
KUJAKU, GET OUT OF THE WAY! THAT THING'S AFTER YOU!

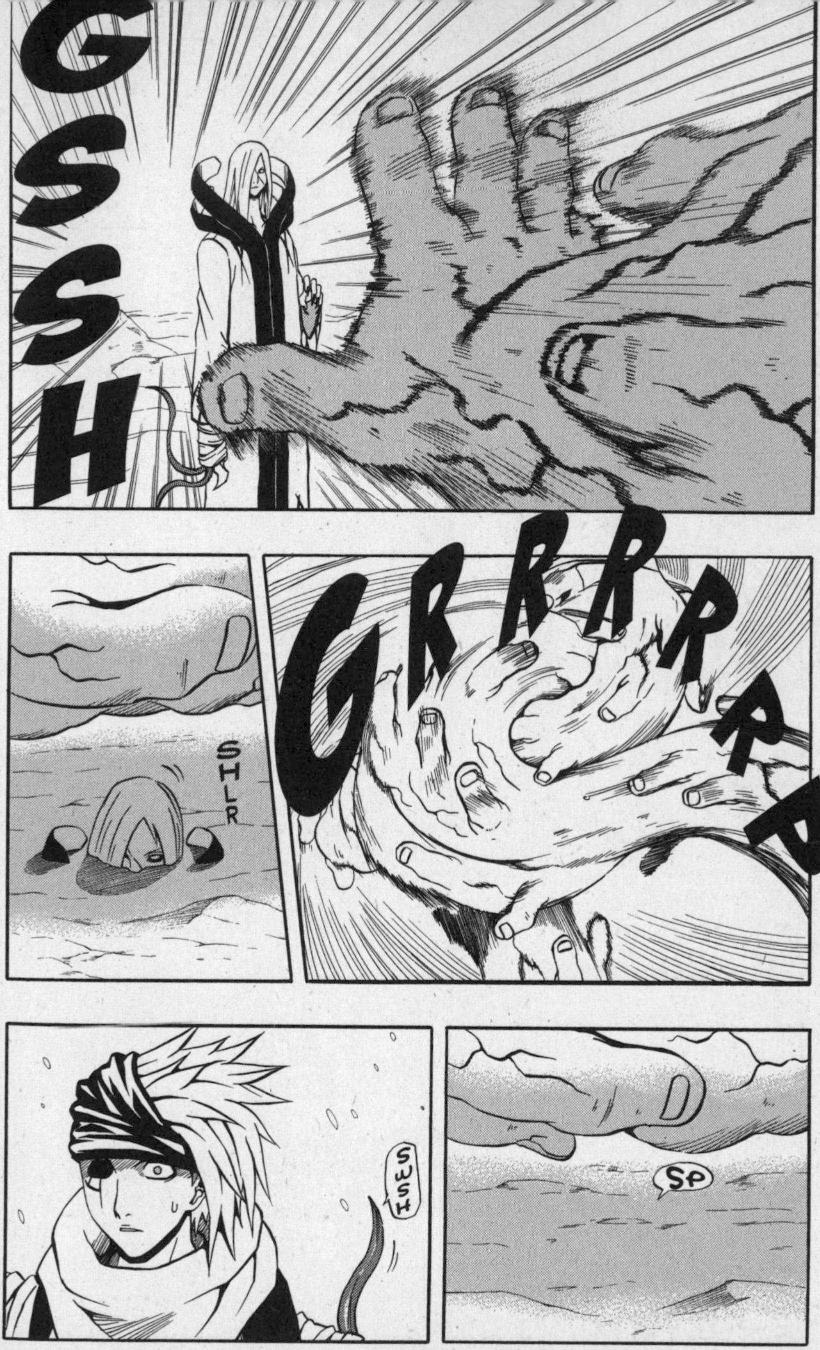
GSSH
GRRRRRP
SHLR
SP
SWSH

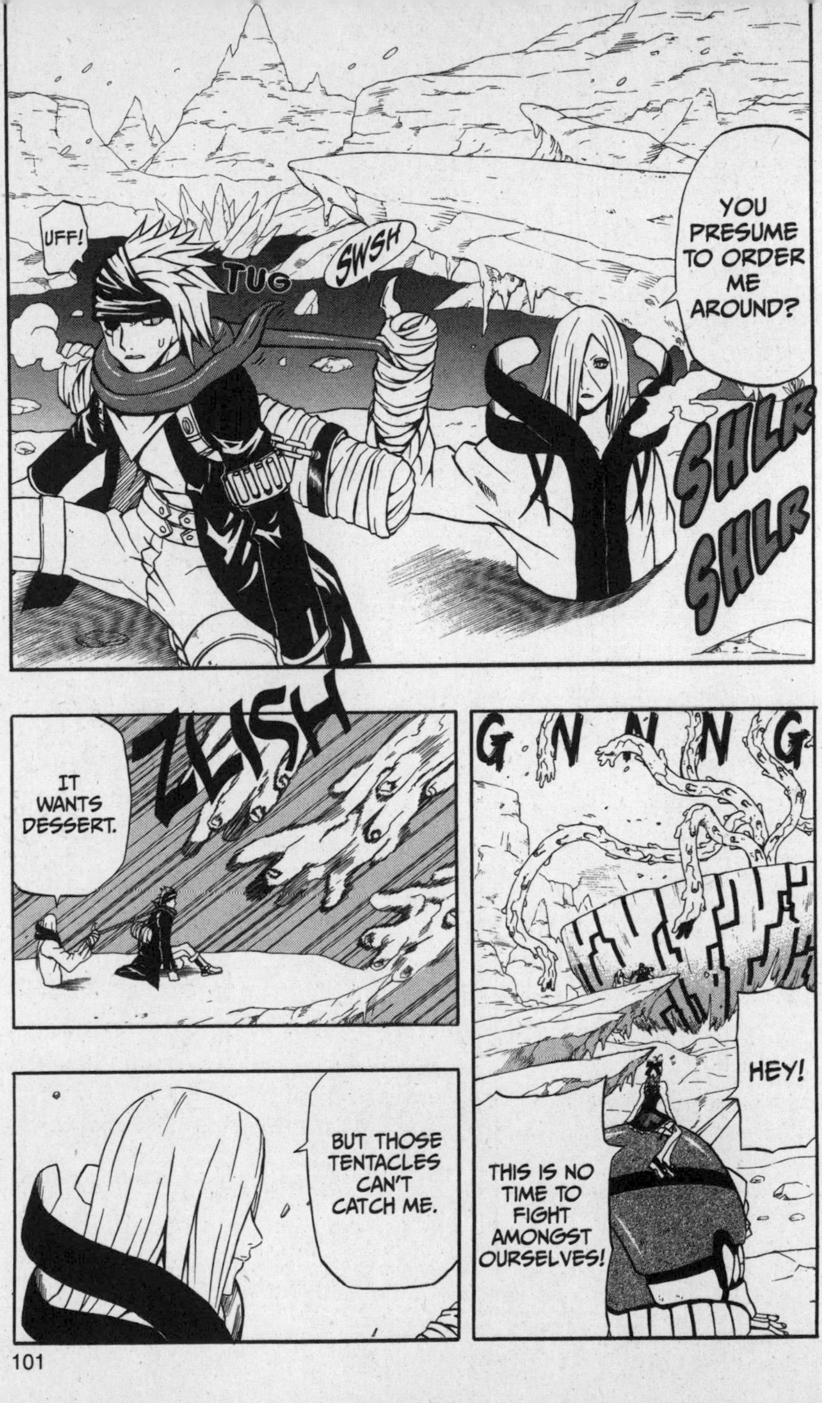
YOU PRESUME TO ORDER ME AROUND?
SHLR SHLR
SWSH
TUG
UFF!
GNNNG
HEY!
THIS IS NO TIME TO FIGHT AMONGST OURSELVES!
ZLISH
IT WANTS DESSERT.
BUT THOSE TENTACLES CAN'T CATCH ME.

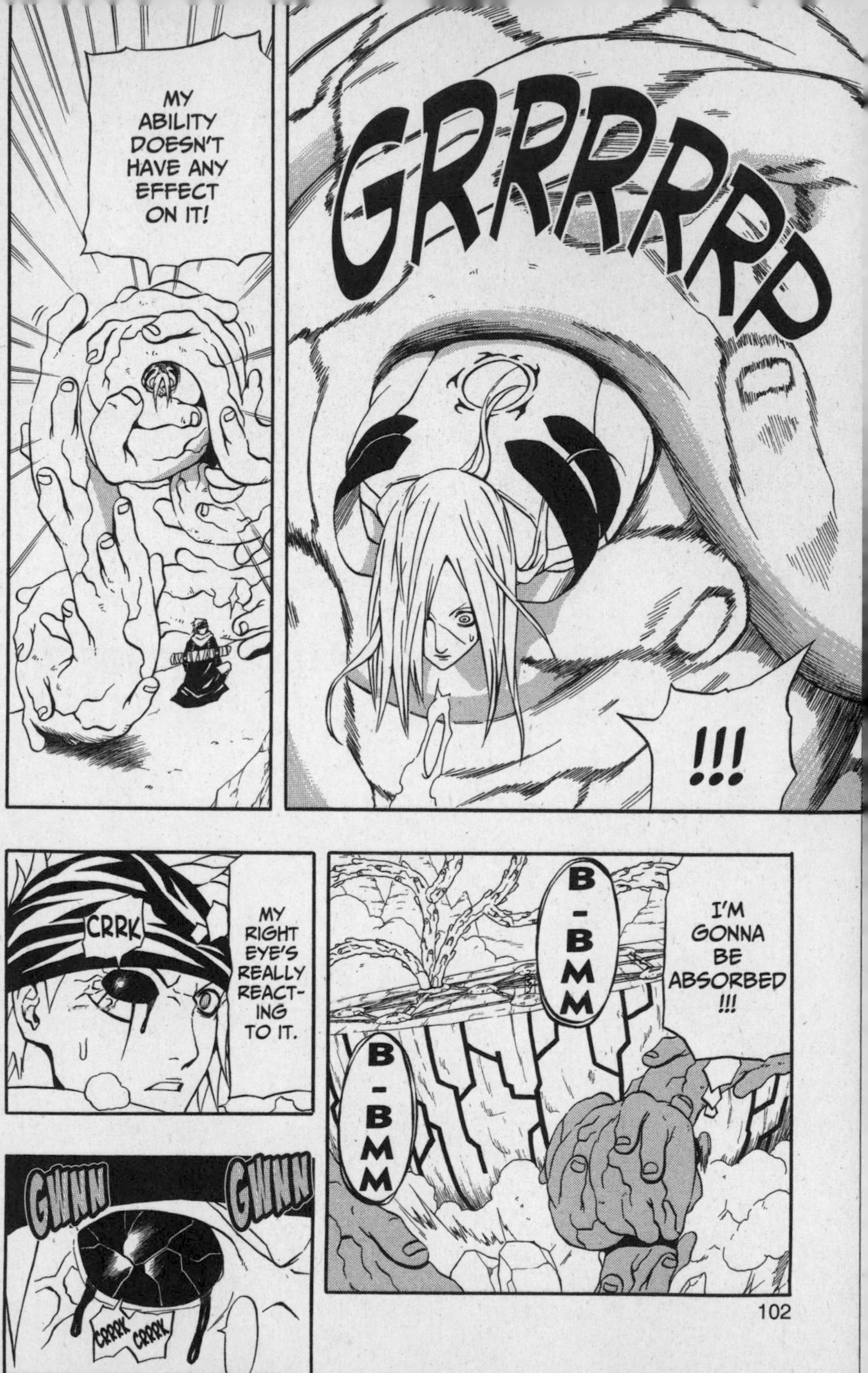
GRRRRRP
!!!
MY ABILITY DOESN'T HAVE ANY EFFECT ON IT!
I'M GONNA BE ABSORBED!!!
B-BMM
B-BMM
CRRK
MY RIGHT EYE'S REALLY REACT-ING TO IT.
GWNN
GWNN
CRRRK
CRRRK

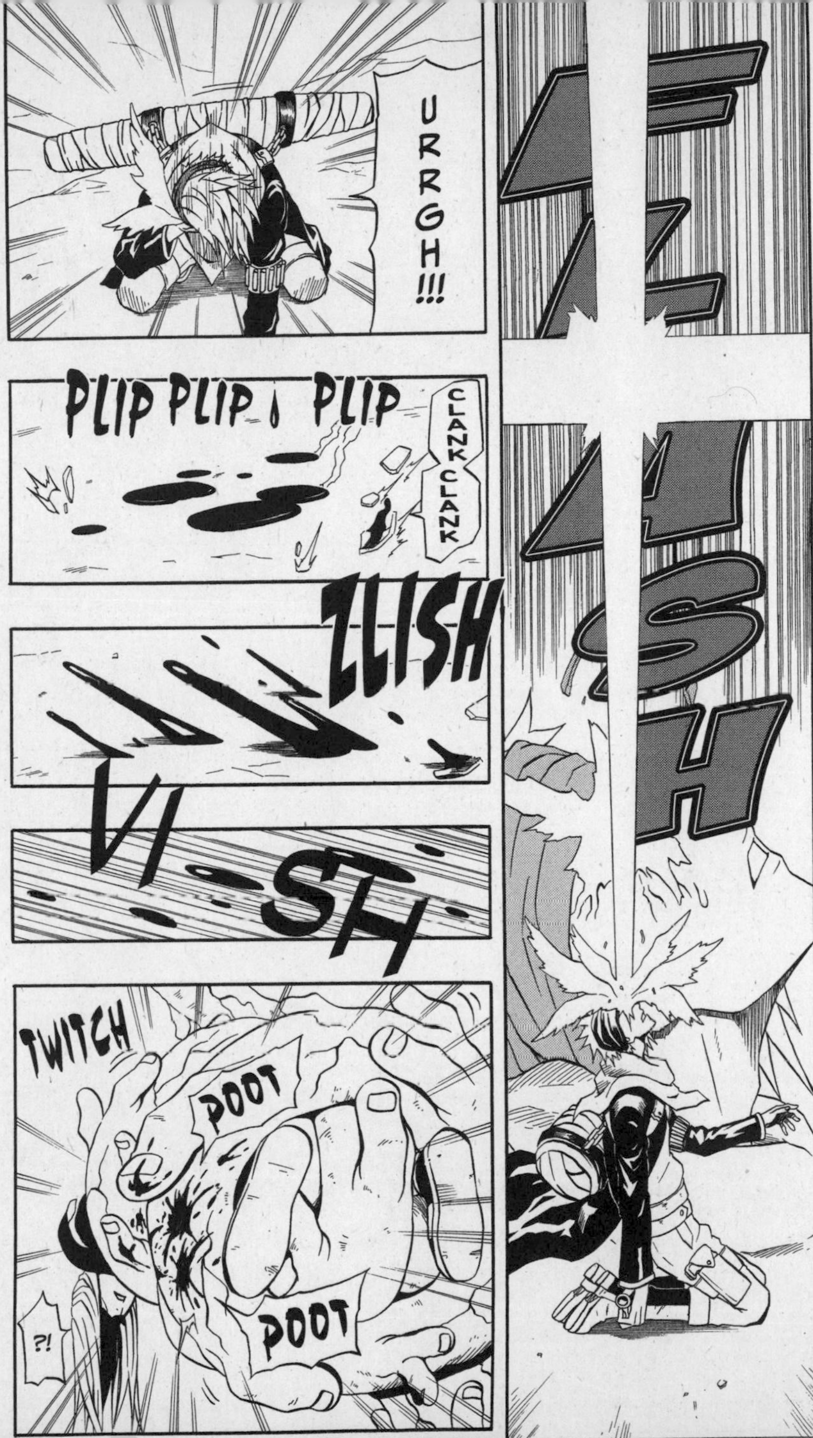
URRGH!!!
CLANK CLANK
PLIP PLIP PLIP
ZLISH
VISH
POOT
TWITCH
POOT
?!

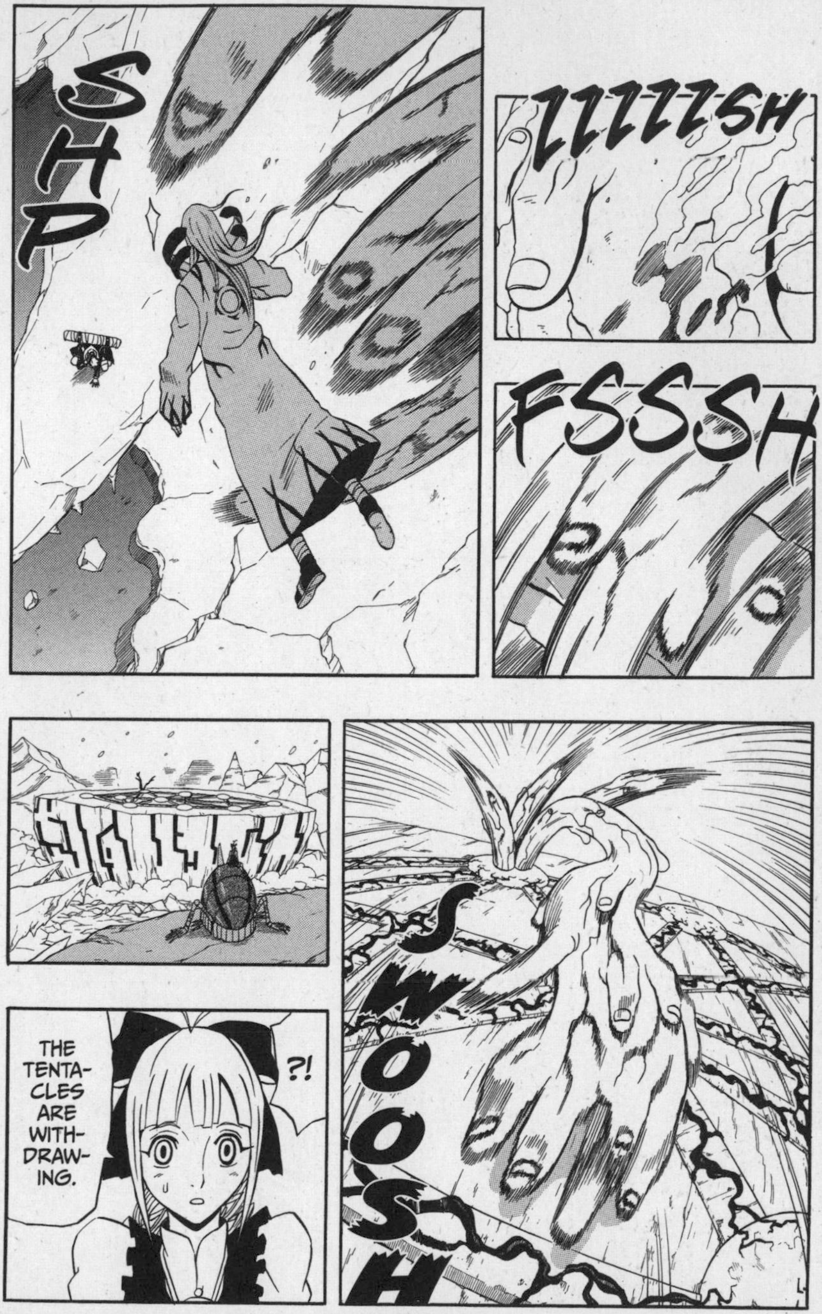

ZZZZZZSH
FSSSH
SHP
SWOOSH
THE TENTACLES ARE WITHDRAWING.
?!

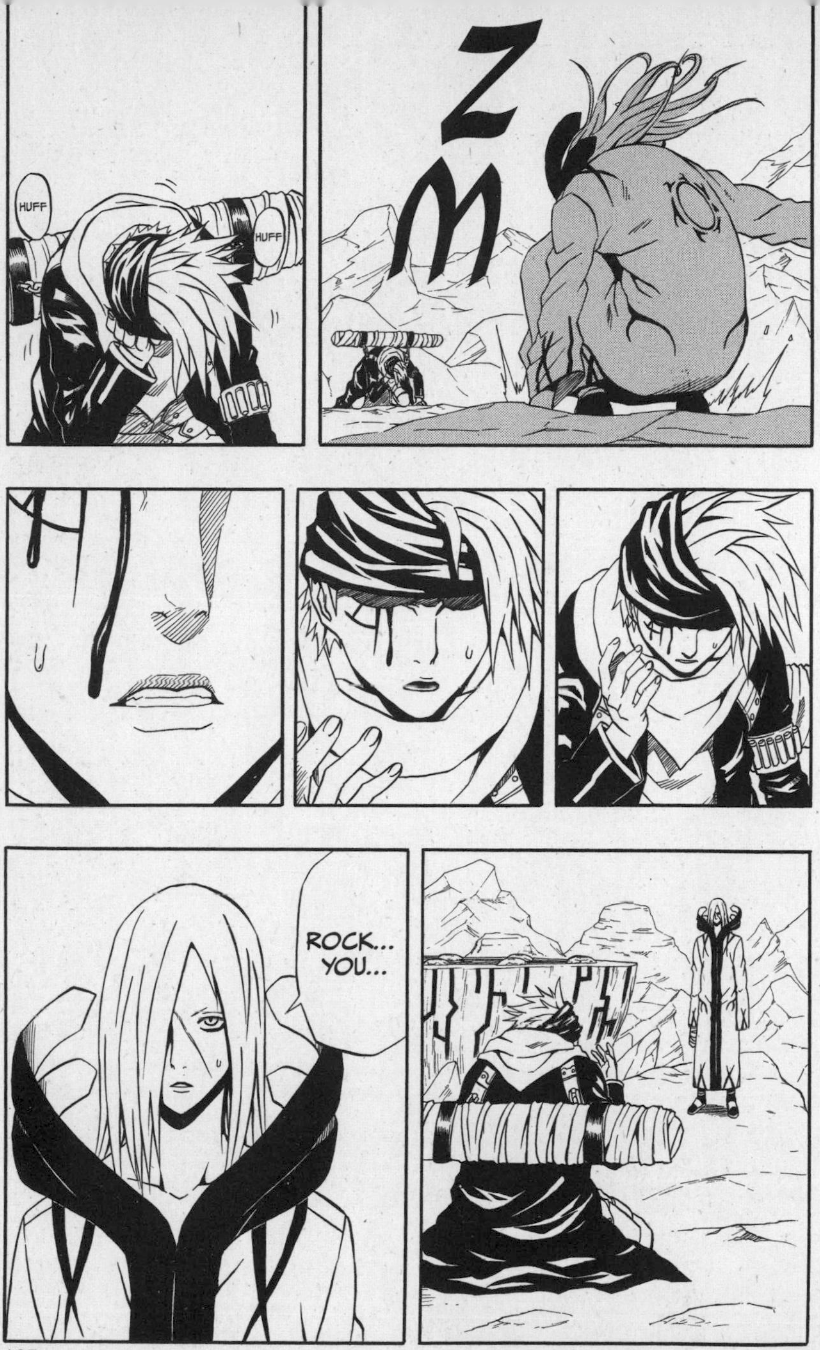
ZM
HUFF
HUFF
ROCK... YOU...

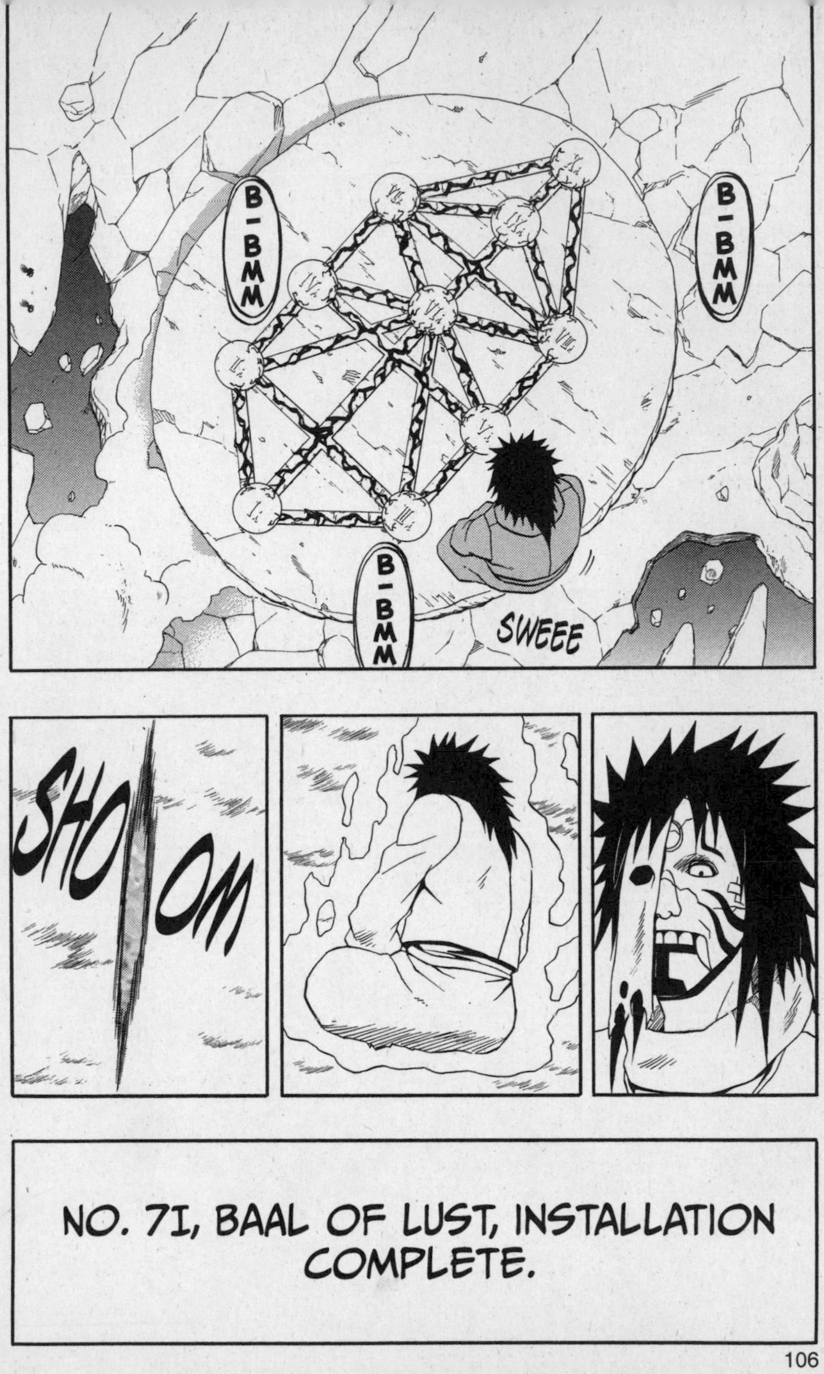
B-BMM
B-BMM
B-BMM
SWEEE
SHOOM
NO. 71, BAAL OF LUST, INSTALLATION COMPLETE.

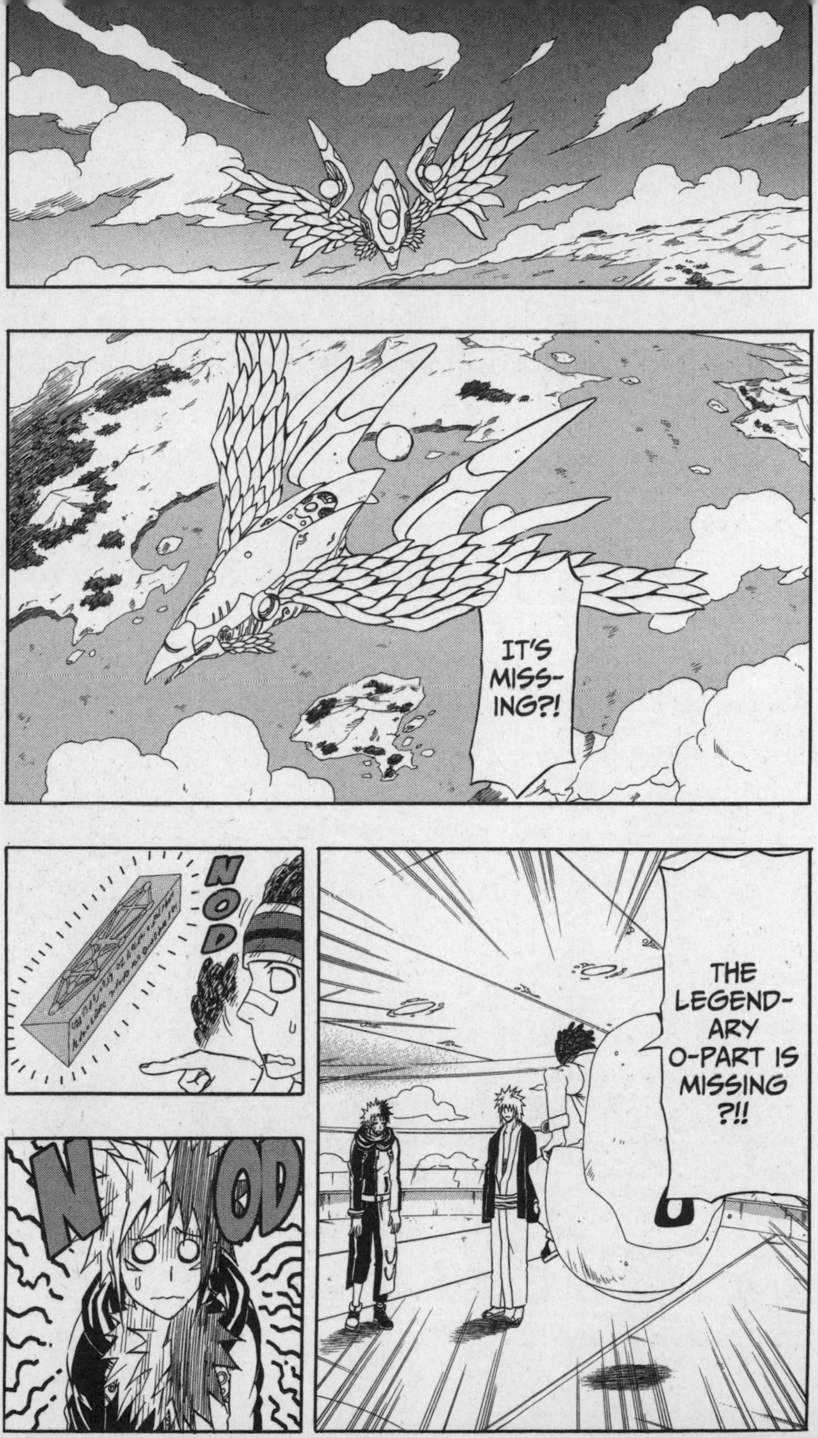
IT'S MISSING?!
THE LEGENDARY O-PART IS MISSING?!!
NOD NOD
NOD

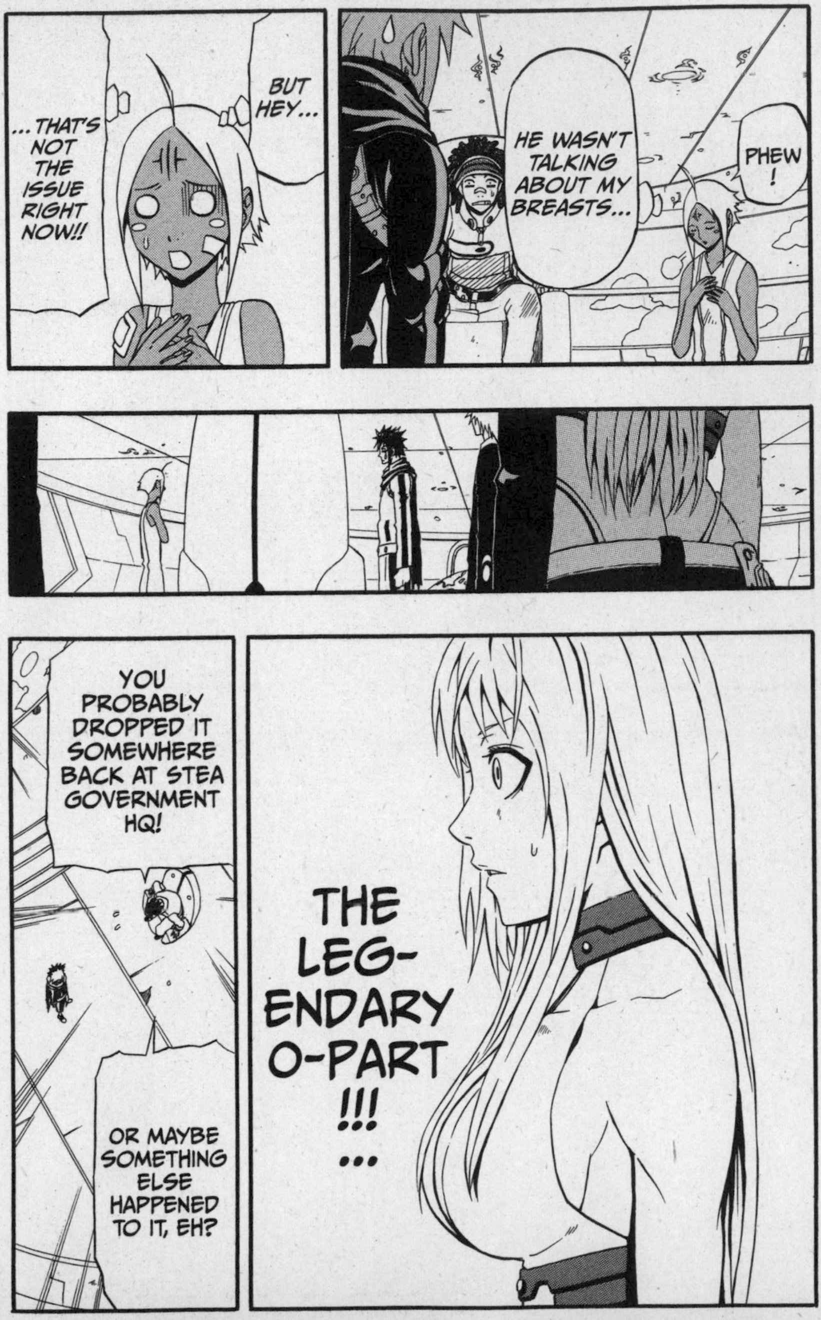
PHEW!
HE WASN'T TALKING ABOUT MY BREASTS...
BUT HEY...
...THAT'S NOT THE ISSUE RIGHT NOW!!
THE LEG-ENDARY O-PART!!! ...
YOU PROBABLY DROPPED IT SOMEWHERE BACK AT STEA GOVERNMENT HQ!
OR MAYBE SOMETHING ELSE HAPPENED TO IT, EH?

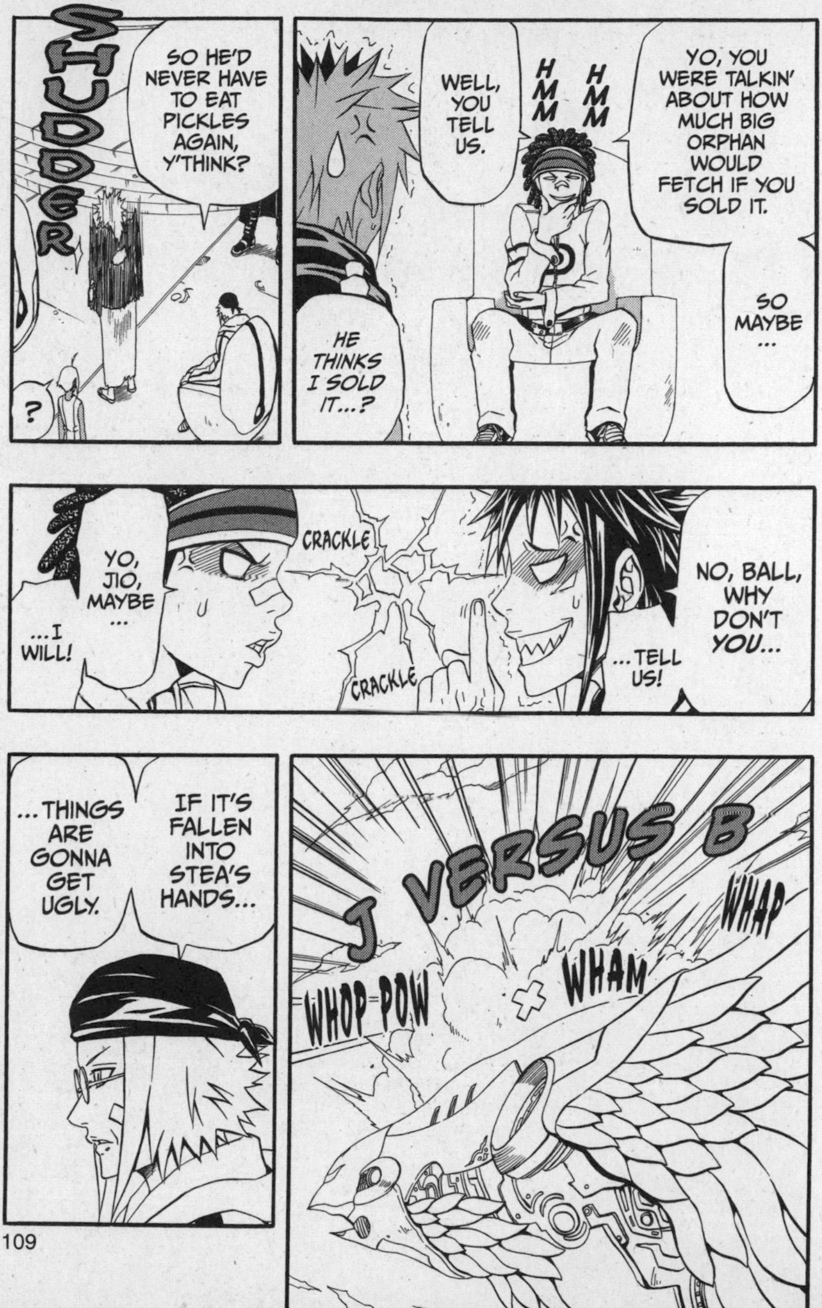
YO, YOU WERE TALKIN' ABOUT HOW MUCH BIG ORPHAN WOULD FETCH IF YOU SOLD IT.
SO MAYBE ...
HMM HMM
WELL, YOU TELL US.
HE THINKS I SOLD IT...?
SO HE'D NEVER HAVE TO EAT PICKLES AGAIN, Y'THINK?
SHUDDER
?
NO, BALL, WHY DON'T *YOU*...
...TELL US!
CRACKLE
CRACKLE
YO, JIO, MAYBE ...
...I WILL!
J VERSUS B
WHAP
WHAM
WHOP POW
IF IT'S FALLEN INTO STEA'S HANDS...
...THINGS ARE GONNA GET UGLY.

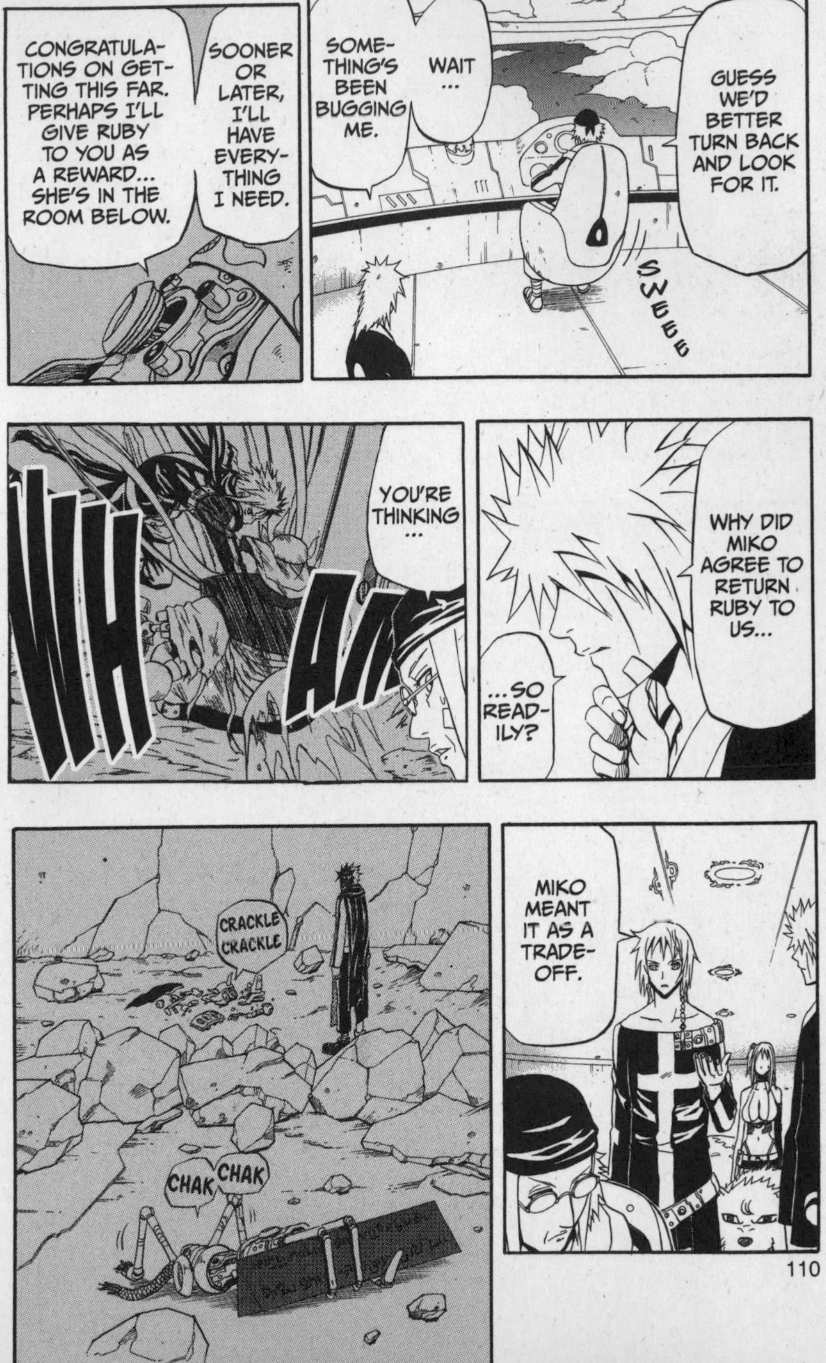
GUESS WE'D BETTER TURN BACK AND LOOK FOR IT.
WAIT ...
SOMETHING'S BEEN BUGGING ME.
SWEEE
SOONER OR LATER, I'LL HAVE EVERYTHING I NEED.
CONGRATULATIONS ON GETTING THIS FAR. PERHAPS I'LL GIVE RUBY TO YOU AS A REWARD... SHE'S IN THE ROOM BELOW.
WHY DID MIKO AGREE TO RETURN RUBY TO US...
...SO READILY?
YOU'RE THINKING ...
MIKO MEANT IT AS A TRADE-OFF.
CRACKLE CRACKLE
CHAK
CHAK

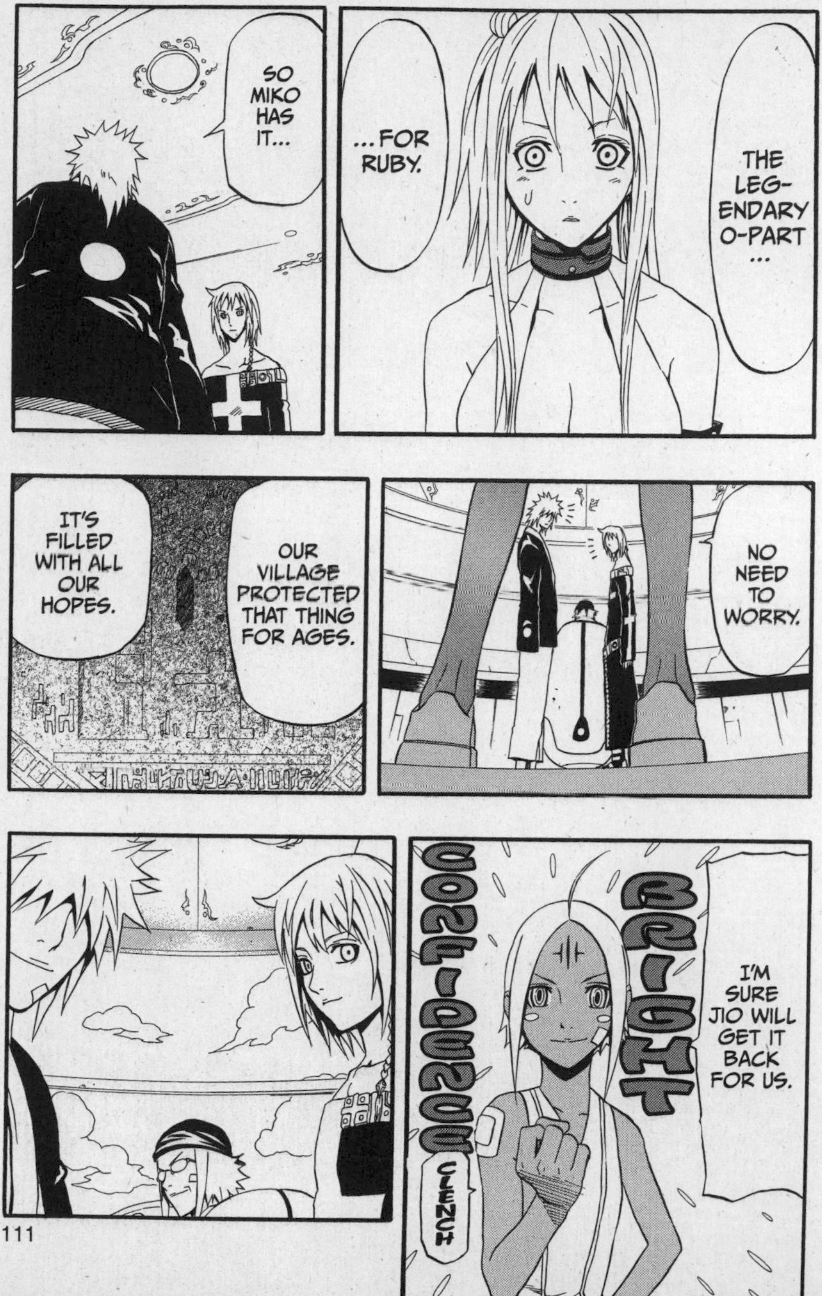
THE LEGENDARY O-PART...
...FOR RUBY.
SO MIKO HAS IT...
NO NEED TO WORRY.
OUR VILLAGE PROTECTED THAT THING FOR AGES.
IT'S FILLED WITH ALL OUR HOPES.
I'M SURE JIO WILL GET IT BACK FOR US.
BRIGHT
CONFIDENCE
CLENCH

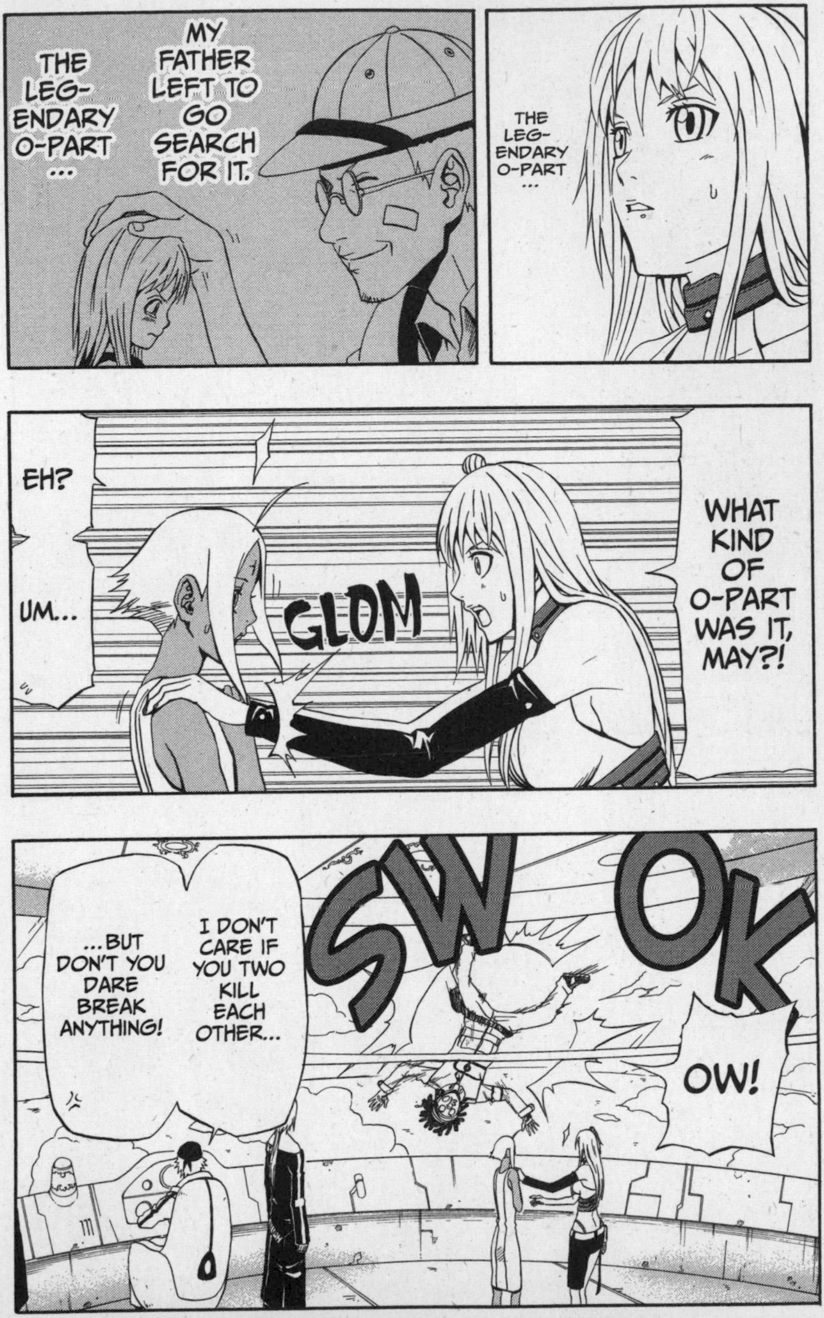
THE LEG-ENDARY O-PART ...
MY FATHER LEFT TO GO SEARCH FOR IT.
THE LEG-ENDARY O-PART ...
WHAT KIND OF O-PART WAS IT, MAY?!
GLOM
EH?
UM...
SWOOK
OW!
I DON'T CARE IF YOU TWO KILL EACH OTHER...
...BUT DON'T YOU DARE BREAK ANYTHING!

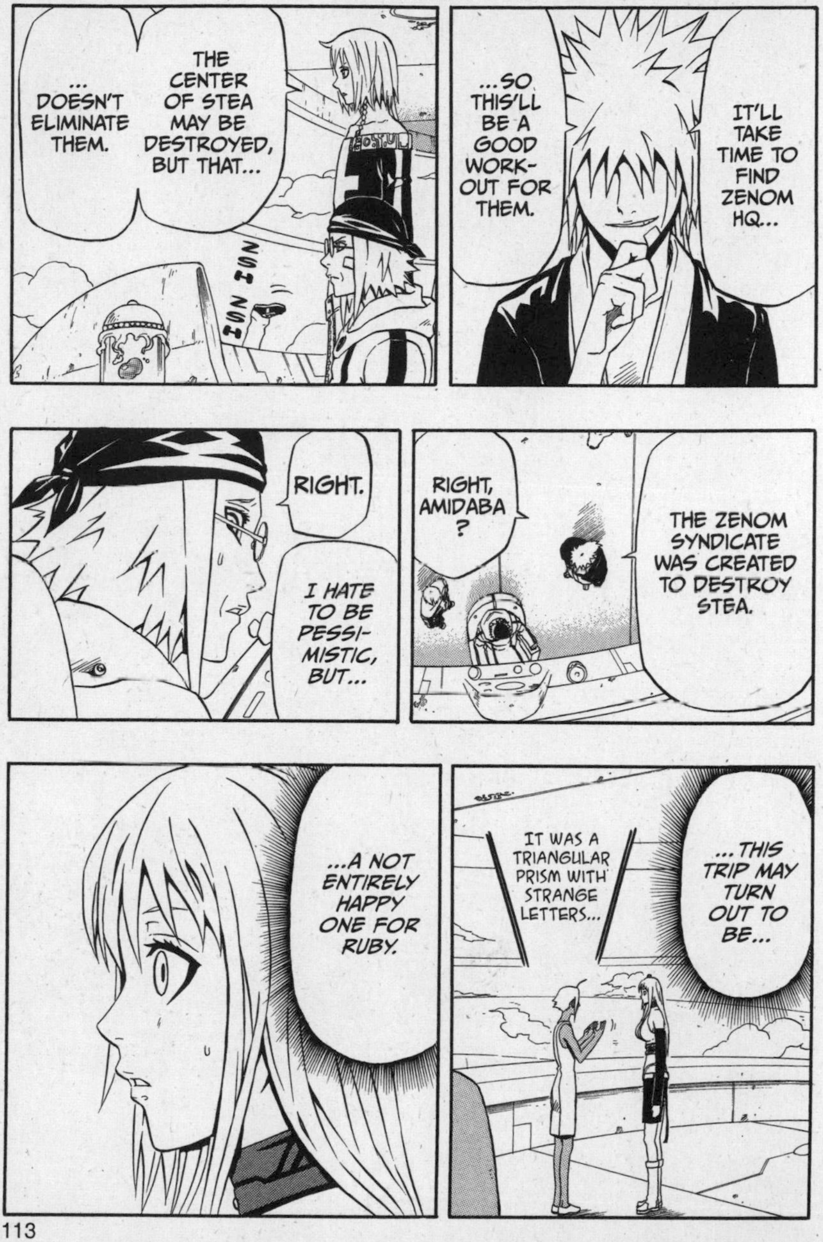
IT'LL TAKE TIME TO FIND ZENOM HQ...
...SO THIS'LL BE A GOOD WORK-OUT FOR THEM.
THE CENTER OF STEA MAY BE DESTROYED, BUT THAT...
...DOESN'T ELIMINATE THEM.
ZSH ZSH
THE ZENOM SYNDICATE WAS CREATED TO DESTROY STEA.
RIGHT, AMIDABA?
RIGHT.
I HATE TO BE PESSIMISTIC, BUT...
...THIS TRIP MAY TURN OUT TO BE...
IT WAS A TRIANGULAR PRISM WITH STRANGE LETTERS...
...A NOT ENTIRELY HAPPY ONE FOR RUBY.

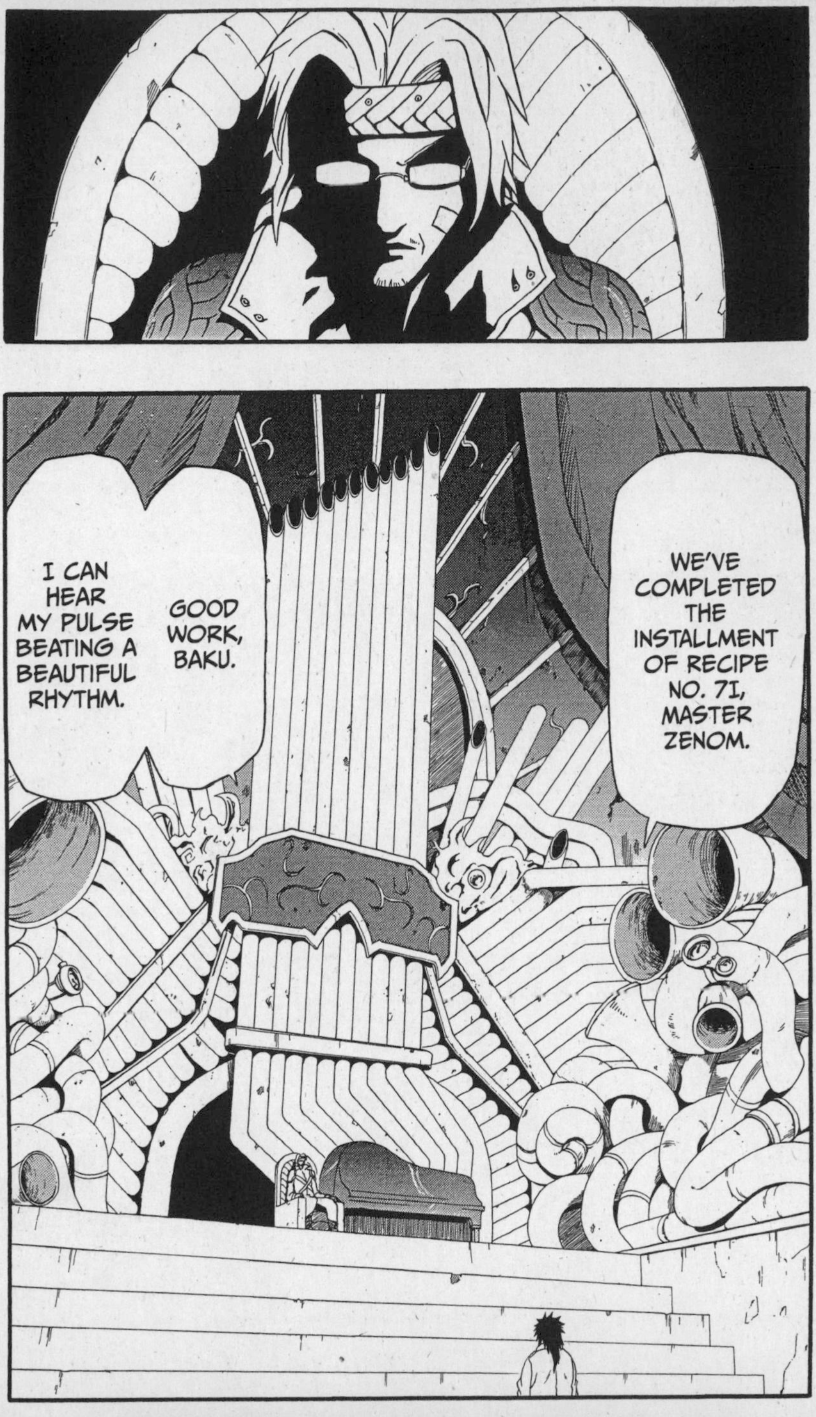
WE'VE COMPLETED THE INSTALLMENT OF RECIPE NO. 71, MASTER ZENOM.
GOOD WORK, BAKU.
I CAN HEAR MY PULSE BEATING A BEAUTIFUL RHYTHM.

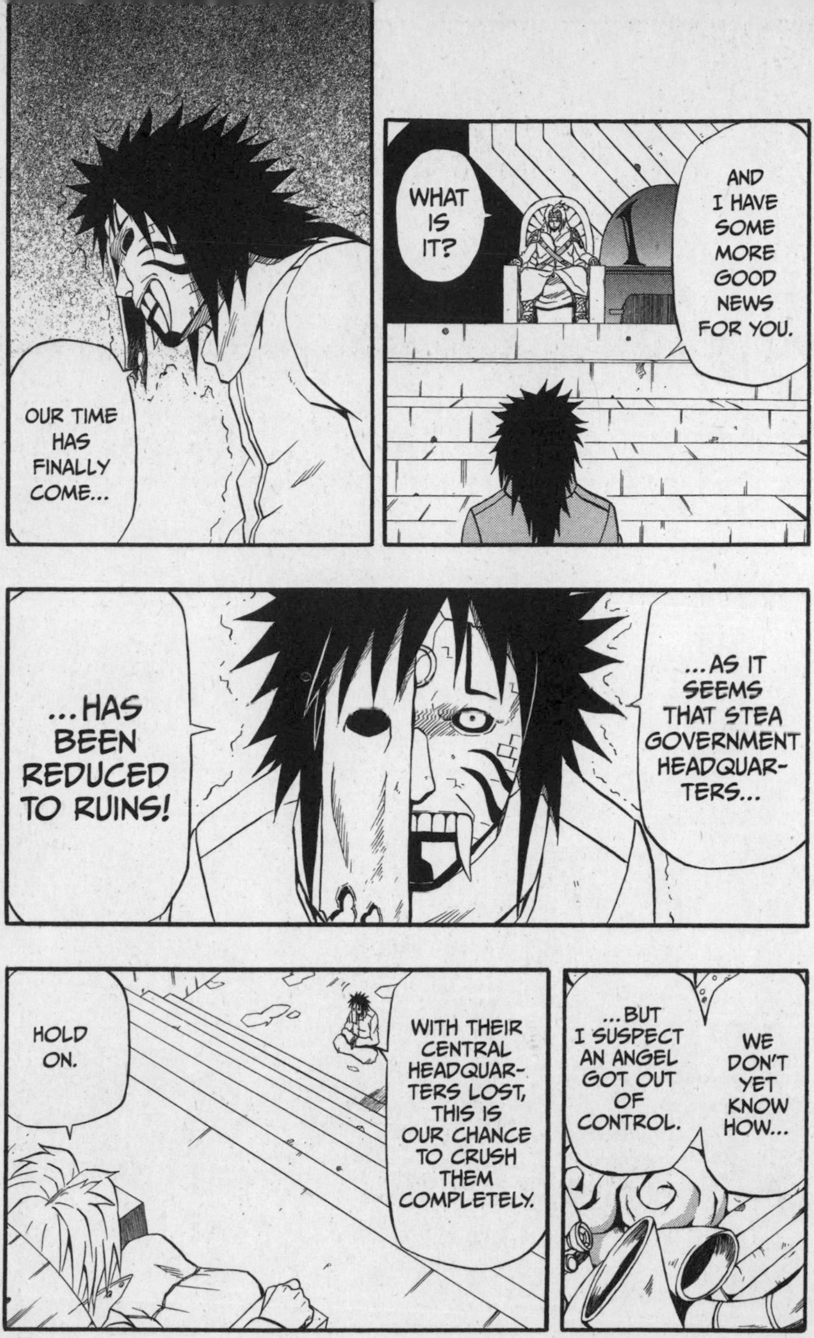
AND I HAVE SOME MORE GOOD NEWS FOR YOU.
WHAT IS IT?
OUR TIME HAS FINALLY COME...
...AS IT SEEMS THAT STEA GOVERNMENT HEADQUARTERS...
...HAS BEEN REDUCED TO RUINS!
WE DON'T YET KNOW HOW...
...BUT I SUSPECT AN ANGEL GOT OUT OF CONTROL.
WITH THEIR CENTRAL HEADQUARTERS LOST, THIS IS OUR CHANCE TO CRUSH THEM COMPLETELY.
HOLD ON.

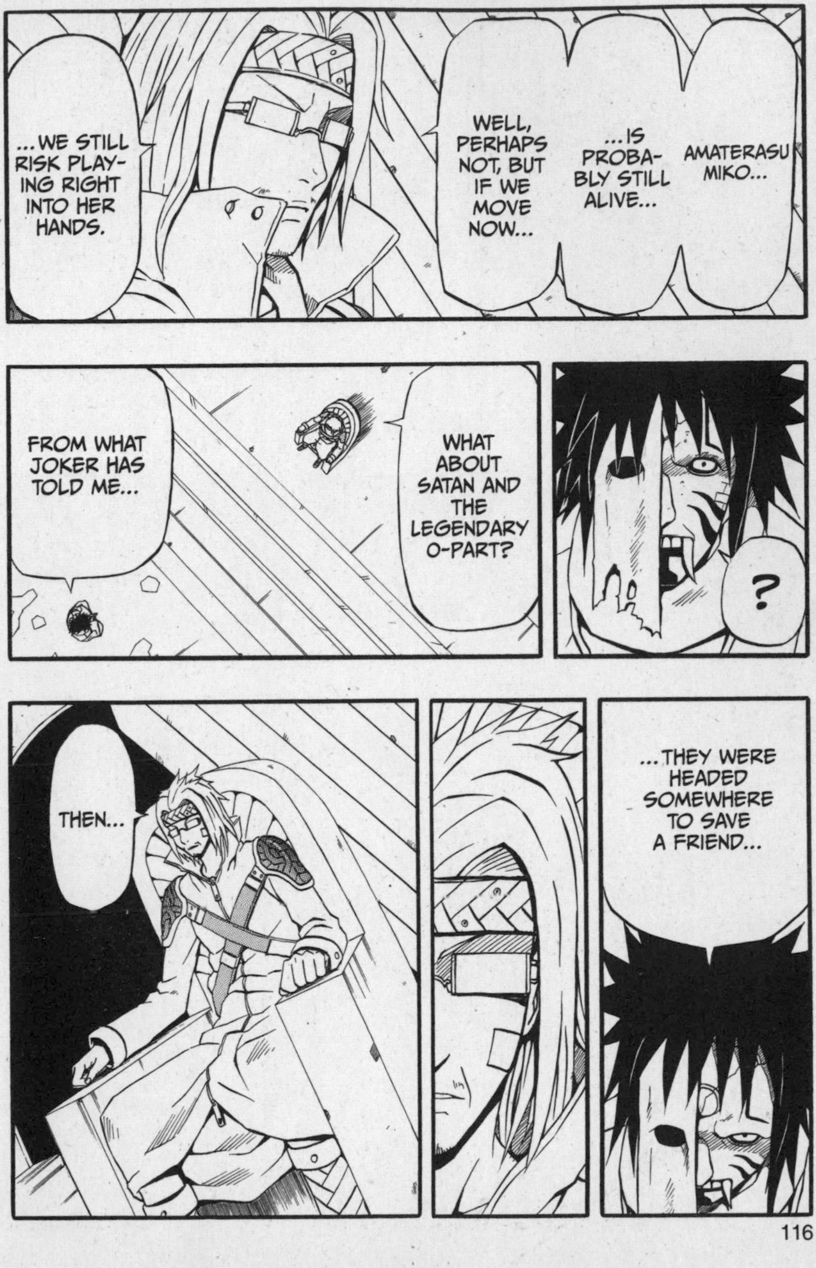
AMATERASU MIKO...
...IS PROBABLY STILL ALIVE...
WELL, PERHAPS NOT, BUT IF WE MOVE NOW...
...WE STILL RISK PLAYING RIGHT INTO HER HANDS.
?
WHAT ABOUT SATAN AND THE LEGENDARY O-PART?
FROM WHAT JOKER HAS TOLD ME...
...THEY WERE HEADED SOMEWHERE TO SAVE A FRIEND...
THEN...

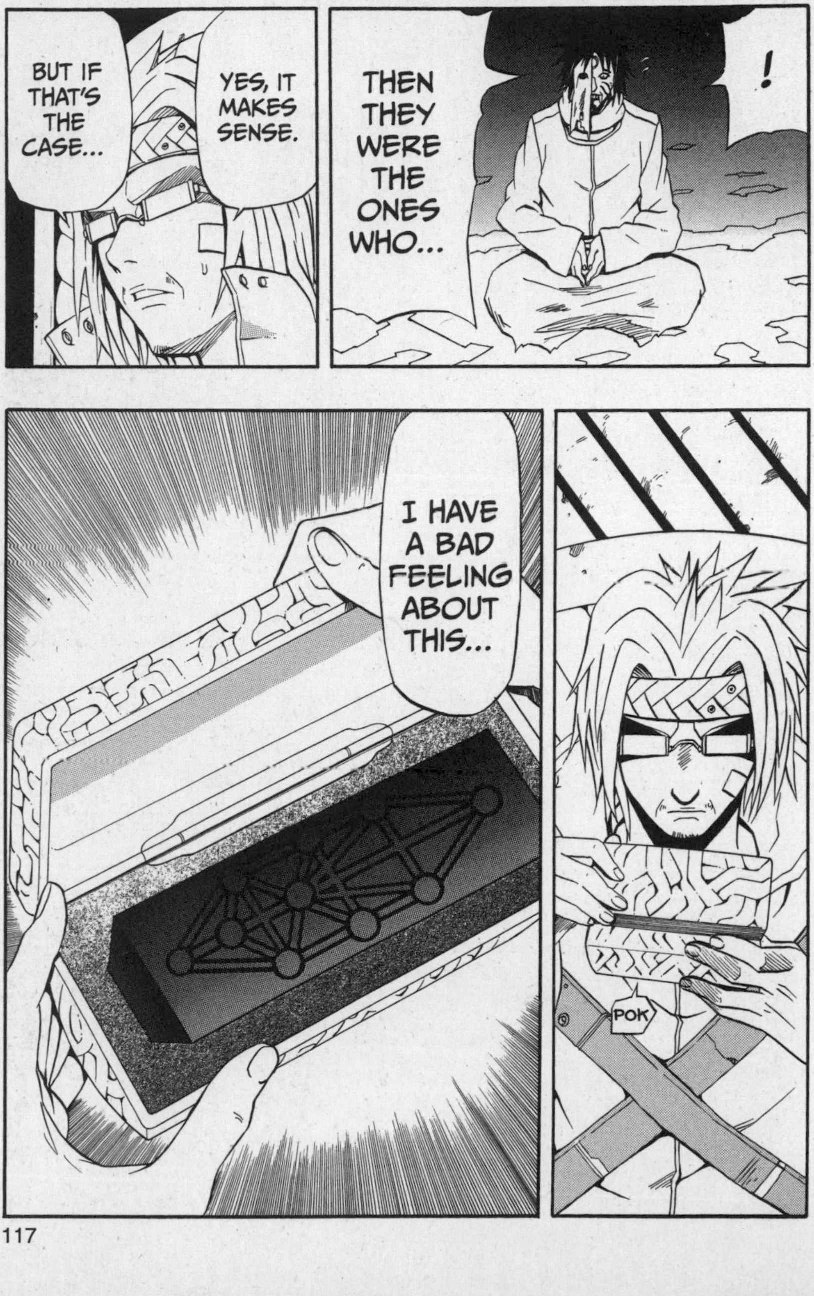
THEN THEY WERE THE ONES WHO...
!
YES, IT MAKES SENSE.
BUT IF THAT'S THE CASE...
POK
I HAVE A BAD FEELING ABOUT THIS...

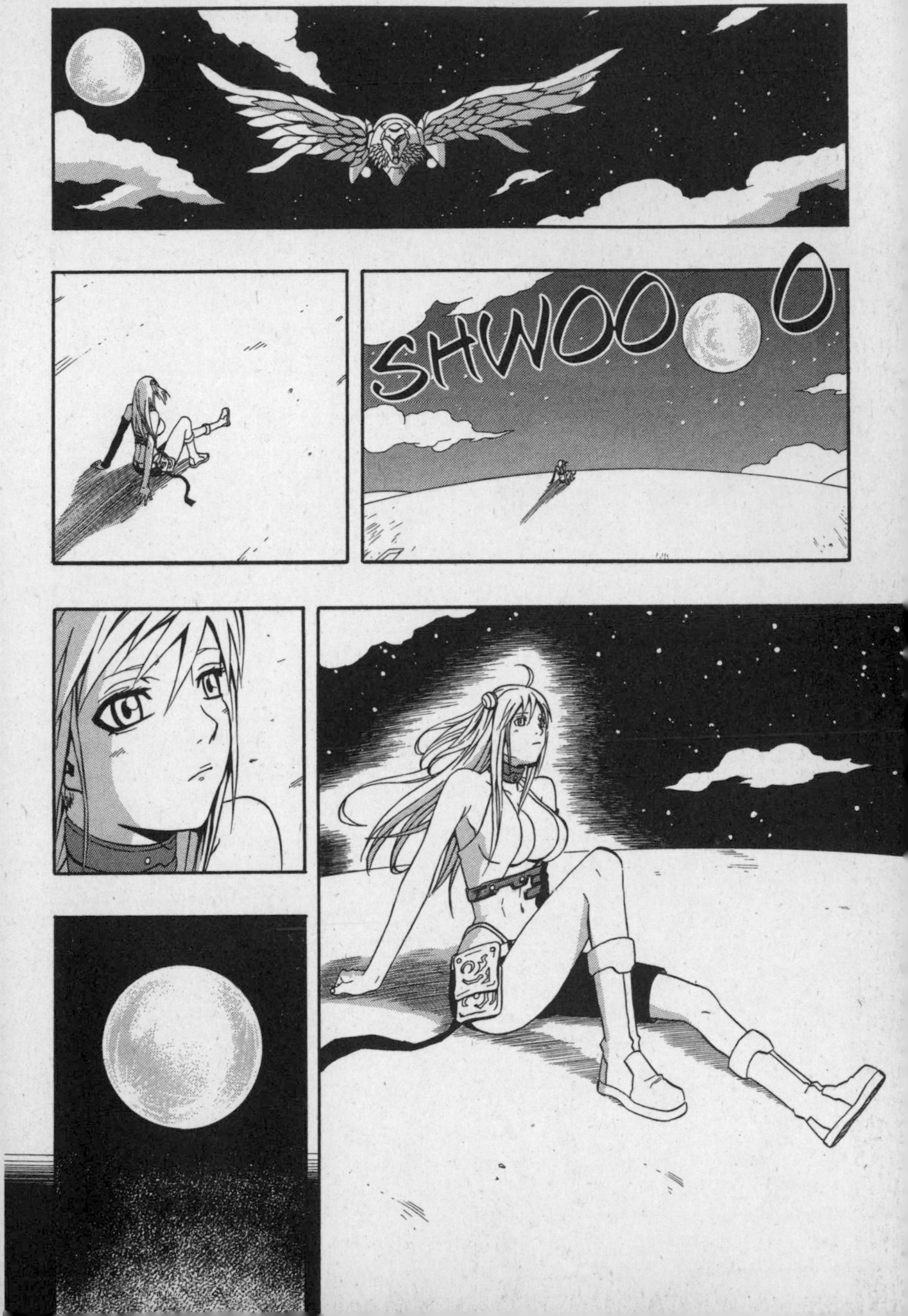
SHWOOOO

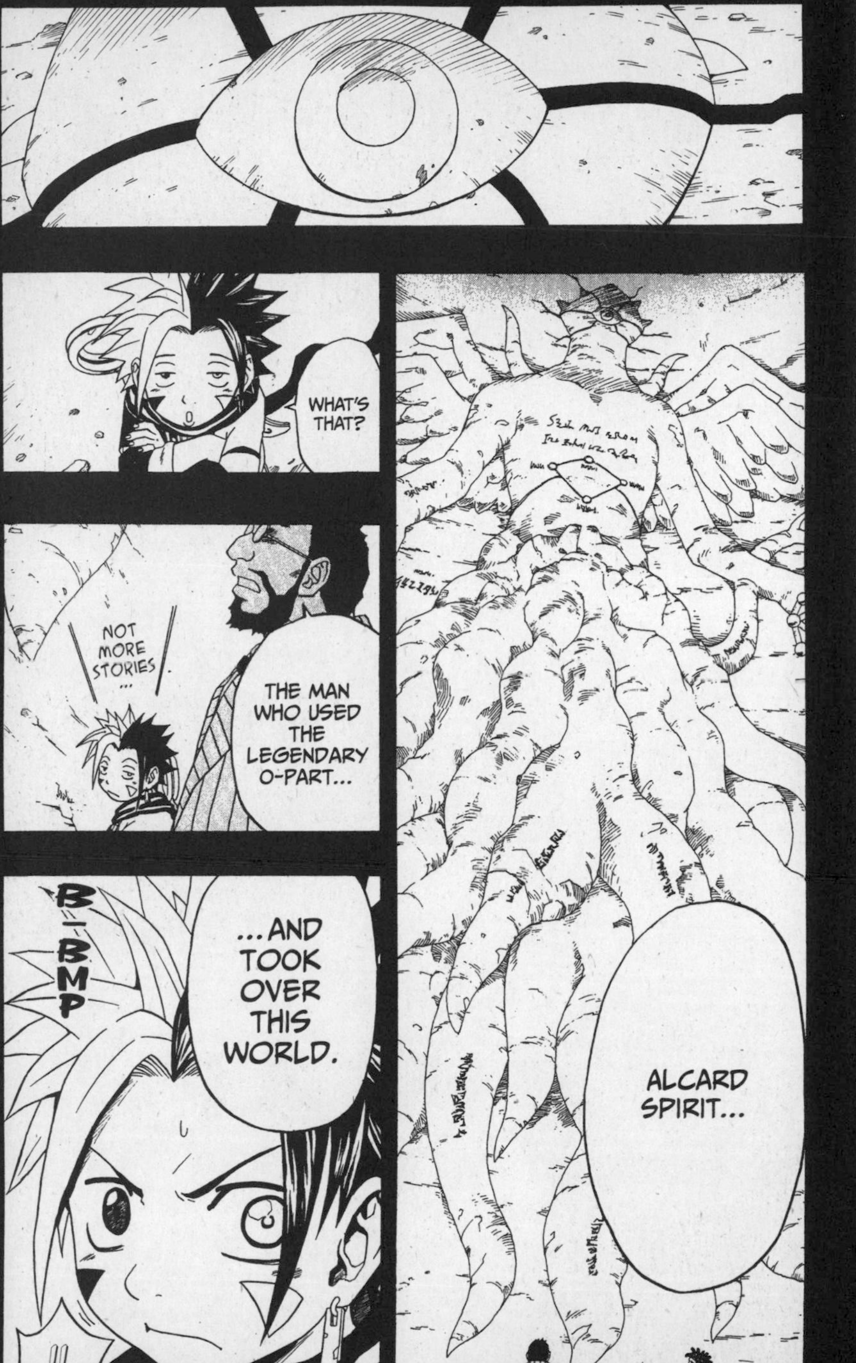
ALCARD SPIRIT...
WHAT'S THAT?
NOT MORE STORIES...
THE MAN WHO USED THE LEGENDARY O-PART...
...AND TOOK OVER THIS WORLD.
B-BMP
!!

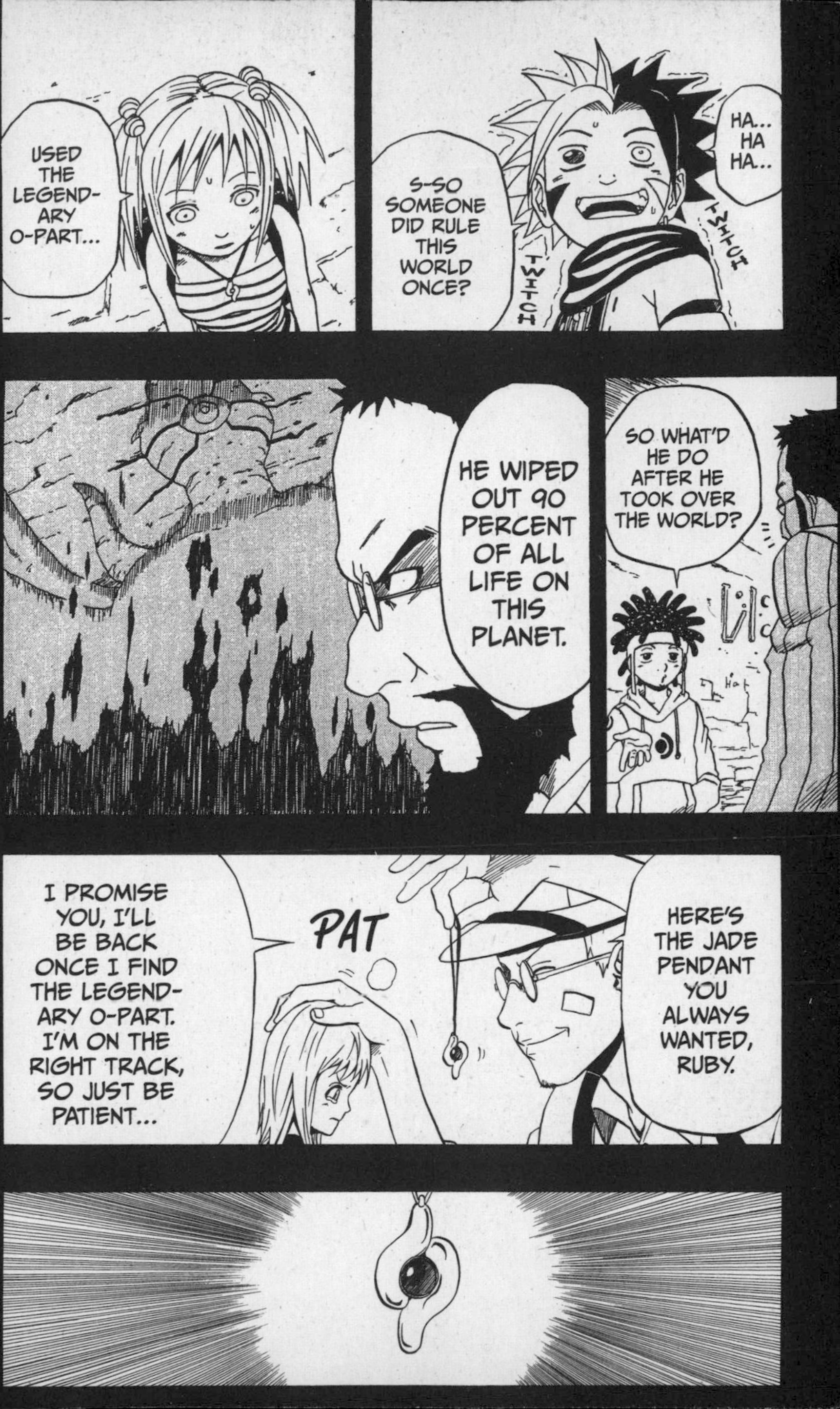

HA... HA HA...
TWITCH
S-SO SOMEONE DID RULE THIS WORLD ONCE?
TWITCH
USED THE LEGEND-ARY O-PART...
SO WHAT'D HE DO AFTER HE TOOK OVER THE WORLD?
HE WIPED OUT 90 PERCENT OF ALL LIFE ON THIS PLANET.
HERE'S THE JADE PENDANT YOU ALWAYS WANTED, RUBY.
PAT
I PROMISE YOU, I'LL BE BACK ONCE I FIND THE LEGEND-ARY O-PART. I'M ON THE RIGHT TRACK, SO JUST BE PATIENT...

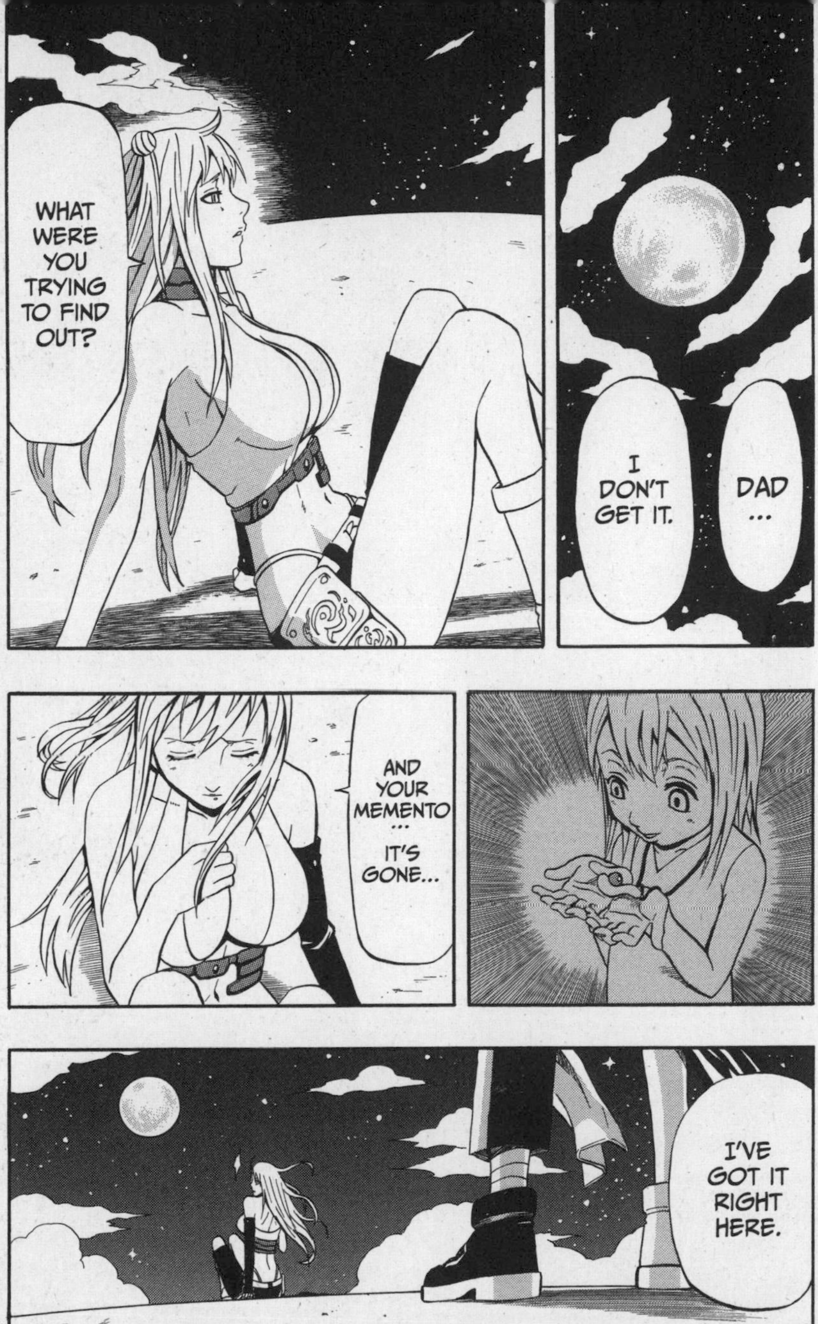
DAD...
I DON'T GET IT.
WHAT WERE YOU TRYING TO FIND OUT?
AND YOUR MEMENTO... IT'S GONE...
I'VE GOT IT RIGHT HERE.

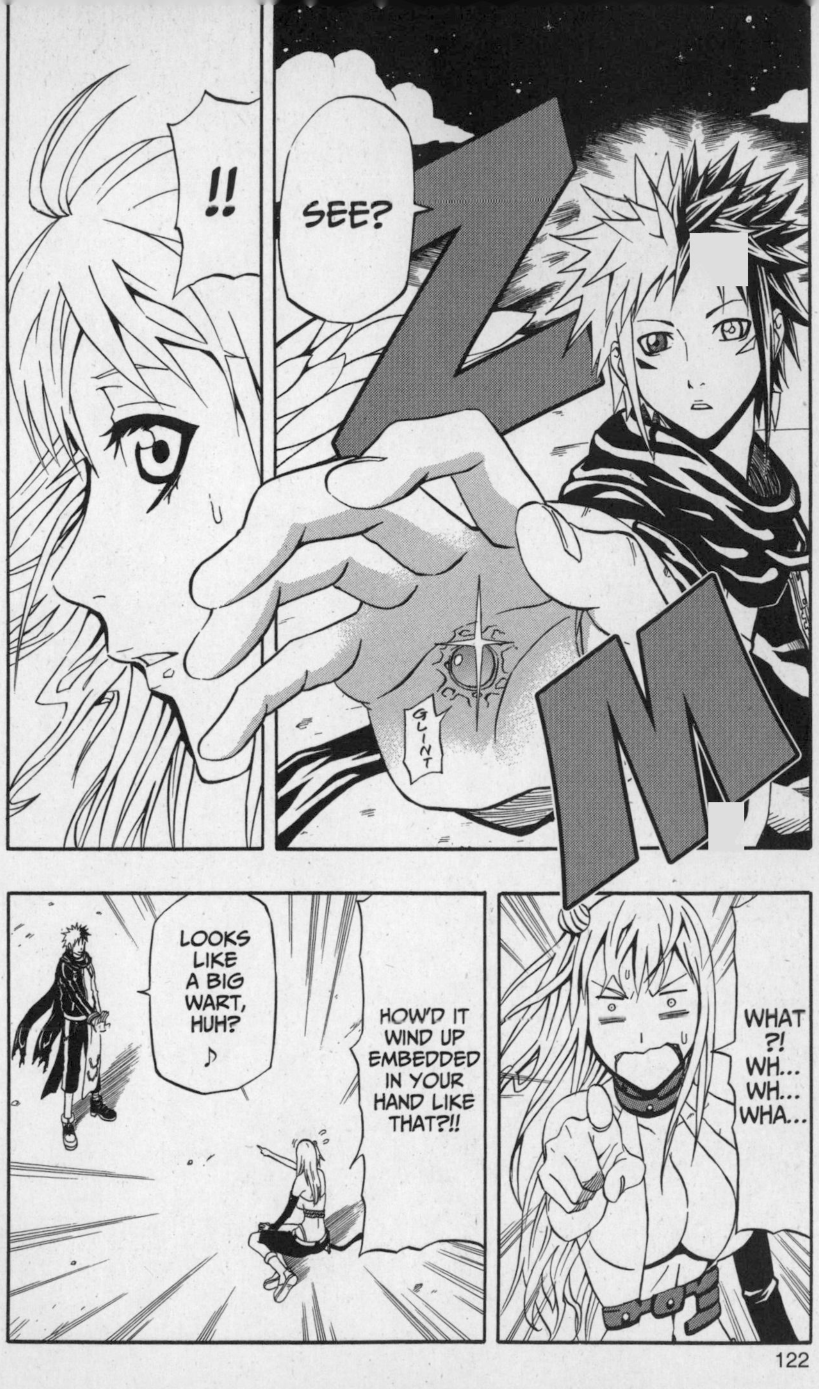
SEE?
Z
M
GLINT
!!
WHAT?! WH... WH... WHA...
LOOKS LIKE A BIG WART, HUH? ♪
HOW'D IT WIND UP EMBEDDED IN YOUR HAND LIKE THAT?!!

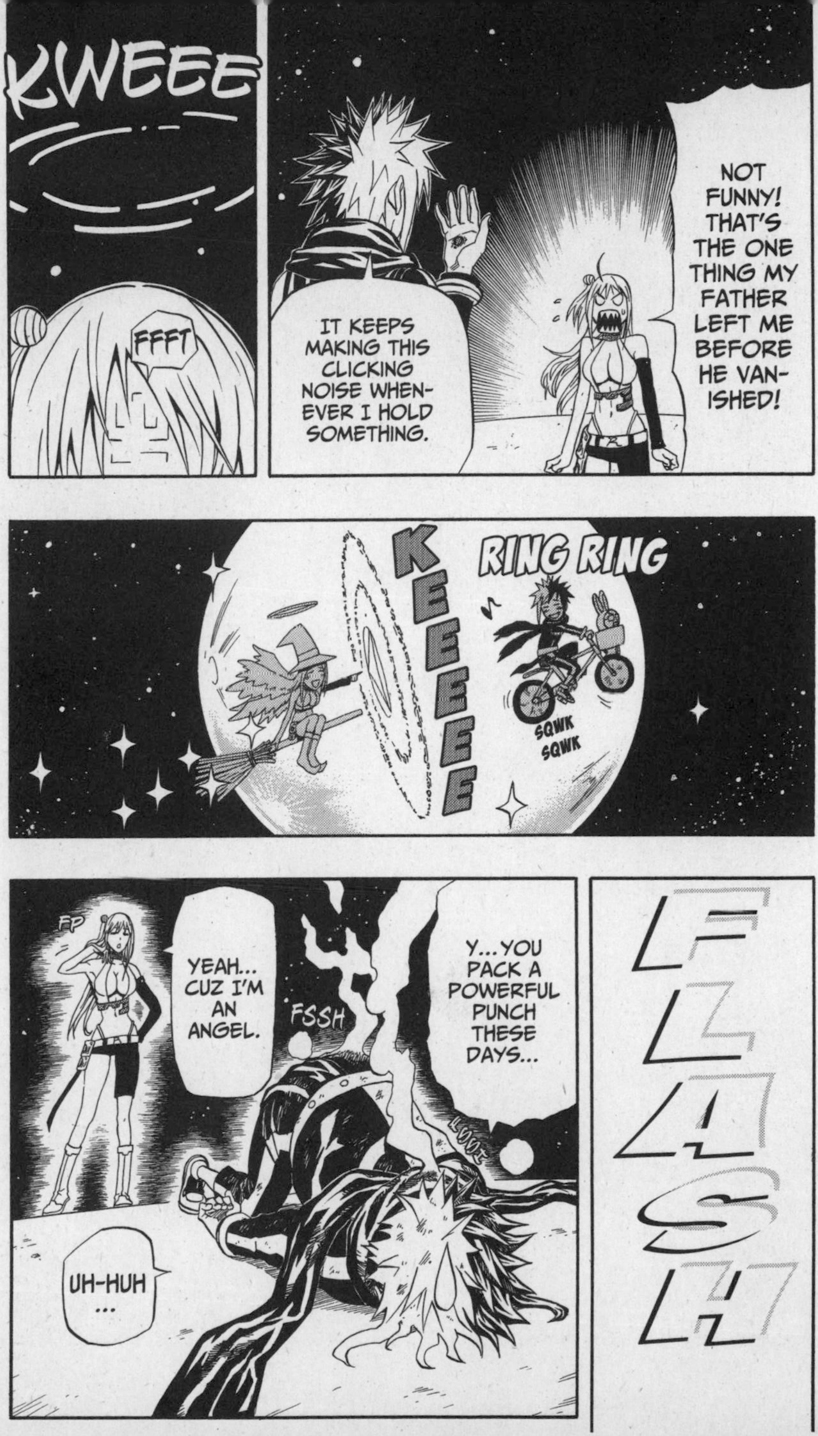
NOT FUNNY! THAT'S THE ONE THING MY FATHER LEFT ME BEFORE HE VAN-ISHED!
IT KEEPS MAKING THIS CLICKING NOISE WHEN-EVER I HOLD SOMETHING.
KWEEE
FFFT
RING RING
KEEEEEE
SQWK SQWK
FLASH
Y...YOU PACK A POWERFUL PUNCH THESE DAYS...
YEAH... CUZ I'M AN ANGEL.
FP
FSSH
UH-HUH ...

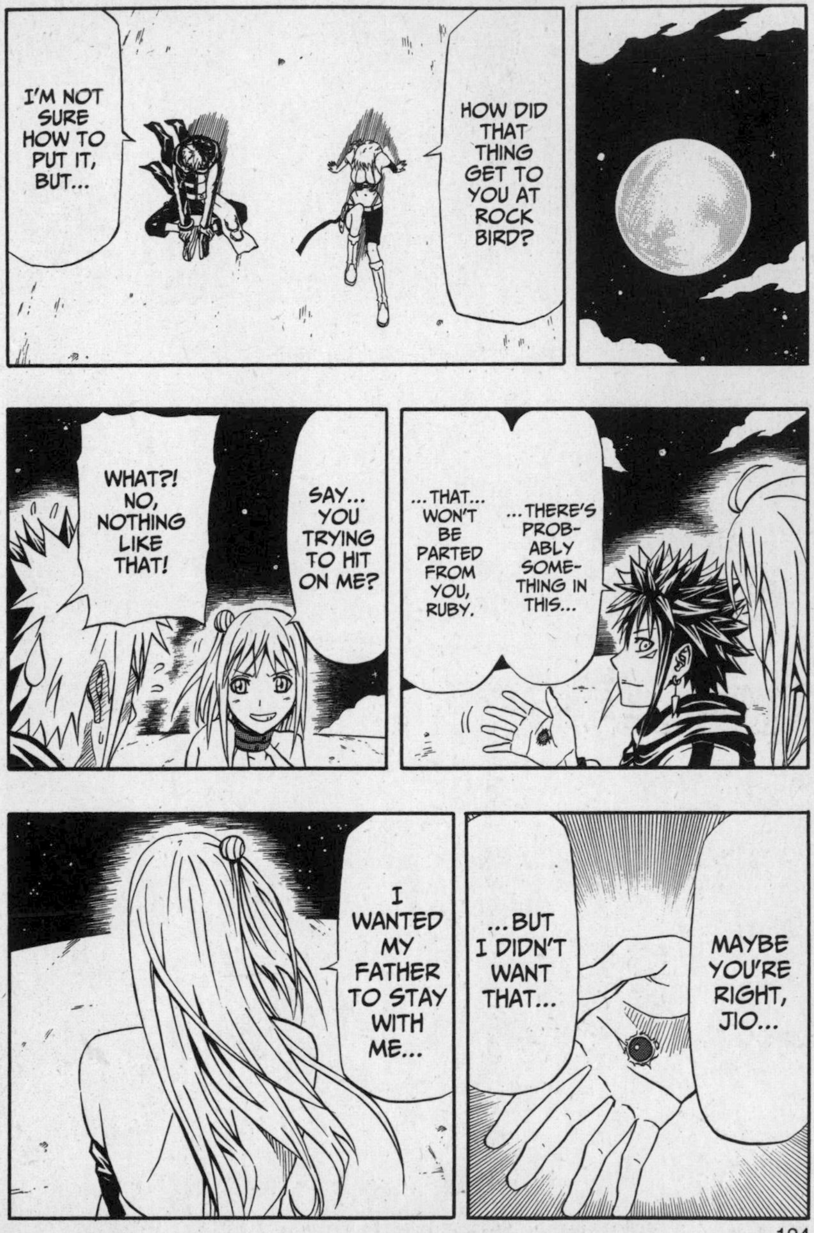
HOW DID THAT THING GET TO YOU AT ROCK BIRD?
I'M NOT SURE HOW TO PUT IT, BUT...
...THERE'S PROBABLY SOMETHING IN THIS...
...THAT... WON'T BE PARTED FROM YOU, RUBY.
SAY... YOU TRYING TO HIT ON ME?
WHAT?! NO, NOTHING LIKE THAT!
MAYBE YOU'RE RIGHT, JIO...
...BUT I DIDN'T WANT THAT...
I WANTED MY FATHER TO STAY WITH ME...

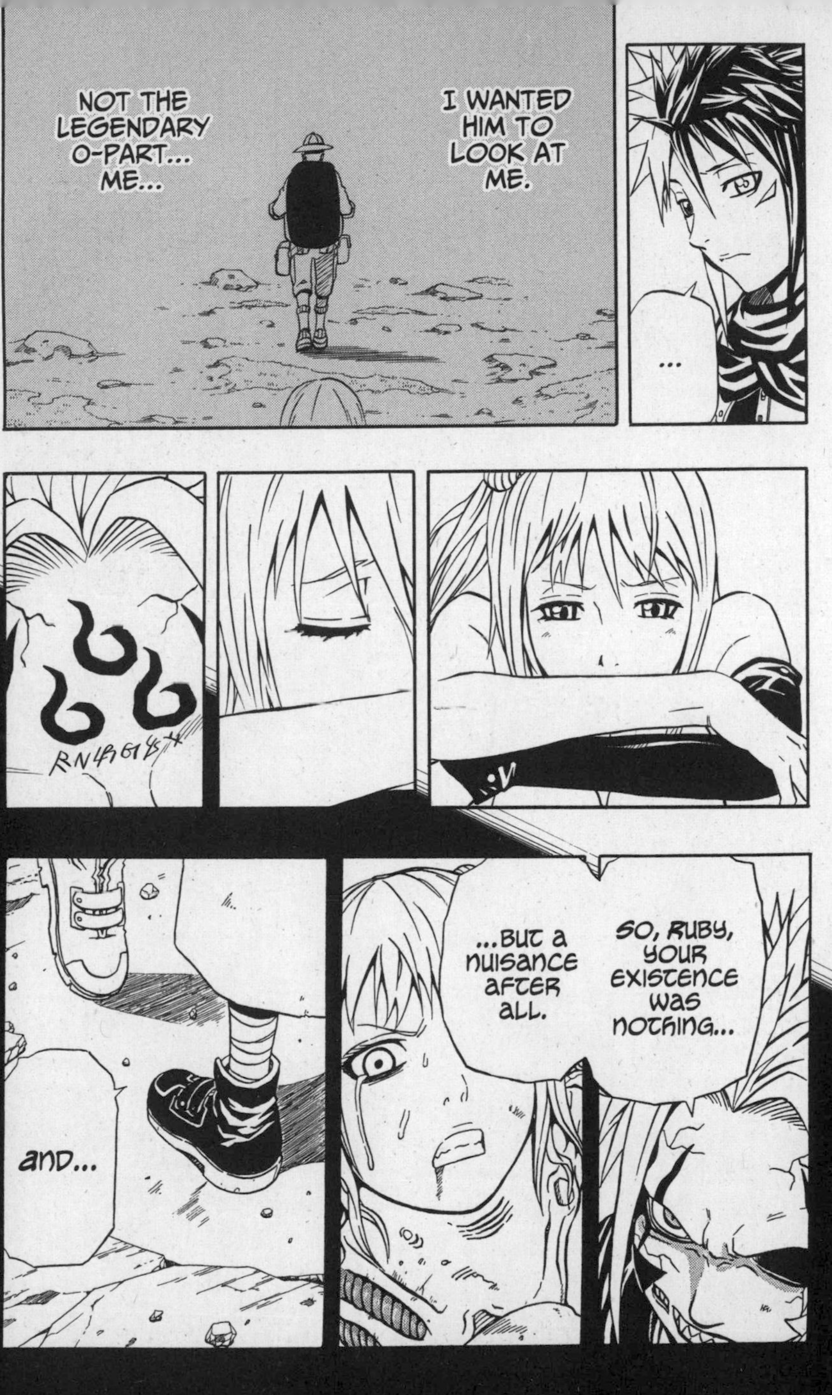
...
I WANTED HIM TO LOOK AT ME.
NOT THE LEGENDARY O-PART... ME...
SO, RUBY, YOUR EXISTENCE WAS NOTHING...
...BUT A NUISANCE AFTER ALL.
AND...

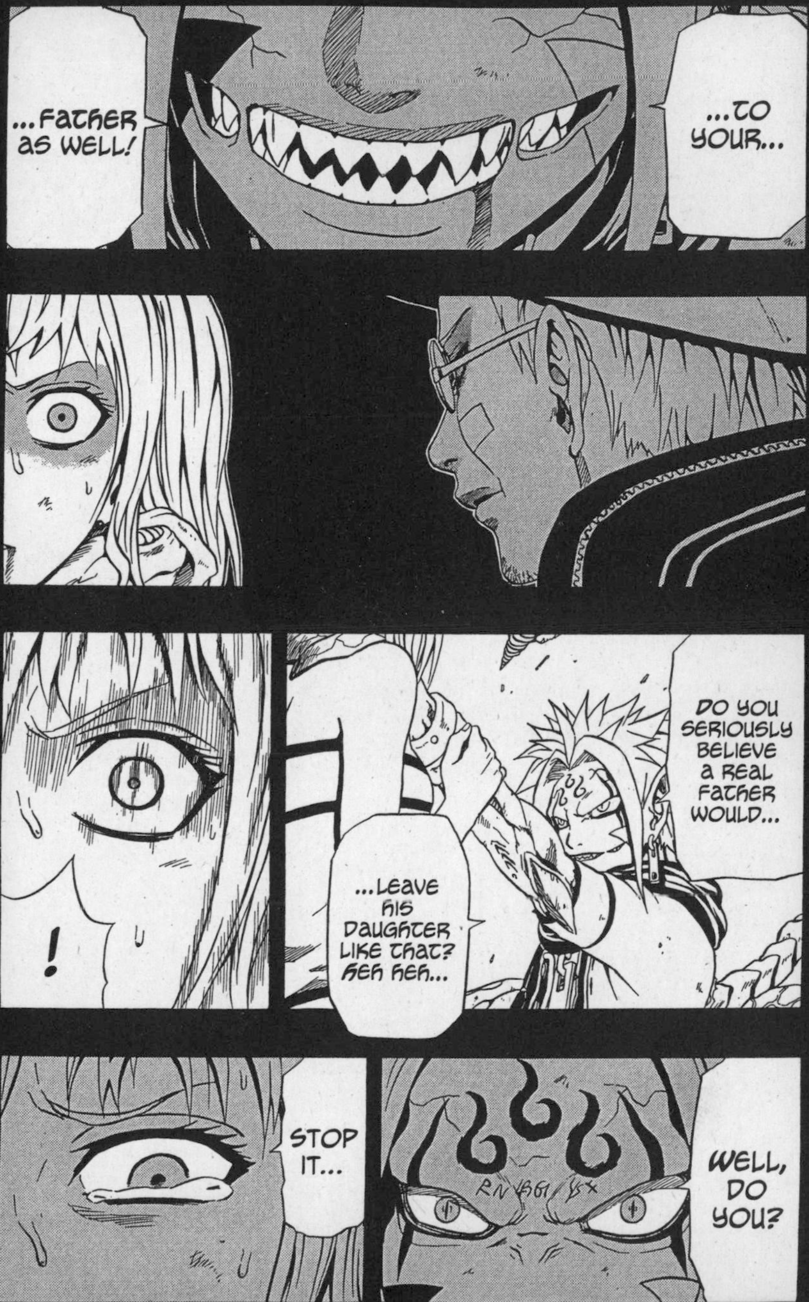
...TO YOUR...
...FATHER AS WELL!
DO YOU SERIOUSLY BELIEVE A REAL FATHER WOULD...
...LEAVE HIS DAUGHTER LIKE THAT? HEH HEH...
!
WELL, DO YOU?
STOP IT...

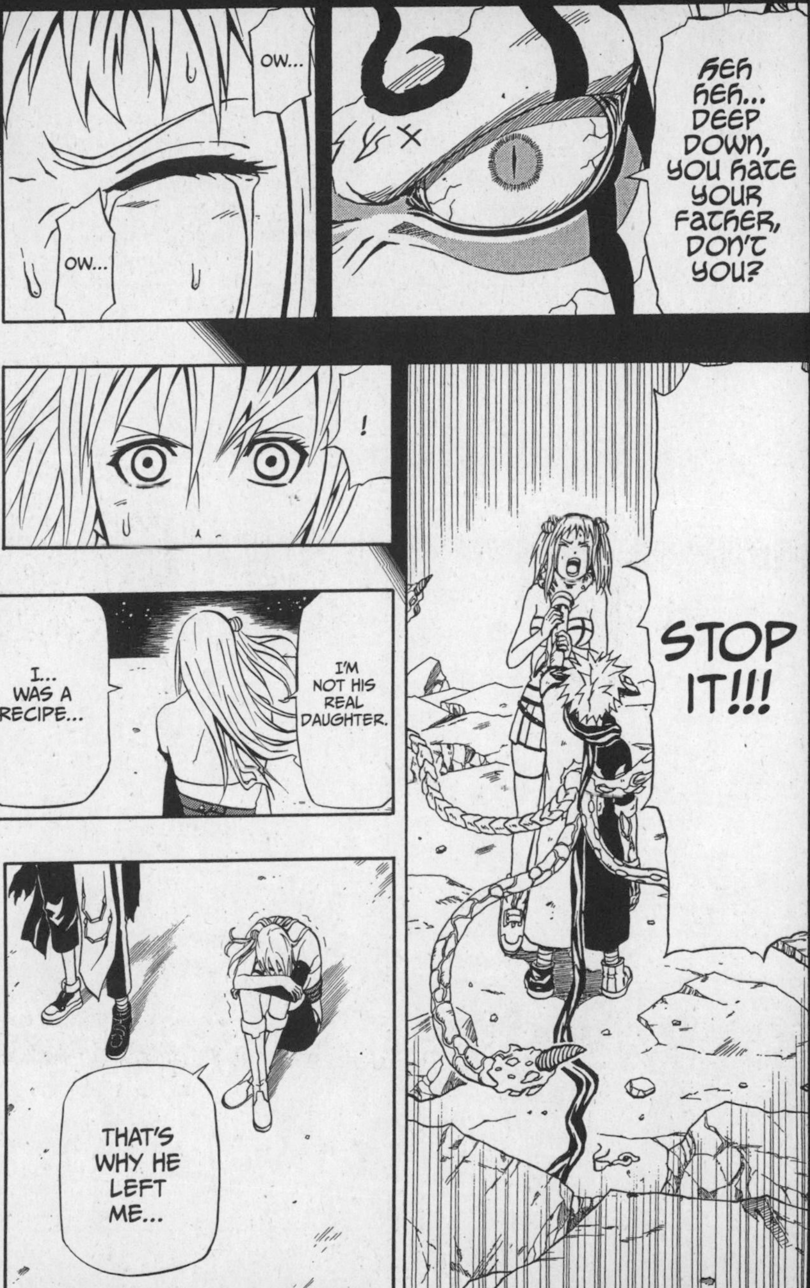
HEH HEH... DEEP DOWN, YOU HATE YOUR FATHER, DON'T YOU?
OW...
OW...
STOP IT!!!
!
I'M NOT HIS REAL DAUGHTER.
I... WAS A RECIPE...
THAT'S WHY HE LEFT ME...

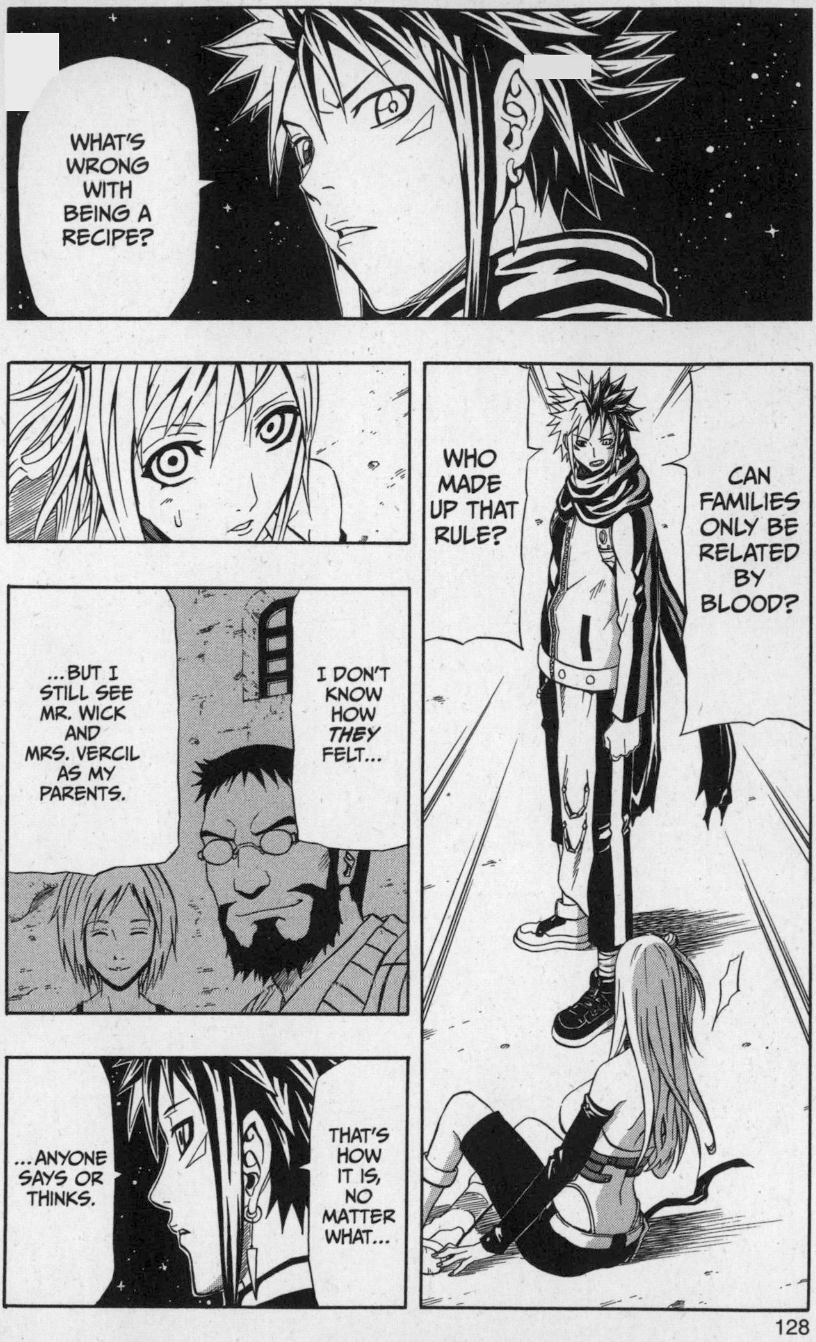
WHAT'S WRONG WITH BEING A RECIPE?
CAN FAMILIES ONLY BE RELATED BY BLOOD?
WHO MADE UP THAT RULE?
I DON'T KNOW HOW *THEY* FELT...
...BUT I STILL SEE MR. WICK AND MRS. VERCIL AS MY PARENTS.
THAT'S HOW IT IS, NO MATTER WHAT...
...ANYONE SAYS OR THINKS.

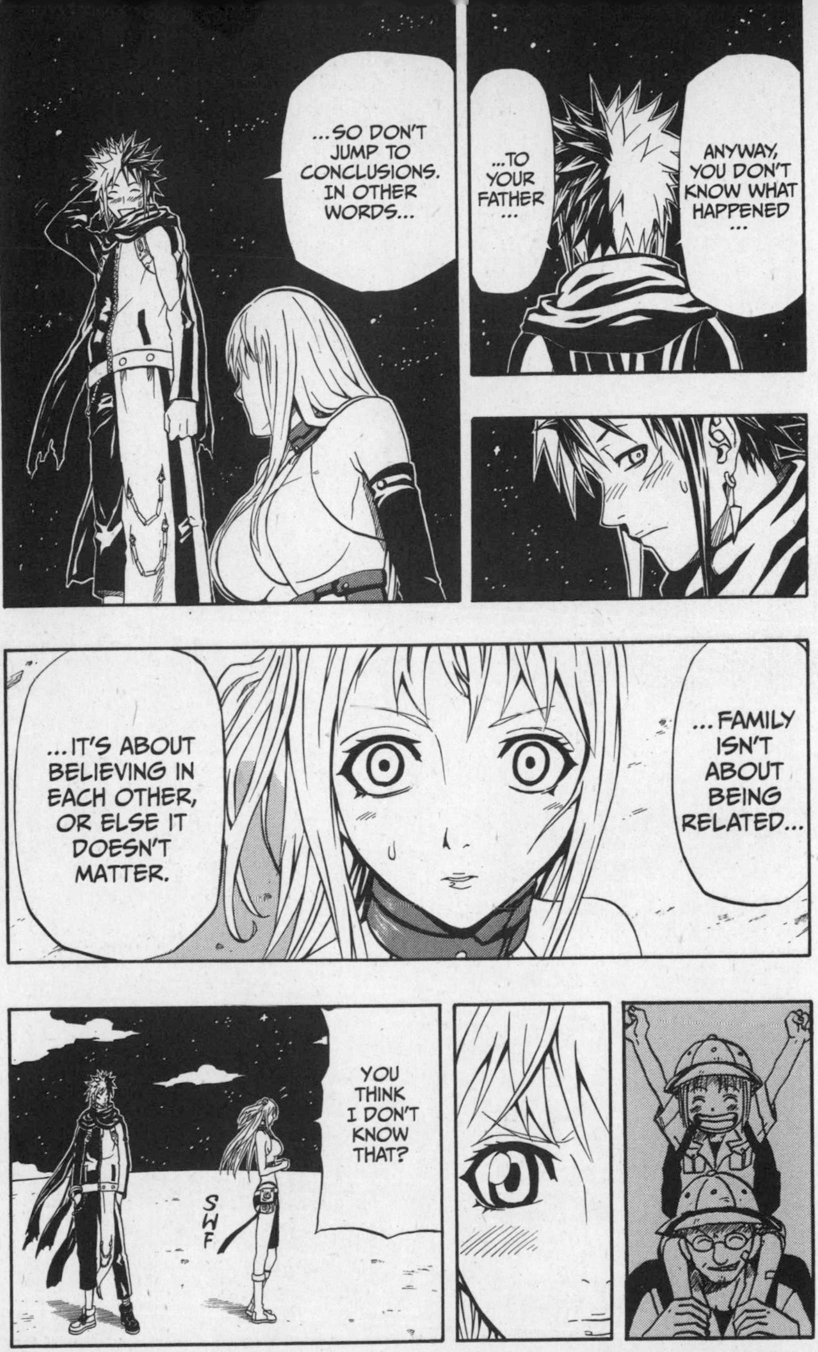
ANYWAY, YOU DON'T KNOW WHAT HAPPENED ...
...TO YOUR FATHER ...
...SO DON'T JUMP TO CONCLUSIONS. IN OTHER WORDS...
...FAMILY ISN'T ABOUT BEING RELATED...
...IT'S ABOUT BELIEVING IN EACH OTHER, OR ELSE IT DOESN'T MATTER.
YOU THINK I DON'T KNOW THAT?
SWF

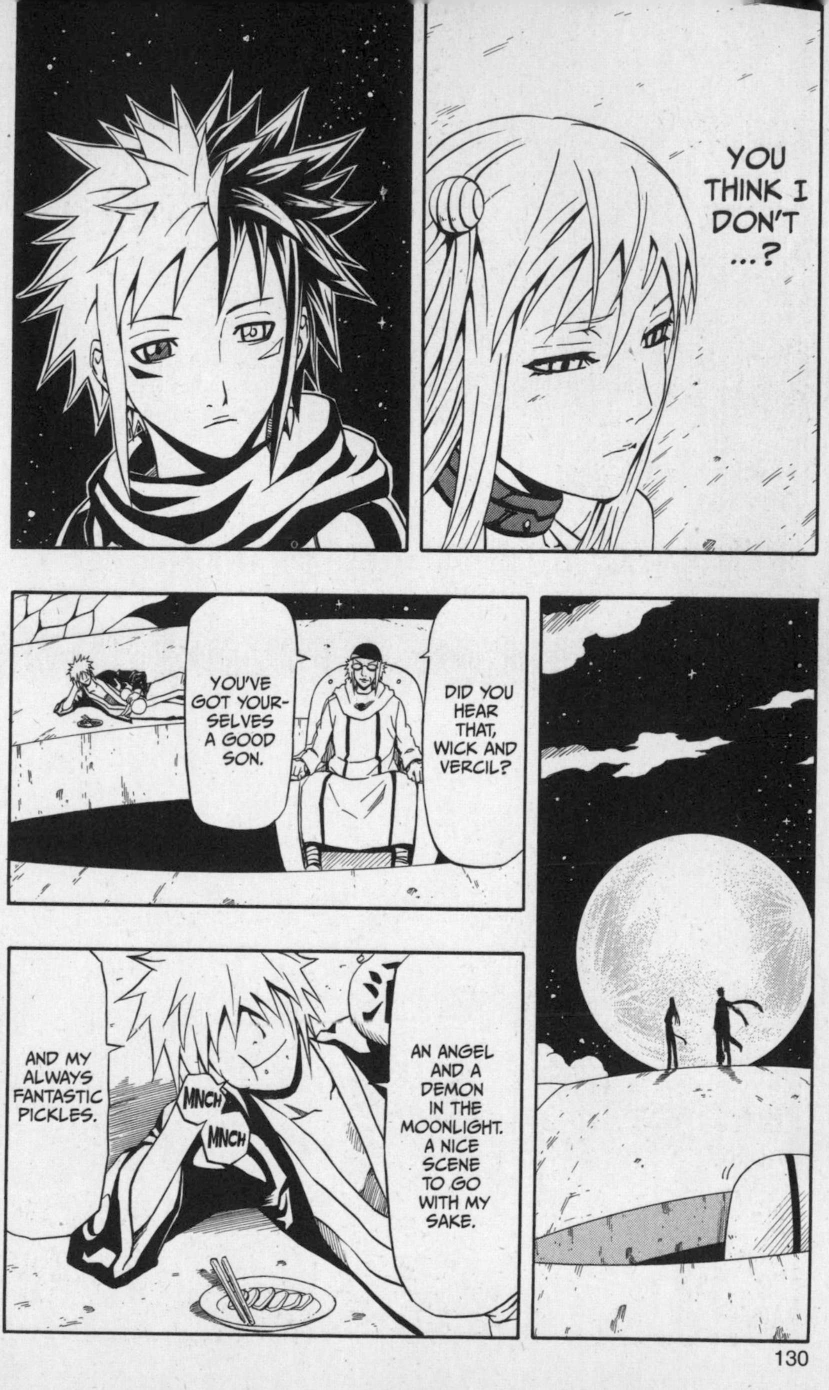
YOU THINK I DON'T ...?
DID YOU HEAR THAT, WICK AND VERCIL?
YOU'VE GOT YOUR-SELVES A GOOD SON.
AN ANGEL AND A DEMON IN THE MOONLIGHT. A NICE SCENE TO GO WITH MY SAKE.
MNCH
MNCH
AND MY ALWAYS FANTASTIC PICKLES.

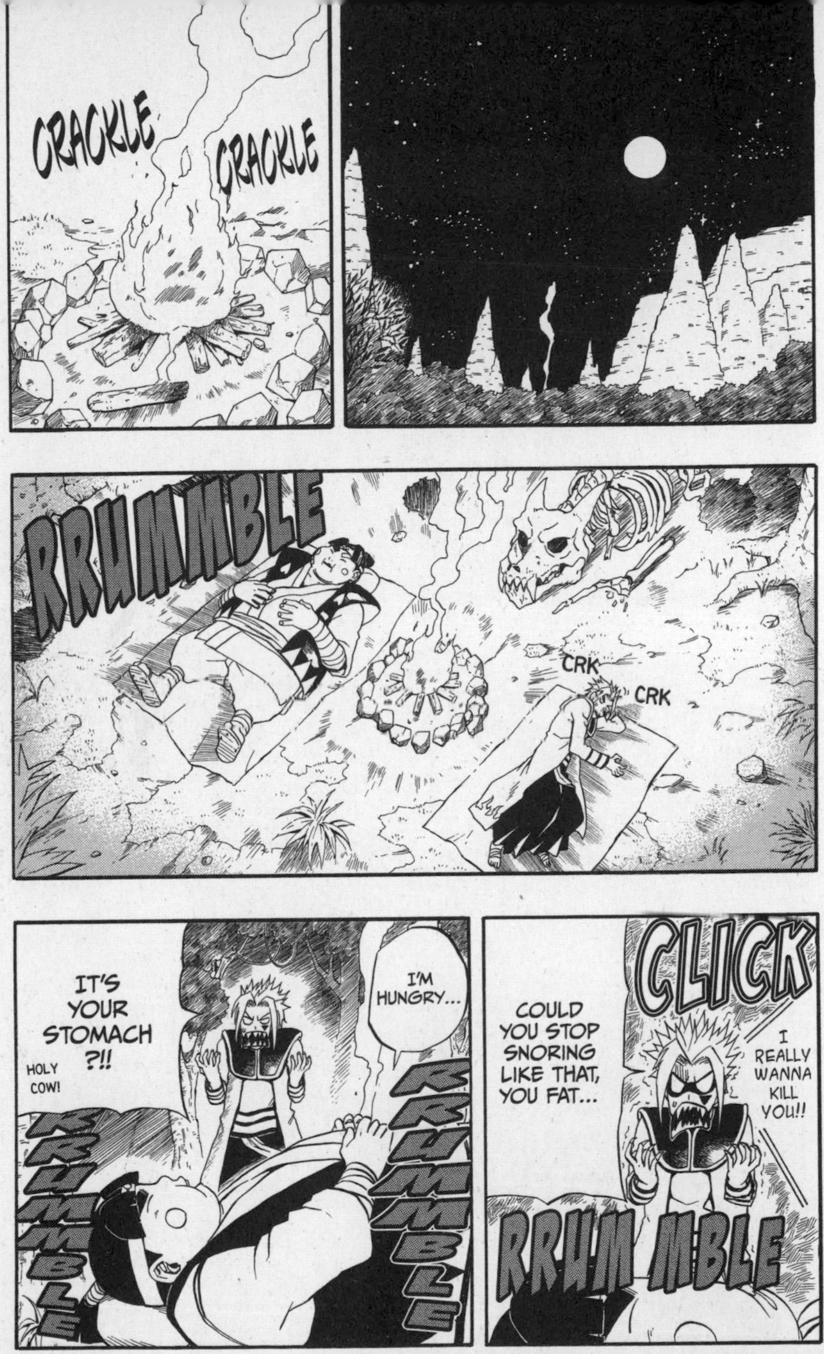
CRACKLE
CRACKLE
RRUMMBLE
CRK
CRK
CLICK
I REALLY WANNA KILL YOU!!
COULD YOU STOP SNORING LIKE THAT, YOU FAT...
RRUMMBLE
I'M HUNGRY...
RRUMMBLE
IT'S YOUR STOMACH?!!
HOLY COW!
RRUMMBLE

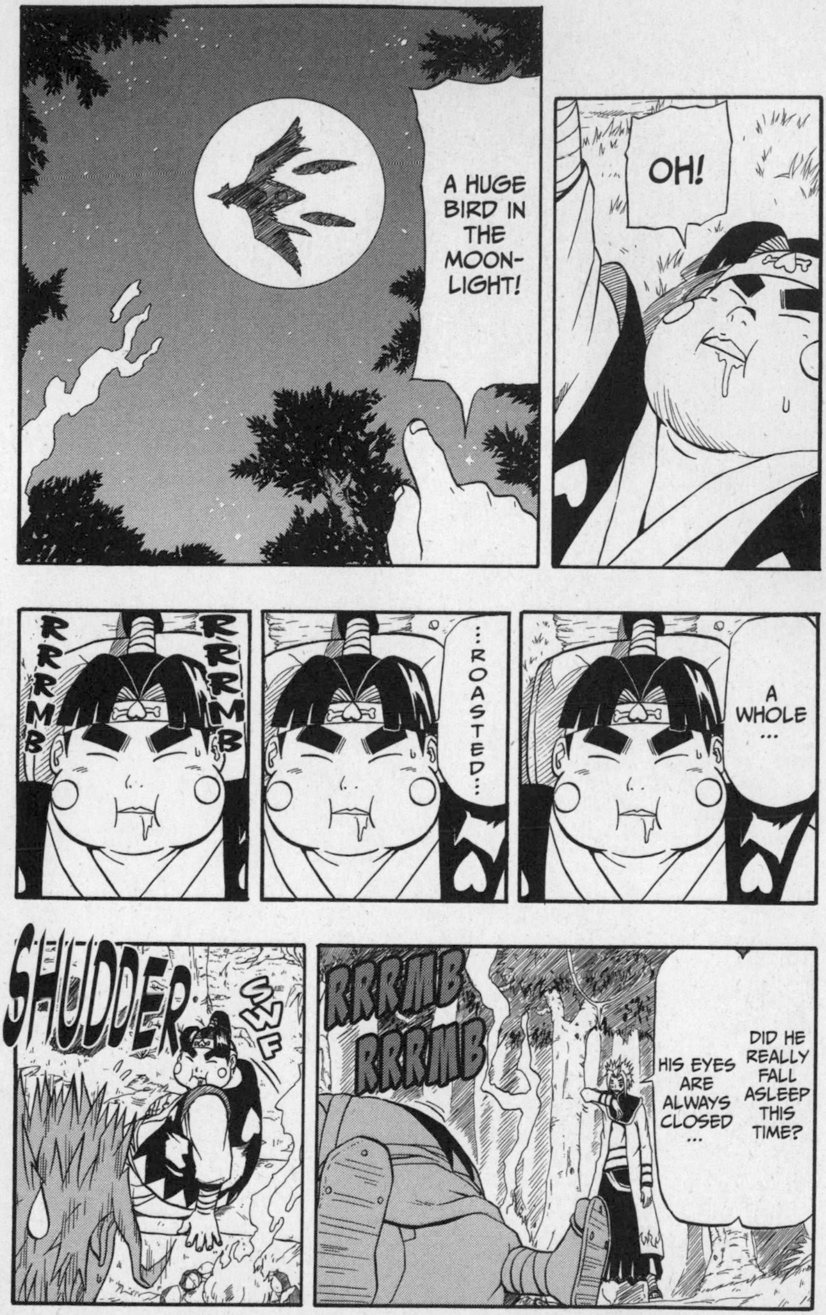
OH!
A HUGE BIRD IN THE MOON-LIGHT!
A WHOLE ...
...ROASTED...
RRRRMB
RRRRMB
DID HE REALLY FALL ASLEEP THIS TIME?
HIS EYES ARE ALWAYS CLOSED ...
RRRMB
RRRMB
SWF
SHUDDER

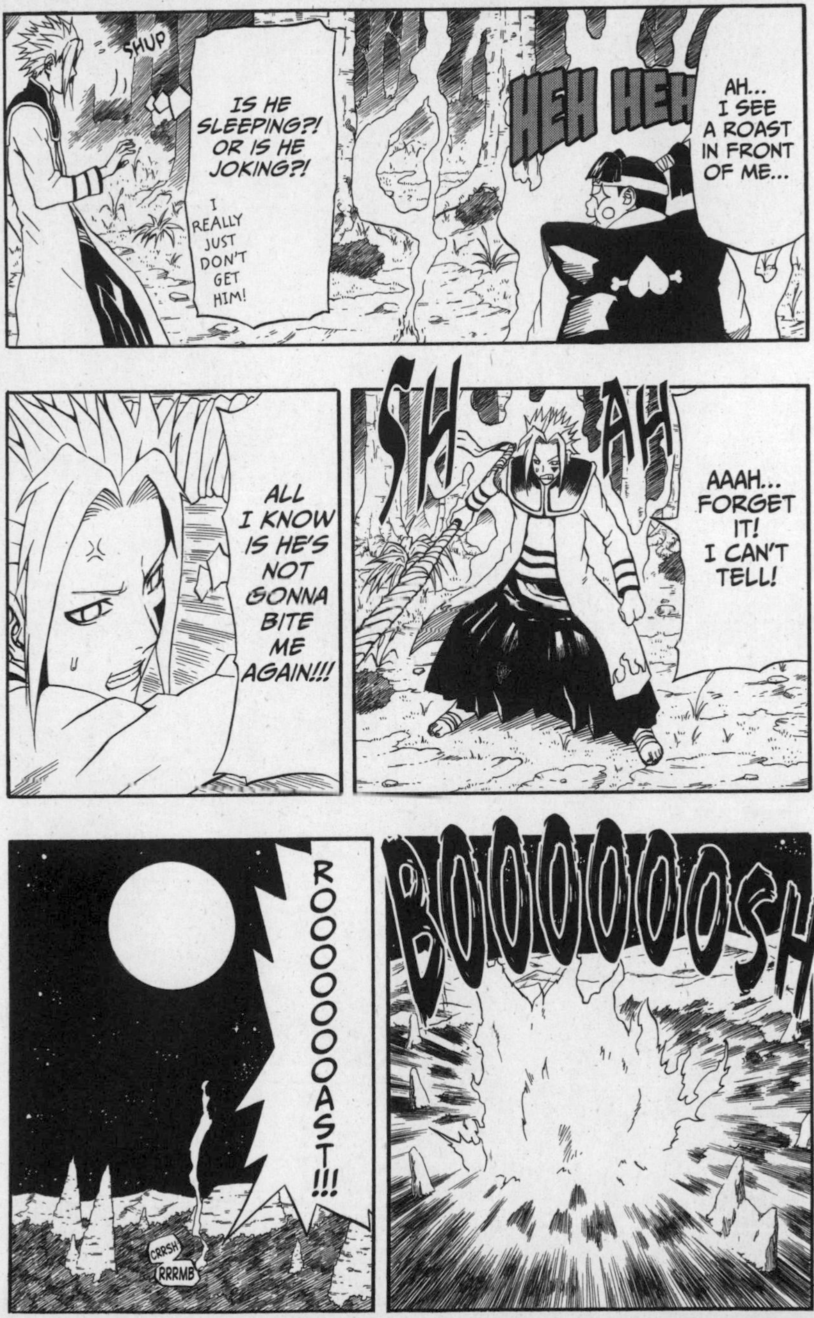
HEH HEH
AH... I SEE A ROAST IN FRONT OF ME...
SHUP
IS HE SLEEPING?! OR IS HE JOKING?!
I REALLY JUST DON'T GET HIM!
SH AH
AAAH... FORGET IT! I CAN'T TELL!
ALL I KNOW IS HE'S NOT GONNA BITE ME AGAIN!!!
BOOOOOOOSH
ROOOOOOOAST!!!
CRRSH
RRRMB

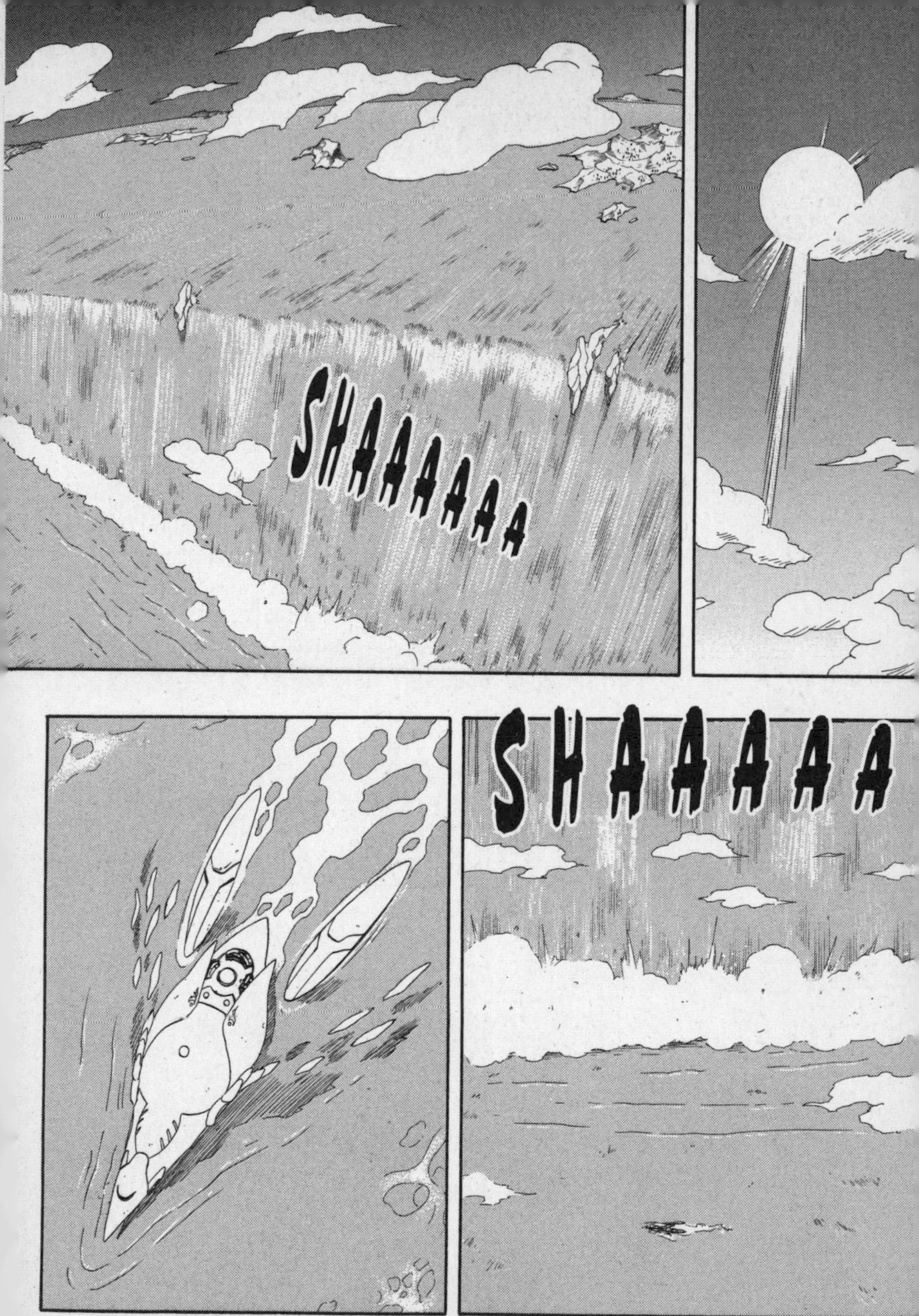
SHAAAAAAA
SHAAAAA

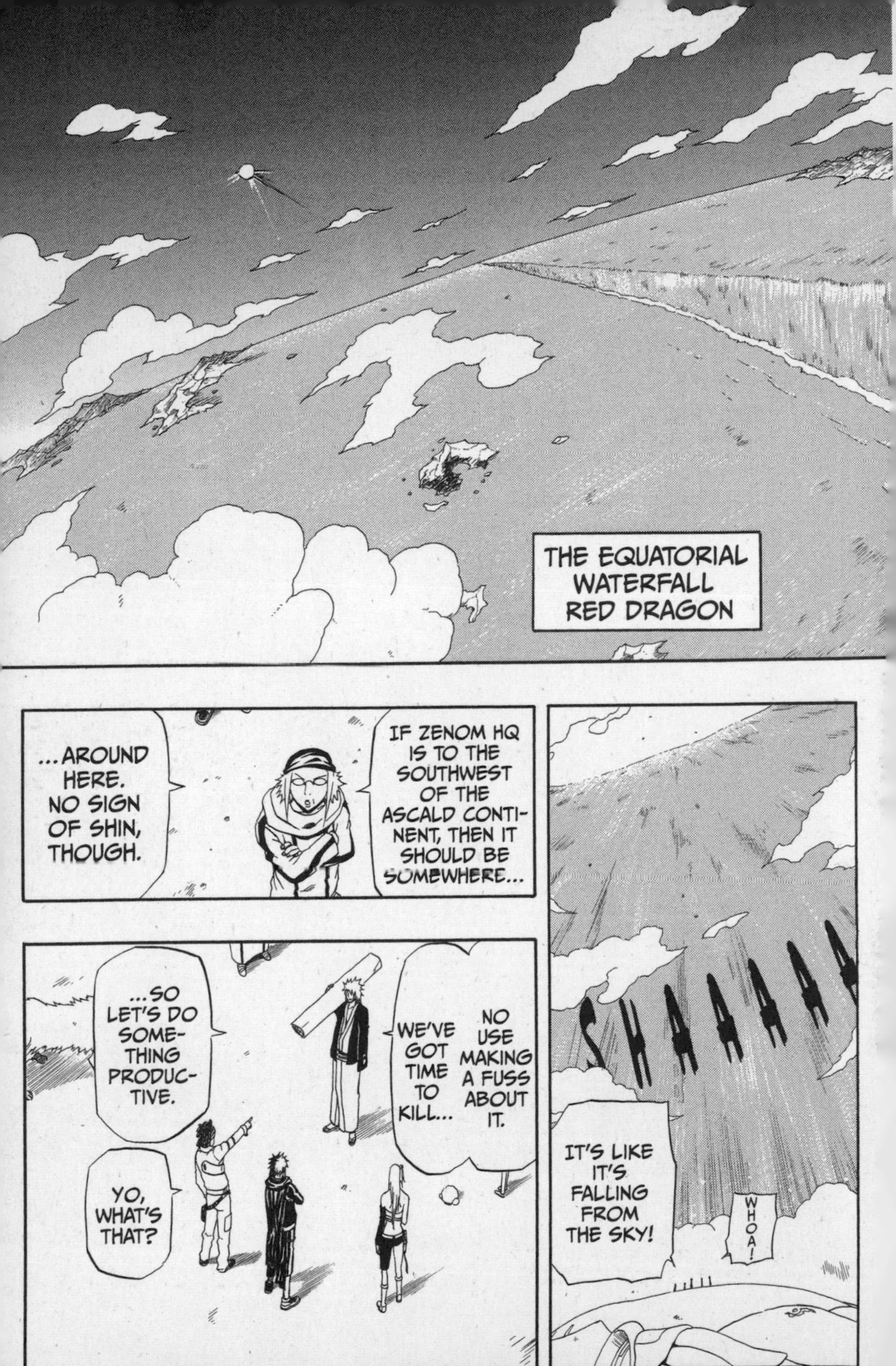
THE EQUATORIAL WATERFALL RED DRAGON
SHAAAAA
IT'S LIKE IT'S FALLING FROM THE SKY!
WHOA!
IF ZENOM HQ IS TO THE SOUTHWEST OF THE ASCALD CONTI-NENT, THEN IT SHOULD BE SOMEWHERE...
...AROUND HERE. NO SIGN OF SHIN, THOUGH.
NO USE MAKING A FUSS ABOUT IT.
WE'VE GOT TIME TO KILL...
...SO LET'S DO SOME-THING PRODUC-TIVE.
YO, WHAT'S THAT?

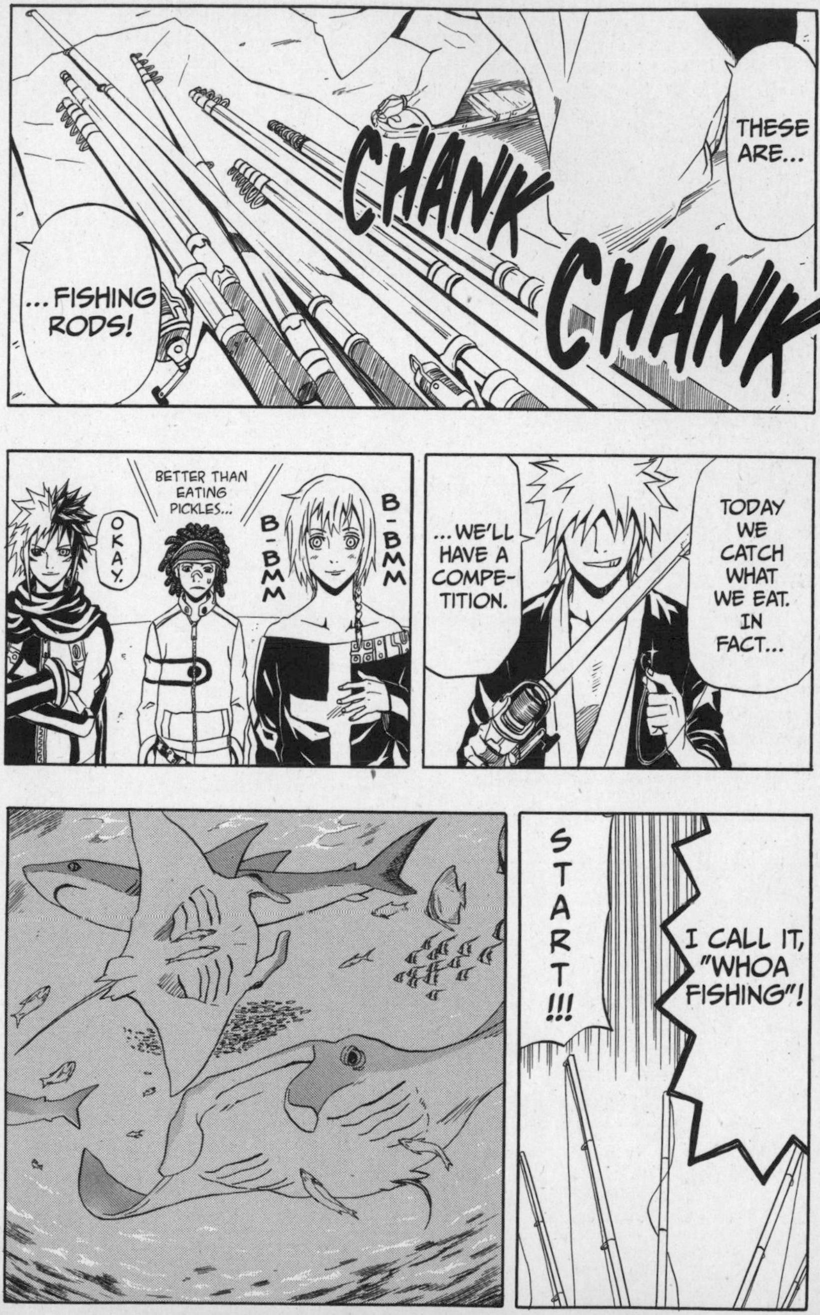
THESE ARE...
CHANK
CHANK
...FISHING RODS!
TODAY WE CATCH WHAT WE EAT. IN FACT...
...WE'LL HAVE A COMPE-TITION.
B-BMM
B-BMM
BETTER THAN EATING PICKLES...
OKAY.
I CALL IT, "WHOA FISHING"!
START!!!

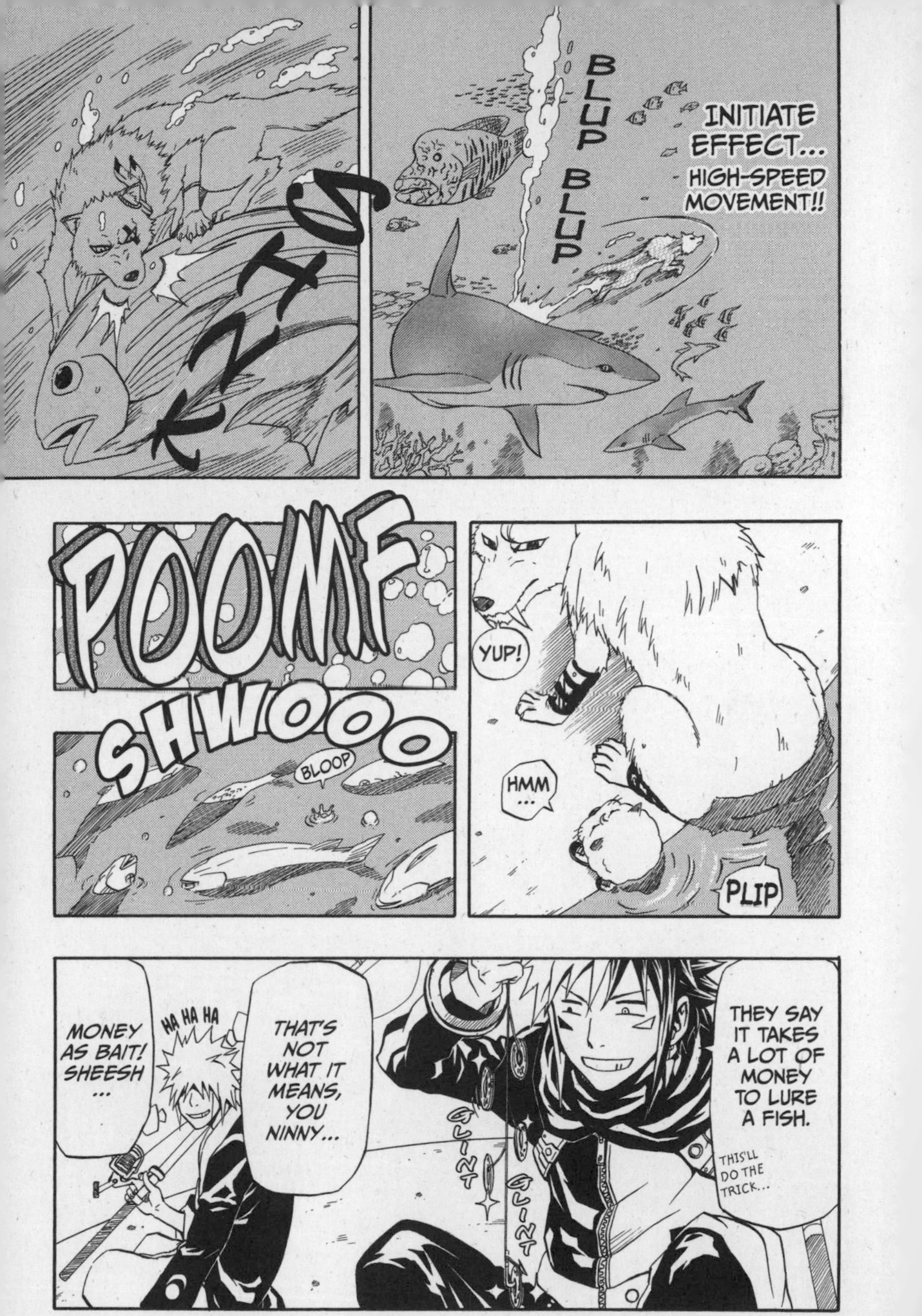
BLUP BLUP
INITIATE EFFECT...
HIGH-SPEED MOVEMENT!!
YUP!
HMM ...
PLIP
POOMF
SHWOOO
BLOOP
THEY SAY IT TAKES A LOT OF MONEY TO LURE A FISH.
THIS'LL DO THE TRICK...
GLINT
GLINT
THAT'S NOT WHAT IT MEANS, YOU NINNY...
HA HA HA
MONEY AS BAIT! SHEESH ...

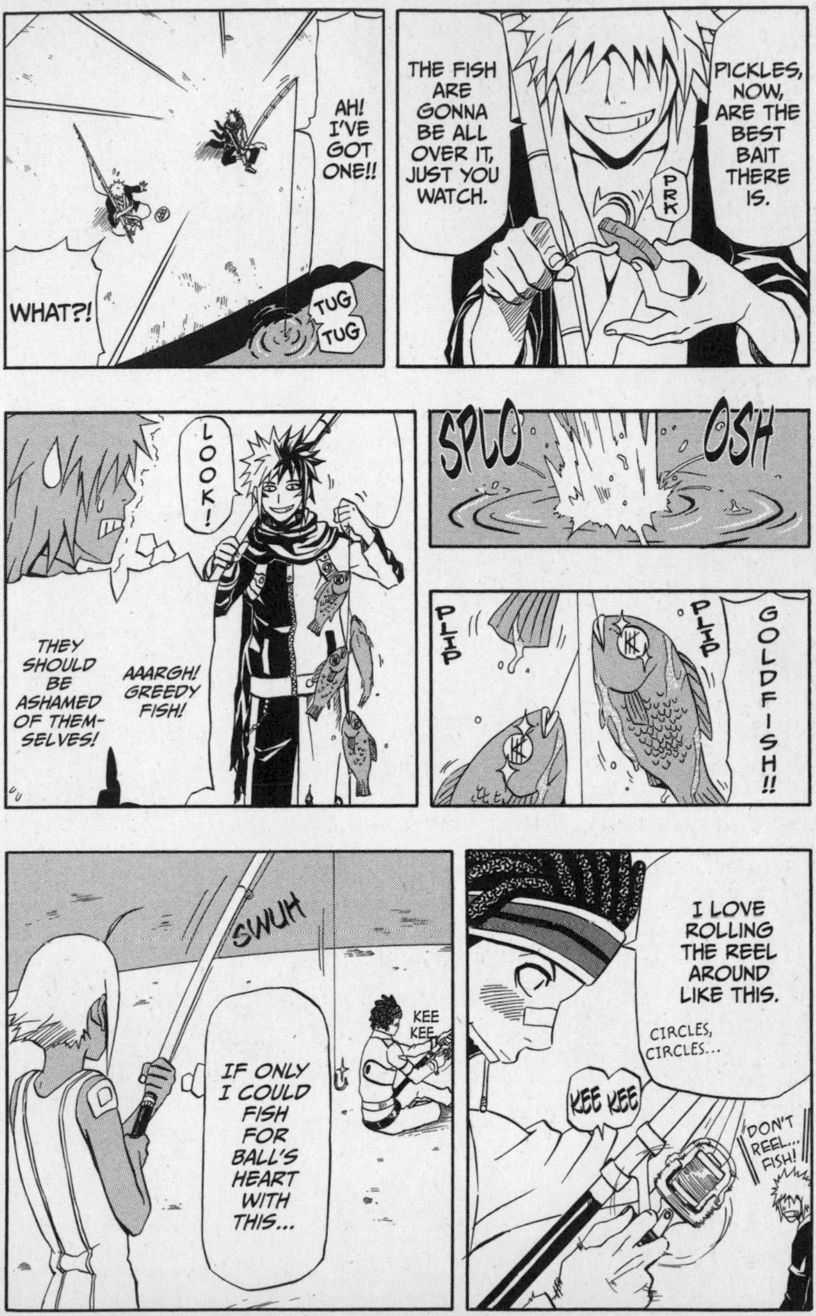
PICKLES, NOW, ARE THE BEST BAIT THERE IS.
PRK
THE FISH ARE GONNA BE ALL OVER IT, JUST YOU WATCH.
AH! I'VE GOT ONE!!
TUG TUG
WHAT?!
SPLO OSH
GOLDFISH!!
PLIP
PLIP
LOOK!
AAARGH! GREEDY FISH!
THEY SHOULD BE ASHAMED OF THEM-SELVES!
I LOVE ROLLING THE REEL AROUND LIKE THIS.
CIRCLES, CIRCLES...
KEE KEE
DON'T REEL... FISH!
SWUH
KEE KEE
IF ONLY I COULD FISH FOR BALL'S HEART WITH THIS...

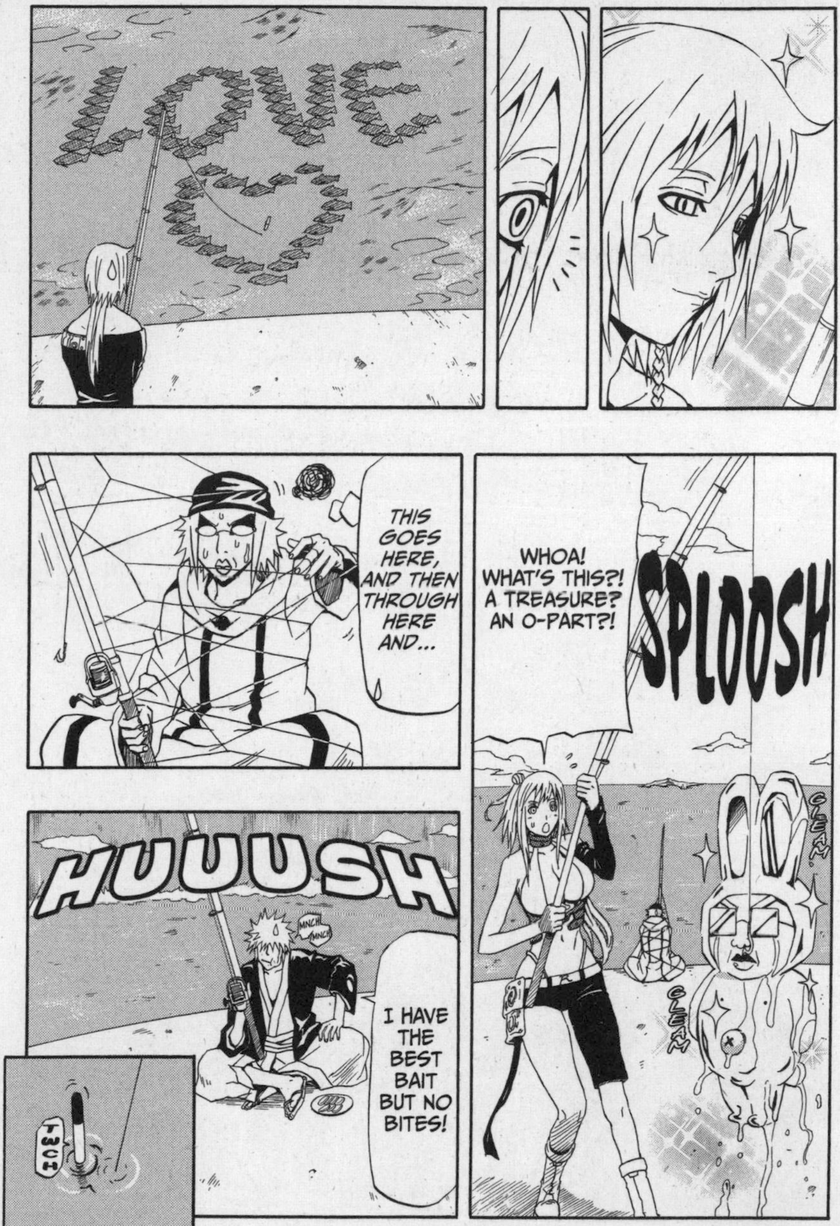
LOVE
SPLOOSH
WHOA! WHAT'S THIS?! A TREASURE? AN O-PART?!
GLEAM
GLEAM
THIS GOES HERE, AND THEN THROUGH HERE AND...
HUUUSH
MNCH MNCH
I HAVE THE BEST BAIT BUT NO BITES!
TWCH

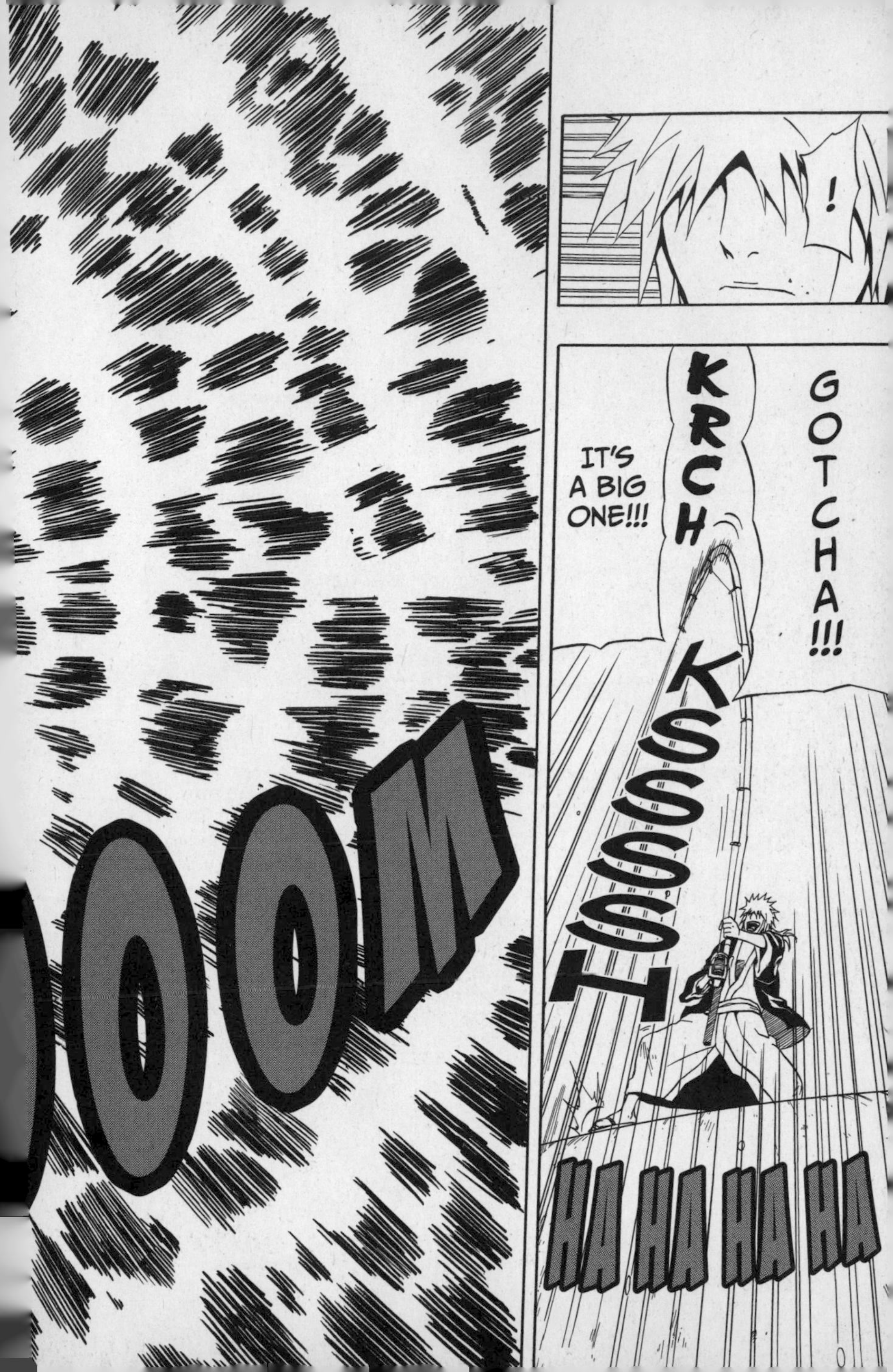
!
GOTCHA!!!
KRCH
IT'S A BIG ONE!!!
KSSSSH
HA HA HA HA HA
OOOM

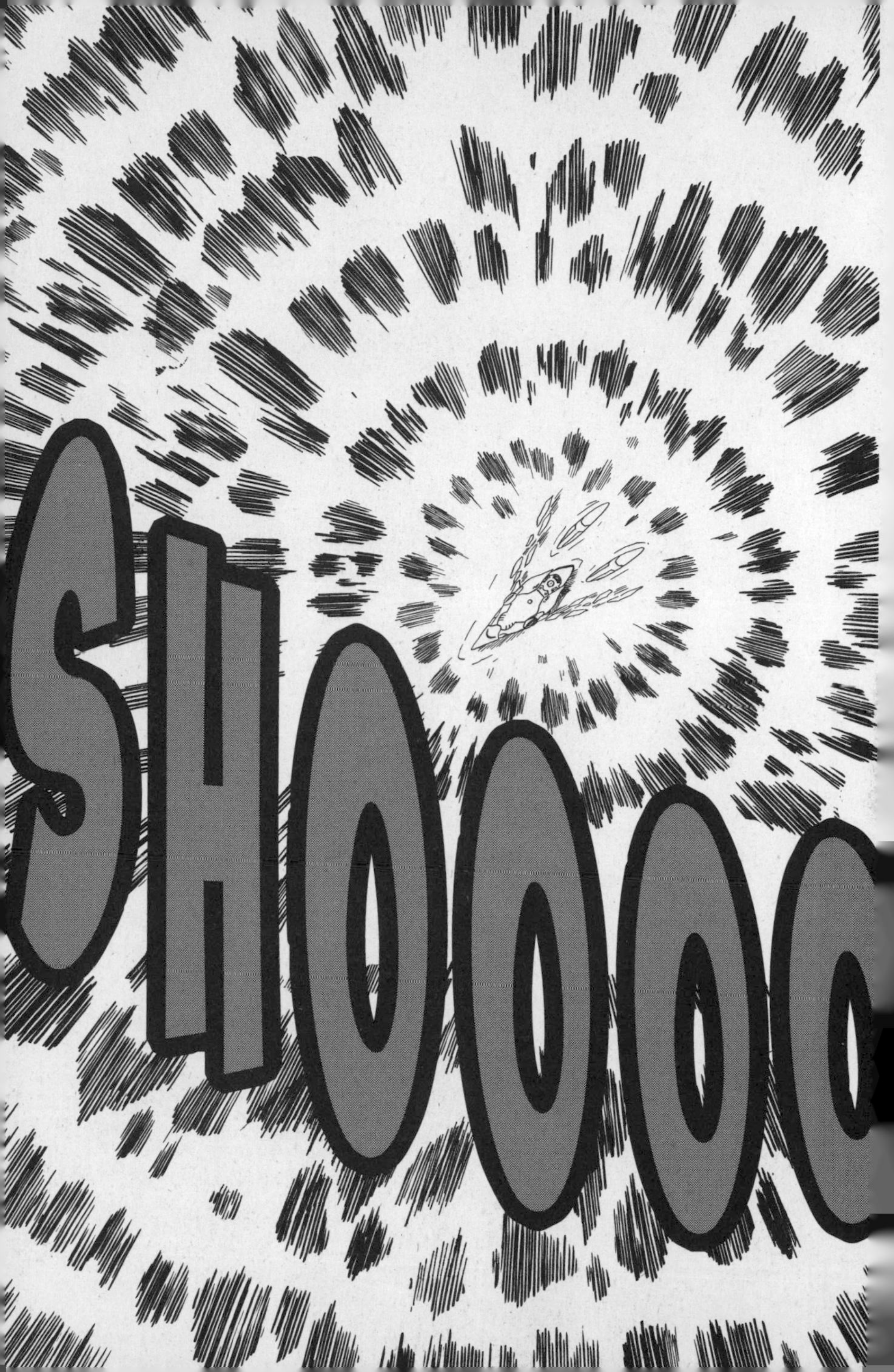
SHOOOO

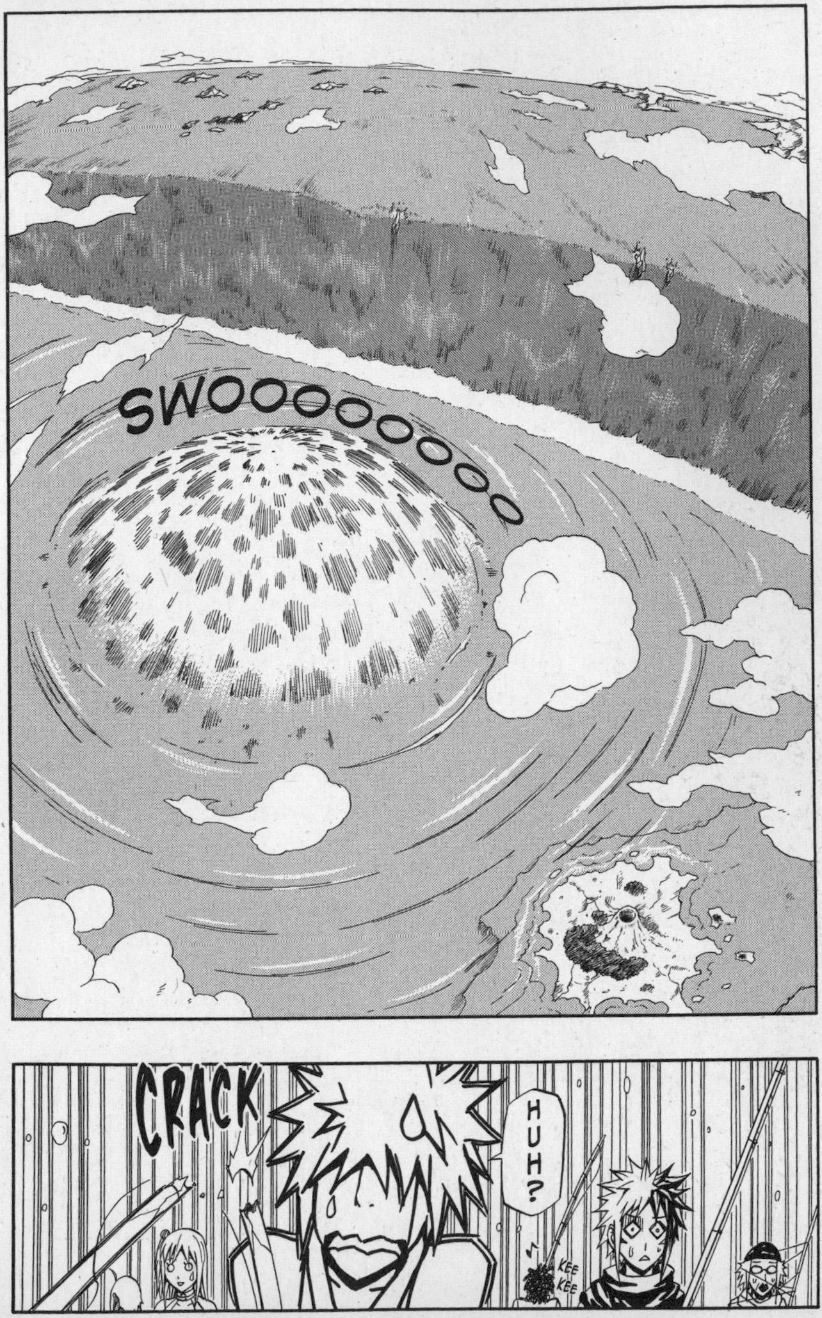
SWOOOOOOOO
HUH?
CRACK
KEE KEE

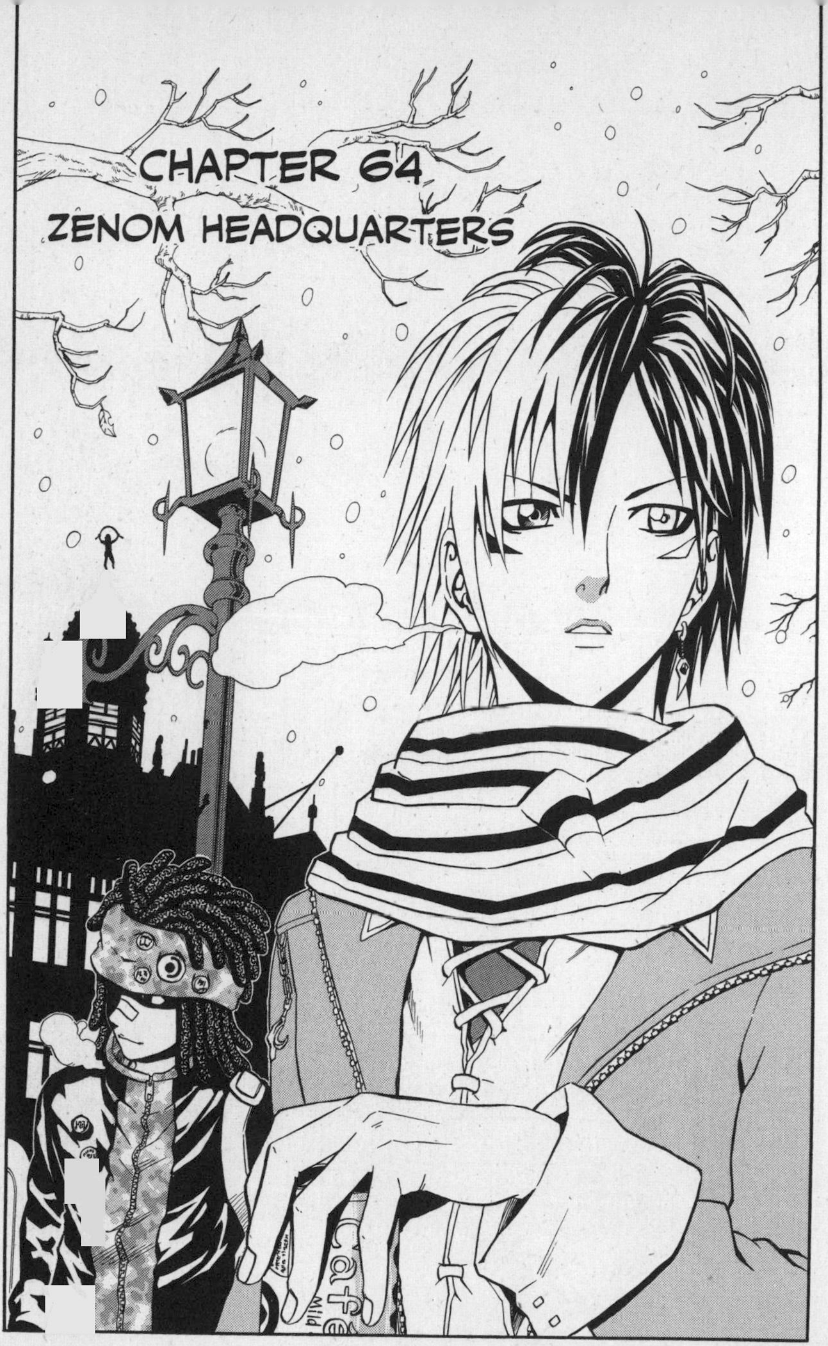
CHAPTER 64
ZENOM HEADQUARTERS
cafe
Mild

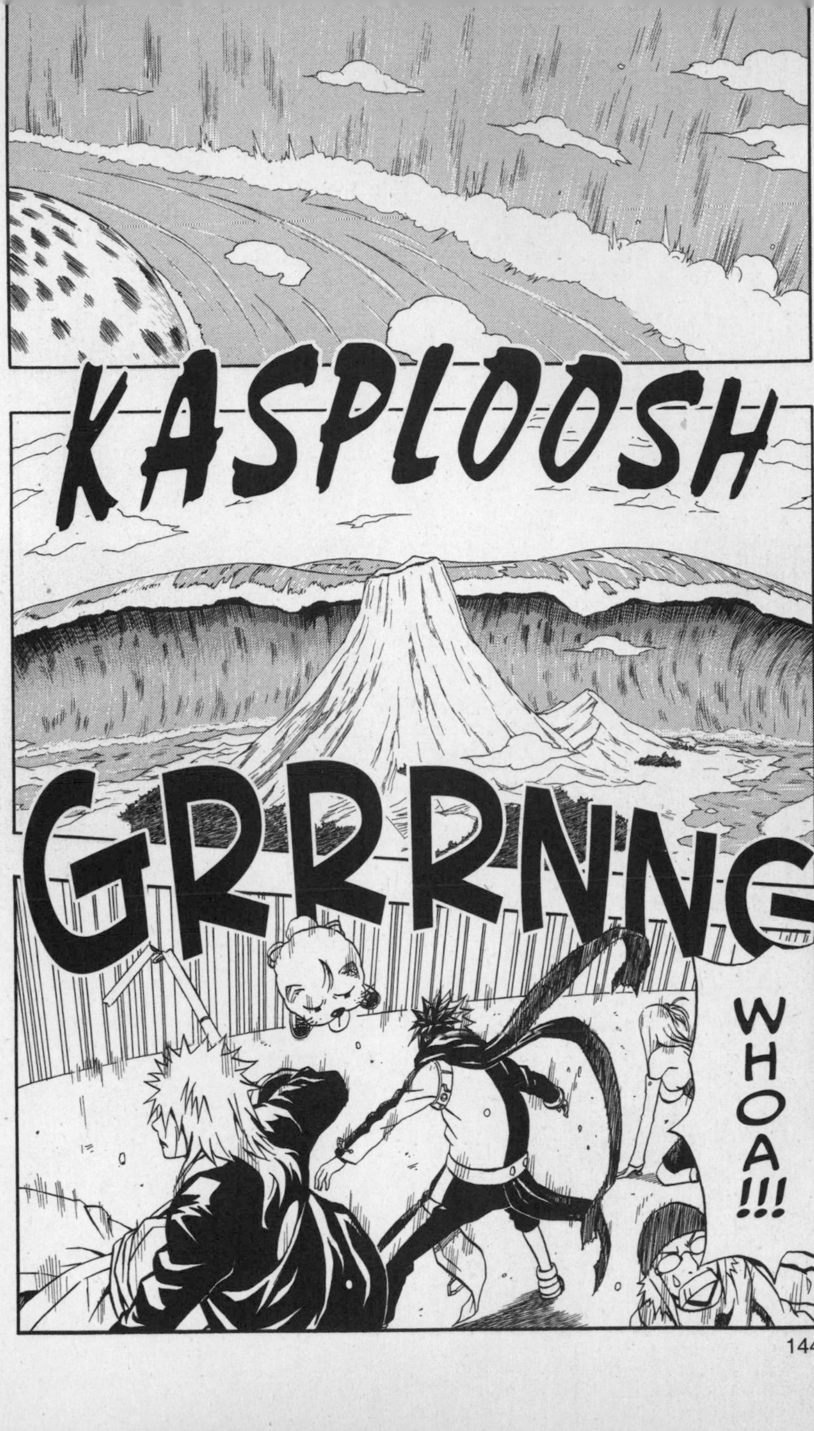
KASPLOOSH
GRRRNNG
WHOA!!!

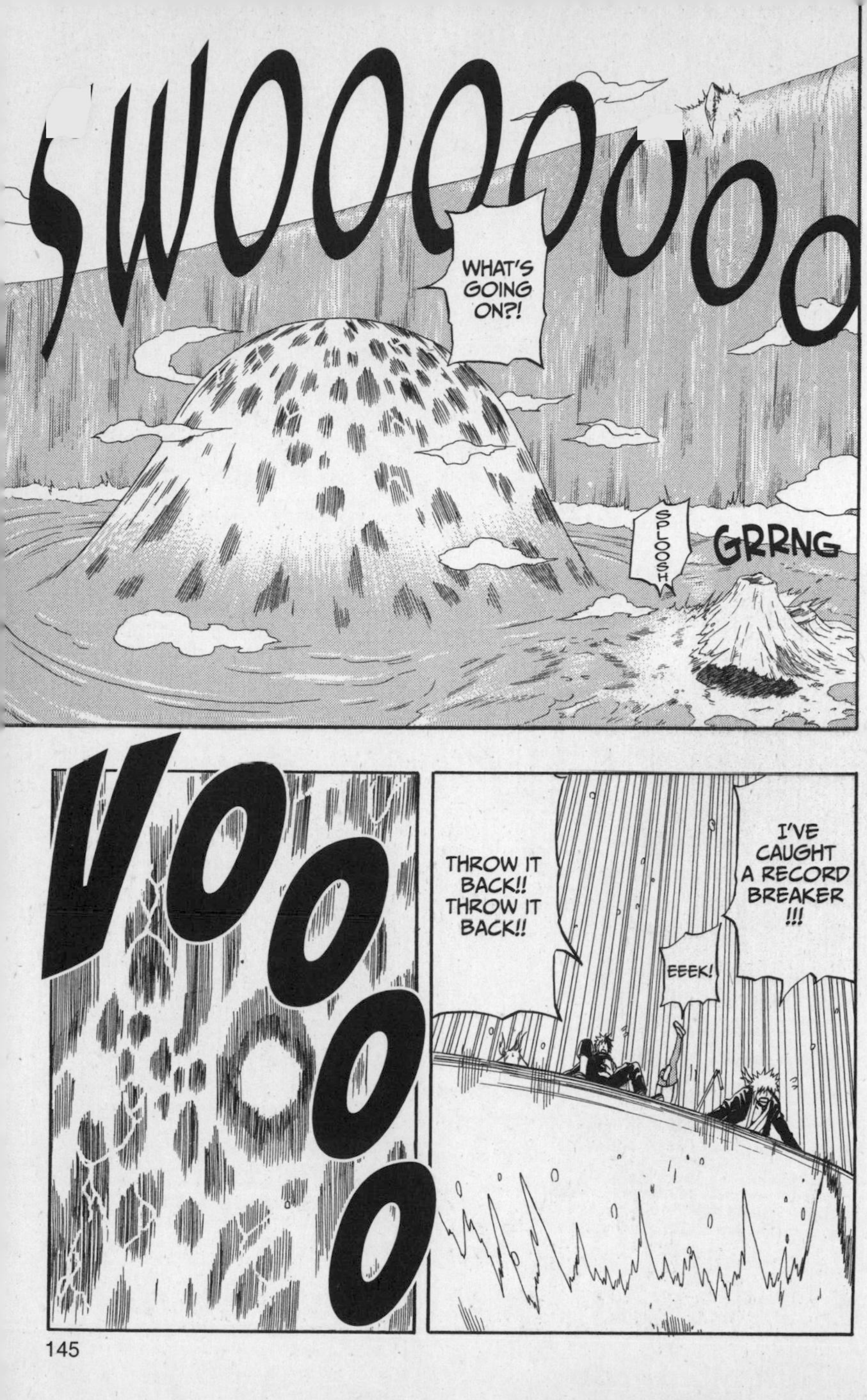
SWOOOOOOOO
WHAT'S GOING ON?!
GRRNG
SPLOOSH
I'VE CAUGHT A RECORD BREAKER !!!
THROW IT BACK!! THROW IT BACK!!
EEEK!
VOOOOOO

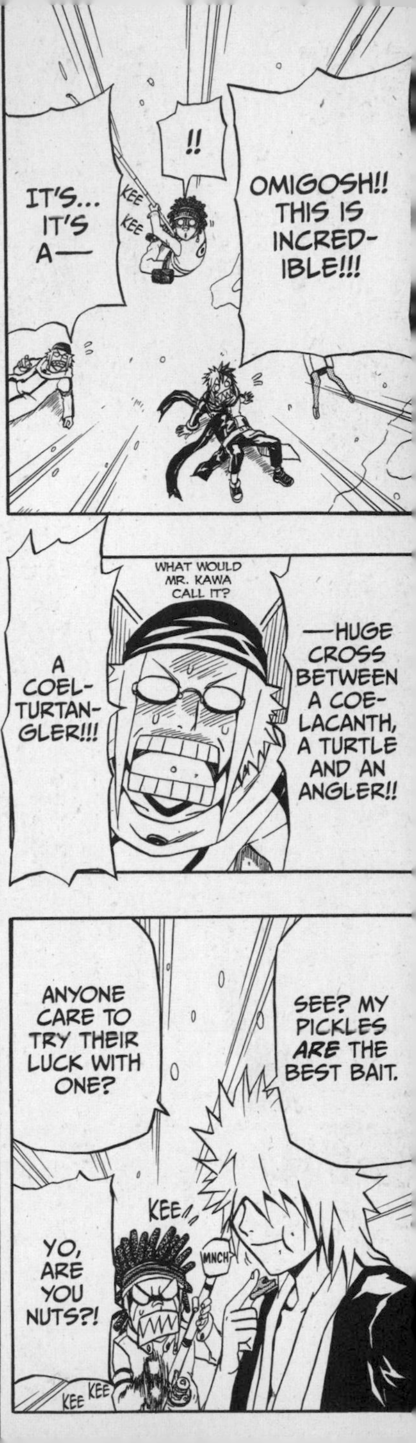
OMIGOSH!! THIS IS INCRED-IBLE!!!
!!
KEE KEE
IT'S... IT'S A—
—HUGE CROSS BETWEEN A COE-LACANTH, A TURTLE AND AN ANGLER!!
WHAT WOULD MR. KAWA CALL IT?
A COEL-TURTAN-GLER!!!
SEE? MY PICKLES *ARE* THE BEST BAIT.
ANYONE CARE TO TRY THEIR LUCK WITH ONE?
KEE
MNCH
YO, ARE YOU NUTS?!
KEE KEE
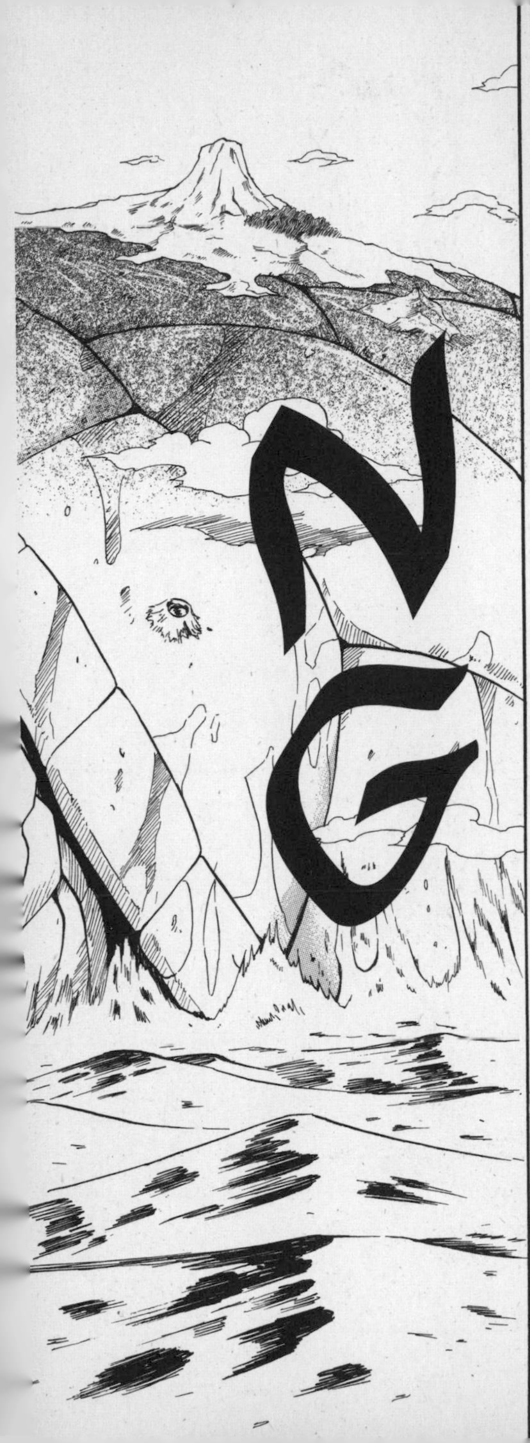
NG

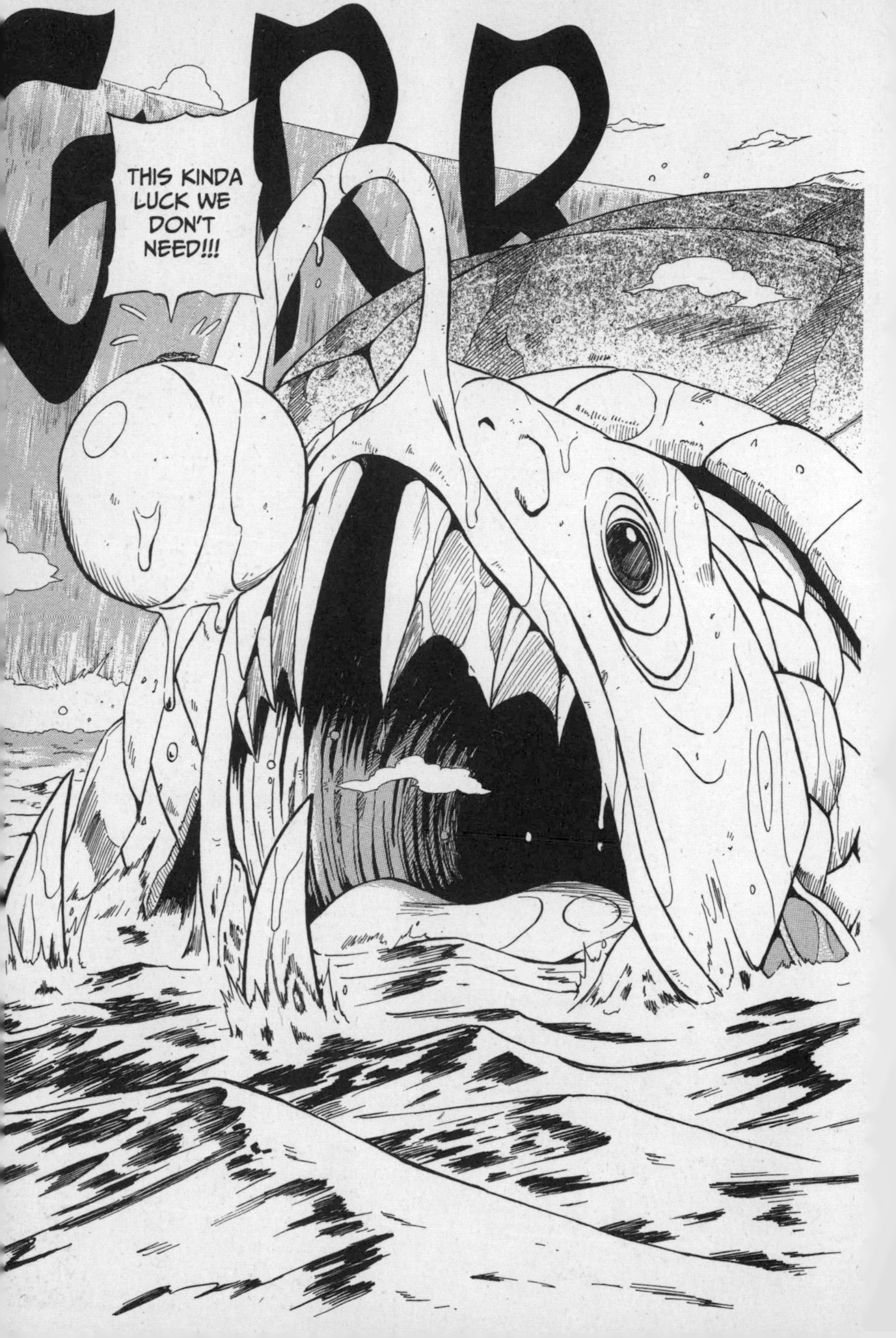
GRR
THIS KINDA LUCK WE DON'T NEED!!!

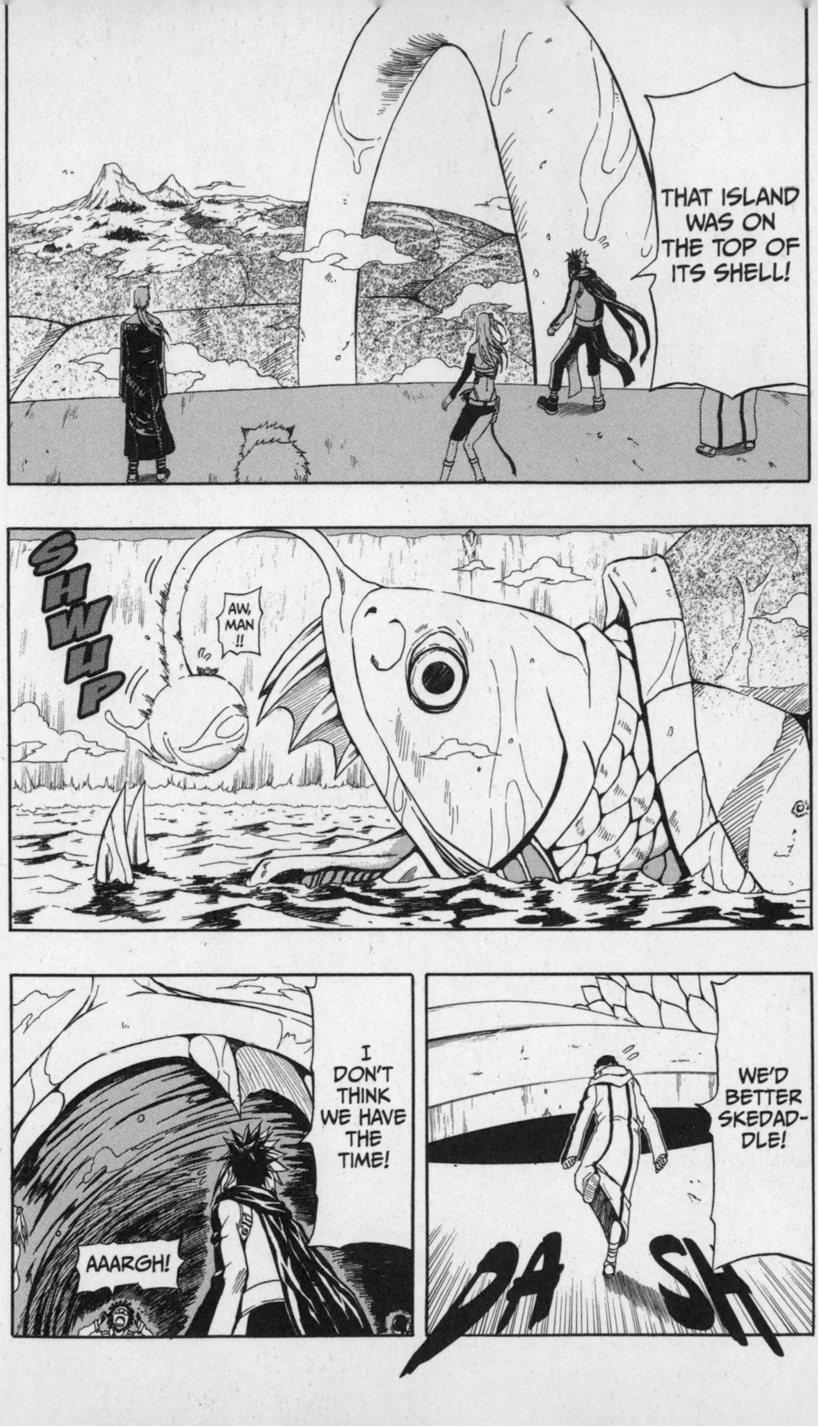
THAT ISLAND WAS ON THE TOP OF ITS SHELL!
SHWUP
AW, MAN!!
WE'D BETTER SKEDADDLE!
DASH
I DON'T THINK WE HAVE THE TIME!
AARGH!

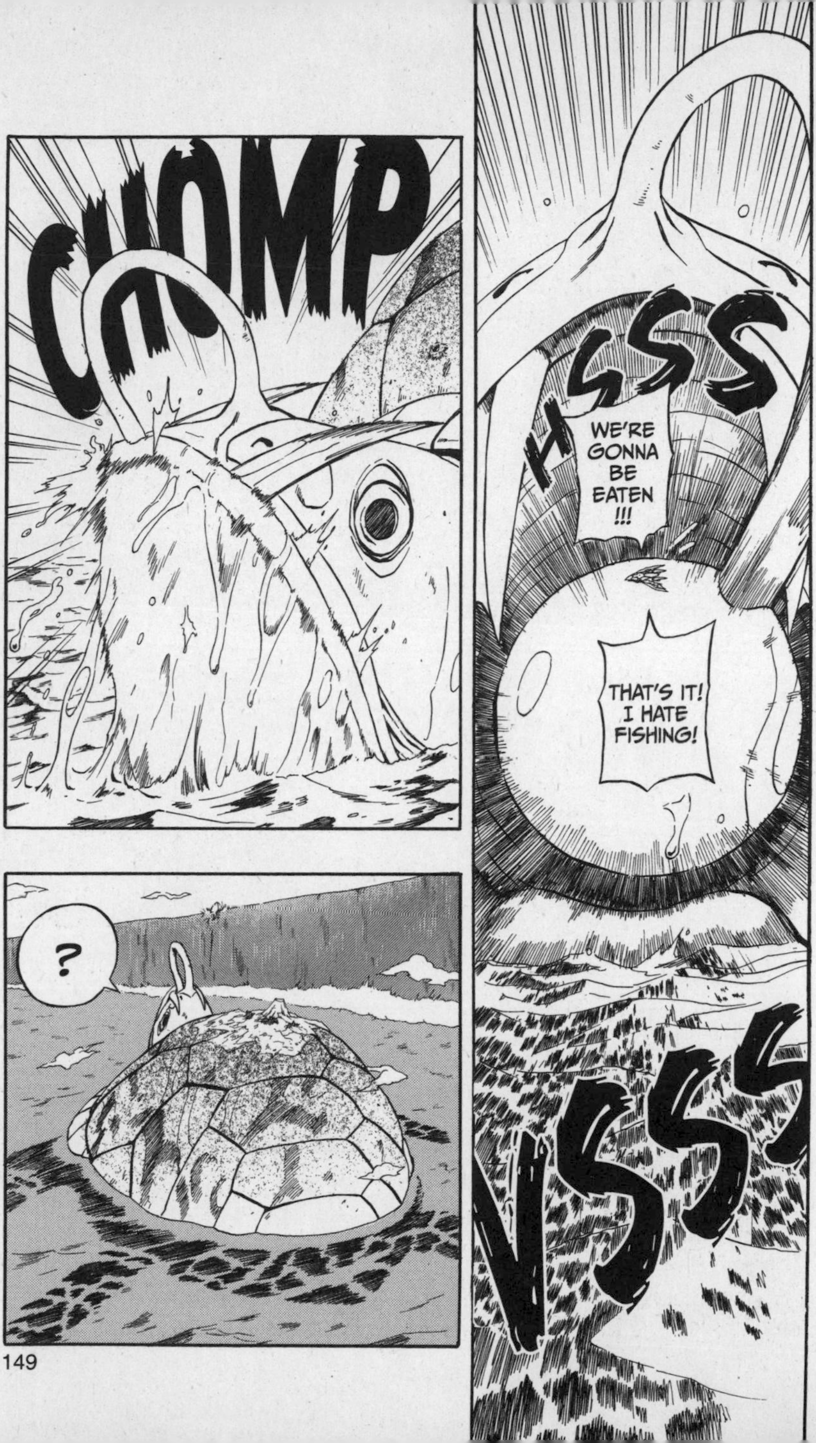
HSSS
WE'RE GONNA BE EATEN!!!
THAT'S IT! I HATE FISHING!
CHOMP
?

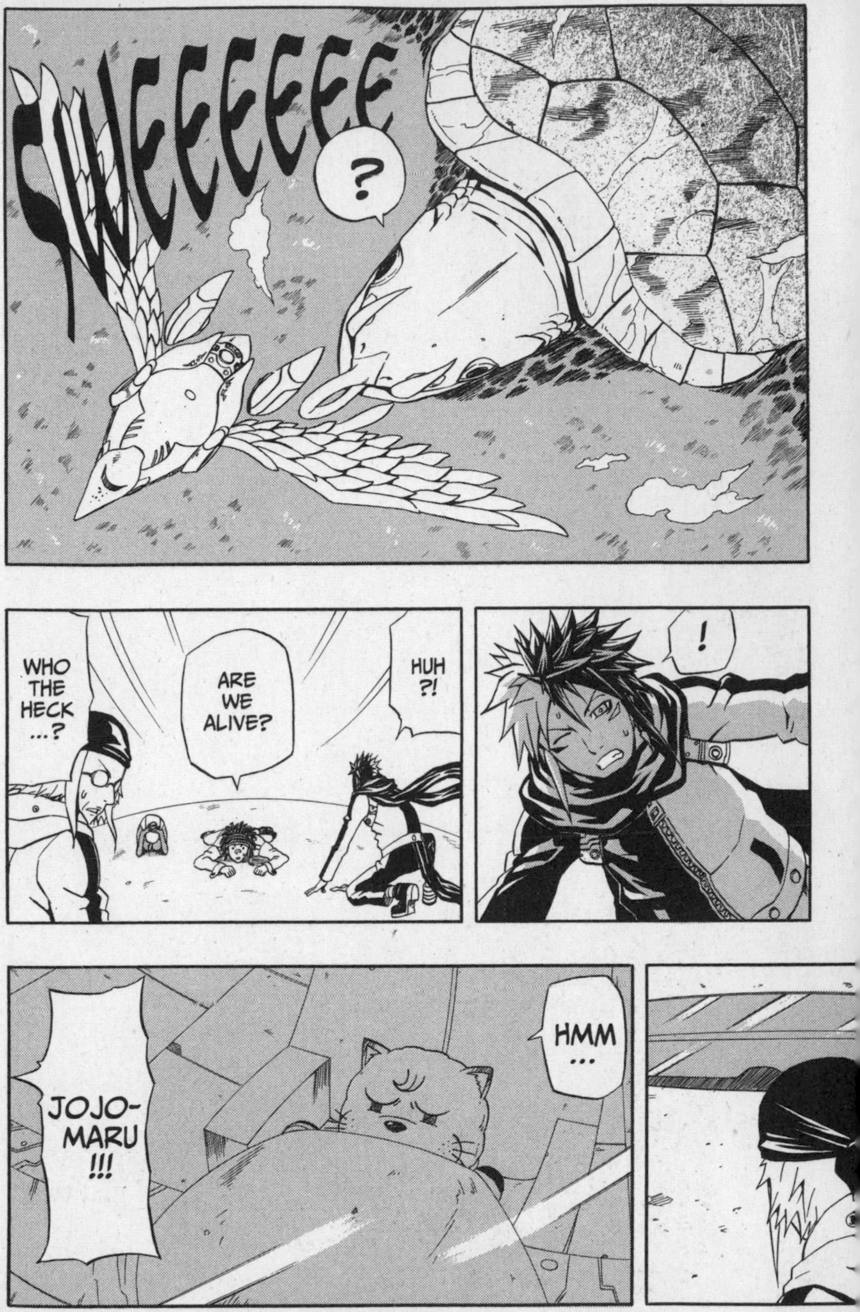
SWEEEEEE
?
!
HUH?!
ARE WE ALIVE?
WHO THE HECK...?
HMM...
JOJO-MARU!!!

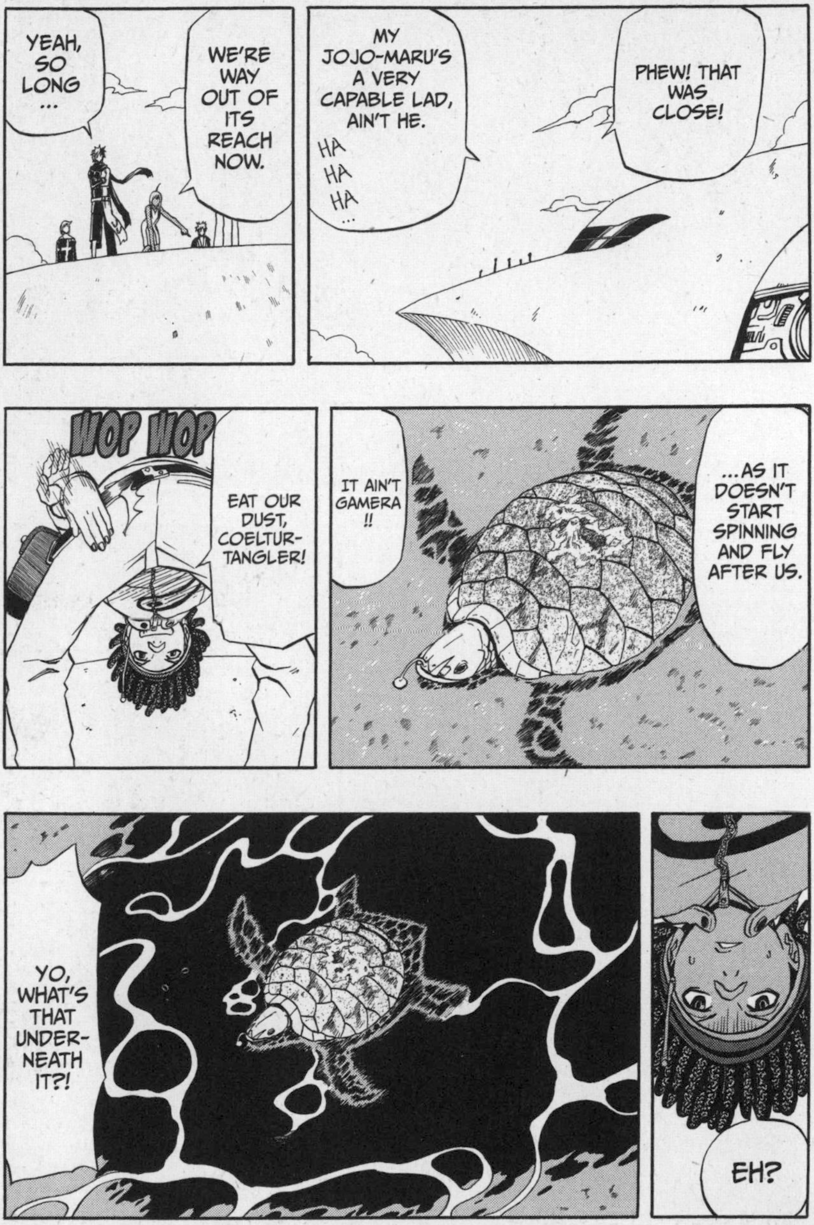
PHEW! THAT WAS CLOSE!
MY JOJO-MARU'S A VERY CAPABLE LAD, AIN'T HE.
HA HA HA ...
WE'RE WAY OUT OF ITS REACH NOW.
YEAH, SO LONG ...
...AS IT DOESN'T START SPINNING AND FLY AFTER US.
IT AIN'T GAMERA !!
WOP WOP
EAT OUR DUST, COELTUR-TANGLER!
EH?
YO, WHAT'S THAT UNDER-NEATH IT?!

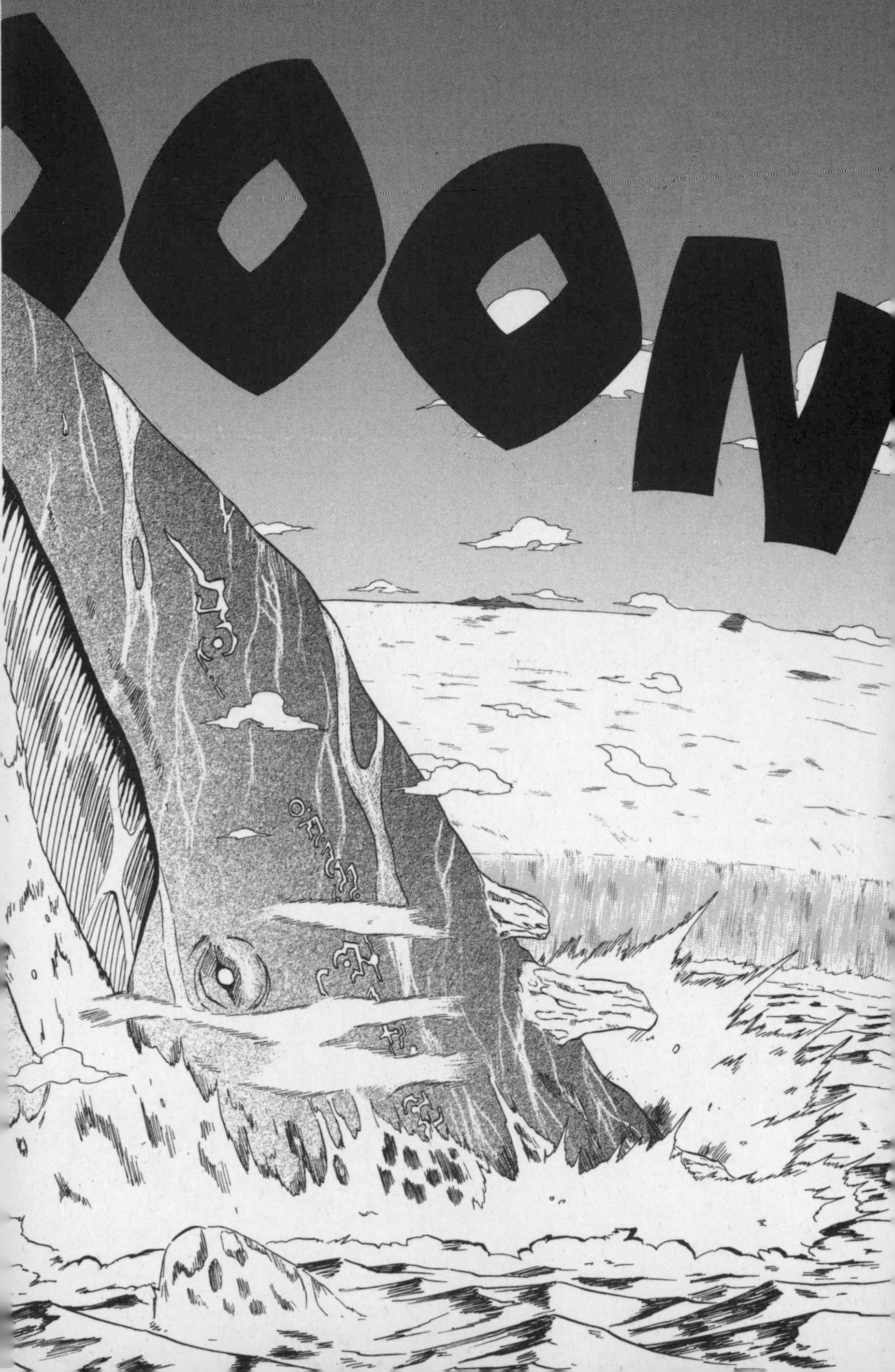
OON

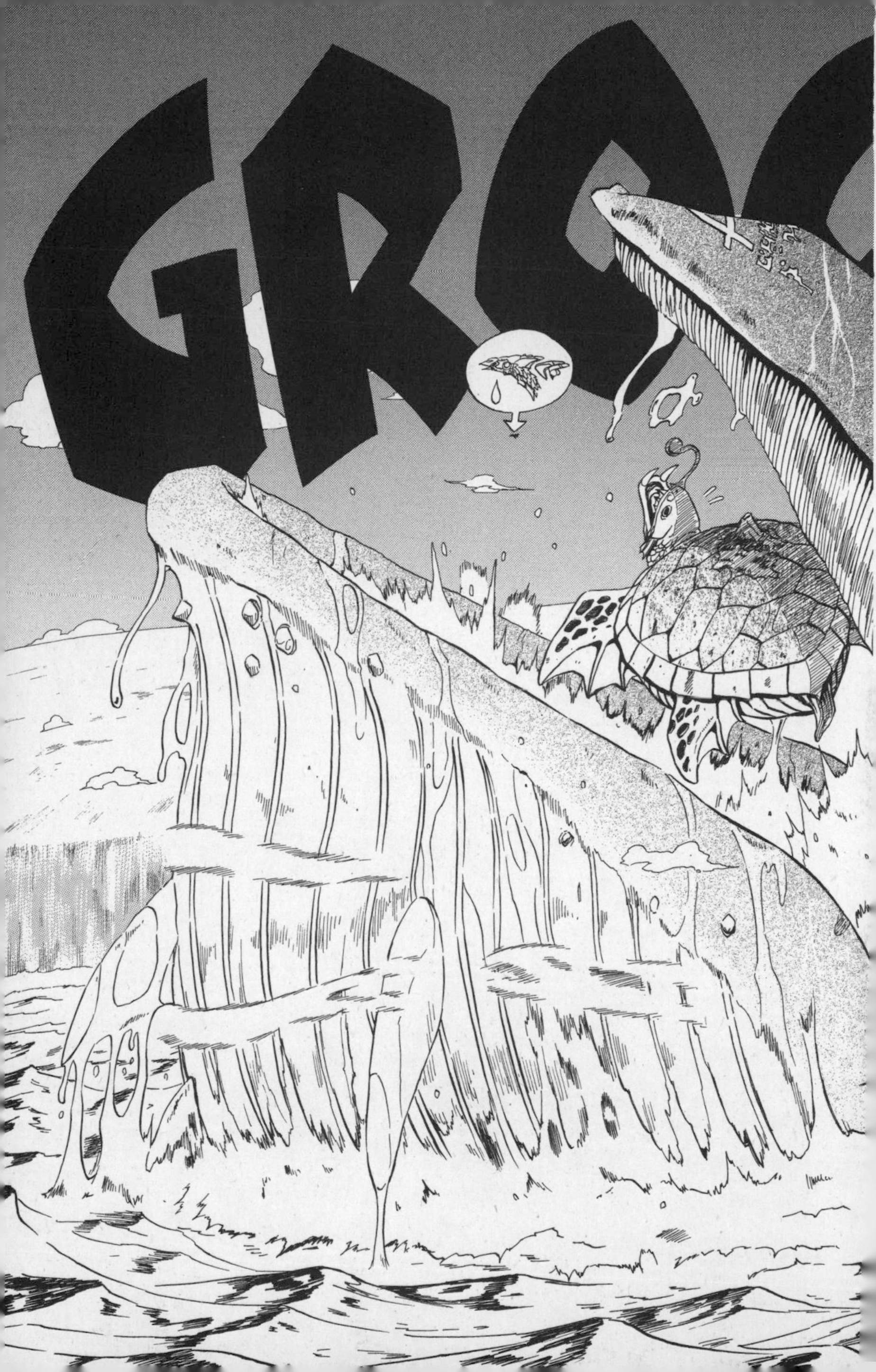
GRO

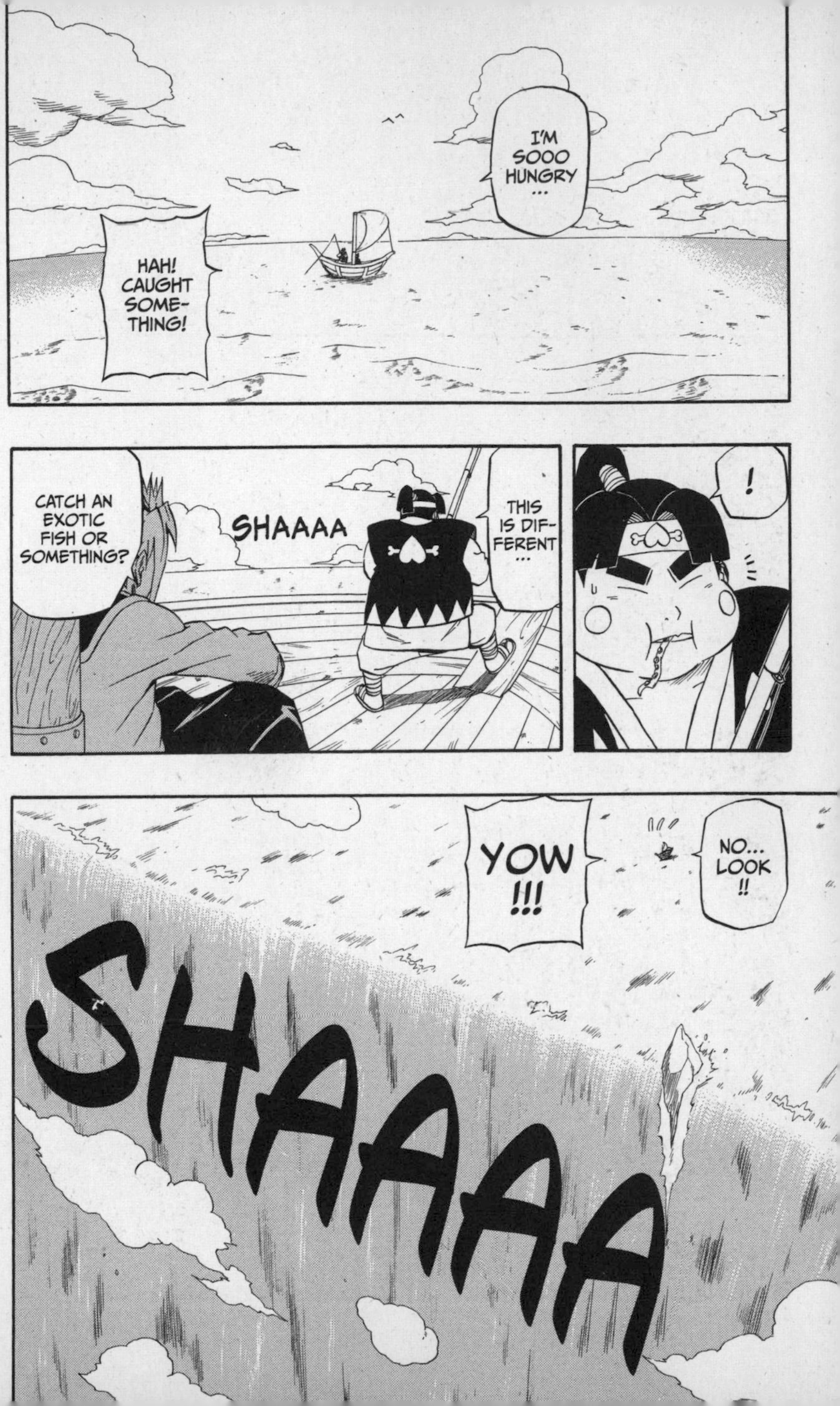

I'M SOOO HUNGRY...
HAH! CAUGHT SOME-THING!
!
THIS IS DIF-FERENT...
CATCH AN EXOTIC FISH OR SOMETHING?
SHAAAA
NO... LOOK!!
YOW!!!
SHAAAAA

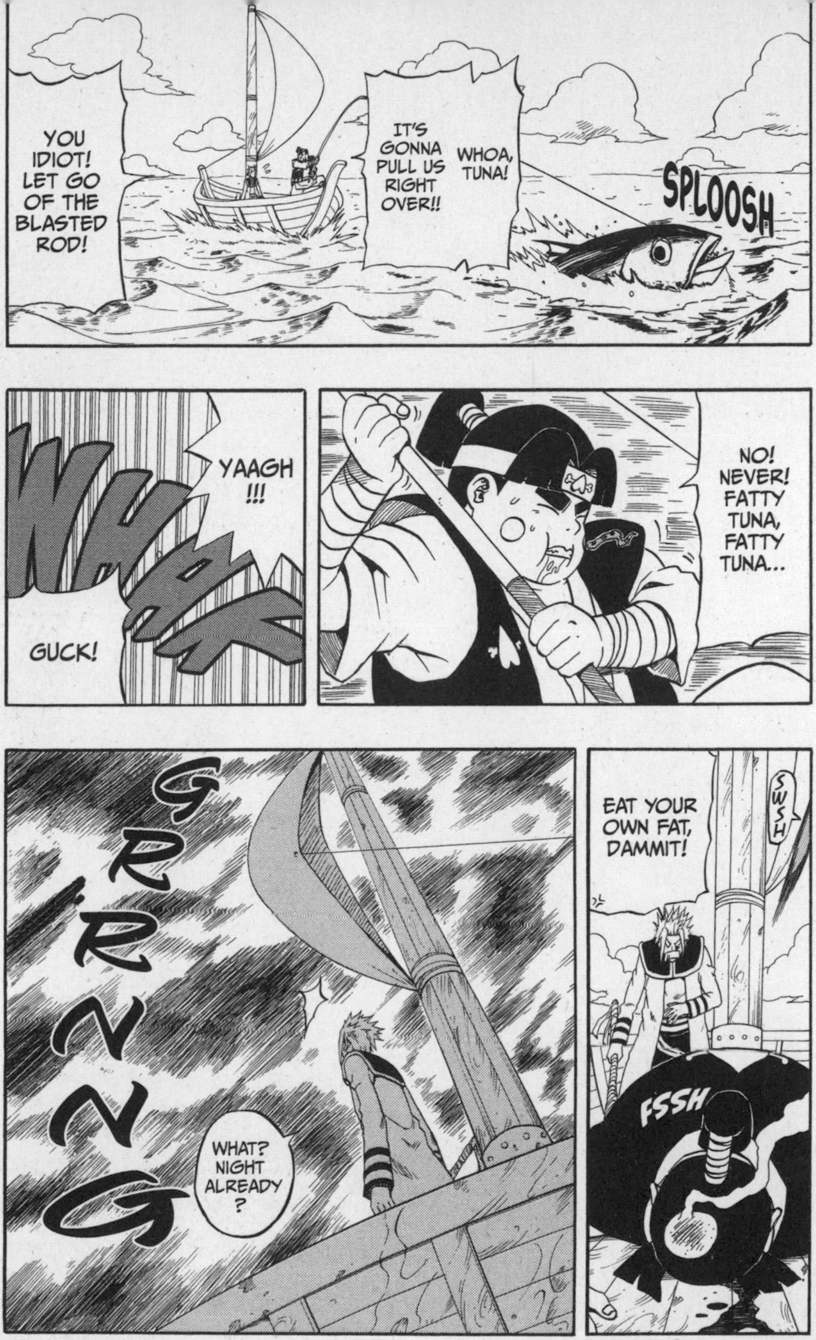
SPLOOSH
WHOA, TUNA!
IT'S GONNA PULL US RIGHT OVER!!
YOU IDIOT! LET GO OF THE BLASTED ROD!
NO! NEVER! FATTY TUNA, FATTY TUNA...
YAAGH!!!
WHAK
GUCK!
SWSH
EAT YOUR OWN FAT, DAMMIT!
FSSH
GRRNNG
WHAT? NIGHT ALREADY?

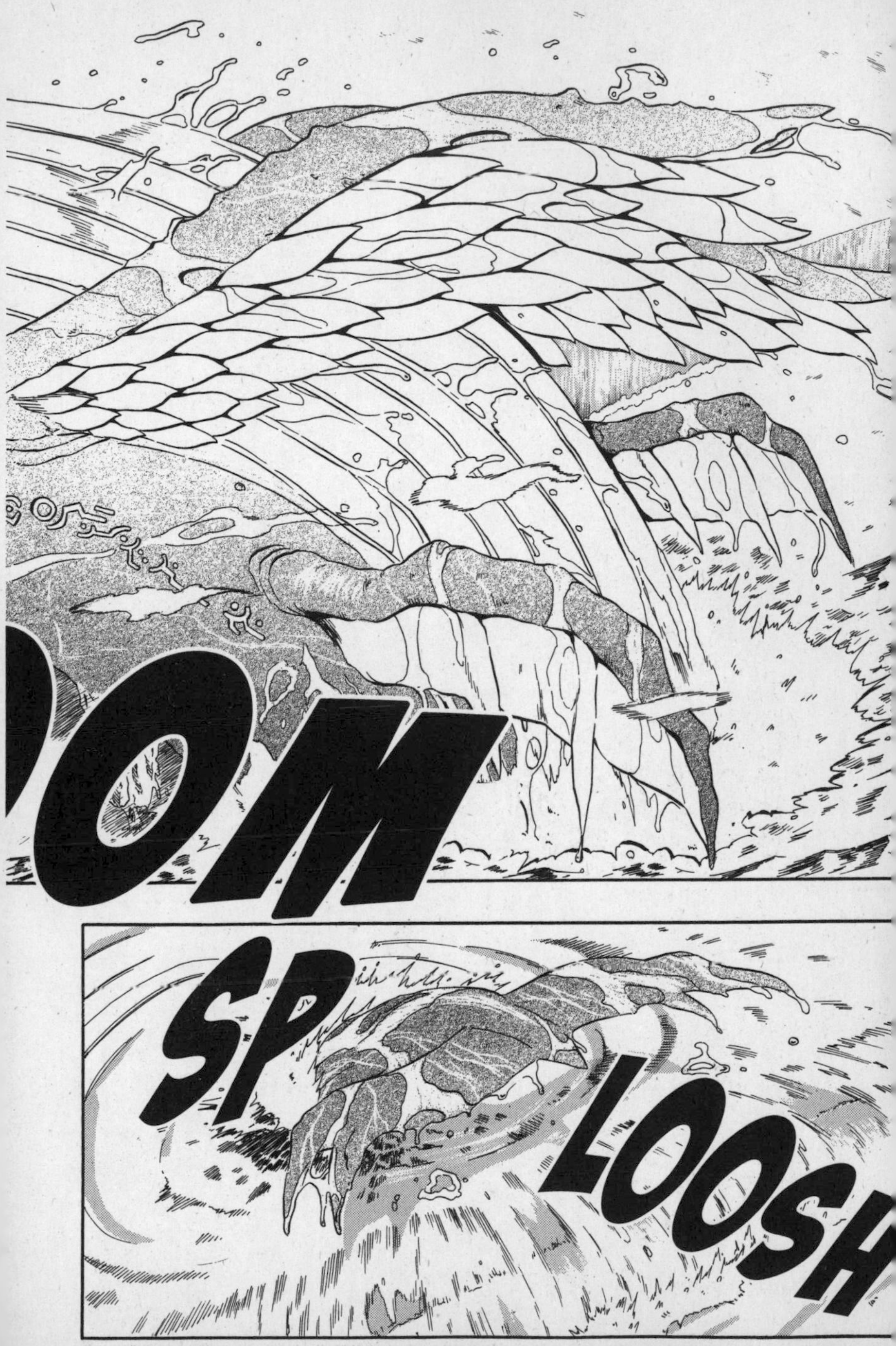
OM
SPLOOSH

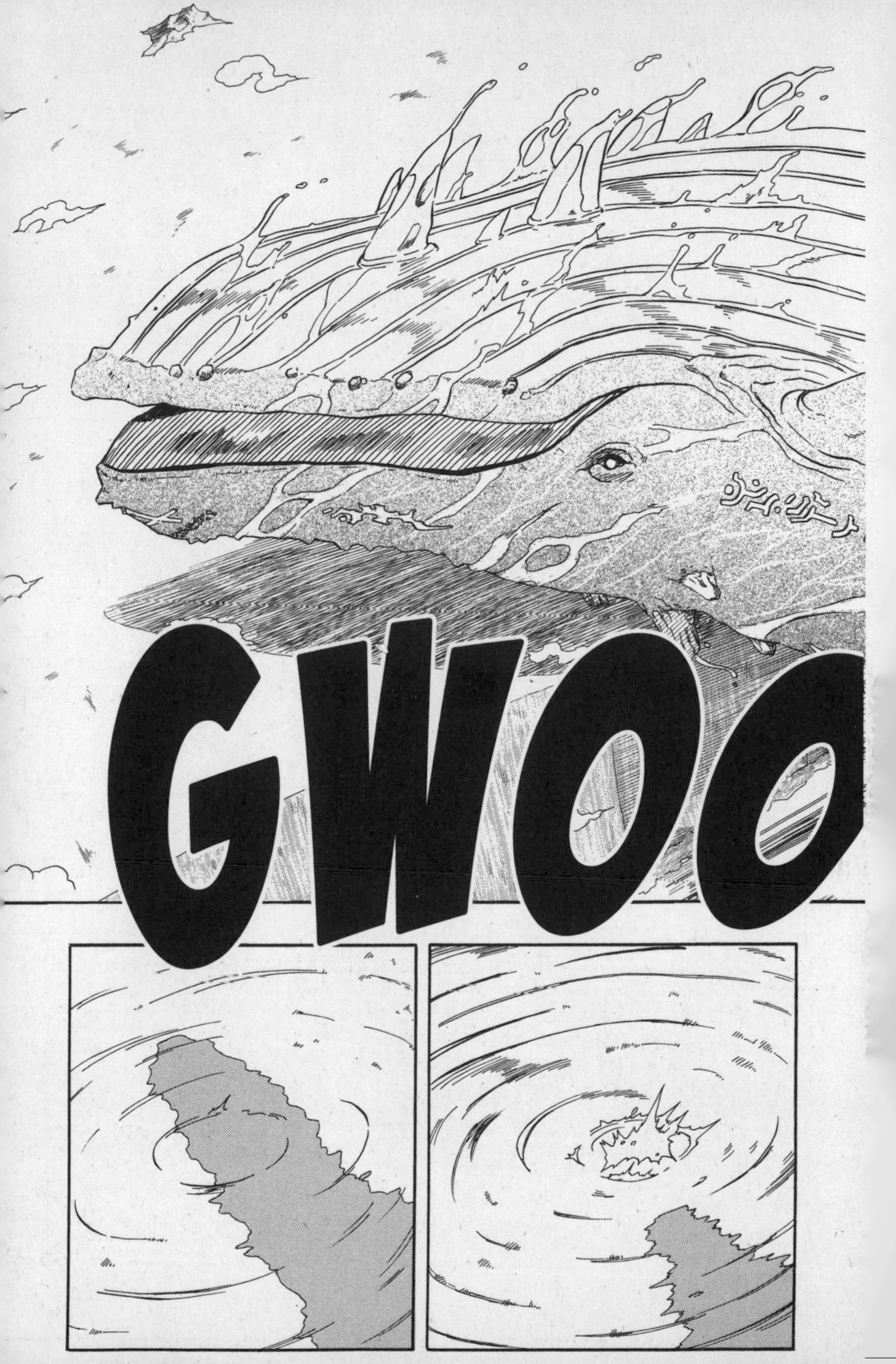
GWOO

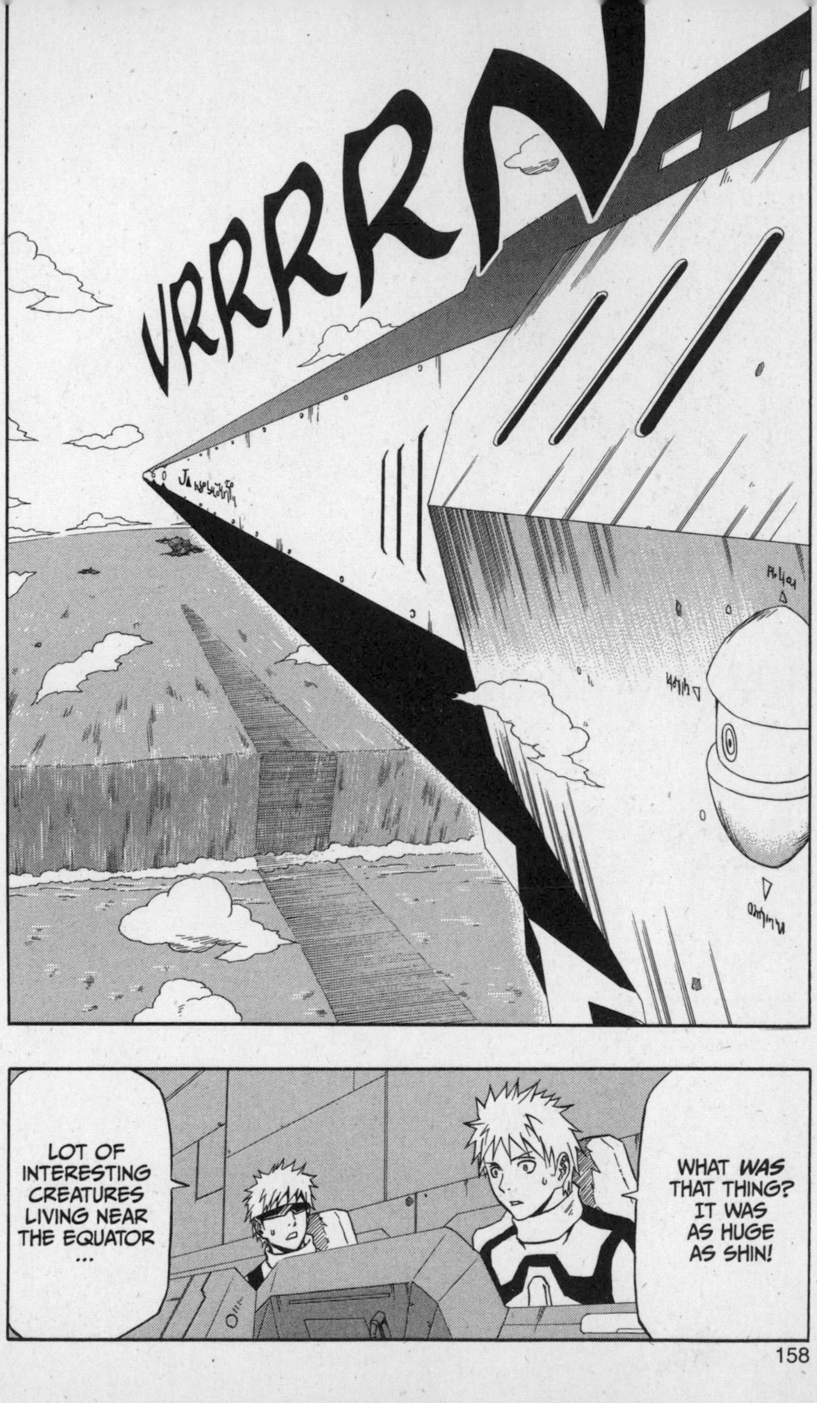
VRRRRN
WHAT WAS THAT THING? IT WAS AS HUGE AS SHIN!
LOT OF INTERESTING CREATURES LIVING NEAR THE EQUATOR ...

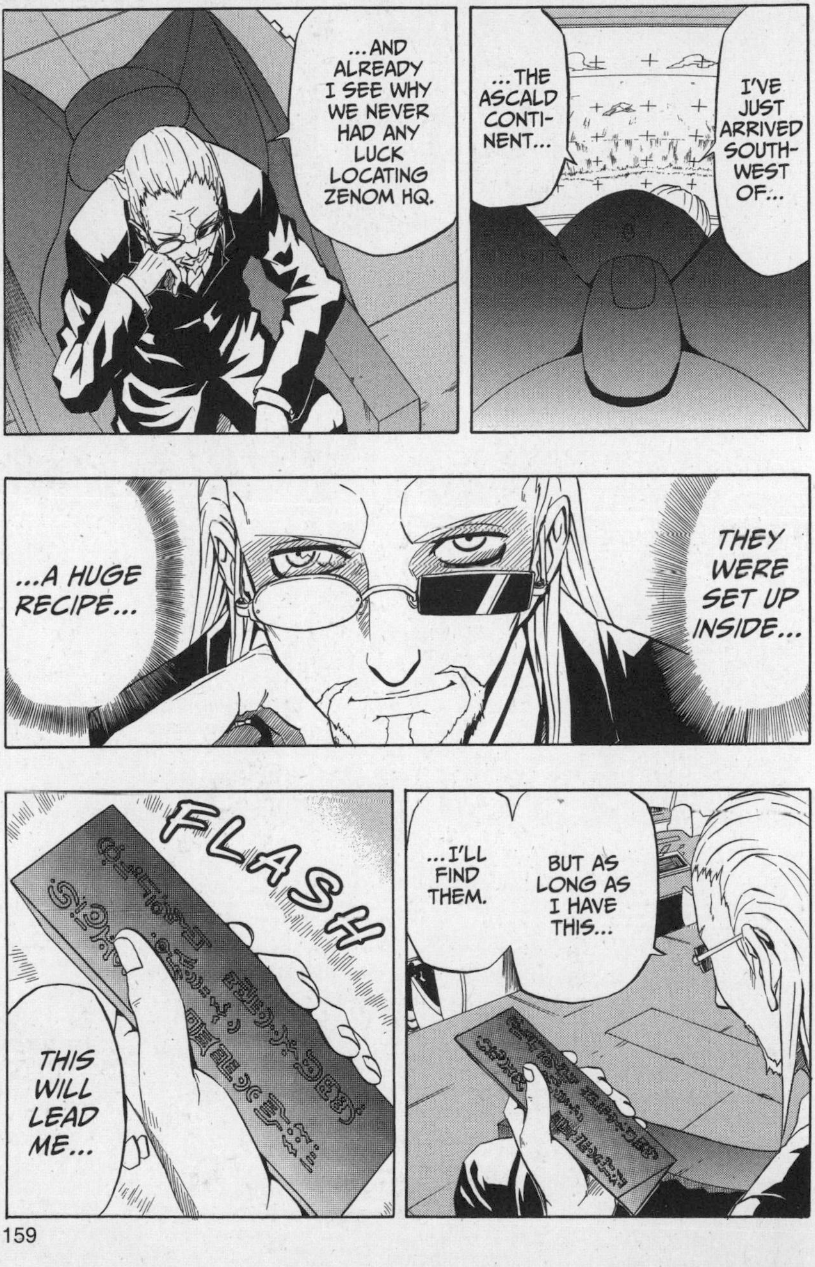
I'VE JUST ARRIVED SOUTH-WEST OF...
...THE ASCALD CONTI-NENT...
...AND ALREADY I SEE WHY WE NEVER HAD ANY LUCK LOCATING ZENOM HQ.
THEY WERE SET UP INSIDE...
...A HUGE RECIPE...
BUT AS LONG AS I HAVE THIS...
...I'LL FIND THEM.
FLASH
THIS WILL LEAD ME...

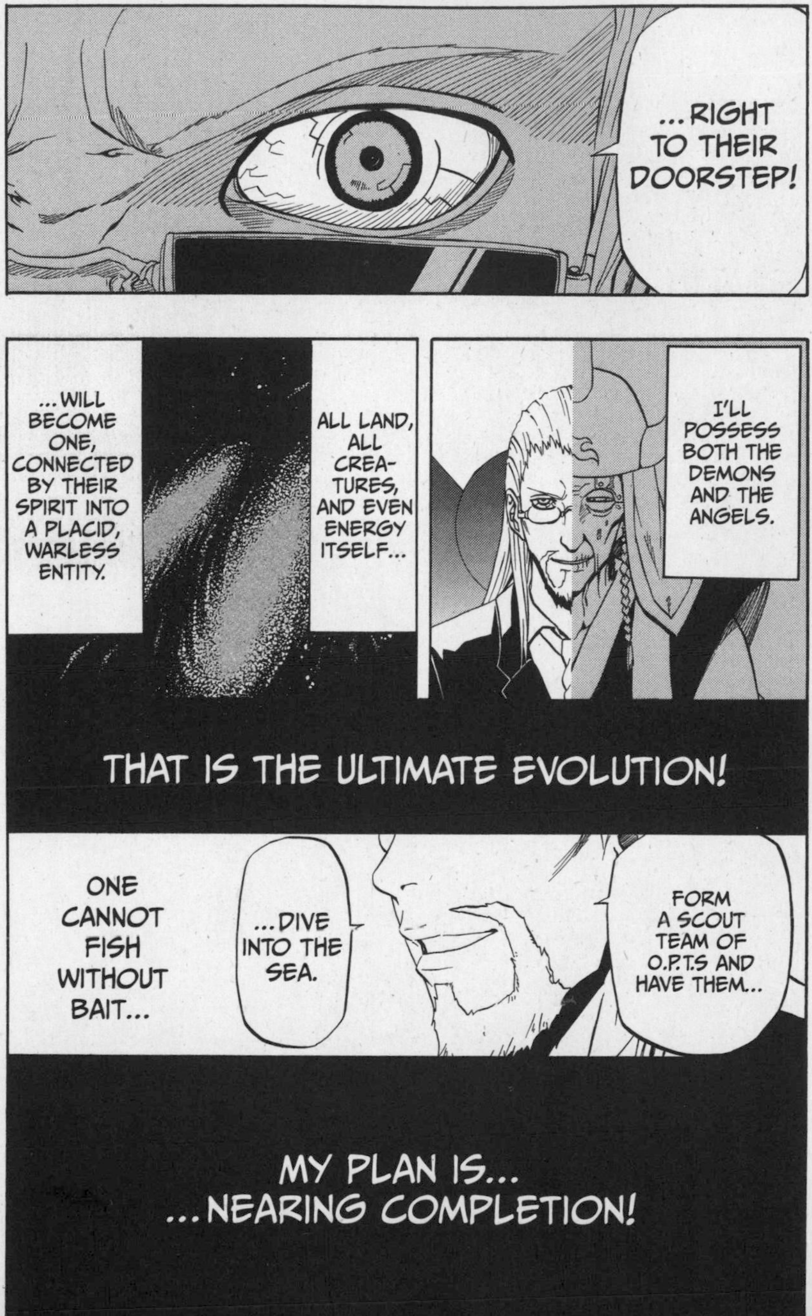
...RIGHT TO THEIR DOORSTEP!
I'LL POSSESS BOTH THE DEMONS AND THE ANGELS.
ALL LAND, ALL CREA-TURES, AND EVEN ENERGY ITSELF...
...WILL BECOME ONE, CONNECTED BY THEIR SPIRIT INTO A PLACID, WARLESS ENTITY.
THAT IS THE ULTIMATE EVOLUTION!
FORM A SCOUT TEAM OF O.P.T.S AND HAVE THEM...
...DIVE INTO THE SEA.
ONE CANNOT FISH WITHOUT BAIT...
MY PLAN IS...
...NEARING COMPLETION!

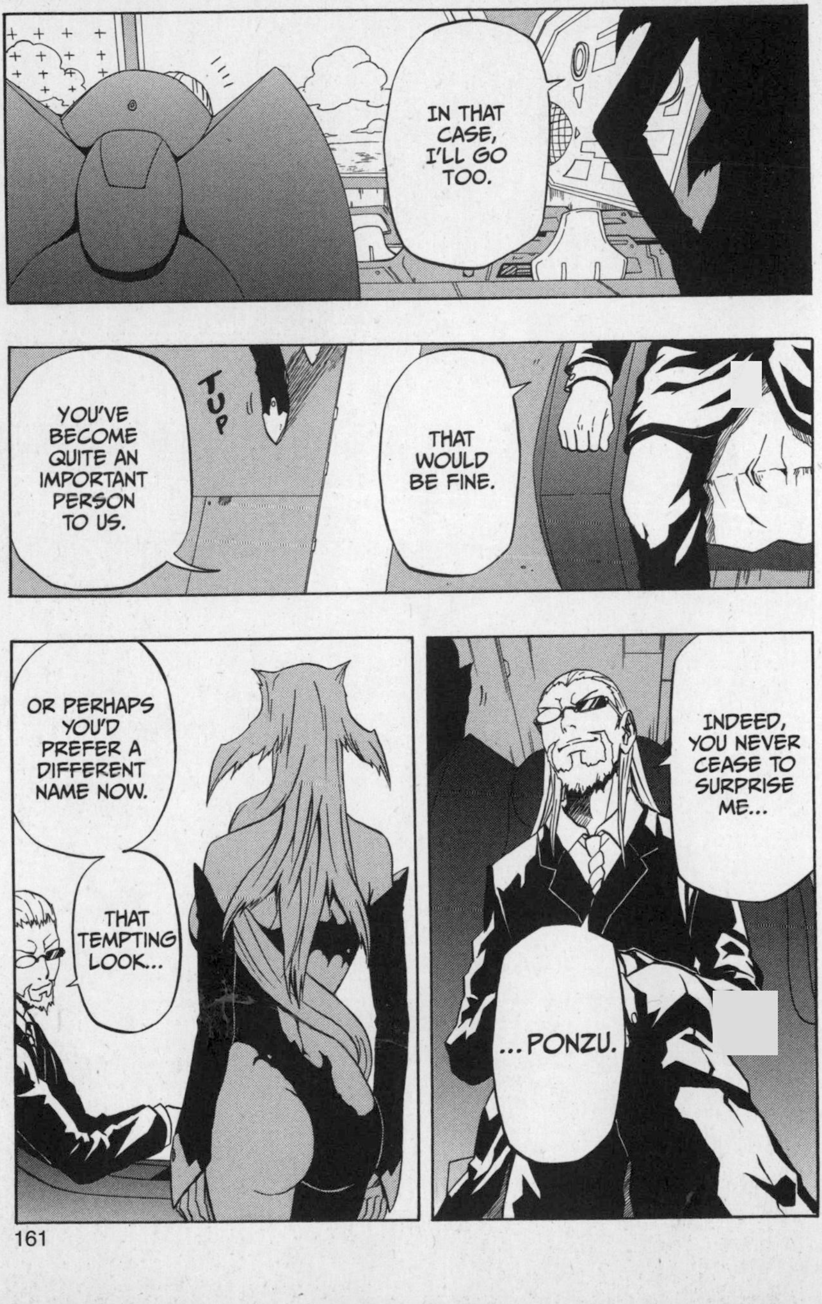
IN THAT CASE, I'LL GO TOO.
THAT WOULD BE FINE.
TUP
YOU'VE BECOME QUITE AN IMPORTANT PERSON TO US.
INDEED, YOU NEVER CEASE TO SURPRISE ME...
...PONZU.
OR PERHAPS YOU'D PREFER A DIFFERENT NAME NOW.
THAT TEMPTING LOOK...

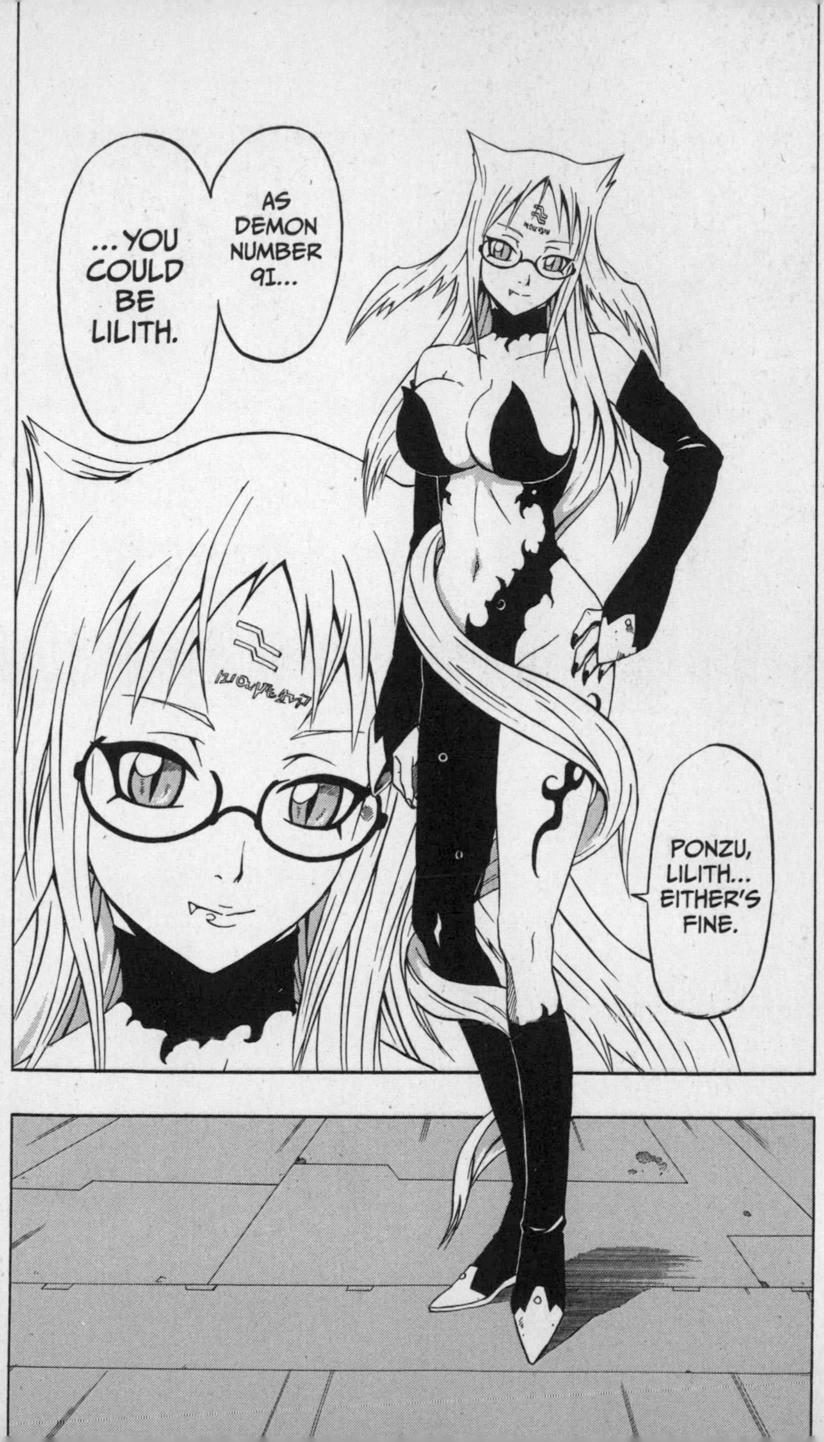
AS DEMON NUMBER 91...
...YOU COULD BE LILITH.
PONZU, LILITH... EITHER'S FINE.

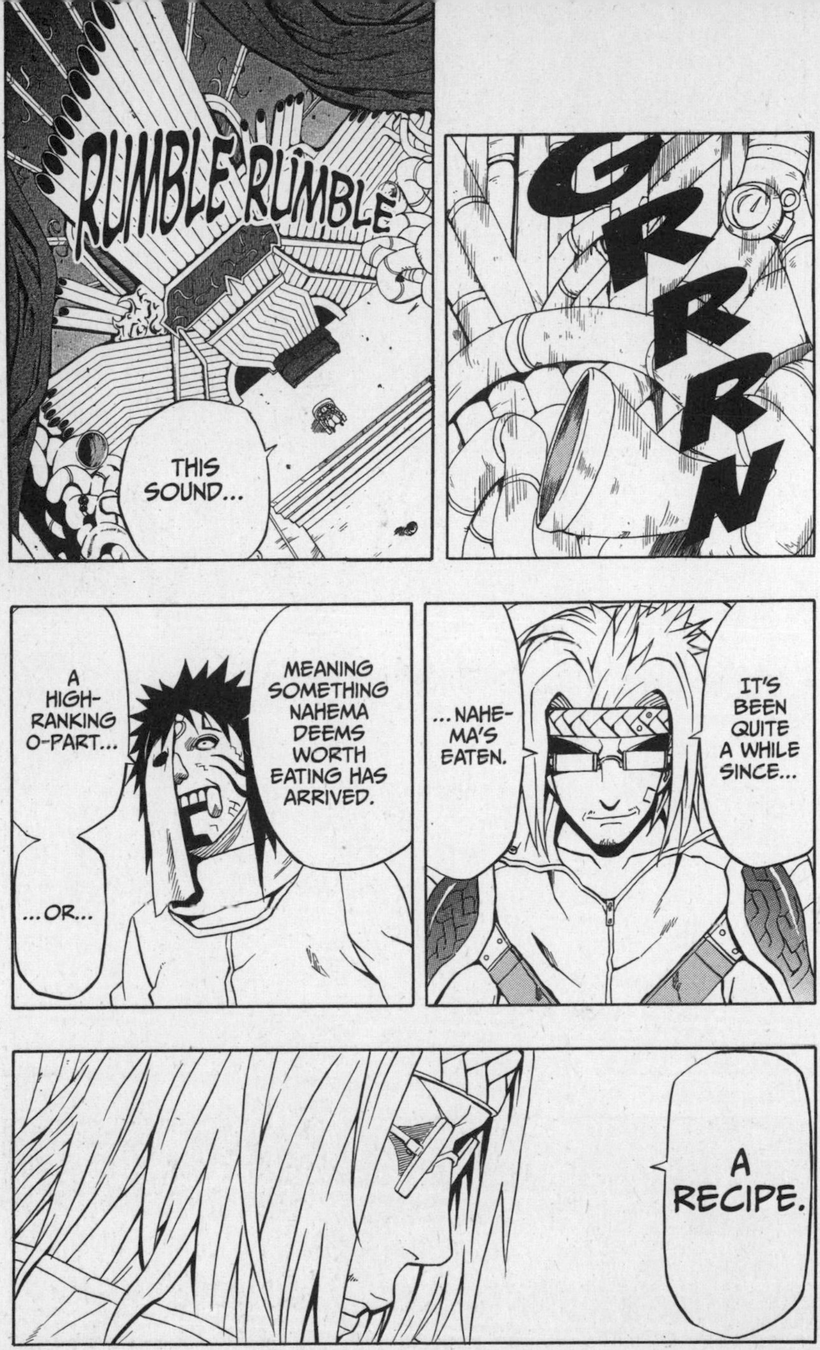
GRRRN
RUMBLE RUMBLE
THIS SOUND...
IT'S BEEN QUITE A WHILE SINCE...
...NAHEMA'S EATEN.
MEANING SOMETHING NAHEMA DEEMS WORTH EATING HAS ARRIVED.
A HIGH-RANKING O-PART...
...OR...
A RECIPE.

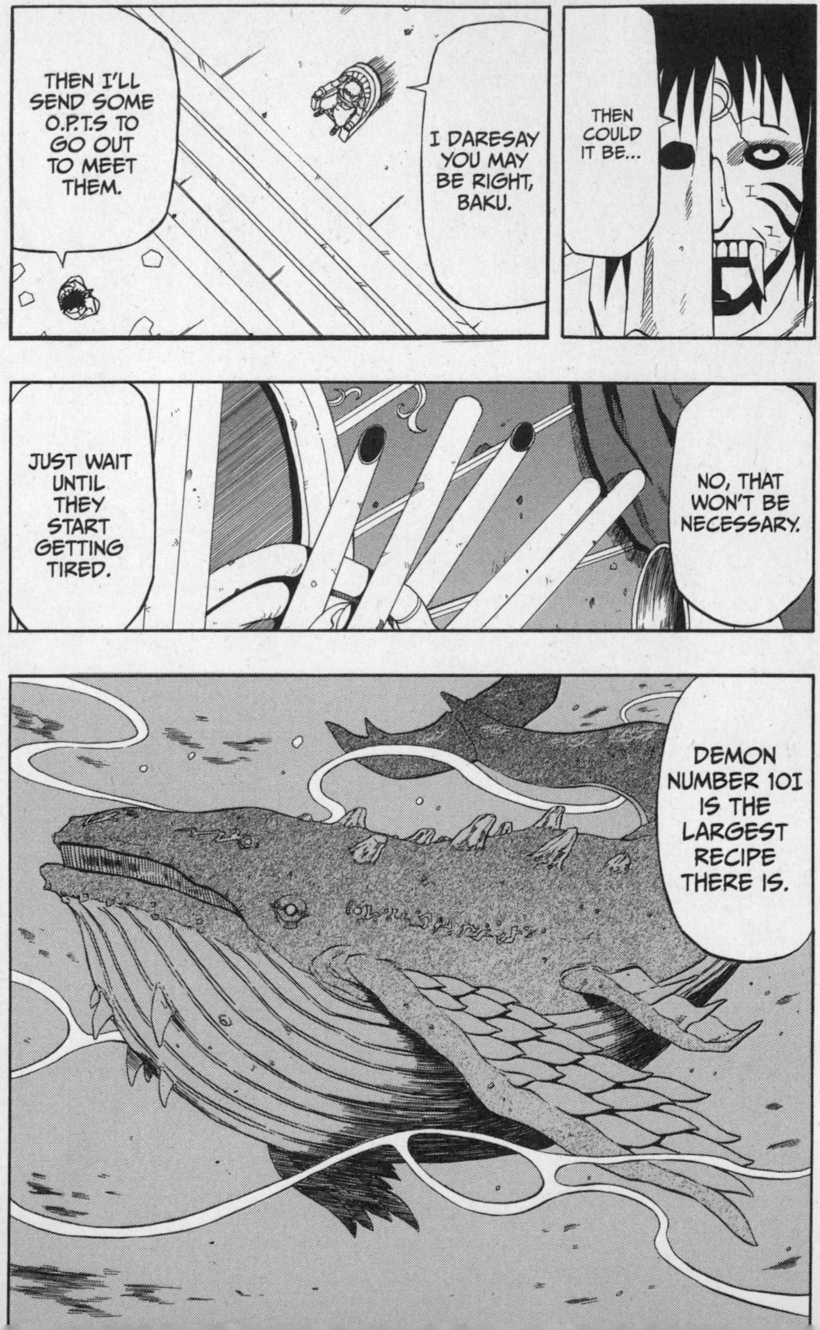
THEN COULD IT BE...
I DARESAY YOU MAY BE RIGHT, BAKU.
THEN I'LL SEND SOME O.P.T.S TO GO OUT TO MEET THEM.
NO, THAT WON'T BE NECESSARY.
JUST WAIT UNTIL THEY START GETTING TIRED.
DEMON NUMBER 101 IS THE LARGEST RECIPE THERE IS.

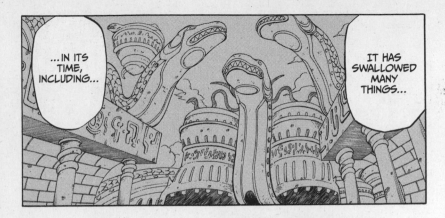

IT HAS SWALLOWED MANY THINGS...
...IN ITS TIME, INCLUDING...
...ALL SORTS OF DEVICES AND TRAPS...
FLASH
!
IF, AS I SUSPECT, MIKO HAS THE OTHER HALF OF THIS, THEN SHE HAS ARRIVED AS WELL.
GOT A STURDY FISHING ROD, MIKO? YOU'LL NEED IT!
FLASH

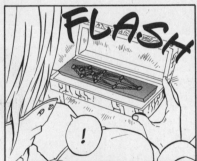

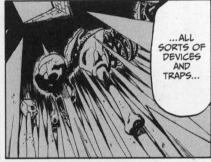

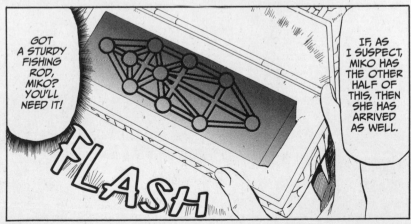

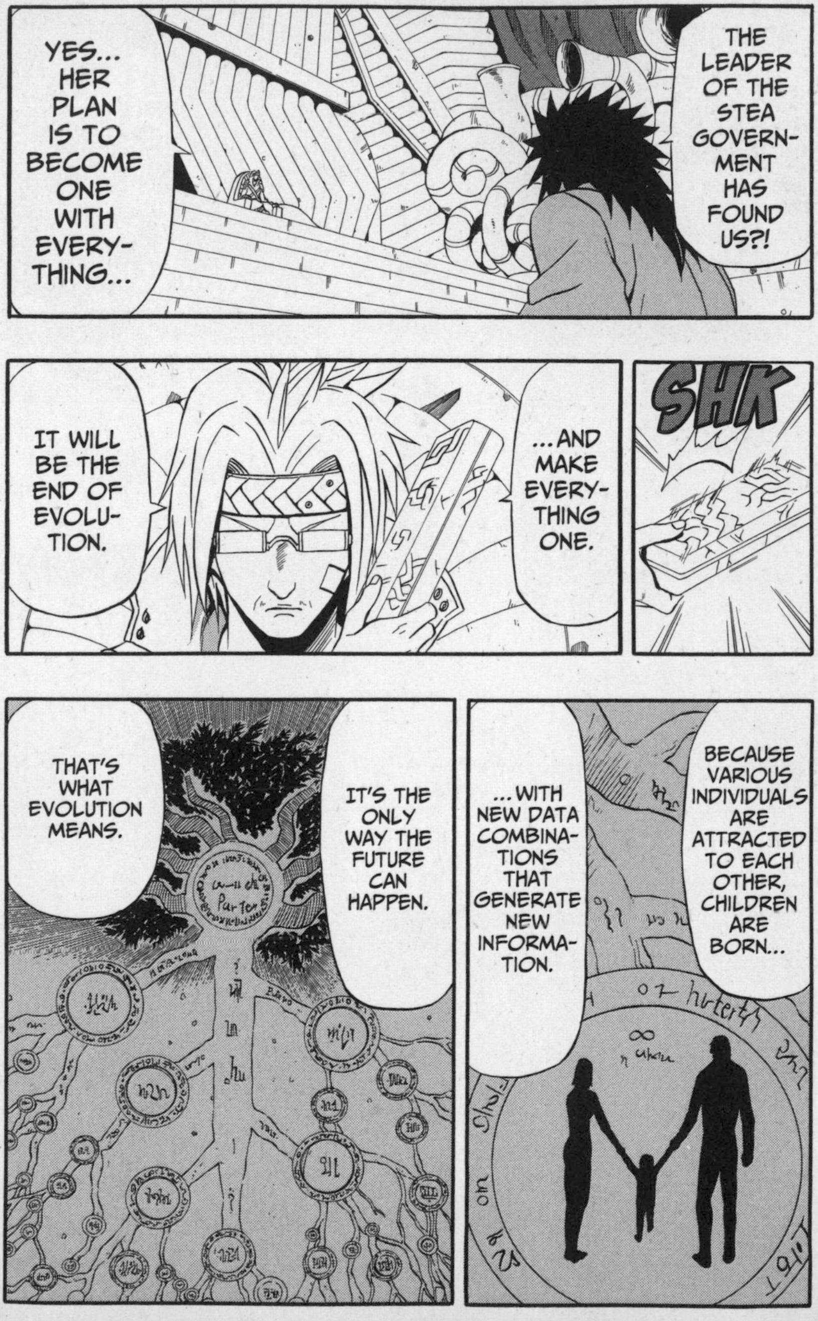
THE LEADER OF THE STEA GOVERN-MENT HAS FOUND US?!
YES... HER PLAN IS TO BECOME ONE WITH EVERY-THING...
SHK
...AND MAKE EVERY-THING ONE.
IT WILL BE THE END OF EVOLU-TION.
BECAUSE VARIOUS INDIVIDUALS ARE ATTRACTED TO EACH OTHER, CHILDREN ARE BORN...
...WITH NEW DATA COMBINA-TIONS THAT GENERATE NEW INFORMA-TION.
IT'S THE ONLY WAY THE FUTURE CAN HAPPEN.
THAT'S WHAT EVOLUTION MEANS.

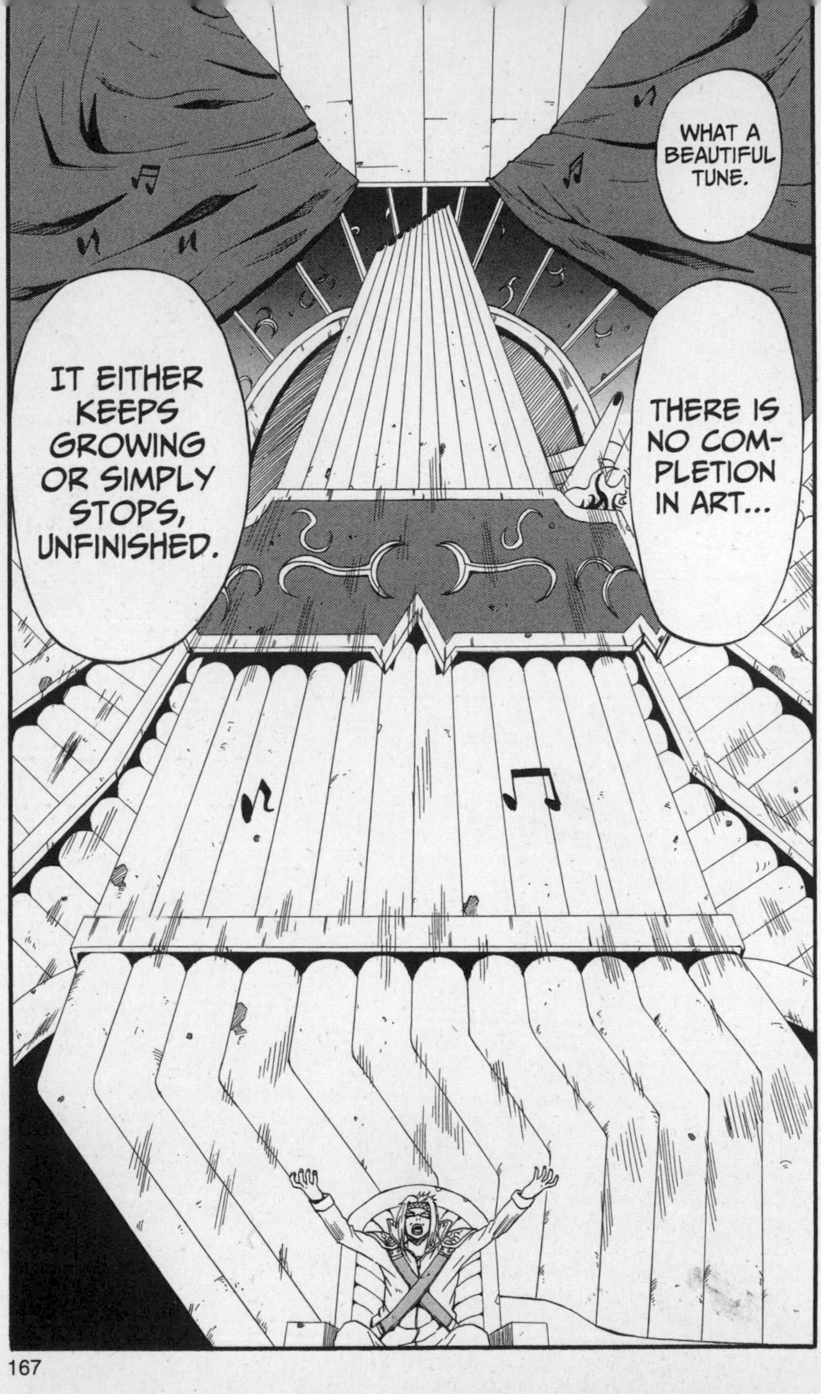
WHAT A BEAUTIFUL TUNE.
THERE IS NO COMPLETION IN ART...
IT EITHER KEEPS GROWING OR SIMPLY STOPS, UNFINISHED.

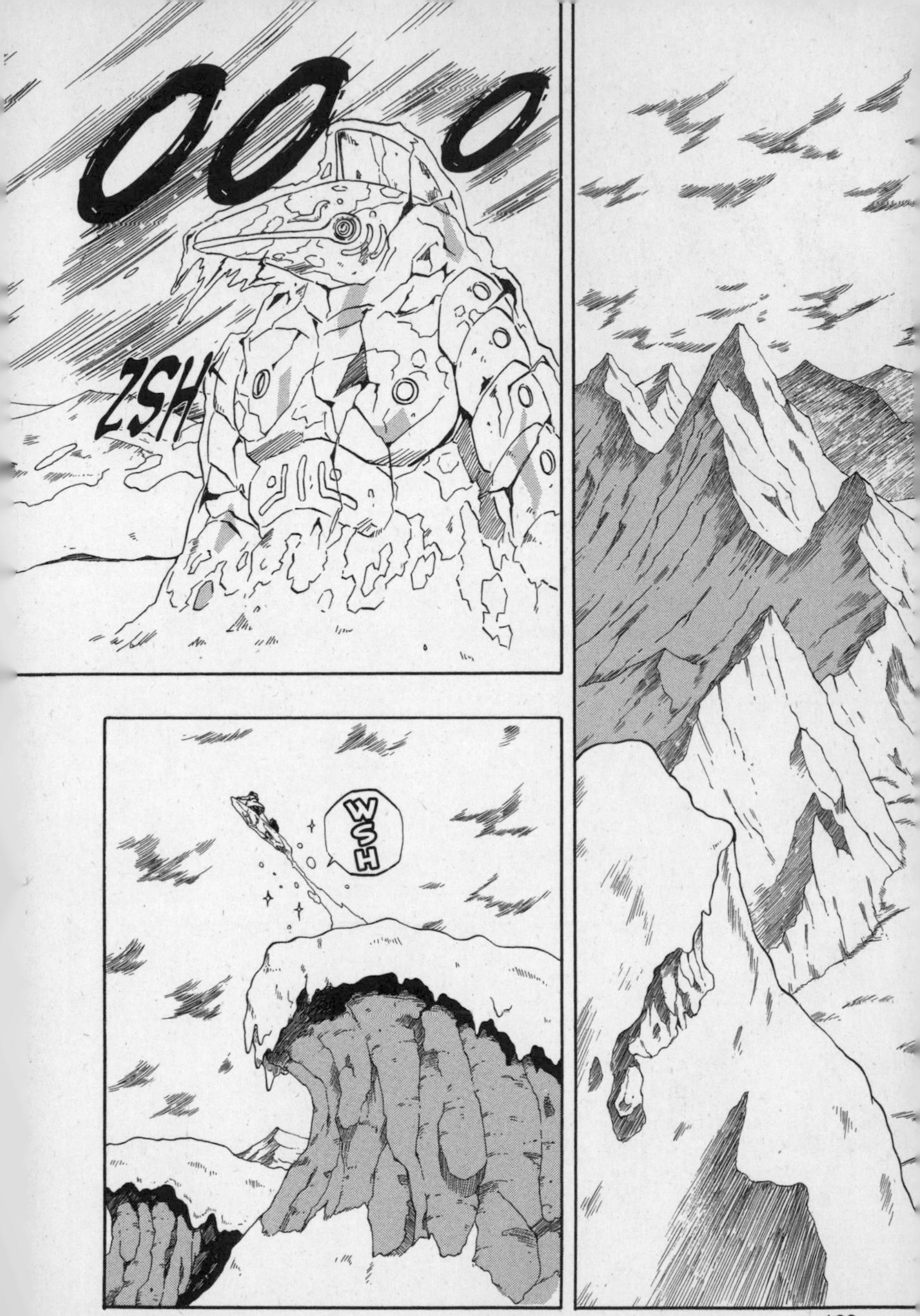
OOO
ZSH
WSH

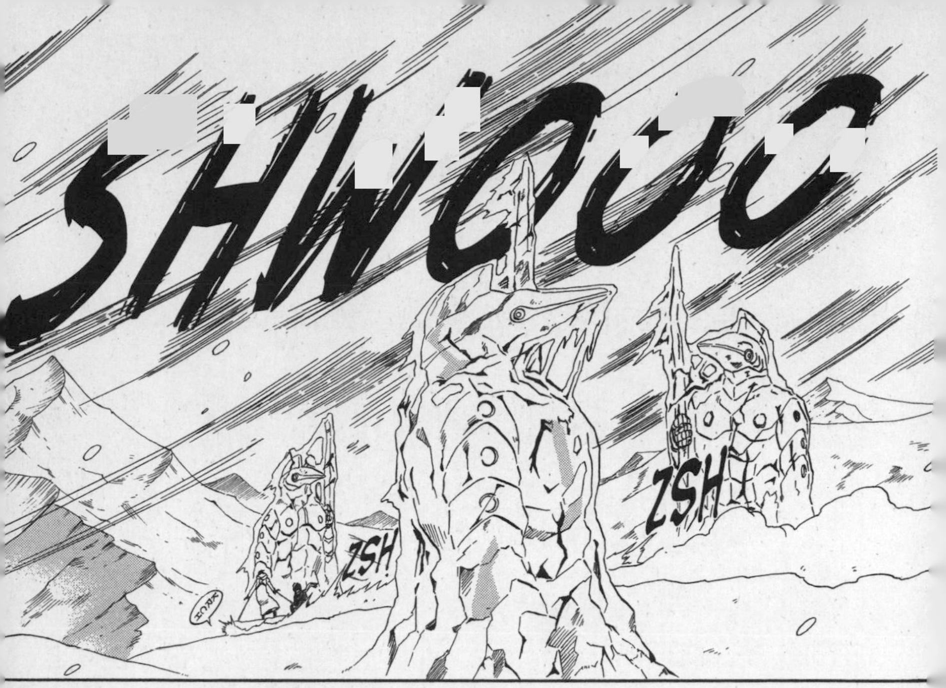
SHWOOO
ZSH
ZSH!
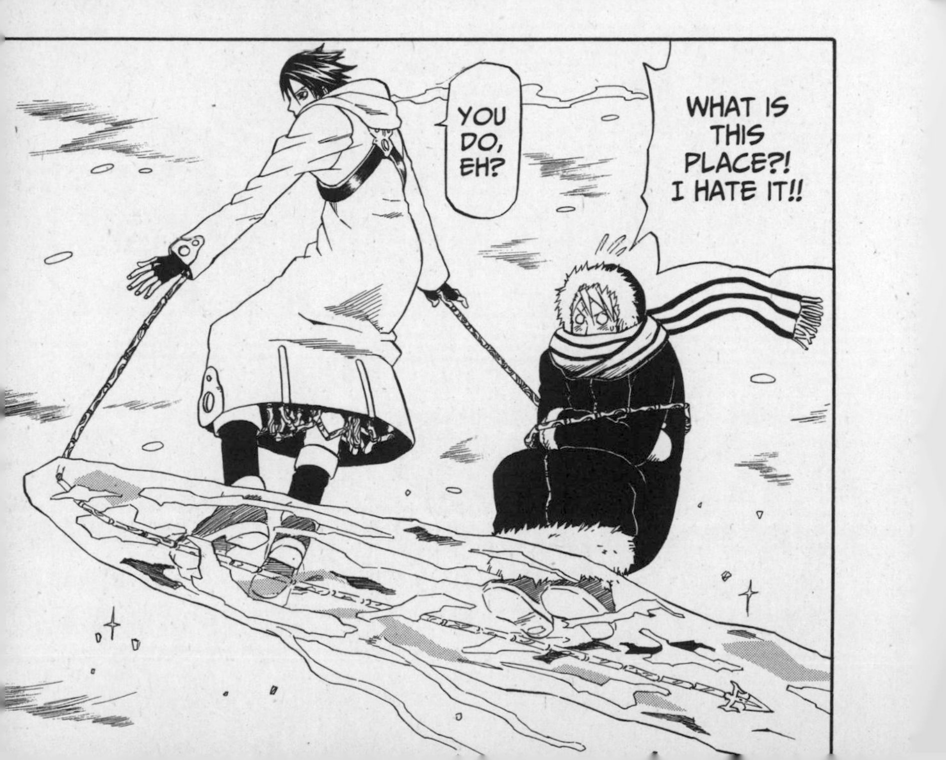
WHAT IS THIS PLACE?! I HATE IT!!
YOU DO, EH?

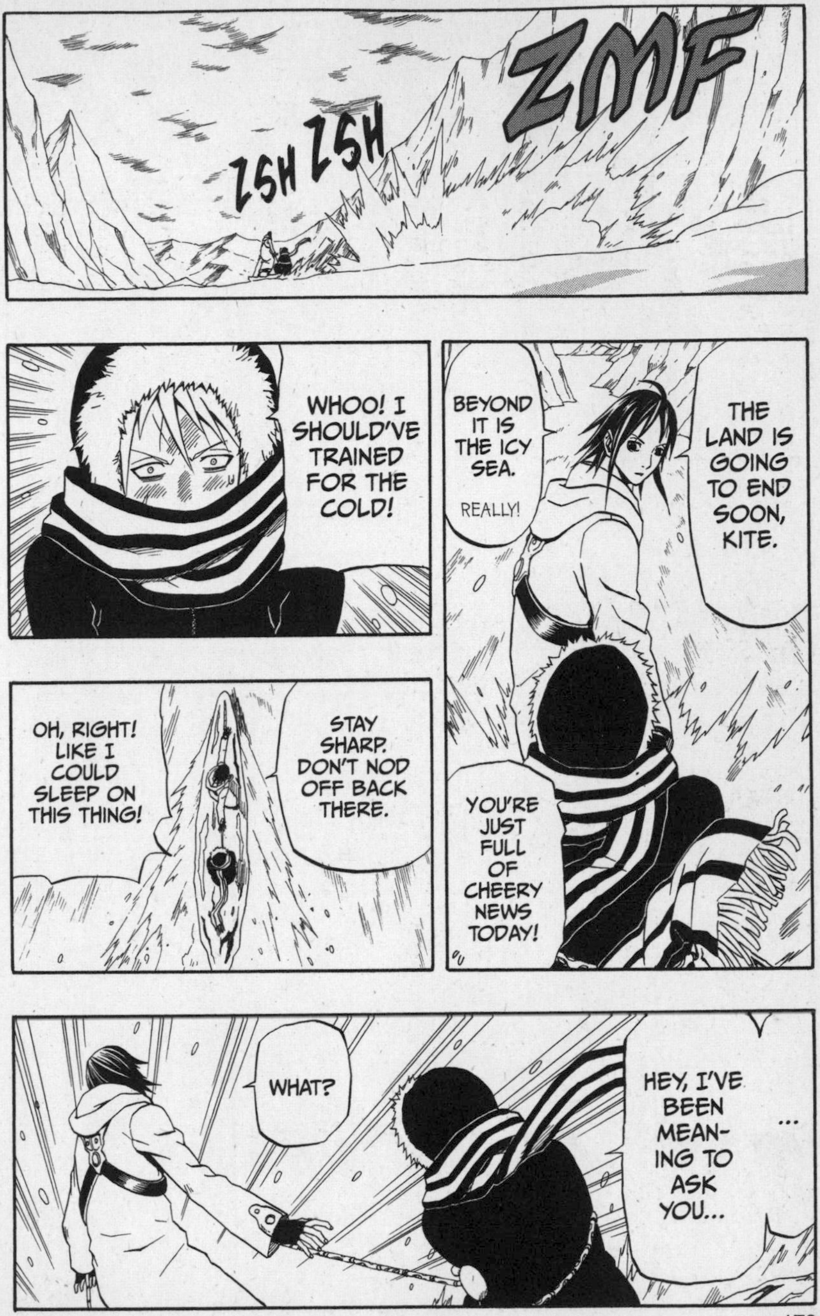
ZMF
ZSH ZSH
THE LAND IS GOING TO END SOON, KITE.
BEYOND IT IS THE ICY SEA.
REALLY!
YOU'RE JUST FULL OF CHEERY NEWS TODAY!
WHOO! I SHOULD'VE TRAINED FOR THE COLD!
STAY SHARP. DON'T NOD OFF BACK THERE.
OH, RIGHT! LIKE I COULD SLEEP ON THIS THING!
HEY, I'VE BEEN MEANING TO ASK YOU...
...
WHAT?

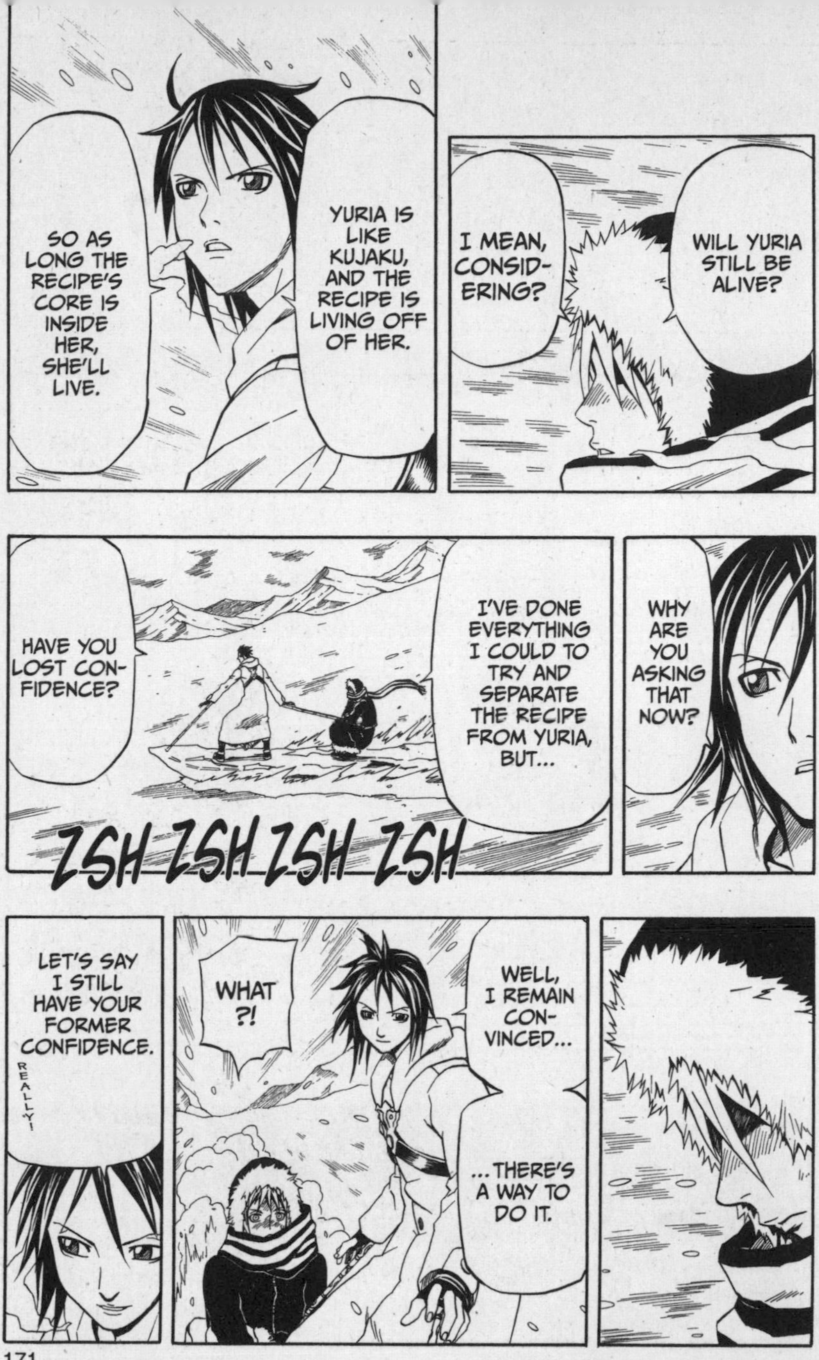

WILL YURIA STILL BE ALIVE?
I MEAN, CONSIDERING?
YURIA IS LIKE KUJAKU, AND THE RECIPE IS LIVING OFF OF HER.
SO AS LONG THE RECIPE'S CORE IS INSIDE HER, SHE'LL LIVE.
WHY ARE YOU ASKING THAT NOW?
I'VE DONE EVERYTHING I COULD TO TRY AND SEPARATE THE RECIPE FROM YURIA, BUT...
HAVE YOU LOST CONFIDENCE?
ZSH ZSH ZSH ZSH
WELL, I REMAIN CONVINCED...
...THERE'S A WAY TO DO IT.
WHAT?!
LET'S SAY I STILL HAVE YOUR FORMER CONFIDENCE.
REALLY!

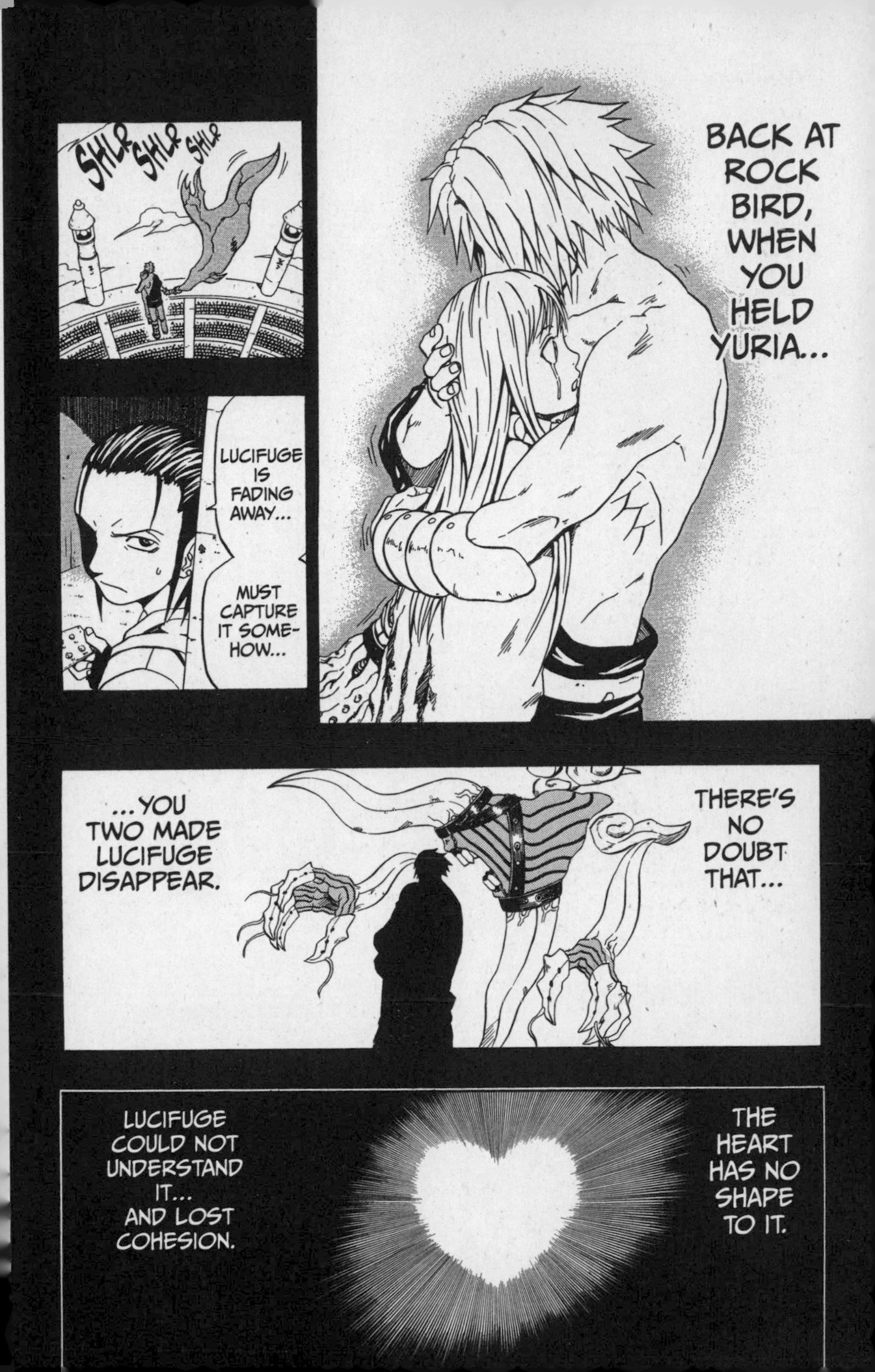
BACK AT ROCK BIRD, WHEN YOU HELD YURIA...
SHLR SHLR SHLR
LUCIFUGE IS FADING AWAY...
MUST CAPTURE IT SOME-HOW...
THERE'S NO DOUBT THAT...
...YOU TWO MADE LUCIFUGE DISAPPEAR.
THE HEART HAS NO SHAPE TO IT.
LUCIFUGE COULD NOT UNDERSTAND IT...
AND LOST COHESION.

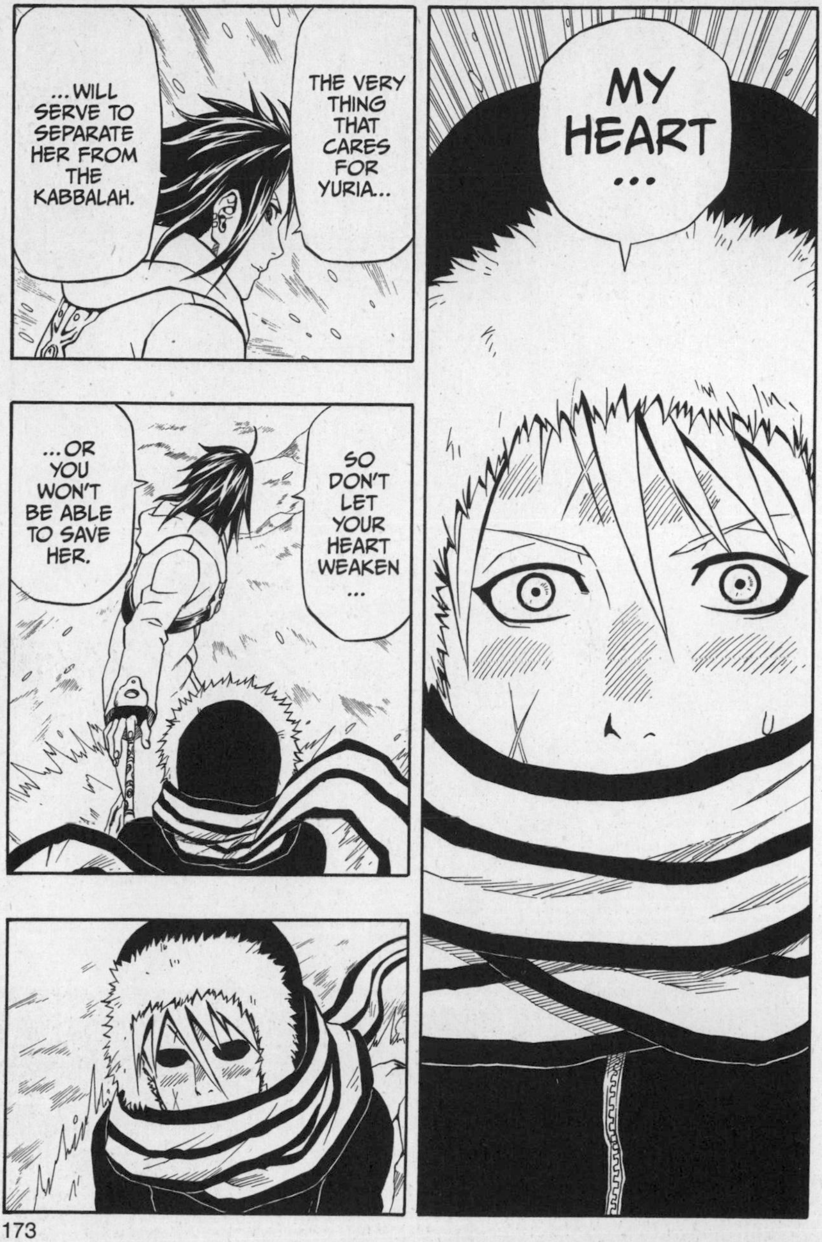
MY HEART ...
THE VERY THING THAT CARES FOR YURIA...
...WILL SERVE TO SEPARATE HER FROM THE KABBALAH.
SO DON'T LET YOUR HEART WEAKEN ...
...OR YOU WON'T BE ABLE TO SAVE HER.

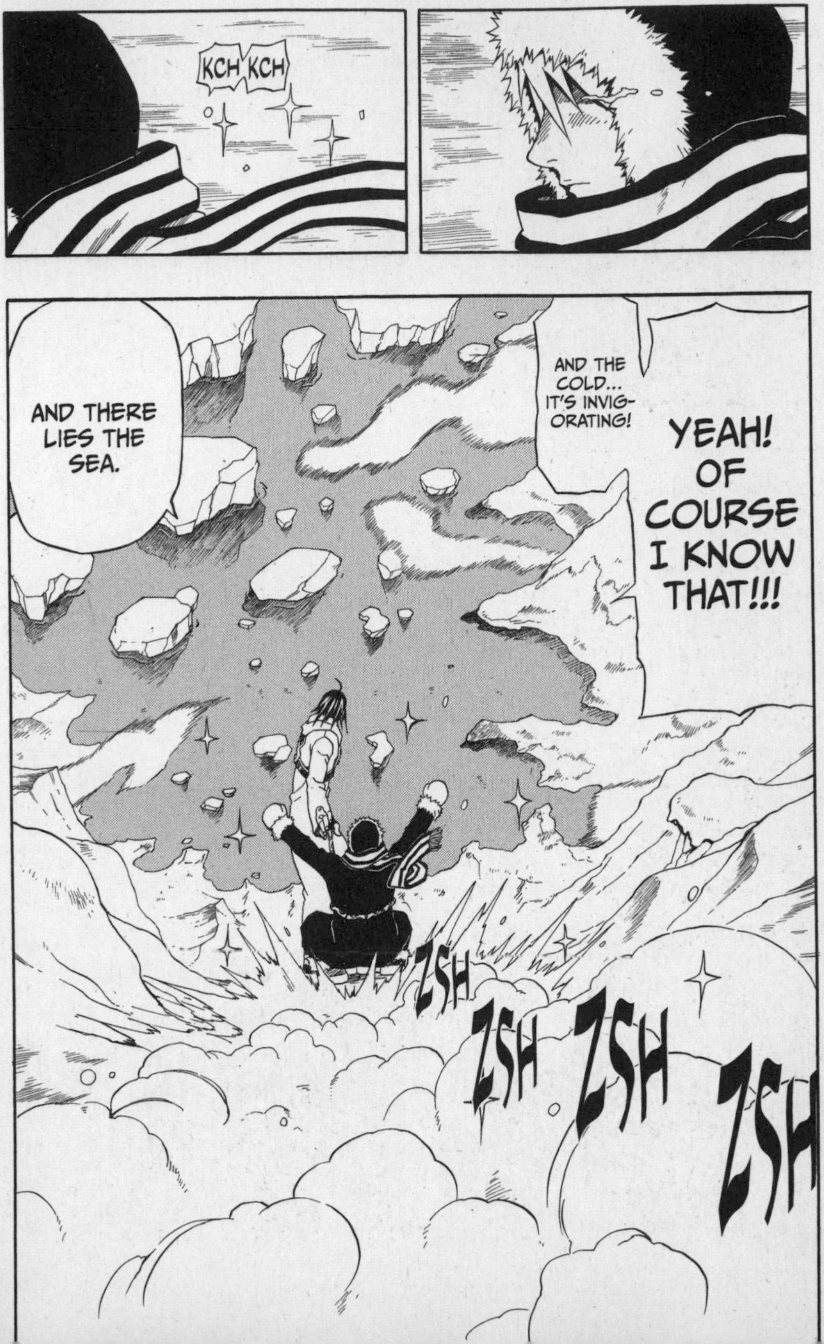
KCH KCH
AND THE COLD... IT'S INVIG-ORATING!
AND THERE LIES THE SEA.
YEAH! OF COURSE I KNOW THAT!!!
ZSH
ZSH ZSH
ZSH

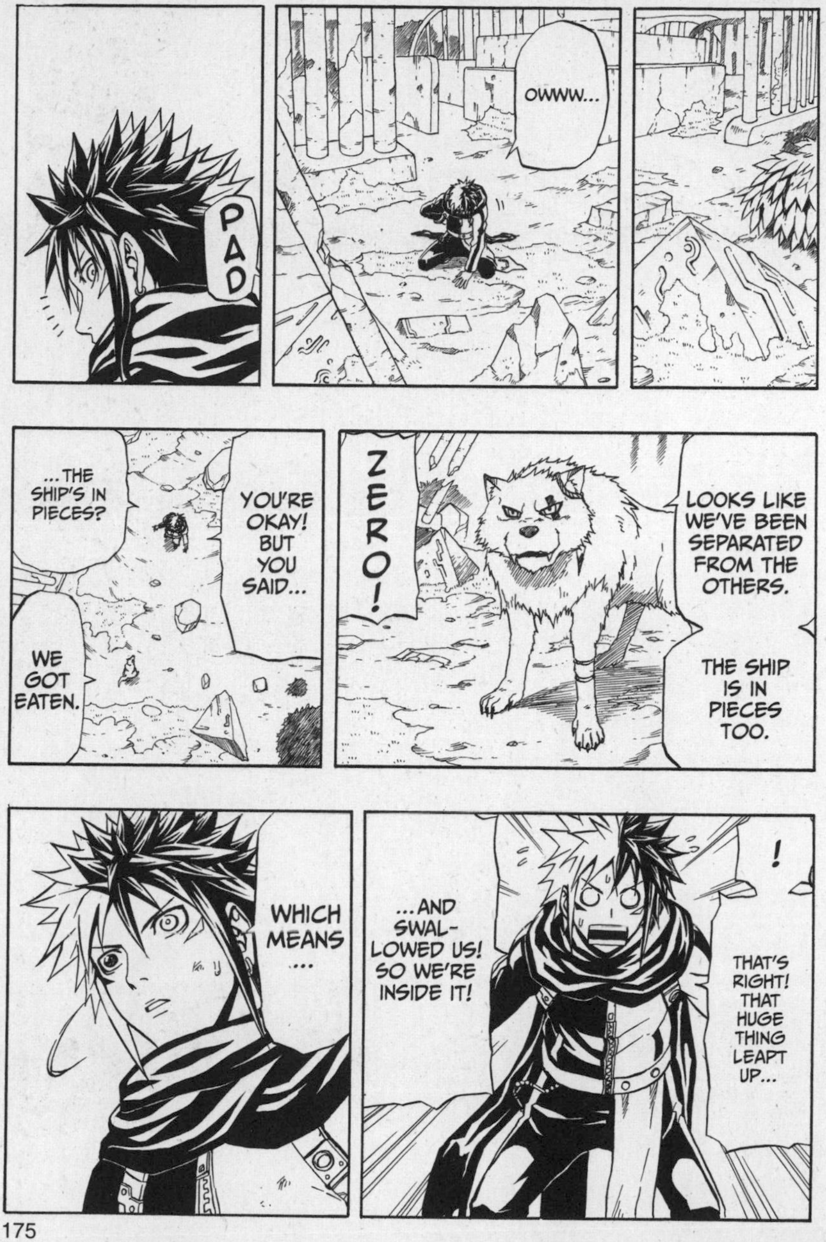
OWWW...
PAD
LOOKS LIKE WE'VE BEEN SEPARATED FROM THE OTHERS.
ZERO!
THE SHIP IS IN PIECES TOO.
YOU'RE OKAY! BUT YOU SAID...
...THE SHIP'S IN PIECES?
WE GOT EATEN.
!
THAT'S RIGHT! THAT HUGE THING LEAPT UP...
...AND SWAL-LOWED US! SO WE'RE INSIDE IT!
WHICH MEANS ....

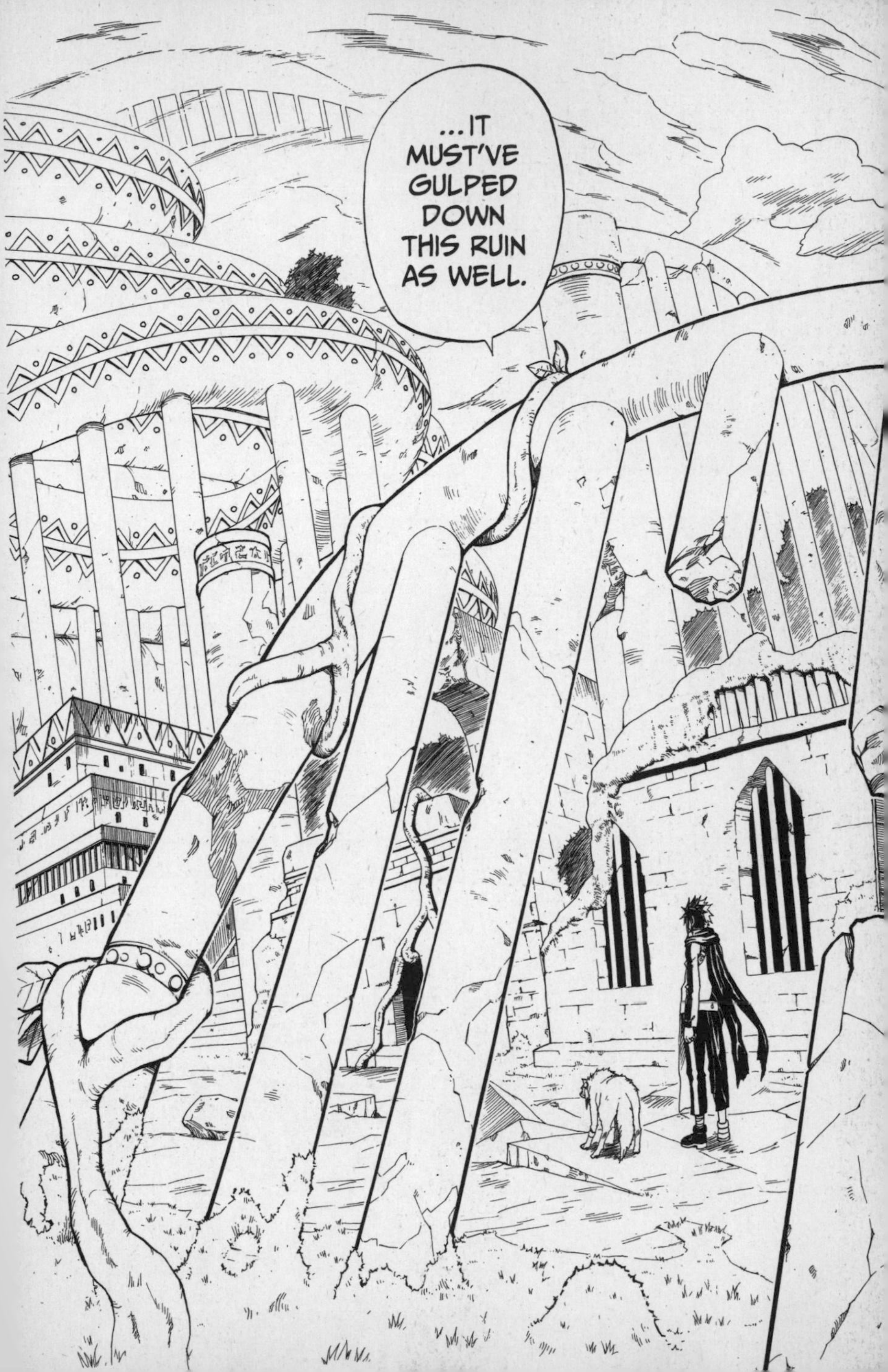
...IT MUST'VE GULPED DOWN THIS RUIN AS WELL.

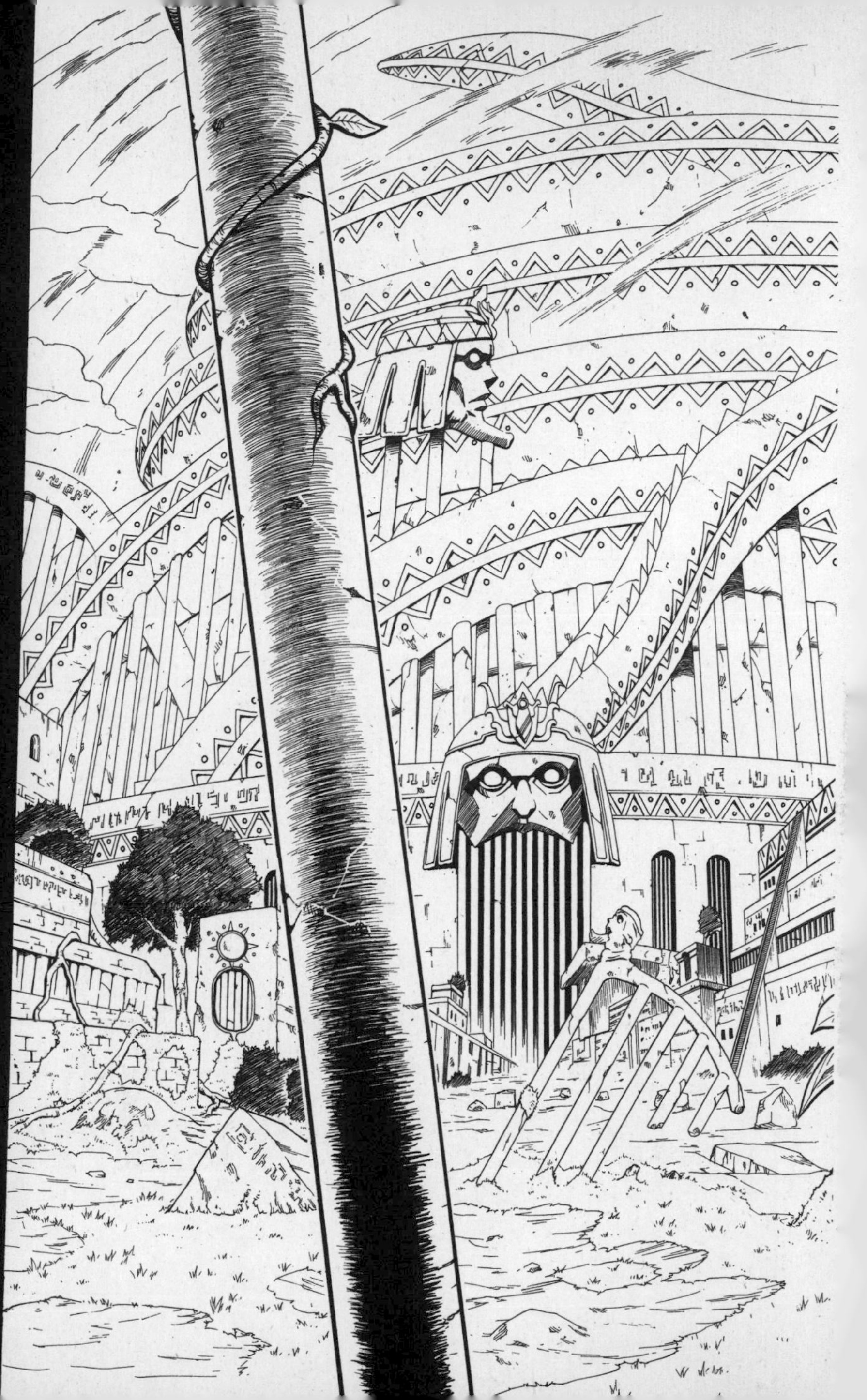

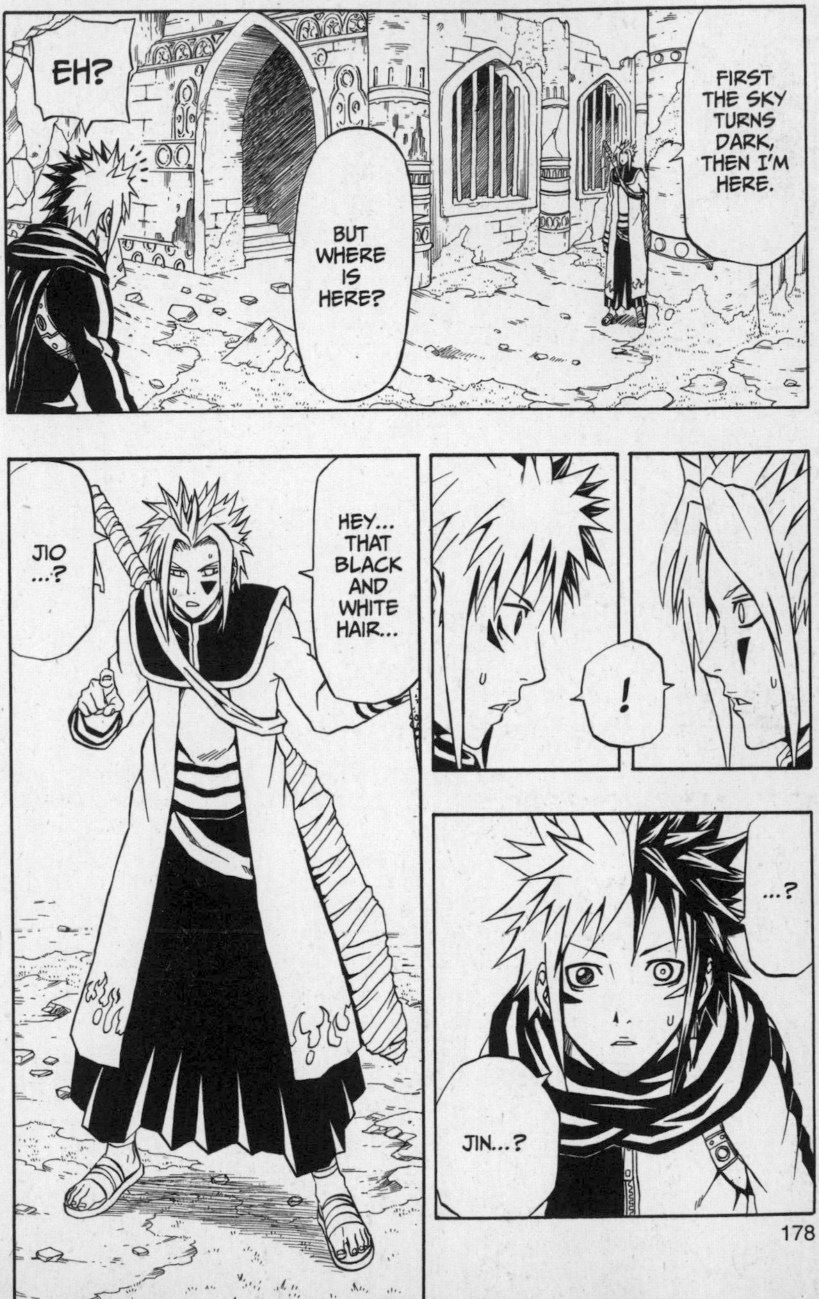
FIRST THE SKY TURNS DARK, THEN I'M HERE.
BUT WHERE IS HERE?
EH?
!
...?
JIN...?
HEY... THAT BLACK AND WHITE HAIR...
JIO ...?

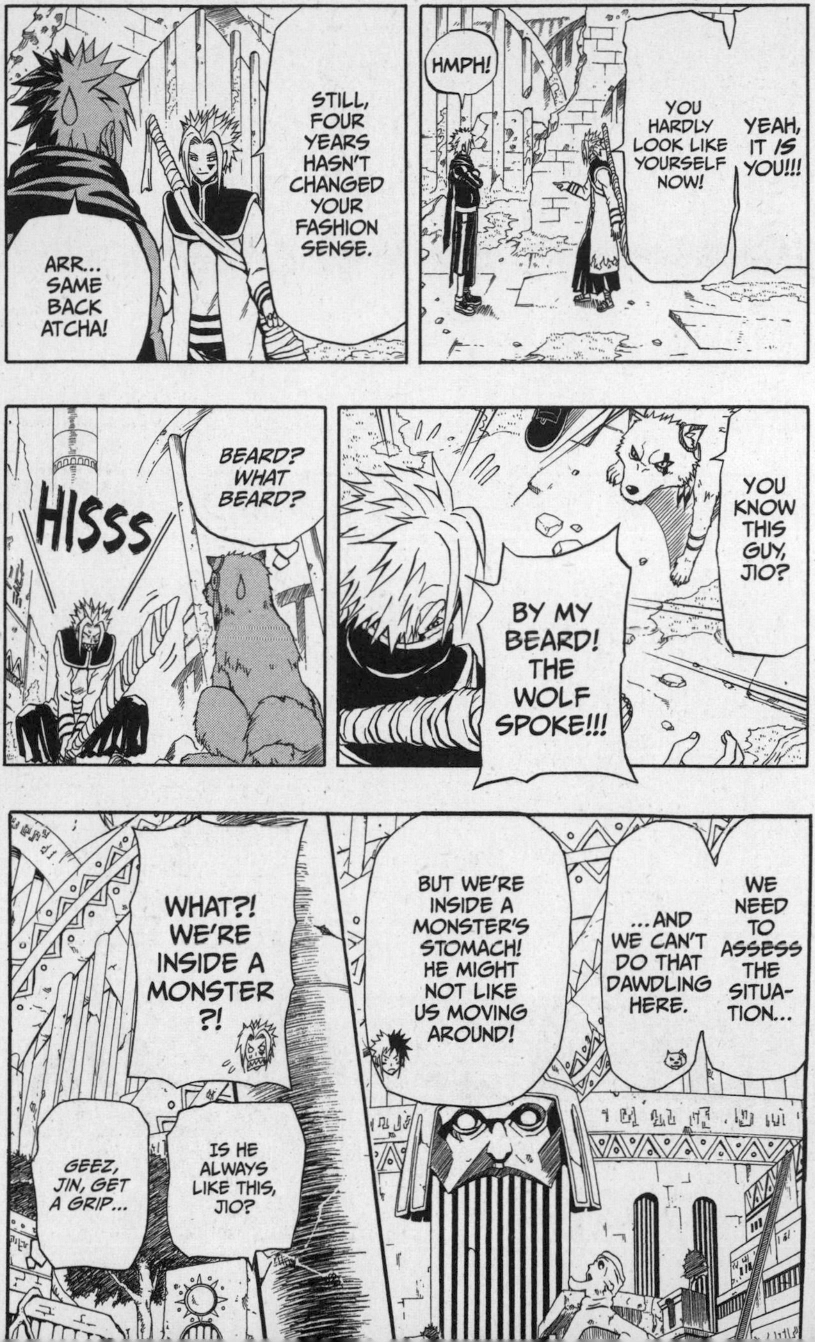
YEAH, IT *IS* YOU!!!
YOU HARDLY LOOK LIKE YOURSELF NOW!
HMPH!
STILL, FOUR YEARS HASN'T CHANGED YOUR FASHION SENSE.
ARR... SAME BACK ATCHA!
YOU KNOW THIS GUY, JIO?
BY MY BEARD! THE WOLF SPOKE!!!
BEARD? WHAT BEARD?
HISSS
WE NEED TO ASSESS THE SITUATION...
...AND WE CAN'T DO THAT DAWDLING HERE.
BUT WE'RE INSIDE A MONSTER'S STOMACH! HE MIGHT NOT LIKE US MOVING AROUND!
WHAT?! WE'RE INSIDE A MONSTER?!
IS HE ALWAYS LIKE THIS, JIO?
GEEZ, JIN, GET A GRIP...

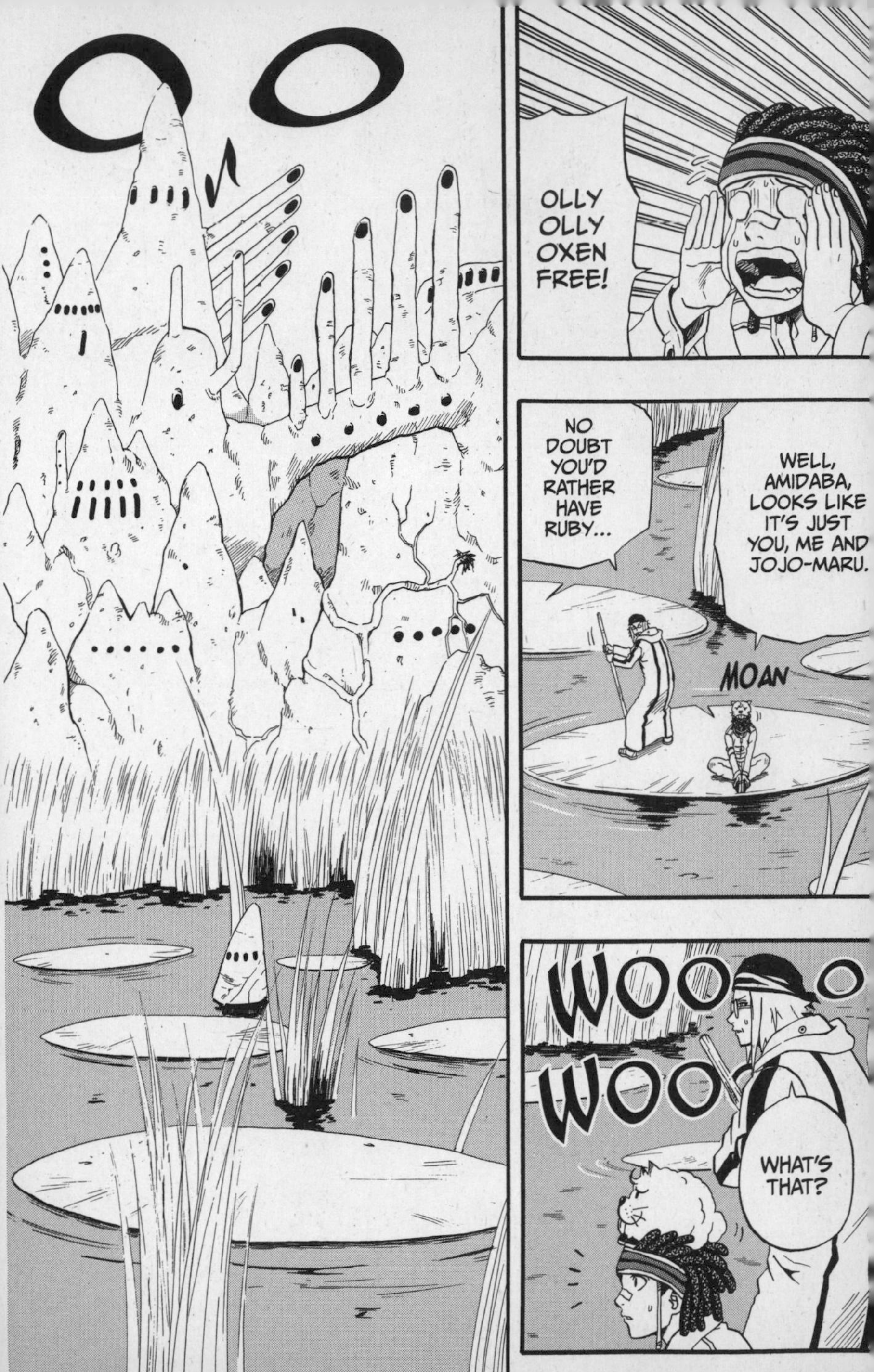
OLLY OLLY OXEN FREE!
WELL, AMIDABA, LOOKS LIKE IT'S JUST YOU, ME AND JOJO-MARU.
NO DOUBT YOU'D RATHER HAVE RUBY...
MOAN
WOOO O
WOOO
WHAT'S THAT?
OO

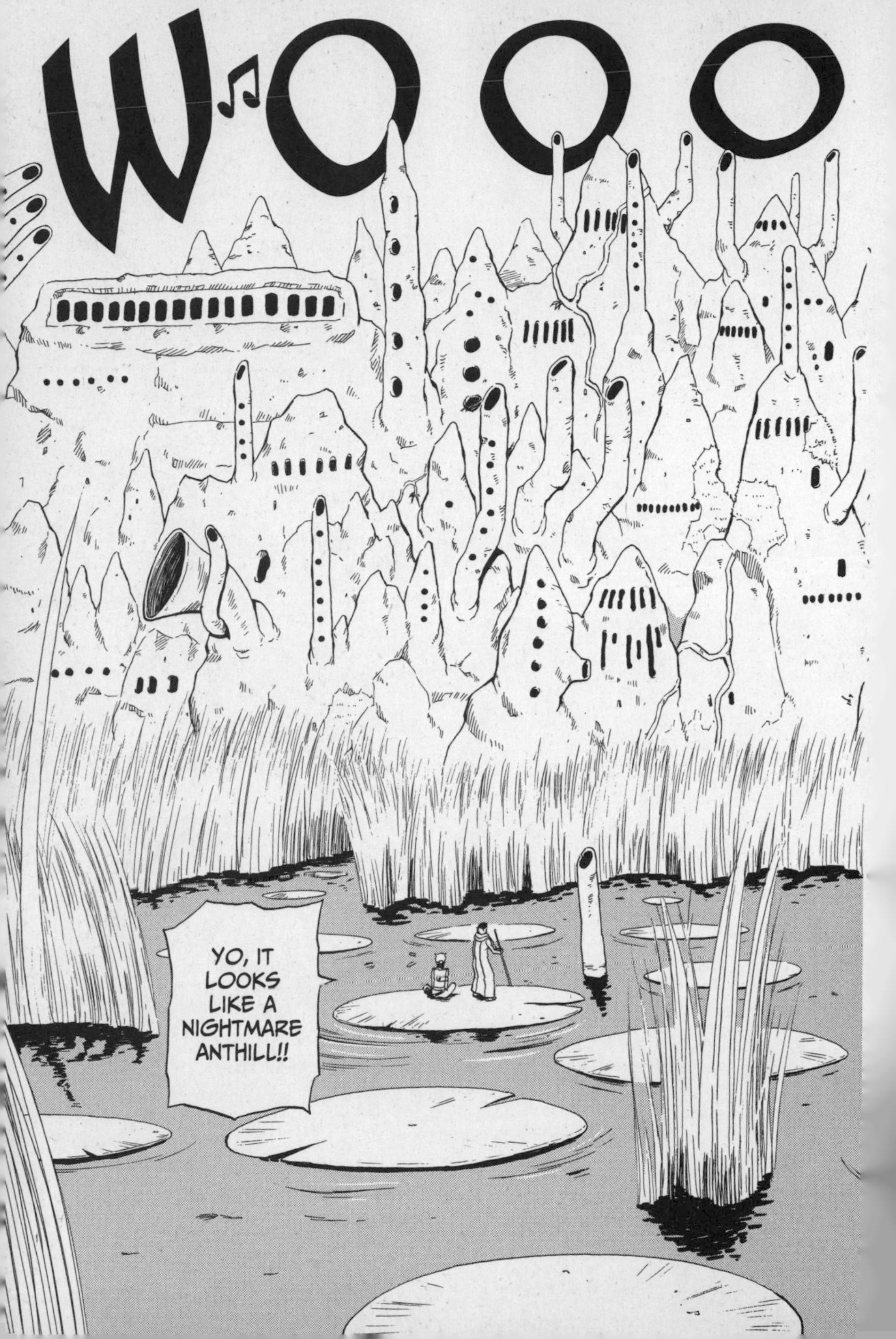
WOOO
YO, IT LOOKS LIKE A NIGHTMARE ANTHILL!!

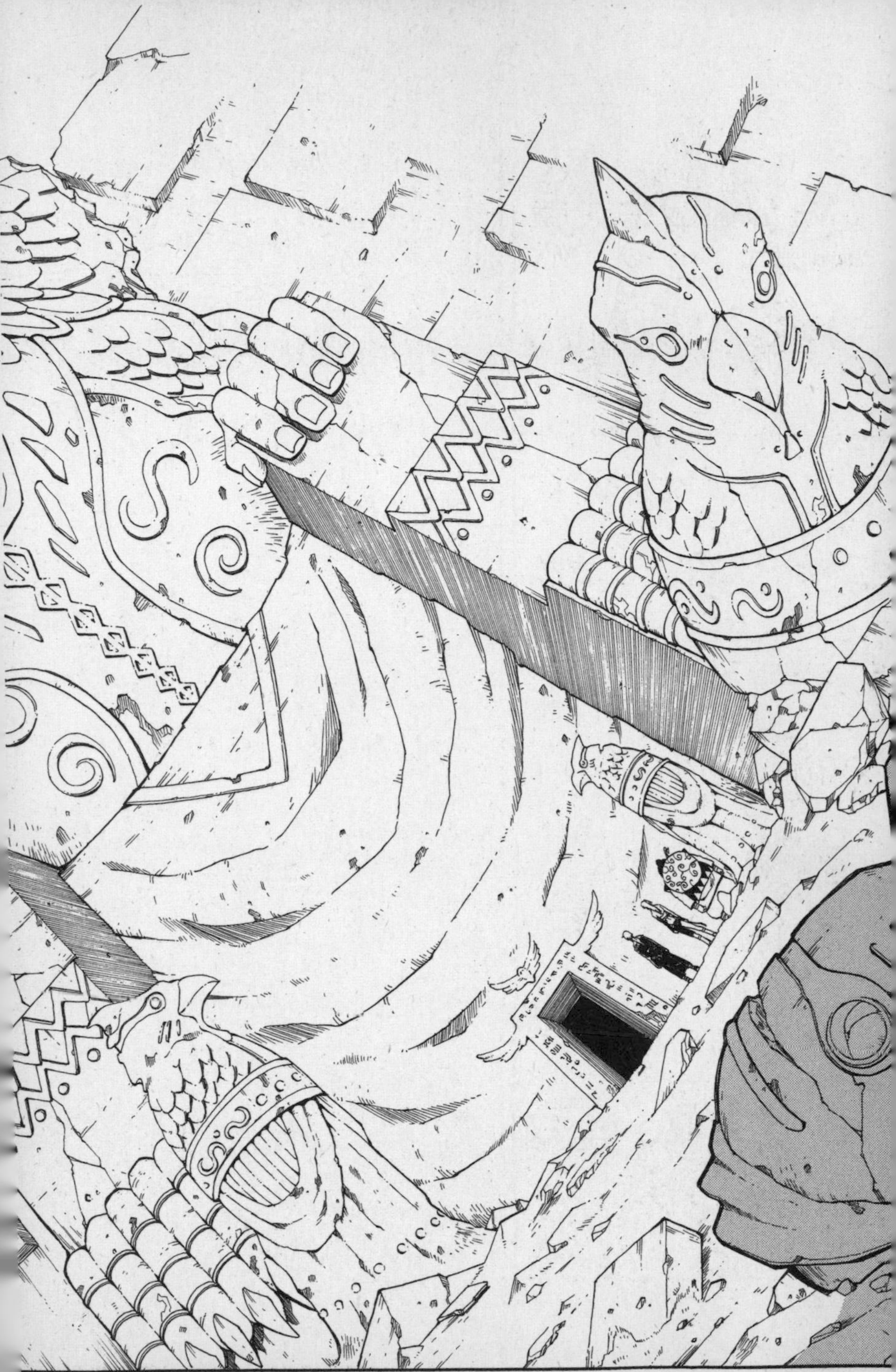

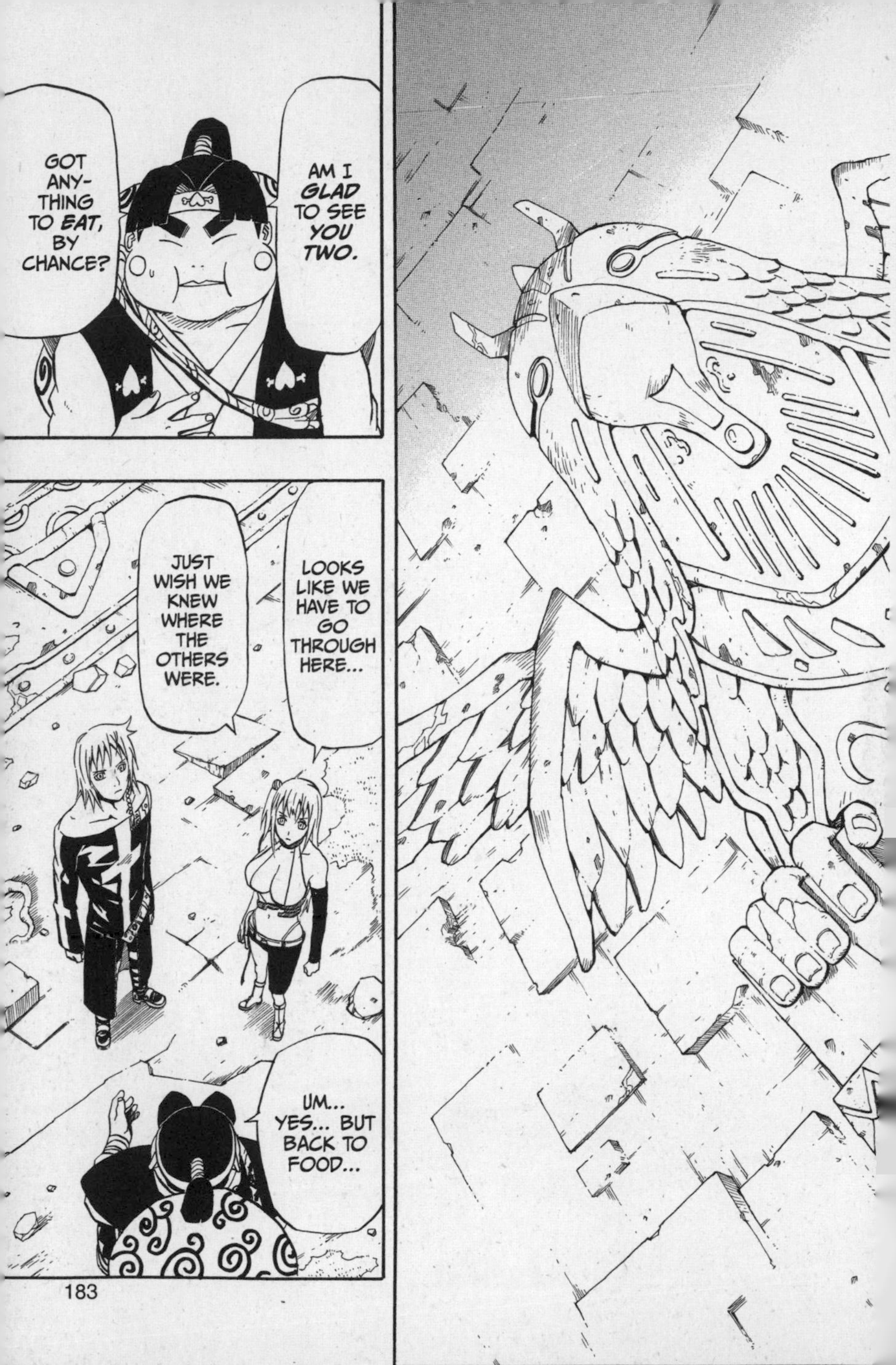
AM I GLAD TO SEE YOU TWO.
GOT ANYTHING TO EAT, BY CHANCE?
LOOKS LIKE WE HAVE TO GO THROUGH HERE...
JUST WISH WE KNEW WHERE THE OTHERS WERE.
UM... YES... BUT BACK TO FOOD...

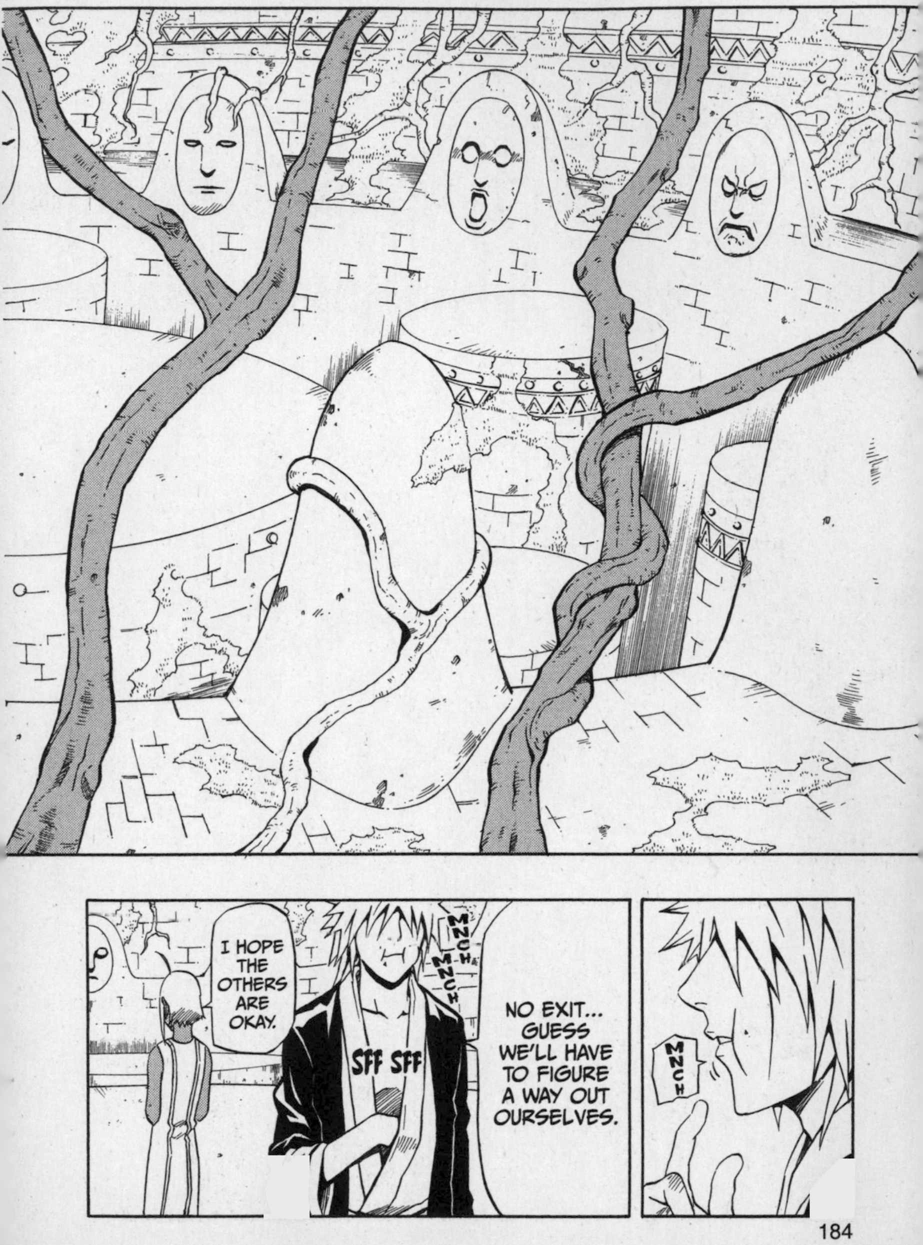
MNCH
MNCH MNCH
NO EXIT... GUESS WE'LL HAVE TO FIGURE A WAY OUT OURSELVES.
SFF SFF
I HOPE THE OTHERS ARE OKAY.

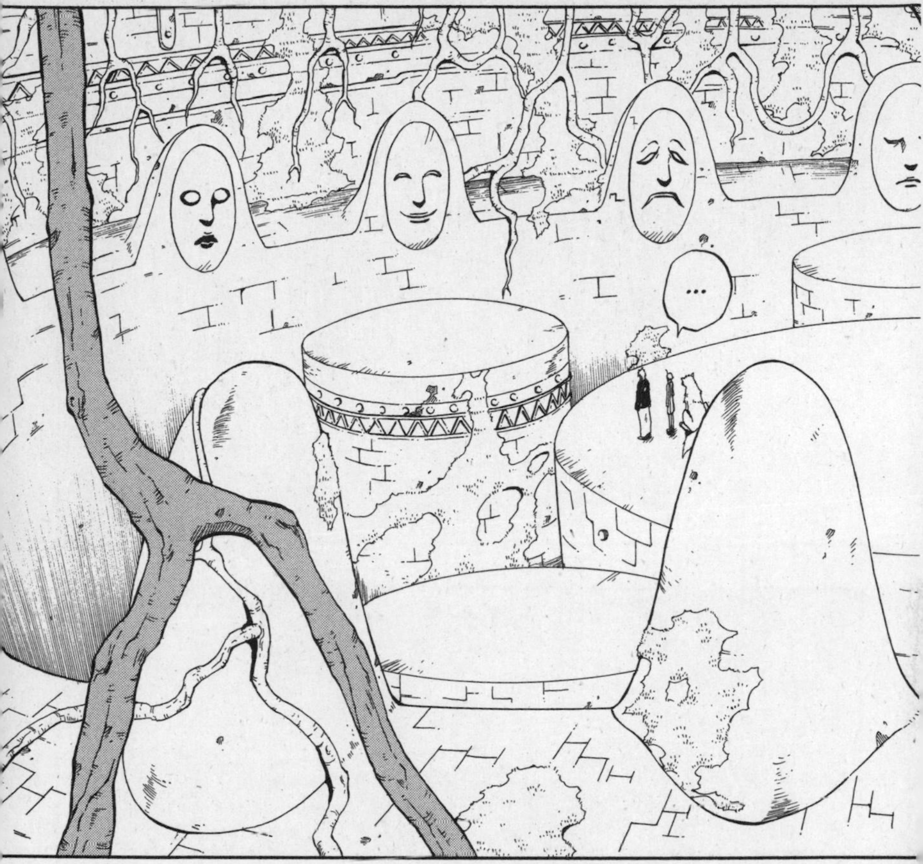
...

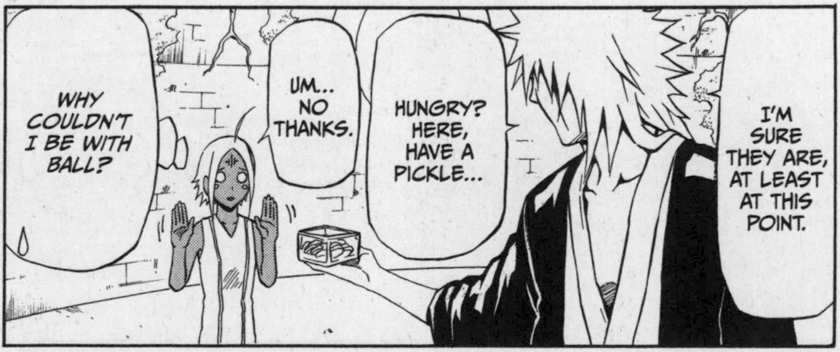
I'M SURE THEY ARE, AT LEAST AT THIS POINT.
HUNGRY? HERE, HAVE A PICKLE...
UM... NO THANKS.
WHY COULDN'T I BE WITH BALL?

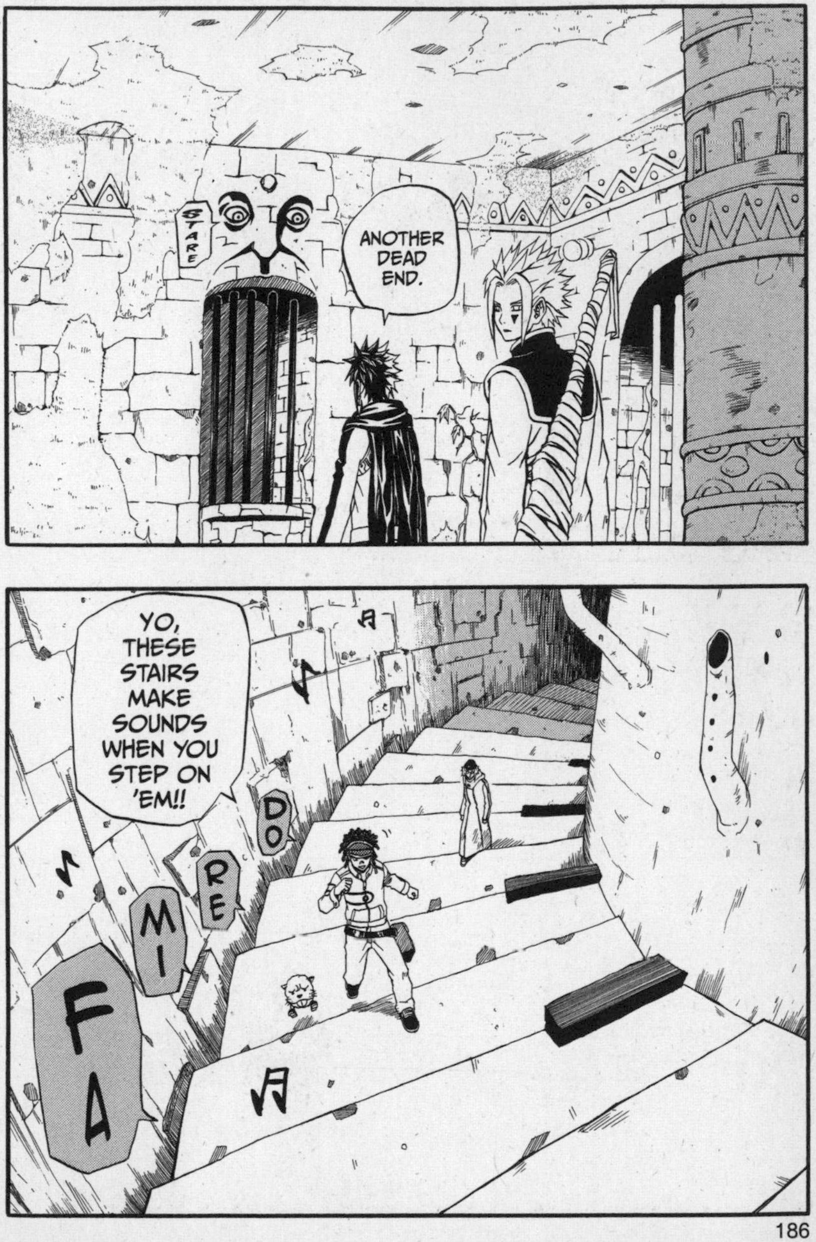
STARE
ANOTHER DEAD END.
YO, THESE STAIRS MAKE SOUNDS WHEN YOU STEP ON 'EM!!
DO
RE
MI
FA

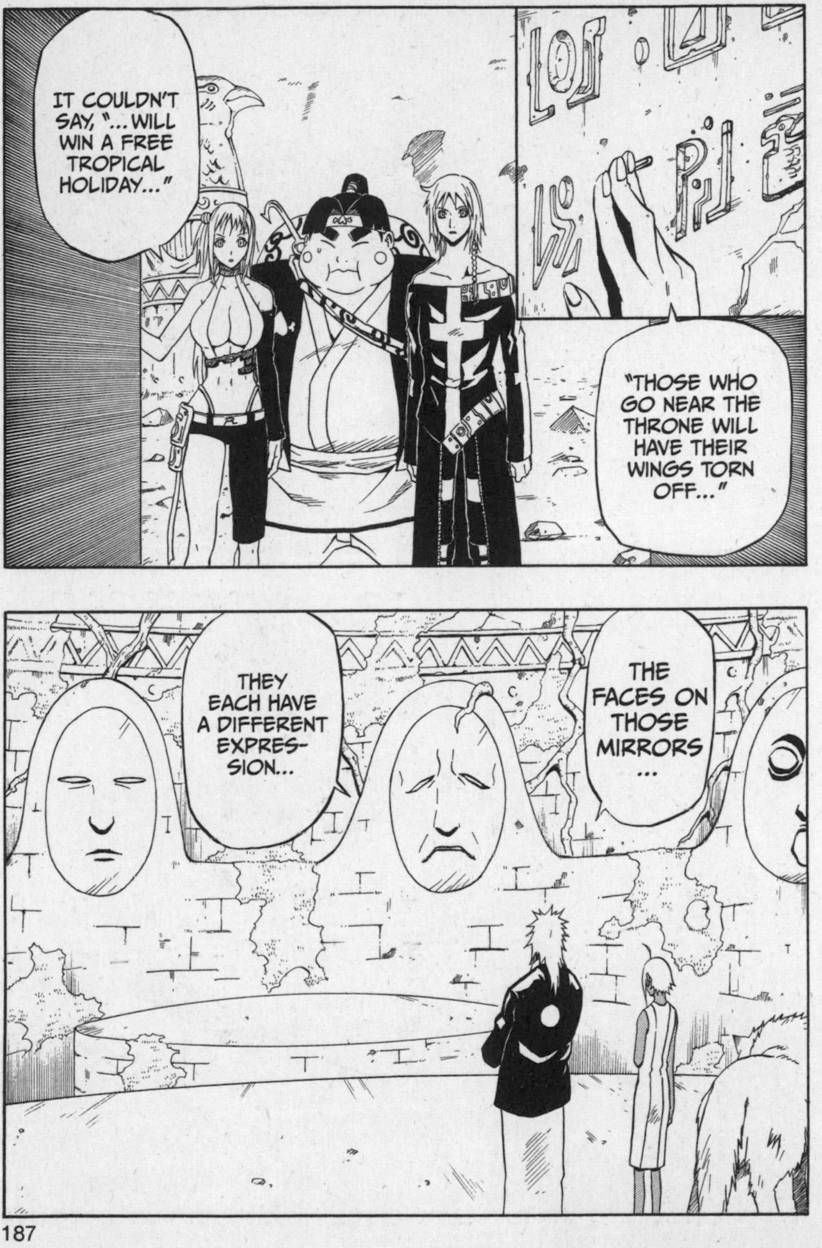
"THOSE WHO GO NEAR THE THRONE WILL HAVE THEIR WINGS TORN OFF..."
IT COULDN'T SAY, "...WILL WIN A FREE TROPICAL HOLIDAY..."
THE FACES ON THOSE MIRRORS ...
THEY EACH HAVE A DIFFERENT EXPRES-SION...

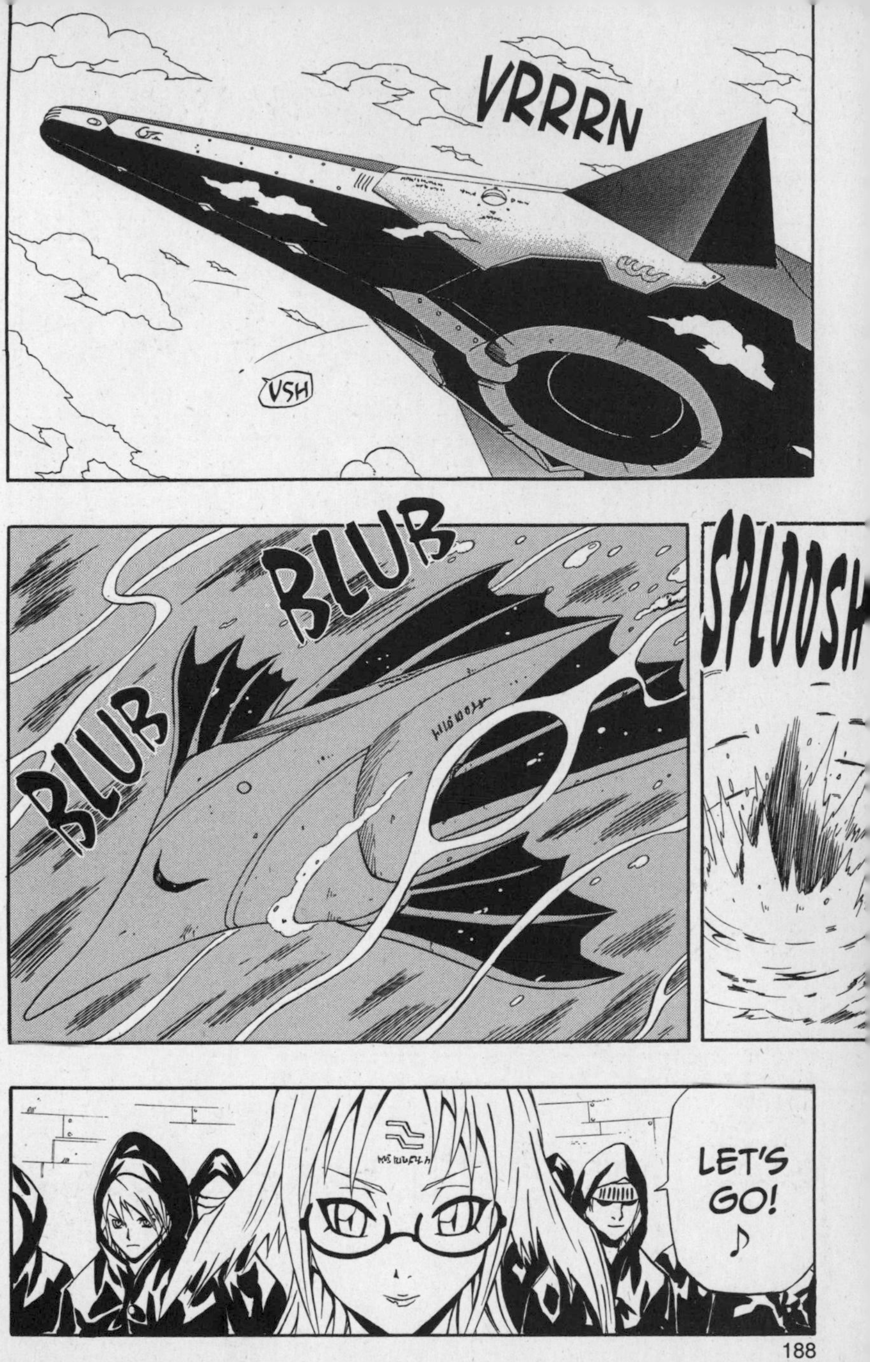
VRRRN
VSH
SPLOOSH
BLUB BLUB
LET'S GO! ♪

SEISHI AND THE ORANGE POLE

WHAT'S THIS ORANGE POLE?
I PUT MY FOOT ON IT...
KRUK
WBBL
WHOA!
BWING
RUBBER ?!
TUMP
WHUMP
A FEW DAYS LATER...
OH!
RUBBER?!
BWING

SEISHI AND THE SOFTBALL MATCH

ONE DAY I TRIPPED OVER MY MOTOR-BIKE...
URF!
SKSSSH
NEXT DAY I PLAYED SOFT-BALL...
C'MON, HIT ONE TO DADDY...
POMF
COMIN' ATCHA!
GOT IT!
TOK
I LEARNED THAT SCRAPED PALMS DON'T HEAL SO QUICK!
TWITCH
TWITCH
TM
TM

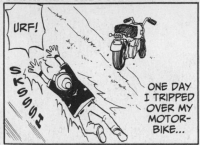

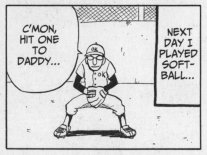

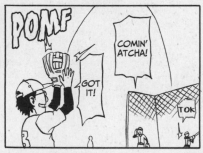

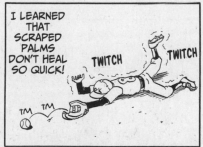

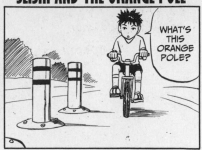

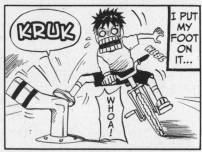

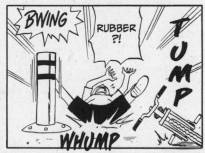

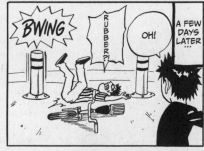

O-Parts CATALOGUE ⑯

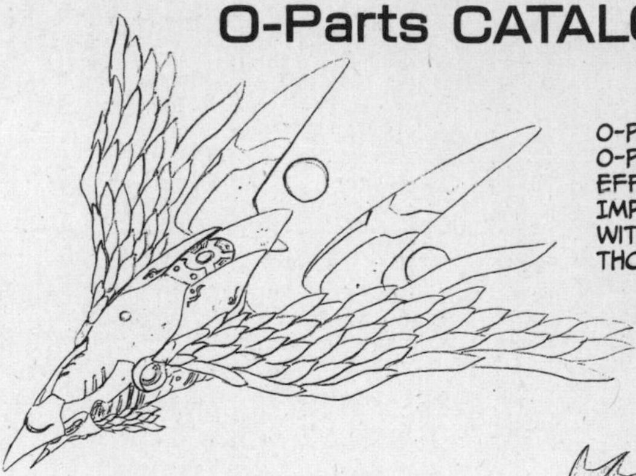

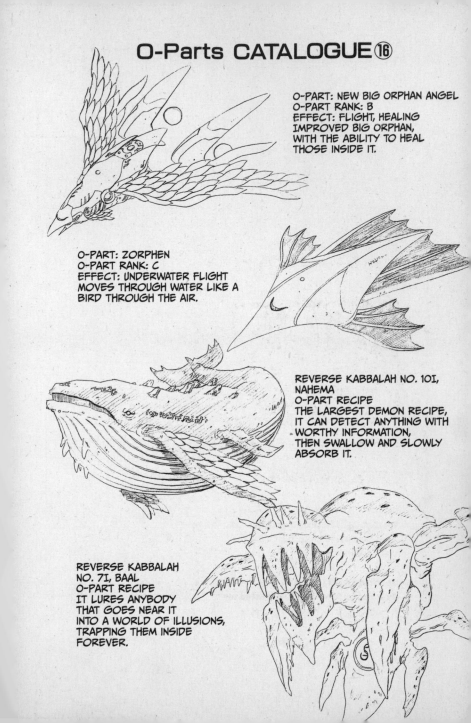

O-PART: NEW BIG ORPHAN ANGEL
O-PART RANK: B
EFFECT: FLIGHT, HEALING
IMPROVED BIG ORPHAN,
WITH THE ABILITY TO HEAL
THOSE INSIDE IT.

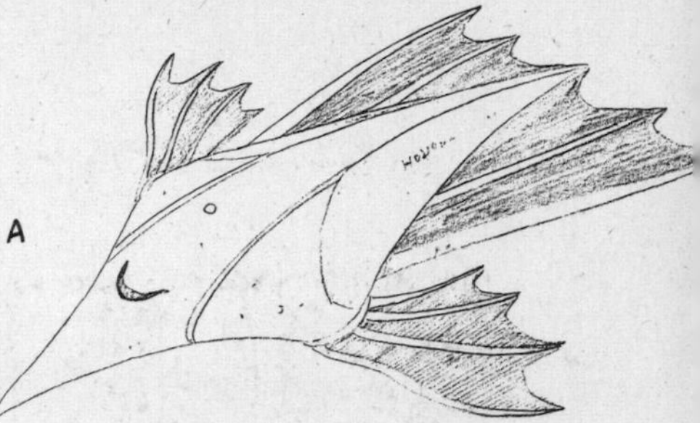

O-PART: ZORPHEN
O-PART RANK: C
EFFECT: UNDERWATER FLIGHT
MOVES THROUGH WATER LIKE A
BIRD THROUGH THE AIR.

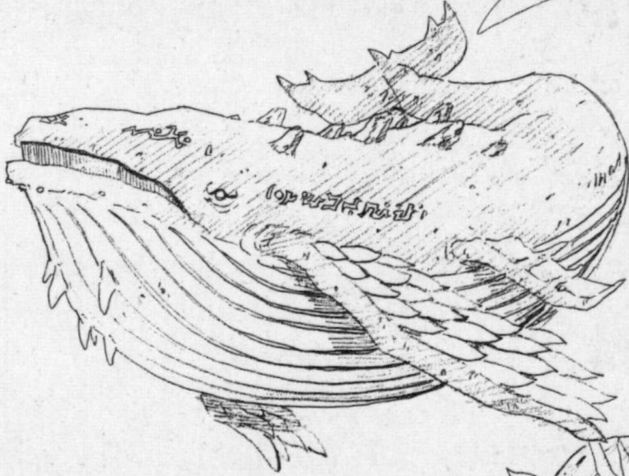

REVERSE KABBALAH NO. 101,
NAHEMA
O-PART RECIPE
THE LARGEST DEMON RECIPE,
IT CAN DETECT ANYTHING WITH
WORTHY INFORMATION,
THEN SWALLOW AND SLOWLY
ABSORB IT.

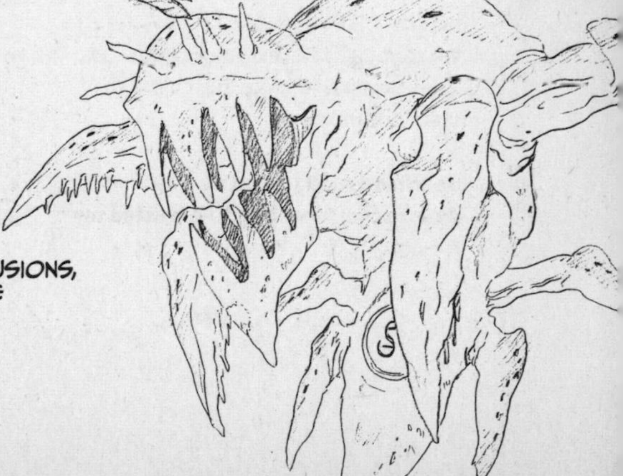

REVERSE KABBALAH
NO. 71, BAAL
O-PART RECIPE
IT LURES ANYBODY
THAT GOES NEAR IT
INTO A WORLD OF ILLUSIONS,
TRAPPING THEM INSIDE
FOREVER.

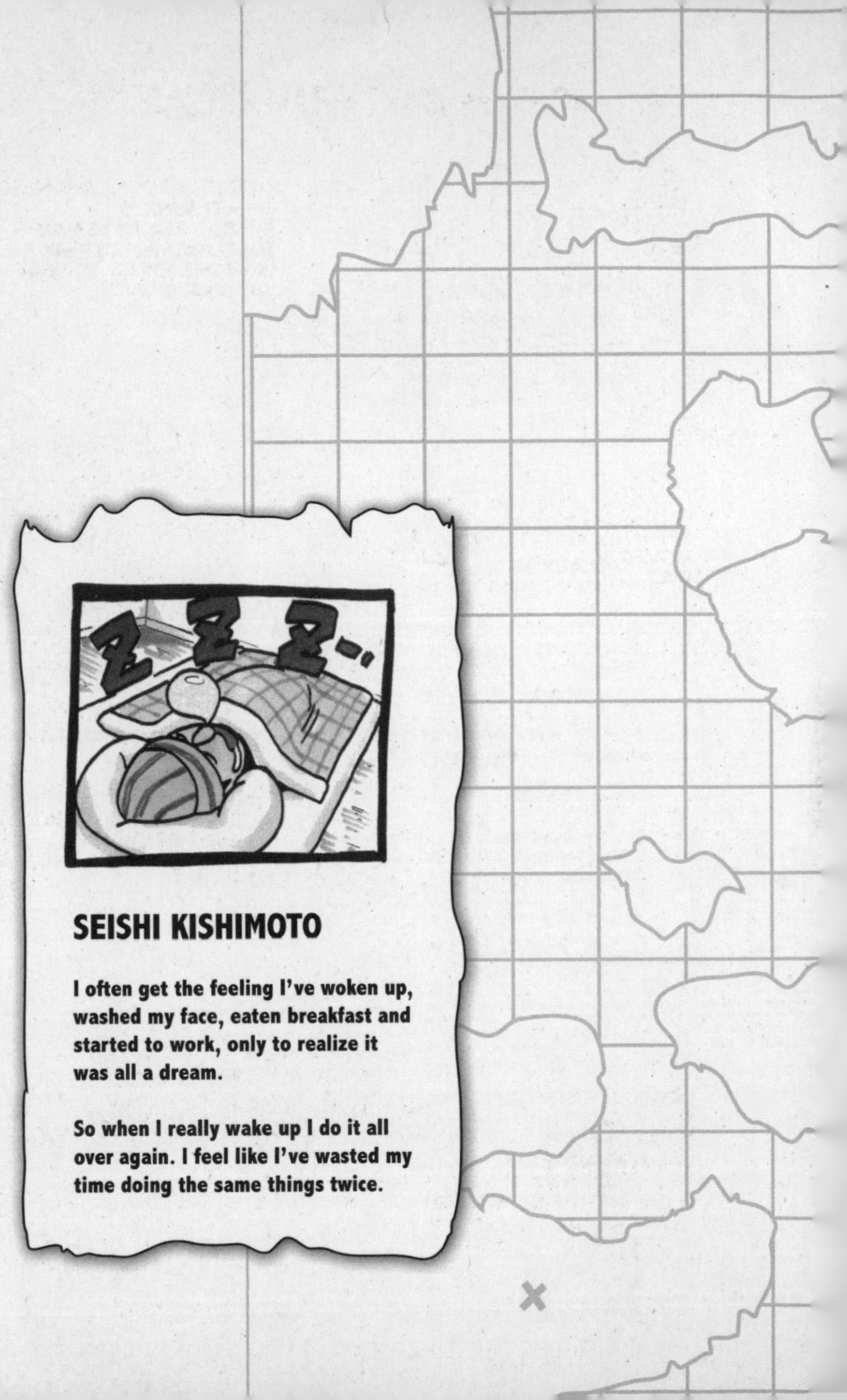
ZZZ..

SEISHI KISHIMOTO

I often get the feeling I've woken up, washed my face, eaten breakfast and started to work, only to realize it was all a dream.

So when I really wake up I do it all over again. I feel like I've wasted my time doing the same things twice.

O-Parts HUNTER 16

VIZ Media Edition
STORY AND ART BY SEISHI KISHIMOTO

English Adaptation/Tetsuichiro Miyaki
Touch-up Art & Lettering/HudsonYards
Design/Andrea Rice
Editor/Gary Leach

Editor in Chief, Books/Alvin Lu
Editor in Chief, Magazines/Marc Weidenbaum
VP, Publishing Licensing/Rika Inouye
VP, Sales & Product Marketing/Gonzalo Ferreyra
VP, Creative/Linda Espinosa
Publisher/Hyoe Narita

Printed in the U.S.A.

Published by VIZ Media, LLC
P.O. Box 77010
San Francisco, CA 94107

10 9 8 7 6 5 4 3 2 1
First printing, June 2009

www.viz.com
store.viz.com

PARENTAL ADVISORY
O-PARTS HUNTER is rated T+ for Older Teen and is recommended for ages 16 and up. This volume contains realistic and fantasy violence and adult situations.
ratings.viz.com